The Music of the Jews in the Diaspora
(up to 1800)

Süsskind of Trimberg, the Jewish Minstrel (13th century). From the Manasseh Codex. (Courtesy of the Heidelberg University Library).

The Music of the Jews in the Diaspora
(up to 1800)

A CONTRIBUTION
TO THE SOCIAL AND CULTURAL HISTORY
OF THE JEWS

By Alfred Sendrey

THOMAS YOSELOFF

New York • South Brunswick • London

Thomas Yoseloff, Publisher
Cranbury, New Jersey 08512

Thomas Yoseloff Ltd
108 New Bond Street
London W1Y OQX, England

ML
160
.S 417
.M 9

SBN
498-06647-9

To The University of Judaism
in Los Angeles

Contents

Table of Transliterations*

Hebrew and Aramaic

Consonants

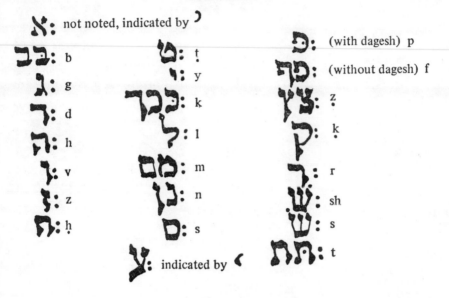

א: not noted, indicated by ʾ

ב: b

ג: g

ד: d

ה: h

ו: v

ז: z

ח: ḥ

ט: ṭ

י: y

כ: k

ל: l

מ: m

נ: n

ס: s

ע: indicated by ʿ

פ: (with dagesh) p

פ: (without dagesh) f

צ: ẓ

ק: ḳ

ר: r

ש: sh

ש: s

ת: t

Vowels

◌ָ : a, o	◌ֵ : e	◌ִ : i	◌ֻ : u	◌ֳ : c
◌ְ : e	◌ָ : o	◌ַ : a	◌ֲ : a	◌ֱ : e
◌ִי : i	◌ֻ : u		◌ֹ : o	◌ֹ : o

Kameẓ hatuf is represented by *o*. The so-called "Continental" pronunciation of the English vowels is implied.

The Hebrew article is transcribed as *ha*, followed by a hyphen, without doubling the following letter.

The presence of *dagesh lene* is not noted, except in the case of *pe*. *Dagesh forte* is indicated by doubling the letter.

* We follow the system of transliteration as employed by the *Jewish Encyclopedia*.

List of Abbreviations

Abrahams	Abrahams, Israel, *Jewish Life in the Middle Ages*, 1932
Adler	Adler, Israel, *La pratique musicale savante dans quelques communautés Juives en Europe aux XVIIe et XVIIIe siècles*, 1966
AdlerRise	Adler, Israel. *The Rise of Art Music in the Italian Ghetto*. In: *Jewish Medieval and Renaissance Studies*, ed. by Alexander Altmann, pp. 321–364, 1967
BaronCom	Baron, Salo W., *The Jewish Community*, 1942
BaronSoc (1937)	Baron, Salo W., *A Social and Religious History of the Jews*, 1937 (3 vols.)
BaronSoc (1958)	Baron, Salo W., *A Social and Religious History of the Jews*, 1958 (8 vols.)
Berliner	Berliner, Abraham, *Aus dem Leben der Juden Deutschlands im Mittelalter*, 1927
Chabaneau	Chabaneau, Camille, *Les Biographies des Troubadours en Langue Provençale*, 1885
DurantFaith	Durant, Will, *The Age of Faith*, 1950
DurantLouis	Durant, Will, *The Age of Louis XIV*, 1963
Faral	Faral, Edmond, *Les Jongleurs en France au Moyen Age*, 1910
Farmer	Farmer, Henry George, *A History of Arabian Music*, 1929
Grad	Gradenwitz, Peter, *The Music of Israel, its Rise and Growth*, 1949
Graetz	Graetz, Heinrich Hirsch, *History of the Jews* (Engl. ed.), 1898
HUCA	*Hebrew Union College Annual*
Idelsohn	Idelsohn, Abraham Zevi, *Jewish Music in its Historical Development*, 1929
IdelsohnThes	Idelsohn, Abraham Zevi, *Thesaurus of Oriental Hebrew Melodies*, 1914–1933 (Engl. ed. 1923–38). (10 vols.)

Jacobs	Jacobs, Joseph, *An Inquiry into the Sources of the History of the Jews in Spain*, 1894
J.E.	*Jewish Encyclopedia* 1901–1906 (12 vols.)
JQR	*Jewish Quarterly Review*
M	*Mishnah*
Marcus	Marcus, Jacob R., *The Jew in the Medieval World*, 1938
Menéndez	Menéndez, Pidal Ramón, *La epopeya a través de la literatura Española*, 1945
MenéndezPoesía	Menéndez, Pidal Ramón, *Poesía juglaresca y origenes da las literaturas romanicas*, 1957
MGG	*Die Musik in Geschichte und Gegenwart*, ed. by Friedrich Blume, 1949 (13 vols.)
MGWJ	*Monatsschrift für Geschichte und Wissenschaft des Judentums*
Midr	*Midrash*
MQ	*Musical Quarterly*
Neumann	Neumann, Abraham A., *The Jews in Spain*, 1942
PfeifferIntro	Pfeiffer, Robert Henry, *Introduction to the Old Testament*, 1941
REJ	*Revue des Études Juives*
Roth	Roth, Cecil, *The Jews in the Renaissance*, 1959
RothVenice	Roth, Cecil, *A History of the Jews in Venice*, 1930
SachsGeist	Sachs, Curt, *Geist und Werden der Musikinstrumente*, 1929
SachsHist	Sachs, Curt, *The History of Musical Instruments*, 1940
Stein C.B.	Steinschneider, Moritz, *Catalogus librorum Hebraeorum in Bibliotheca Bodleiana*, 1852–1860 (3 vols.)
SteinLiter (1905)	Steinschneider, Moritz, *Die Geschichtsliteratur der Juden in Druckform und Handschriften*, 1905
SteinLiter (1965)	Steinschneider, Moritz, *Jewish Literature from the Eighth to the Eighteenth Century*, 1965
T.B.	*Babylonian Talmud*
T.Y.	*Palestinian Talmud*
U.J.E.	*Universal Jewish Encyclopedia*, 1939–1942 (10 vols.)
WernerSource	Werner, Eric, *The Oldest Sources of Synagogal Chant*, 1947

List of Illustrations

Frontispiece

Süsskind of Trimberg, the Jewish Minstrel (13th century). From the Manasseh Codex. (Courtesy of the Heidelberg University Library).

To follow page 128

Facsimile of a page from a popular Judaeo-Spanish book printed at Smyrna in the sixteenth century. The example shown is an endecha *(dirge) for* Tishab-ꞌAb.

Galician-Portuguese juglar *playing the* vihuela *with a bow. Singer with* pandero. *(Canc. de Ajuda).*

Large vihuelas *played with bows. Tenth century. (Beato de Liébana).*

Juglares *with* rabel *and lute. (Cant. de Santa María).*

Castilian juglar *singing, accompanied by a Moorish* juglar. *(Cant. de Santa María).*

Galician-Portuguese troubadour with a juglar *playing the harp. (Canc. de Ajuda).*

Juglares *playing the* canon. *(Cant. de Santa María).*

Juglares *playing the* cedra *and* citola. *(Cant. de Santa María).*

Dance of the soldadera, *accompanied by a psaltery. (Canc. de Ajuda).*

Juglares *of the thirteenth century, playing the* sinfonía; *one of them a cleric. (Cant. de Santa María).*

Alfonso X exhorts his singers and musicians to honor the Virgin with songs, accompanied by dancers. (Cant. de Santa María).

Disputation between Jews and Christians. From Seelen-Wurzgarten *(Ulm, 1483).*

The first printed pictures of Jews. (After Lee M. Friedman). In: HUCA, *vol. XXIII, part 2 (1950–51), pp. 433–448.*

To follow page 256

Facsimile of Süsskind's last poems. From the Manasseh Codex. (Courtesy of the Heidelberg University Library).

13

A page of the Locheim Songbook, written by Wölflein von Locheim ca. 1450, with the dedication in Hebrew characters in the last line.

Facsimile of page 20 of the Locheimer songbook. Lyrics in Middle-High-German:

> *Ein vroulein edel von naturen*
> *hefft my myn hertt zo zeer ghewont.*
> *Trost sy my niet in corter stont*
> *niet langer mach myn leuen duren.*

Facsimile of the Manuscript Adler, in the Library of the Jewish Theological Seminary of America (New York).

Facsimile (recto and verso) of the Fragment Cincinnati ENA 4096 b.

Facsimile of the Kedushah-Motet.

To follow page 384

Facsimile of a page from the Cairuan Codex (ca. 1400). Song of Songs. In: Semitic Studies in Memory of Immanuel Löw *(Budapest, 1947), p. 131.*

Page from the earliest Hebrew book printed with ta'amim: Pentateuch (Bologna, 1482). Original size 7½ x 11 inches. (Courtesy of the Jewish Theological Seminary of America, New York).

Facsimile of the title page of Böschenstein's Hebrew Grammar. *(Hagenau, 1520).*

Facsimile of the title page of Kirchan's Simhat ha-Nefesh. *(Fürth, 1727).*

Hazzan, *bass and singer in a Jewish service. From a* Maḥ sor *(fourteenth century). (Courtesy of the University Library, Leipzig).*

Probably Guglielmo da Pesaro and his pupils. (Bibliothèque Nationale, Paris, Manusc. Fonds Ital., 973).

Facsimile of the tenor part of Allegro Porto's Book of Madrigals. *(Courtesy of the University Library, Uppsala).*

Facsimile of the title page of the tenor part of Allegro Porto's Book of Madrigals, *dedicated to the Emperor Ferdinand II. (Courtesy of the University Library, Uppsala).*

Facsimile of a page from Salomone Rossi's Ha-Shirim Asher LiShelomoh. *(Venice, 1622).*

Marriage Procession. From Kirchner, Jüdisches Ceremoniel. *(Nüremberg, 1726).*

Musicians in a Purim Procession. (Woodcut, Amsterdam, 1723).

List of Musical Examples

Foreword

What memory is to an individual, history is to a people. And just as there seem to be specialized brain cells which preserve for the individual on the conscious or subconscious level the memory of past experiences, so there are in all human societies individuals who preserve for the group the memory of its past experiences. Recent study of the activities of the brain seems to indicate so high a degree of specialization among its cells that it would not be at all surprising to discover that different cells remember different types of experiences.

The experiences of a people are, of course, far more varied and infinitely more numerous than that of any individual and the preservation of its memories requires a vast army of highly specialized "cells"—men and women who devote their lives with singular tenacity to the study and the recording of some one area of the vicissitudes and achievements of the group. The debt the group owes to these individuals is inestimable, for a group's memories are as invaluable to it as the individual's memories to him.

Dr. ALFRED SENDREY belongs to this precious company of rare, highly specialized "memory cells" of our people. Throughout his long life he has concentrated his abundant, well-disciplined physical and intellectual resources upon the role of music in the life of the Jewish people and has recorded his findings in a number of volumes widely recognized for their comprehensiveness and authenticity. He has thus greatly enriched our "group memory" of this vital aspect of our historic experience. The present substantial volume of *The Music of the Jews in the Diaspora (up to 1800)* places us even more greatly in his debt for a number of reasons. He has in the first place here gathered the essence of what generations of research have brought to light in this field of inquiry. He has, moreover, related the various musical activities of the Jews to the time and place in which they occurred. This work, therefore, presents in broad outline a panorama of the musical activities of all the peoples among whom Jews lived during some eighteen centuries and that included practically all the peoples of the Mediterranean basin and of Europe. In addition, we are given a summary account of the salient political, social and economic factors that shaped the life of the Jewish community so that the musical component in the culture of the people is seen as an integral part of the culture as a whole.

Musicians and historians of music will find here scholarly discussions of fine points concerning musical scales, musical instruments, the development of the musical notations used in the Synagogue and similar matters to gratify the specialist. All will delight in the biographies of individual Jewish Troubadours and Jongleurs, the history of the Cantorate, the account of the rise of the music of the Chassidim and scores of other fascinating details.

Dr. ALFRED SENDREY is not merely an objective historian. He is a musician and a Jew and as such he is emotionally profoundly involved in his subject. The reader cannot but be deeply affected by the love and the wonder that inform every page of the work, the love of his subject and of the people whose music he is discussing and the wonder that this constantly harassed people could rise above the burden of hate and persecution which constantly sought to crush it and create such a vast variety of musical forms through which to express not only its sorrows, but its irrepressible "joie de vivre" and its determination ever to sing a "new song unto the Lord."

SIMON GREENBERG
Chancellor
University of Judaism
at Los Angeles

Acknowledgments

IT IS THE AUTHOR'S PLEASANT DUTY TO EXPRESS HIS GRATITUDE TO the persons who assisted him in the final shaping of this volume.

Sincere thanks are due Dr. Joseph Yasser, Dr. Israel J. Katz, Professor of Columbia University in New York, and Dr. Stephen Kayser, Professor in Residence at the University of California in Los Angeles, who read the entire manuscript and whose invaluable advice and suggestions were a steady encouragement and inspiration for the author.

Dr. David Aronson, Professor at the University of Judaism in Los Angeles, gave valuable advice in rabbinical matters, for which he earned the author's indebtedness.

Two Professors at the University of California at Los Angeles, Stephen C. Nichols and Carlo L. Golino, graciously provided translations of medieval French and Italian texts. For their cooperation the author conveys his sincere gratitude.

Mr. Shimeon Brisman, Bibliographer of Hebraica and Judaica at the University of California in Los Angeles, contributed generously from his rich knowledge in this field, and earned the author's deep-felt thanks.

Dr. Robert Strassburg devoted much time and effort in assisting the author during the entire growth of the work. His help in reading the proofs is especially appreciated.

Los Angeles, California, February 1970

ALFRED SENDREY

The Music of the Jews in the Diaspora
(up to 1800)

Introduction

THIS BOOK GREW OUT OF A SERIES OF LECTURES GIVEN AT THE UNIversity of Judaism in Los Angeles during the academic year 1963-64. At first, it was a mere assemblage of data, historical, sociological and artistic, data relevant and peripherical, that were used for oral elaboration. In viewing this ample information from a higher vantage point, it became evident that Jewish musical life after the destruction of the Jewish national existence (70 c.e.) until the Emancipation (end of the eighteenth century) shows an organic development which deserves, nay, commands a more intensive treatment.

The various aspects of Jewish musical practice in the Diaspora had been treated repeatedly, not only in a haphazard manner, but mostly as the by-product of the Jewish social life during the Diaspora. Quite a number of writers—historians, sociologists, musicologists—have attempted to tackle this subject from their specific point of view. They failed to visualize the musical life of medieval Jewry as a valuable cultural asset of Jewish spiritual force, because they regarded this musical life as a sideline of general Jewish civilization, a sort of undercurrent of the religious, social, and emotional conditions, in which the Jews lived in the dispersion. However, it is the synthesis of the many isolated elements of medieval Jewish musical life which yields a composite picture of convincing force, showing an unbroken chain. This disproves the almost unanimous belief that Jewish music, Jewish musical life, were dormant or even extinct during the many centuries of oppression in the Middle Ages. We can never fully understand the survival of Jewish musical culture in those fateful centuries if we imagine that the medieval Jews were dejected in spirit and weak in soul. All the evidence points to the contrary. It seems that the persecutions, the denial of elementary human rights to an entire people released forces which enabled this

23

people not only to survive physically, but to keep alive its intellectual and spiritual powers. Without this inner force, the survival of Jewish musical culture would be unimaginable. Occasionally it was concealed under the surface, but it erupted vigorously as soon as the external conditions proved favorable.

The author's aim was to assemble all relevant historical data, scattered in many places, in an attempt to present a comprehensive picture of Jewish musical life during an epoch in which, according to the general consensus, Jews and Jewry were allegedly devoid of their own musical culture. This epoch embraces many centuries of human history generally called the Middle Ages.

Now, the important question arises: when did the "Middle Ages" *actually* occur in terms of Jewish history?

Historiography is somewhat vague in its definition of what constitutes the Middle Ages in general, where it began, where it ended. Historians almost generally accept the idea that this period begins with the fall of the Roman Empire, when it succumbed to the assault of barbarian hordes and ceased to be a world power. Its end is seen roughly in the rise of the Renaissance, at which time the modern era supposedly began. The period of the Middle Ages embraces a millennium of turmoil, disasters, wars, and social unrest. It was encompassed on one side, spiritually, by the iron grip of the Church on human society, as well as on the individual, with the lack of personal liberty; and on the other side politically, by the overwhelming imprint of the feudal system. Viewed from this aspect, it was appropriately called "the Dark Ages" of human history.

However, scholars of our age have different ideas as to what constitutes the Middle Ages in human history. To begin with, the notion of Middle Ages was first devised by a Dutch professor named HORN, in Leiden, in the seventeenth century. He denoted by it the *European* history, as well as the region in which the Latin language was paramount, dominating the Church and—through the influence of ecclesiastical thinking—the world of science and learning at large. The subdivision of history into "ancient," "medieval," and "modern" followed automatically, with "ancient," and "modern" becoming, so to say, the pillars on which this arbitrary denomination had to rest. Now, this system of ancient-medieval-modern is, according to OSWALD SPENGLER (1880-1936), "an incredibly jejune and meaningless scheme,"[1] which for a long time has entirely dominated our historical thinking.[2] The cultures that each of these arbitrarily created epochs brought forth are more meaningful than the simple rectilinear progression in which historiography recorded each successive century of human struggle for self-assertion. What SPENGLER meant by culture" is the sum total of everything expressed by an inner symbolism that keeps the people of a specific era and a specific part of the world together. With a drastic simile, SPENGLER defined this "traditional" method of professional historians as "a sort of tapeworm industriously adding to itself one epoch after another."[3]

He considered the fundamental question of higher history not merely as a succession of events or as a sequel of the ups and downs of the clerical, dynastic, and social struggles of the nations and masses. It is rather the image of the failure and fulfillment of mankind's struggle to assert its civilization. He saw "civilization as the inevitable *destiny* of the culture," each civilization having its own ways of self-expression, which arises, flourishes, and decays. In applying SPENGLER's thoughts to Jewish history, we may come closer to a definition of the time span that constitutes the *Jewish* Middle Ages.

ARNOLD TOYNBEE disagrees with SPENGLER's theory according to which civilizations arise, flourish, and decline, and all this in an unvarying conformity to an unchanging time table. To TOYNBEE this seems dogmatic and deterministic, and it is, indeed, a scheme too rigid to be applied to Western history, let alone to the history of the Jewish people. As TOYNBEE sees it, "civilizations, like nations, are plural, not singular; there are different civilizations which meet and, of their encounters, societies of another species, and most important, the higher religions are born into this world."[4]

It is well known how TOYNBEE has been attacked by Jews and non-Jews alike for his absurd statement that the Jews represent a surviving fossil of the ancient Syrian civilization.[5] Yet, in another statement, he gives full credit to the Jewish contributions to our *Weltanschauung*. As he puts it, "in the vision seen by the Prophets of Israel and Judah, history is not a cycle and not a mechanical process. It is the masterful and progressive execution, on the narrow stage of this world, of a divine plan which is revealed to us in this fragmentary glimpse, but which transcends our human powers of vision and understanding in every dimension. Moreover, the Prophets, through their own experience, anticipated Aeschylus' discovery that learning comes through suffering—a discovery which we, in our time and circumstances, have been making too, a statement that has an even higher significance for the Jewish people.[6]

TOYNBEE sees history as the cyclical flowering and dying of *contemporaneous* cultures. In his reasoning, the kingdoms of Israel and Judah, two of the many states of the ancient Syrian world, were prematurely and permanently overthrown with the result that the extinction of all the political hopes for their existence as independent states brought the *religion of Judaism* to birth. TOYNBEE leaves the question open as to whether Abraham and Moses were historical personages, but, as he says, "it can be taken as certain that they represent historical stages of religious experience."[7] He surmises that Moses and Abraham received their enlightenment and their promise at the dissolution, in the nineteenth or eighteenth century B.C.E. of the ancient civilizations of Sumer and Akkad, this being, as far as we know today, the earliest case of a civilization going to ruin.[8]

The destiny of the Jews, after the destruction of their national existence, at no time paralleled that of the people among whom they lived. Their fate was determined by their own living conditions and by the attitude expressed toward them by the surrounding cultures. Thus, it may be postulated that the Middle Ages of the general European history does not necessarily coincide with the Middle Ages of the Jews. Both SPENGLER and TOYNBEE are unanimous in maintaining that the Middle Ages of European history are not applicable to other continents, other civilizations, nor other peoples. For us, the Middle Ages of Jewish existence have other criteria than simply paralleling it with the fate of one continent, one society, one civilization. To us, it seems to be logical that the Middle Ages of the Jews began with the destruction of their national state, and its continuance up to the Emancipation when the ghetto walls were broken down. By this, we may be at variance with general historiography. But the fate of the Jewish people, so different from that of other nations, certainly warrants a different approach in evaluating its historical, social, and cultural aspects.

Therefore, in examining the main streams of Jewish history, we would probably be justified in maintaining that the period of the Middle Ages for the Jews embraces all the centuries of persecution, suffering, oppression—and survival.

Considering, however, the fact that this new concept of the Jewish Middle Ages coincides historically and culturally with the life of the Jews in the European Diaspora up to the year 1800, we shall retain the latter idea for the title of the present book, as well as for the literary exposition of its text. This will help the reader to avoid the many confusions that might arise from the use of the same technical terms for different historical situations—Jewish and non-Jewish.

Before starting our investigation, it would seem to be appropriate to point out certain analogies as well as differences which exist between the intellectual and spiritual climate of Christian and Jewish life especially when both religions coexisted in an epoch that constitutes the European Middle Ages.

1. Both were overwhelmingly dominated by their respective religions: Christian life under the undisputed tyranny of the papacy and the clergy; Jewish life under strong rabbinical ruling, which left no liberty for individual thinking.

There was, however, an intrinsic difference between the two. The Christian religion was expanding, embracing voraciously more and more peoples, nations, continents, influencing politically and administratively—through their secular arm—the social and economic life of the believers. In contrast to this, the Jewish religion was introspective, self-contained, with no political aspirations, only striving to keep alive the tradition of the Fathers.

2. Both were ruled politically by a small segment of the population, the Christian world by the power of a well-rooted feudal system, exercised by the princes and the nobility; the Jews by the

authority invested in the Rabbis. In reality, the Rabbis not only were the spiritual leaders of the Jews, but reigned supreme, almost autocratically, over the destinies, the thinking, and emotional life of their co-religionists. Their edicts and ordinances, couched in a religious garment, invoking the Mosaic law, had just as much force for the Jews as decrees issued by the secular authorities.

3. In both worlds the individual had neither freedom of conscience nor choice but to follow blindly the way of life prescribed by the masters of their destiny. Individuals who dared to have different ideas from those generally sanctioned were considered heretics, outcasts, who had to suffer the consequences of their convictions. This amounted in the Christian world mostly to the stake, in the Jewish world to excommunication, with all its horrors for those who were subjected to such a fate.

4. In both worlds, the Christian as well as the Jewish, the intellectual life was governed exclusively by the tenets of the religion. It is evident that in such an atmosphere sciences could not thrive. The scholarship of the Church and the Rabbis was devoted almost exclusively to the expounding of sacred texts, of theological hair-splitting, of interpretation and definition of the "word." The few examples of the courageous who showed signs of individual thinking stand out as beacons in a dark night.

1

The Early Diaspora

Eastern Settlements

WE NEED NOT WAIT AS LATE AS THE YEAR 315 C.E., WHICH WAS THE official date of historiography for the beginning of the European Middle Ages. The Jewish Middle Ages began at the time when they lost their national independence, and from this it follows that the early records of Jewish Middle Ages coincide with the scriptural Talmudic epoch.

In this period, Jewish music and its practice were supposed to be extinct. So goes the saying, at least. For, as we know, after the loss of the Jerusalem Sanctuary severe interdictions by zealous rabbis were issued, prohibiting the "loud" *i.e.*, public cultivation of music, instrumental as well as vocal, with the possible exception of some sacred songs and hymns in the synagogal liturgy. Had these interdictions been carried out rigorously, this would have been the end of Jewish music. Yet, what happened in reality? How did such prohibitions work out in everyday life?

Before answering this question let us go several centuries back to Jewish history.

After the destruction of the First (Solomon's) Temple in 586 B.C.E., NEBUCHADREZZAR deported the flower of the Jewish population to Babylonia. First they lived there oppressed, captives, bewailing their national and personal misfortune, toiling and struggling for daily necessities. However, as time went by, their fate improved, the external hardships of their life were alleviated and, with the usual and often proven aptitude of the Jewish people to adapt themselves to new circumstances, they succeeded in creating for themselves a new home in an alien country. They multiplied, prospered, and, with improved conditions, they revived their ancient spiritual and cultural activities, among them music. Zion was far off. The loss of the Temple, though considered a severe blow of fate, was not felt by Babylonian Jewry as acute as perhaps by those who remained in the homeland. Thus, Babylonian Jews put up with the existing conditions and eventually reconciled themselves to the idea that Babylon was an acceptable substitute for their lost country.

They were never seriously handicapped in the exercise of their religion, and this alone was a strong reason for being satisfied with their new life. Thus, after nearly half a century in exile, only a relatively small part of them, led by ZERUBBABEL, returned to Zion (638 B.C.E.). About eighty years later, a second and a much smaller wave of exiled Jews, under the leadership of EZRA the Scribe, returned to the ancient homeland, still leaving behind a substantial part of the Jewish population in Babylon. Here, the remaining Jews, by the sheer number of their inhabitants and even more so by the spiritual climate, which they established in their new homeland, became, even during the existence of the Second Commonwealth, the most important intellectual settlement of Jews outside the Holy Land.

Then came the Roman assault upon Jerusalem (70 C.E.). While the final phases of the struggle for the life and death of the Jewish nation were still in progress, the spiritual leaders of Palestinian Jewry already thought of, and made plans for, preserving at least the religious and intellectual life of Judaism. After the inevitable catastrophe, the leaders of the surviving Jews acted at once.

JOHANAN ben ZAKKAI and his disciples asked the victorious Romans and obtained their permission to establish outside of Jerusalem a central, nonpolitical institution for the preservation and continuation of Jewish spiritual life under the changed circumstances. They had chosen a small but historically important settlement, Yabneh, situated on the Mediterranean coast. Their aim was nothing less than the creation of a supranational leadership for the lost Jewish state, and they achieved this by setting up a supreme authority with the purpose of concentrating all Jewish energies toward one goal: religious and spiritual survival, with the exclusion of everything that did not directly serve their higher aims. To what extent they succeeded is evidenced by the subsequent destiny of Jewry, showing the world the complete religious unity of a people torn nationally to shreds, while unbroken in spirit.

Here in Yabneh was founded the first of the academies where Jewish learning continued and developed to unprecedented heights. During the period following the revolt of BAR KOKBA (131-135 C.E.), the Academy at Yabneh was transferred to Usha in Galilee, then to Bet-Shearim, and later to Sepphoris. It was there that R. YUDAH edited the *Mishnah*. Eventually, the center of learning was moved to Tiberias, where the great legal discussion by the Amoraim ("expounders," "interpreters") on the text of the *Mishnah* began. This led to the completion of the Palestinian Talmud about 400 C.E. At the end of the eleventh century, during the Crusades, the Palestinian academies ceased to exist.

Meanwhile, however, stimulated apparently by the reawakening of the intellectual life in the homeland, especially after the Roman victory, and taking advantage of the favorable spiritual climate of Babylonia, further academies were created in this most important Jewish settlement outside of Palestine. Here, at the beginning of the third century, the first important Babylonian academy was established in Nehardea, soon followed by a similar institution in Sura. When in 259 C.E. the city of Nehardea was destroyed, its academy was transferred to Pumbedita. This latter center of learning became the leading force of intellectual life for Babylonian Jewry and retained that position until the end of the Gaonic period.

The Academy of Sura lasted until 946 C.E., that of Pumbedita another century. Thus there existed simultaneously in Babylonia two separate academies which, being remote from one another, did not interfere with each other's decisions.

For centuries the various Babylonian academies had their ups and downs, those of Sura and Pumbedita gaining eventually lasting prominence. They were considered the only important seats of learning: ". . . their heads were the undisputed authorities, whose decisions were sought from all sides and were accepted wherever Jewish communal life existed."[1]

The official designation of the Babylonian academies was the

Aramaic *metibta* (Hebr. *yeshibah*). The head of the academy was accordingly called *resh meshibta* (*rosh yeshibah*). In these academies the Babylonian Talmud was completed by the Gaonim and Saboraim ("reasoners") at about 500 C.E.

All these academies, in Palestine as well as in Babylonia, were instrumental in preserving and developing the Jewish intellectual heritage, the *Midrash* and *Mishnah*. They also prepared the way for a systematic treatment of the Talmudic *Halakah* and *'Aggadah* as well as the Biblical exegesis.

With all these undeniable merits, the great deficiency of all the academies cannot be overlooked, since they completely failed to preserve one of the most significant parts of the ancient national heritage: the music of the Forefathers. The strong rabbinical prohibition with regard to music after the fall of Jerusalem was only one reason for this neglect by the academies; the other was the complete misconception of the sages about the importance of music in the people's life. They did not realize, or did not *want* to realize, what solace, what moral uplifting and promise for the future music had for a downtrodden and persecuted people. In this respect, all the scholarly institutions failed completely. And had the people themselves not continued to cling to their musical practice, as much as possible in the face of prohibitions and the existing dangerous circumstances, Jewish music would have become irremediably extinct at that time. Therefore, the distinction of having saved Jewish music does not belong to the scholarly men but to the people itself.

The learned men of the academies were only the spiritual leaders of Babylonian Jewry. Furthermore, the inhabitants of this settlement, the largest in the East, established for themselves a secular head who reigned over them with a veritable royal authority from the second through the eleventh century C.E.

This was the office of the Exilarch ("*rosh golah*" or "*resh galuta*"), a title given to the head of the Babylonian Jews, a position of honor, recognized by the kings and monarchs of Babylonia. The office, as first, was elective, and thereafter became hereditary in a family that traced its descent back to the house of David.

The Exilarch collected taxes for the secular government and was the supreme judge of the Jewish people. He was responsible for the public security and, furthermore, he controlled the trade and commerce of the Jewish community.

The sublime authority of the Exilarch was characterized by the fact that—like the Oriental heads of state—he lived in luxury and splendor. Some of the Exilarchs dressed entirely in silk,[2] gave sumptuous banquets, and enjoyed a veneration by the people not unlike that accorded to a crowned monarch.

The Exilarchs gathered a large retinue of scholars around them who were called *rabban di-bey resh galuta,* "scholars of the house of the Exilarch." They wore certain badges on their garments to indicate their status.[3] Furthermore, as befitted the exalted office, the Exilarch had numerous servants attached to their home; these servants, basking in the splendor of their master, would often insult and mistreat guests and even reputed scholars who came visiting the Exilarch. The Talmud contains several anecdotes about the indignities that persons of standing had to suffer at the hands of some insolent servants.[4]

The sublime authority of the Exilarchs is aptly characterized by the fact that, like most Oriental potentates, they kept some musicians permanently employed at their court. The Talmud tells us that the Exilarch rose in the morning with music (a veritable *lever* like that of the French kings of later times), and retired for the night with music,[5] as fitting for a highly placed person. Arabic writers also stated that the Exilarch maintained a number of musicians at his court.

Under the Moslem rule in Babylonia, the Exilarch was accepted by the Caliph not only as the spiritual but also as the secular head of all the Jews in Babylonia, Turkestan, Armenia, Persia, and Yemen. One of the Exilarchs, HUNA ben NATHAN, visited a Babylonian king, who with his own hands girded him with the belt that was the sign of the Exilarch's office. BENJAMIN of Tudela in his report about his journey to the Orient in the twelfth century, writes that all subjects of the Caliph were required to "rise in the presence of the Prince of Captivity and to salute him respectfully."

The installation ceremony of a newly elected Exilarch shows

the veneration accorded him by the members of his community. This ceremony took place on the Sabbath. The first homage was paid him on Thursday in the synagogue, and the event was announced by trumpet blasts. (It is reasonable to assume that the *shofar* was used for this ceremony, although BENJAMIN's report does not specify the type of instrument, and we know furthermore that in Talmudic times the terms for the two instruments, trumpet and *shofar*, were often used interchangeably.) On Thursday and Friday the Exilarch gave great banquets to which all persons of standing and the leading scholars of the town were invited. Though the existing records do not state it explicitly, it is certain that the house musicians participated at these banquets.

On Sabbath morning the elders of the community called for the Exilarch and marched with him in a solemn cortège to the synagogue. Here, a wooden platform (*bima*) had been erected, covered entirely with costly cloth. Under this platform "a selected choir of sweet-voiced youths well versed in the liturgy had been placed," singing responsively with the leader of the prayer.[6] Their singing was the highlight of the installation ceremony. After the *Musaf* prayer the entire congregation followed the Exilarch to his house, singing psalms and hymns, set to music, which were familiar to everyone.

Does it appear, from all these reports, that the strong rabbinical prohibitions concerning music and singing were really carried out to the hilt? Not only the report about this inauguration ceremony, but a great number of indications in the Talmudic literature bear out just the contrary conclusion. We quote at random the most significant ones, which will afford an insight into the musical practice of the Jews in the post-Biblical period.

The most important pronouncement in this respect is the Talmudic instruction that the sacred texts always must be taught in conjunction with singing, as stated explicitly: "If one reads the Scripture without a melody or repeats the *Mishnah* without a tune, of him the Scripture says, 'Wherefore I gave them also statutes that were not good.' "[7] One may easily imagine how much the teaching of the young with the aid of singing (or chanting) may have contributed to the preservation of the ancient musical tradition.

The method of teaching by chanting the material to be used was based upon two practical considerations. On the one hand, chanting of the Scriptural text was looked upon as essential for clarity, syntactical intelligibility and, not least, for the solemnity of the lection; on the other hand, the live experience showed that studying with chanting was infinitely more effective than the spoken word alone for memorizing the text. Since the tradition was first transmitted exclusively by oral means, chanting became an indispensable mnemonic aid in learning extended passages from the Scriptures.

As late as the twelfth century, R. PETAḤYAH of REGENSBURG, who had made extensive voyages in the Orient, observed that in places visited by him the entire Talmud was recited with singing (v'kol ha-talmud be-niggun). This chanting practice has been preserved even in the present time for studying the *Talmud*.

The words "singing" and "music" run through rabbinic writings frequently. The *Gemarah* considers singing not only an expression of the joy of living, but also attributes to it the power of raising divine enthusiasm. It states: "What type of worship is done with joy and good heart? You should say: it is song."[8] Such ethical evaluation of singing contradicts the severe interdiction of singing by some overzealous rabbis. Of course, there was a precise distinction between singing for sacred and secular purposes. Still some ultra-orthodox rabbis advocated the abolition of all singing, even in the synagogue. The inborn good sense of other spiritual leaders spared posterity such a calamity; in fact, singing in the synagogue was never seriously menaced.

At the ordination of rabbis, the participating colleagues performed merry songs: "When they ordained him [R. ZIRA], they [the schoolmen] sang before him."[9] At solemn receptions of high religious dignitaries, singing belonged to the honors bestowed upon distinguished guests: "When R. ʾABBAHU arrived at the Emperor's Court [in Caesarea], from College, the ladies of the Court went out to receive him and sang to him: 'Great man of thy people, leader of thy nation, lantern of light, thy coming be blessed with peace.'"[10]

At the Feast of the *Bet ha-Sheʿuba* at Tabernacles, the singing of the rabbis, as accompaniment to the torch dances, was one of the highlights of the water-libation ceremony.[11]

Singing played an all-important role at the most joyful events in the life of the individual, the wedding. At no other festive occasion was there more abundant singing than at weddings. Wise and virtuous rabbis did not consider it beneath their dignity to adorn the wedding ceremonies with their songs; they sang, alone or in groups, in honor of the bridal couple, and at times topped off the songs with dances: "At the marriage feast of MAR, the son of RABINA, . . . the rabbis said to R. HAMNUNA ZUTI: 'Let the master sing for us.' "[12] At the same wedding a group of rabbis participated in singing.[13] Occasional textual fragments of wedding songs are preserved in some of the rabbinical writings.[14]

Wedding songs in Babylonia seem to have differed from those in Palestine, for R. DIMI, returning to Babylon from visiting the mother country, reported: "Thus they sing before the bride in the West [i.e. in Palestine]: 'No powder and no paint and no waving [of the hair], and still a graceful gazelle.' "[15]

The Talmudic 'Aggadah looked upon the wedding song as an indispensable element of joy: "The ministering angels assembled and came to listen like people who assemble and come to watch the [musical] entertainment of a bridegroom and bride at a wedding,"[16]

How widespread singing must have been in Jewish life at this time may be judged from the following Talmudic passage: "The song of thanksgiving was [sung to the accompaniment of] lutes, lyres, and cymbals at every corner and upon every great stone in Jerusalem."[17]

The loss of the Sanhedrin was not the only reason for the rabbinic prohibition of singing and music. The abuses of certain strata of society, whose revelries were accompanied by singing, music, dancing girls, and jesters, aroused the ire of the puritanic rabbis. The religious leaders have justly been alarmed by the unseemly attitude displayed within these social circles, toward singing and music, which deteriorated to a point where the esthetic pleasure turned into a mere voluptous sensation. For moral reasons they felt justified in denouncing this kind of licentious singing. The sensuous charm of the female voice was castigated with particular severity: "Listening to a woman's voice [song] is a sexual incitement."[18] "When men sing and women join in, it is licentiousness; when women sing and men join in, it is like fire in tow."[19]

In a significant parable, the destructive effect of such debased music is aptly characterized: "Thy children have made me as a harp (*kinnor*) upon which they frivolously (*lezim*) play (*menagnim*)."[20] By *lezim* the Talmudic scribe means the ungodly ones, symbolizing the pernicious influence of secular music.

As long as the Sanhedrin existed, it could check such social abuses as the widely expanding pleasure-hunting of the well-to-do. Later, the restraint was no longer effective, so the Talmud of Jerusalem complains: "In olden times the fear of the Sanhedrin was over them, so they did not sing [i.e., revel]. Now the fear of the Sanhedrin is not over them, so they sing."[21]

All this proves that the rabbinical prohibitions of music, generally speaking, did not have much effect. However, in one particular instance, we have an even more drastic indication that the draconic measures of some unyielding religious authorities caused a veritable social calamity. For some reason, which is not divulged by the Talmud, R. Huna had forbidden secular singing. As a result, all mundane feasts ceased, because singing was an indispensable element for all festivities. This prohibition caused a social disaster which, together with an economic crisis, rose to such proportions that the prices of essential commodities fell to a bottomless low. "Hundred geese were priced at a *zuz* and hundred *se'ahs* of wheat at a *zuz* and there was no demand for them [even at that price]." R. Ḥisda, the successor to R. Huna, showed more understanding of human nature and abolished his predecessor's prohibition of singing. Immediately, the prices rose again: "A goose was required [even at the high price of] a *zuz* but was not to be found."[22]

This Talmudic report, however spurious or exaggerated it may appear, is symptomatic of the cheerful conception of life among the Israelites, with its invariable leitmotif of merry singing.

Even long after the destruction of the Temple, the opinions of the sages were divided as to whether all secular singing or merely singing accompanied by instruments should be expressly prohibited. To settle this question, a special inquiry was addressed to the most famous rabbinical authority of those times, the Exilarch MAR 'UKBA (third century C.E.). About this procedure we read in the Talmud: "An inquiry was once addressed to MAR 'UKBA: 'Where does the Scripture tell us that it is forbidden [in these times] to sing [at carousals]?' He sent back [the following quotation] written on lines: Hosea 9:1 (Rejoice not, O Israel, unto exultation, like the peoples, for thou hast gone astray from thy God). Should he not rather have sent the following: Isaiah 24:8-9? (The mirth of tabrets ceaseth, the noise of them that rejoice endeth, the joy of the harp ceaseth. They drink not wine with a song). From this verse I should conclude that only musical instruments are forbidden, but not song."[23] Evidently enough, rabbinical astuteness and discernment always found ways and means to justify and maintain secular singing. The joy of it could not be extirpated among the Israelites, despite the most severe interdictions.

Even if the amount of the mundane pleasures caused by the solemn occasion did not actually measure up to it, the joy of singing compensated the participants for the food shortage. The Talmud reports that once in a Passover meal "there was [only] as much as an olive of the Passover offering [to eat], yet the Hallel split the roofs! [it was sung with such gusto]."[24]

In the religious conception of the Jews, singing was not only a mundane, but also a celestial institution. According to a Talmudic legend, three groups of angels sang daily songs of praise in honor of the Most High.[25] And the same Talmudic passage attributes to the angel who wrestled with Jacob (Gen. 32:26) the words: "I am an angel, and from the day that I was created my time to sing praises [to the Lord] had not come until now."[26] This passage, incidentally, would point indirectly to the existence of an immense multitude of singing angels, according to Jewish conception. Curiously, God prefers the mundane singing to that of the angelic, for the "ministering angels sing praises but once a day, whereas Israel sings praises to the Lord every hour."[27]

According to the naïve conception of the Midrash, God is so pleased with the singing as such that "every day the Holy One

. . . creates a band of new angels who utter a new song before Him and then pass away."[28] And the singing of His chosen people is so agreeable to the Lord that "whenever God hears Israel's song He calls the heavenly host to listen."[29] Even if the Lord has a resentment against His people, He is softened when He hears the singing of Israel: "When Israel . . . praises and extols God, He listens to their voices and is appeased."[30]

There were some tragic occurrences in the life of Israel about which God prohibited singing to the host of angels: "On three occasions the Ministering Angels wished to utter song before the Holy One . . . , but He would not let them [viz. at the Flood, at the drowning of the Egyptians in the Red Sea, and at the destruction of the Temple]."[31]

According to the legend, the Lord Himself indulges in singing: "When the Levites started playing and addressed the whole Israel with high voice (kol rom), you should not read kol rom, but kekolo shel rom, like the voice of the High One. We learn from this that the Lord Himself participates in their music."[32] This corroborates strongly the rabbinical contention that singing is of divine origin. In Job 35:10, God is referred to as a "song-giver."

The importance of singing in the conception of Ancient Israel may be described as a great cycle, the starting point of which is heaven itself. Even before the creation of the world, there was singing in heaven—in daily life singing was regarded as inseparable from man's earthly destiny and closely bound to his joys and sorrows—in addition to this, singing was considered inherently divine, and was capable of transporting man to the source of everything that is lofty and sublime, which were the celestial regions themselves.

In the early centuries of the Diaspora a development took place that proved to have the greatest repercussions on the future of music history in general, and on the history of Christian church music in particular.

Relatively soon after the consolidation of the new religion, Christian music schools had been created. These were modeled after the Levitical schools of music which flourished during all the centuries of the existence of the Temple at Jerusalem. During the nationhood of Ancient Israel the schools of the Levites were instrumental not only in the preservation of the Jewish musical heritage, but they also instructed countless generations in the complex art of liturgical singing.

In the musical service of the early Christian church we encounter the same order as in the Temple: the Christian "lector" corresponds to the Jewish "reader"; the Christian "precentor" to the Jewish *menazzeah,* the soloist of the Levitical choir. We find in the Christian liturgy the ancient Jewish forms of responsorial and antiphonal chant, with this difference, however: while Jewish singing was based upon the Oriental, flexible melodic pattern, governed by the *makam* principle, the Christians used more or less stabilized melodic forms, which in time acquired an almost canonic rigidity, as we witness in the later collections of Ambrosian and Gregorian chants. These Christian schools of music display the strong influences which the Jewish musical practices exerted upon them.

During the centuries of the Dispersion the question would arise again and again whether music, and especially singing, should be abolished altogether, whether it may be permissible on special occasions, or at least in the synagogue service. To clarify this question, the scattered Jewish communities from time to time asked the opinion of the leading religious authorities. The responses they gave constitute a remarkable documentation not only of the religious, but also of the social history of Judaism in the Diaspora.

Of these rabbinical opinions we shall present a succinct survey in a subsequent chapter where the communal life of the Jews in the Western settlements will be investigated.

Western Settlements

As early as during the national statehood of Ancient Israel, the Jews had spread over the whole Mediterranean area. There were Jewish communities in practically every larger city. They were held together by one faith, one ritual, one Bible, and, later, by the Talmud.

After the national disaster of the destruction of Jerusalem, the dispersed Jews settled wherever they were tolerated, wherever they saw an opportunity for survival. At that time the political and religious importance of the lost homeland was at its nadir; the leadership, religious as well as intellectual, had been transferred to Babylonia. The Talmud became the strong link that connected the dispersed Jews living separated from each other in foreign lands, under ruthless rulers, in strange and mostly hostile environments. The Talmud and its study had spread from Babylonia to Egypt, North Africa, Italy, to the Iberian peninsula, and from there to France and Germany. Eventually, these regions were destined to become the abodes for Jewish learning and Jewish spirit; and in all these countries intellectual interest centered in the Talmud.

The Talmud could not be, and should not be, understood merely in terms of history, or even as a code of law destined to regulate everyday life. It was "an organ of survival for a people exiled, destitute, oppressed, and in danger of utter disintegration." Using a bold metaphor, HEINE said that "the Talmud was a portable fatherland; wherever Jews lived, even as fearful enclaves in alien and hostile lands, they could retreat into their own world, where they subjected themselves to the injunctions of their Prophets and rabbis, and bathed their minds and hearts in the ocean of the Law."[1]

There was strong emphasis on ritual in the Talmud, as part of the Jews' defense mechanism against the attempts of Church and state to make him abandon his Law and his ritual, which gave him his sense of identity, bond of unity and continuity, and which functioned as a badge of defiance to a never-forgiving world.

Here and there in these twenty odd volumes of Talmudic commentary, one finds words of hatred for Christianity; but they were for a Christianity that had forgotten the gentleness of Jesus. It was their reaction to a Christianity that persecuted the adherents of the Law which Jeshua (Jesus), the young Jewish rabbi, had enjoined his followers to fulfill; and to a Christianity that had, in view of the Jewish sages, abandoned the monotheism which was the inalienable essence of the Judaic faith, as well as of the early Christian faith.[2]

What kept the Jews as one people throughout the Diaspora was not theology alone, but ritual of such burdensome complexity that only a stubborn and sensitive people could muster the humility and patience necessary to obey it.[3]

)ABBA)AREKA (RAB), the celebrated Babylonian)Amora (interpreter) clearly states the ethical purpose of Jewish life: "The laws were given only for the purpose of disciplining and refining men by their observance." "Refining men" was, and is, the characteristic attitude of the Jews toward study and learning.

Whatever they experienced, whatever tribulations fate bestowed upon them, learning and intellectual striving kept them alive and fit for the struggle which survival demanded.

The Talmudic Jews should not be regarded as abject pessimists, despite the oppression and poverty they suffered. Through centuries of rejection they kept their heads high, sustained by their vision and longing for a restored homeland, supported in their earthly travail by the tenderness and brief beauty of their burdened women and their sensitivity to the splendor of the earth and sky above them.[4]

Despite their tribulations—and they were enormous—the Jews of the Diaspora always recovered. Patiently they rebuilt their ravaged or destroyed synagogues, reorganized their lives, traded, prayed and hoped, increased and multiplied. Just as it had been obligatory in Jerusalem and in all other places of the homeland, so in the Diaspora each settlement was required to maintain at communal expense at least one elementary and one secondary school, which as a rule were in the synagogue (until our days the Jews call the synagogue their "shul"). Scholars were advised not to settle in any town that lacked such schools. R. SIMEON ben YOHAI (disciple of R. 'AKIBA) said: "If you see cities in the land of Israel that are destroyed to their very foundations, know that it is because they did not provide pay for teachers of the Bible and of Tradition."[5]

The language of worship and instruction was Hebrew. The

language of daily speech was Aramaic in the East (the language of both Talmudim) and Greek in Egypt and in the Mediterranean area. Elsewhere, the Jews adopted the language of the host country. After the rise of Mohammedanism, the Jews spoke Arabic in North Africa and Moslem Spain. After the conquest of Iberia by Christian rulers, the Jewish vernacular was Spanish or Portuguese, sometimes mixed with Arabic and Hebrew words. As time went by, this developed into a specific dialect of Sephardic Jewry, the Ladino (Judaeo-Spanish), which still survives among the Jews of the Mediterranean basin.

The study and observance of the Law was the central theme of Jewish education. Secular culture was almost completely ignored. The rabbis and scholars were convinced that dispersed Jewry could maintain itself intact in body and soul only through religious education.[6]

The Talmud was not a code of laws requiring strict obedience; it was a record of rabbinical discussions, opinions, and decisions, "head-splitting hair splitting," as DURANT says, dealing with what might and what might not be done in all walks of life, religious and secular. But the casuistry of the rabbis was directed to mitigating, rather than increasing the terrors of piety. The Talmud is above all a code of religious ethics, applied to every phase of daily conduct, which regulates all imaginable, and unimaginable, situations of human life.

Those who watched over the Talmudic prescriptions and tried to adapt them to the ever changing circumstances were the rabbis. Throughout Jewish history they were admired for their virtues and faults as well as for their devotion to learning. This remarkable aristocracy of the learned men was a unique phenomenon in Western history. The Rabbinate was open to rich and poor alike. and even after achieving renown as teachers, judges, and spiritual leaders most of them continued to earn their living as artisans or merchants, because they were not paid for their services as rabbis. Their wisdom won them special honors not only among their own people, but among the nobility of the Christian world, who recognized, albeit grudgingly, their intellectual attainments. "To this day no people so honors the student and the scholar as do the Jews."[7]

The wisdom of the race bade the Jews keep their festivals and feasts as the Scriptures demanded, and—despite the overtones of sorrow that resounded even in their joys—these observances released the hidden emotions of an oppressed people through singing and dancing, rejoicing and merrymaking—in obvious contradiction to the severe rabbinical prohibitions. It may be said that at no period in Jewish history were the people ever without music.

Following the destruction of Jerusalem by the Romans, the *national* life of the Jews was replaced by the *communal* life.* The Romans reserved for themselves the civil government of the conquered provinces, but otherwise they did not abolish existing communities and, above all, did not interfere with the internal affairs of the townships. For this reason, the Jews remaining in Palestine after their defeat still retained a central authority in the person of the Patriarch (*nasi*), who attended to the communal duties and even had the right to levy taxes. When the Jewish communities of Babylonia were separated from those of the mother country, they established for themselves, as we have seen, their own head, the Exilarch (*resh galuta*), whose authority surpassed even that of the Palestinian Patriarch.[8]

This pattern was adopted by most or all of the Jewish communities that came into being in the Dispersion. In these places the head of the community was called the "Archisynagogue." His tenure of office was for life, and even hereditary. His official title was *rosh ha-keneset,* "head of the assembly," although his authority was confined to liturgical and ritualistic matters. A higher synagogue office was that of the *ḥazzan ha-keneset,* whose functions included all other synagogal and general matters. His influence in communal life was increased considerably when he was designated the *sheliah ẓibbur,* the "delegate of the congregation," a position in which he was regarded as the intermediary between God and the community.

---

* It is not the aim of this study, and it would by far exceed the limits put to it, to give an account of Jewish communal life in the Dispersion. Yet it may be necessary to deal at least with its social implications, as far as musical practice is concerned, in order to examine how music fits into the communal organization of Jewry in the Diaspora. For information about this subject see S. W. Baron, *The Jewish Community* (Philadelphia, 1942). 3 vols.

Until then, the office of the *hazzan ha-keneset* was unpaid. In order to put an end to unpleasant rivalries for leadership in prayer, a salaried reader was soon appointed whose title was simply *hazzan,* but who subsequently was put in charge of some of the musical functions of the liturgy as well. As time went by, the *hazzan* assumed the role of the musical leader of the congregation. (About the *hazzan* more will be said in a subsequent chapter.)

After the decline of the offices of Exilarch and Archisynagogue, the learned rabbis became the spiritual leaders of the communities. As men who spent their lives in study and scholarship, expounding the Scriptures, and attempting to clear up the enigmatic pages of rabbinic literature, they could not be expected to do justice to the ancient musical heritage of the Jews, as well. Still, we know of outstanding rabbis in the early Middle Ages who assumed the functions of the *hazzan,* and were not merely the spiritual, but also the musical leaders of their congregations. Here, however, we can observe a curious fact. While the majority of the rabbis "were not themselves proficient in the musical art, the *bahurim,* or Talmud students of the Middle Ages, were often accomplished musicians."[9] This is an apparent contradiction, inasmuch as the *bahurim* later became rabbis themselves. Therefore, it appears that what constituted a virtue for a student was a vice for a rabbi.

This is self-explanatory if we consider the general attitude of the congregation toward its spiritual leader. The rabbi was expected to be wise, learned, and just; he had to interpret the Scriptures, to further the religious feeling of the congregants, apply the wisdom of Solomon in the case of litigation, and display, in all the circumstances of life, a model of human behavior. For such multiple duties a musical aptitude seemed to be a liability more than an asset. It is therefore understandable that the musical talent of some rabbis was generally passed over in silence, even when they distinguished themselves in this art while still young men. Nevertheless, we will see in the chapter devoted to the activity of the *hazzanim* that quite a number of distinguished rabbis also excelled in the field of music.

Except for a few cities in Spain, there existed in the early Diaspora no marked segregation of Jews from the native population; "usually, however, they lived in a voluntary isolation, for social convenience, physical security, and religious unity."[10] There was one more important reason for the isolation. The synagogue was not only the geographical, social, and religious center of the community, but also the place where the Jews could partake in the only entertainment available to them, singing and dancing. At a later period (since the thirteenth century), and especially in Germanic countries, dance houses sprang up to satisfy the human need for entertainment. But in the early centuries of the Dispersion the only place where the Jews had an outlet for their natural inclination for music was the synagogue, its courtyard, or another small gathering place in its neighborhood. Therefore, the Jews had to live close by, despite the general overcrowding and bad public and private sanitary conditions.

Furthermore, the synagogue was also the communal court, the *Beth Din,* where justice was administered, ordinances issued, and rules established over every aspect of Jewish life, morals, diets, dress, economy, fixing taxes, imposing fines and penalties, including the carrying out of the most dreadful punishment in Jewish life, the *herem,* or total excommunication. This was a frightening ceremony of charges hurled, curses fired, and candles extinguished one by one as a symbol of the accused's spiritual death. During the ceremony *shofar* blasts added the required tonal background to make the act of excommunication even more gruesome.

The *shofar* was also sounded in the synagogue for other extra-religious occasions: prolonged drought which threatened to cause famine; economic calamities; warnings for impending hostilities of the Christian world, etc. Threatened by one of these, or other adversities, the Jews assembled in the synagogue, prayed and fasted; the solemnities of prayer were heightened by the blowing of the *shofar,* which in the subconscious of medieval Jewry retained some of the erstwhile magic connotations. When, after a long drought, rain began to fall, the synagogue was the scene of great rejoicing, with singing of the *Hallel,* the Psalms of Praise.

Throughout their history, the family life of the Jews was exemplary. No people surpassed the Jews in the cheerfulness and serenity of their family life. Every home in Judaism was a sanctuary, every school was a temple of learning, and every father was a patriarch.[11] On the eve of the Sabbath the entire family, together with their servants, assembled before the head of the household, who blessed them individually, and led them in prayer and in singing of *zemirot*, the sacred festive songs.

Just as in Ancient Israel, and later in Babylonia, every synagogue in the Diaspora had a school (*Beth ha-Midrash*, House of Study) for elementary instruction. Many synagogues, especially in the larger communities, established a school for higher learning. This devotion to education, based on Talmudic rulings, resulted in a higher degree of literacy among the Jews than among the Christians in the early medieval era. The students learned by means of verbal repetition, chanted or sung aloud. Sometimes the resulting chorus was so noisy that neighbors were given the right to prevent the creation of a Jewish school in their neighborhood, as they might similarly have prevented the introduction of a trade that created a nuisance.[12]

Since in most cases all learning was done in the synagogue by chanting, we may consider, by implication, that the synagogue was also the music school of the Jews, a function generally overlooked.

The musical practice of the scattered Jews during the early centuries of the Dispersion centered in cantillation. Formerly, in Ancient Israel, the Jews possessed a highly developed instrumental music. Once again in the Western settlements, where they were in constant intercourse with the surrounding peoples, and stimulated by the more advanced musical instruments of the Middle Ages, they took up the practice of instrumental music. But in the intermediate centuries, the musical urge of the Jews was mainly relegated to the vocal art; and in this field cantillation represented the foremost, in some respects the unique, musical outlet for Jewish emotions.

During the centuries of the early Diaspora the art and science of cantillation of the Biblical text underwent a transformation from very limited and often loosely used motivic patterns to a highly systematized practice with rigid rules of chanting.

In Jewish liturgy the term cantillation refers to the intonation, or musical inflection, used for the public readings of the Holy Scriptures, in order to make them more meaningful and impressive. The earliest mention of this manner of presenting the sacred text in a musical or semimusical manner appears in Nehemiah 8:8, where it is said: "They read in the book, in the Law of God, distinctly; and they gave the sense, and caused them to understand the reading." And in a further verse: "For all the people wept when they heard the word of the Law." It is the consensus of Biblical exegesis that these passages clearly indicate the fact that some sort of solemn cantillation might have been used so that "the people wept."

From this primitive manner of chanting to the highly sophisticated system of cantillation is still a long way. But we can follow this way through the early Diaspora by examining the respective statements in rabbinical literature. The earliest mention of a definite form of chanting, similar to that described in Nehemiah 8:8, occurs in the Babylonian Talmud,[13] where R. JOHANAN ben NAPPARA (d. 279 C.E.) declares that "if one reads the Scripture without a melody (ne'ima) or repeats the Mishnah without a tune (zimrah), of him the Scripture says, 'Wherefore I gave them also statutes that were not good' (Ezekiel 20:25)." Rabbi 'AKIBA, too, recommends the study of the Law with chanting.[14] We read further in the Talmud that special instruction had to be given for the pisuḳ ta'amim,[15] which were the terms used for cantillation by the rabbinical writers.[16]

More recent theories deprived the Talmudic ne'ima of its original meaning as the melody proper; it is taken to be some type of intonation in general, referring to the "sweetness" of the singing voice in particular.[17]

The next step in the practice of cantillation was the creation of certain signs, the "accents" or "ta'amim," which originally had mainly syntactical functions, like the signs of interpunction employed today. As time passed, these signs assumed certain musical meanings. There are modern opinions which maintain that it was the rabbis who felt the need of codifying a system by which the preservation of the ancient modes would be assured. This overlooks the historical facts. Cantillation existed long before the Temple of Jerusalem was destroyed by the Romans. At that time the musical part of the sacred service was carried out by the Levites; they alone might have been concerned with preserving in some tangible form, their ancient musical tradition and they

might have applied to the Biblical text certain signs which were
in all probability the graphic form of their choir leaders' gestures
(about which we shall hear more presently) when conducting
the Levitical singers.

The *ta'amim* do not designate tonal values nor any succession
of notes in the Western meaning; they stand for conventional
series or groups of sounds attached to the syllables or words in a
certain manner, so that the meaning of the text as well as its
rhythm received emphasis and illustrations from the chant.[17]
They were not yet a musical "notation" in the proper sense of the
word; but were supposed to aid the reader in remembering certain intonations which were already learned by rote.

As these accents became highly useful for the musically impressive rendering of the Biblical text, the manner in which they
were employed gave birth to two different schools, the Babylonian
and the Palestinian system of accents, with an additional variant
to be found in the Samaritan system.

Although originally mainly graphic symbols of syntax, they
became gradually associated with the concurrently used brief
motives, later termed as *neginoth* (sing. *neginah* = melodicle) or
tropes (Gr. *tropos* = turn, manner, type). We know of their existence in the post-Talmudic period in a rudimentary form from
about the seventh century. The Masoretes perfected them so that
around the year 900 they acquired their final form, as far as a
finality could be achieved in a constantly fluctuating musical or
semimusical system. From then on, this device was designated as
the Tiberian system of the *ta'amim*.

For the Psalms and Proverbs, a simple chanting was employed
for their rendition, later applied to the text of Job as well, which
originally was not to be interpreted with chanting.

The "repetition with song," as the study of religious literature
with chanting was called, survived from Talmudic ages to the
present day. It was universally used in the *yeshibot*, as well as
in other houses of study. But the Scriptural cantillation gained
its supreme importance in the congregations, where it constituted
the life-blood of the synagogue service. The oldest extant manuscript of the Talmud, a fragment of the tractate "*Keritot*," (probably from the eleventh century), is supplied with *ta'amim* for the

use of the students. Later, when the system of the musical values of the *ta'amim* developed, we gained a knowledge of how these signs were interpreted musically.

Modern research attempted to establish the resemblance between some Jewish *ta'amim* and intonations employed in reading the Koran. This is not surprising if we consider that both Jewish as well as Arabian-Turkish music are members of the same Oriental musical family, using the same technique (*maḳamat*) for certain melodic formations, which greatly enhances the likelihood of the resemblance referred to. Some model structures preserved among the Jews closely resemble those of the Byzantine and Armenian tradition as well as the Persian-Arabic melody.[18] This topic is beyond the present study and has been dealt with extensively by specialists in this field.[19] It may be stated only succinctly that the modal feeling of the Jewish synagogue music "is still reminiscent of the musical theory and practice of the Near East, which radiated from Babylon to the Mediterranean" and was taken over by the Jews in the Western settlements."[20]

From Biblical times on, the chanting of the sacred text was accompanied, or better led, by appropriate movements of the hands, indicating the direction (up, down, level) and fluctuations of the melodic line. The Egyptians had already used this device, as seen in numerous wall paintings which clearly show musicians being led by "conductors," whose hands are used to indicate the rise and fall of a melody for singers and instrumentalists. The Greeks developed this technique to a high degree of perfection, and from their language we took over the terms for it, *cheironomy* (*cheiros*, "hand," and *nomos*, "rule"). Thus, the Jews might have adopted this device from the Egyptians or the Greeks, or both. The cheironomic motions were later reproduced in a graphic form which became the accents or *ta'amim*. The technique of hand motions was, of course, no substitute for the written form, and vice versa. The Jewish *ta'amim* are generally considered to be the forerunners of the medieval neumes which later developed into the Western musical notation.

Although it is an important aspect in the development of Jewish musical culture, the limits sets in this study compel us to refrain from delving into the fascinating subject of coeval Biblical cantillation. This was done by a number of specialists in the field, *e.g.*, IDELSOHN, WERNER, and others. Their scholarly works make it superfluous for us to deal with the same subject extensively. The cheironomic practice, too, has been treated repeatedly in special works. Here we only desire to show how this device fits into the musical practice at the period under consideration.

As the Talmud states, the cantillation was always led by appropriate movements of the hand; the right hand indicates the *ta'ame torah*, as the cantillation was called.[21] Not only the hands, but also the fingers in different positions, and sometimes even motions of the head were used to lead the singers in the correct rendering of the cantillation. In Babylonia the schoolmaster, teaching to read the Torah, used his fingers whenever the pupils lost the melody, and they knew instantaneously which tone to sing. RASHI reported as late as the eleventh century that in France and Germany he saw visiting *hazzanim* from Palestine who used hand signs while chanting the Bible.[22] Yet sources long before RASHI contain descriptions of Jewish cheironomic gestures and even give some examples, like f. i. for the *shalsheleth*, the "chain" which was reproduced by a vertical zigzag movement of the hand.

BENJAMIN of TUDELA from Navarre, who traveled extensively in the Orient (from 1160 to 1173), has described the musical service in the synagogues at Bagdad. According to him, Bagdad had at that time twenty-three synagogues, a statement which was certainly somewhat exaggerated. He evidently included the numerous small neighborhood houses of study and prayer. His report seems to be more reliable when he relates that at that time there was in Babylon about a thousand Jewish families and ten *yeshibot*. This number of families evidently needed, besides the elementary schools, a great number of schools for higher learning. It can be assumed with certainty that, together with chanting, cheironomy was practiced in these schools.

BENJAMIN makes reference to the learned ELEAZAR ben ZEMACH, "the master of one of the Hebrew *yeshibot*, who was a descendant of the prophet Samuel and knew the melodies that were sung in the Temple of Jerusalem during the time of its existence."[23] BENJAMIN relates furthermore that the ancient melodies were performed "in traditional manner," that is, with instrumental accompaniment. And in fact, we have other historical evidence to indicate that during the intermediate days of the Feast of Tabernacles singing in the synagogue of Bagdad was accompanied by instrumental music.[24]

Another medieval traveler, R. PETAḤYAH of REGENSBURG, who toured the Orient in the twelfth century, also furnished valuable observations about the customs of the Jews in Babylonia, Ashur, Media, and Persia. In the places referred to he gives significant details about synagogal music; among them he states that psalm singing was accompanied by instruments.[25] PETAḤYAH does not actually mention cheironomic practice, yet from RASHI's statement we gather that cheironomy was universally used in the Orient.

During this epoch, there were other Jewish travelers to the Orient. We also know of YEHUDAH ʾal-ḤARISI, who made an extensive journey in 1218 from Spain to Babylonia. He wrote a book about his experiences, *"Taḥkemoni,"* an imitation of the Arabic book *"Hariri,"* which YEHUDAH translated into Hebrew. Contrary to the reports of BENJAMIN of TUDELA and PETAḤYAH of REGENSBURG, his book does not contain anything concerning music, though it is certain that he attended many Jewish services during his itinerary, in which he must have heard synagogue chants sung.[26]

The backbone and most potent moving power in the musical practice of medieval Jewry was the *ḥazzan*. His role in the preservation of Jewish music in all those centuries of insecurity and turmoil is of such importance that it warrants a more specific consideration besides a thorough analysis, both of which will be dealt with in a subsequent chapter.

These were the centuries in which Jewish music, synagogal as well as secular, received its decisive impetus from outside (non-Jewish) forces. It had to adapt itself to its new surroundings, had to yield to the influences of the environment, and take over and assimilate foreign elements. All this gave it, on the one hand, a powerful stimulus for further development, but constituted, on the other hand, damaging influences for the shaping of a genuine Jewish melos. These influences corrupted the purely Oriental character of Jewish music, with the many extraneous features grafted upon it artificially. This was the period of the birth of Jewish music theory, the forerunner of later Jewish musical science.

The first great Jewish philosopher, SAʿADIA ben JOSEPH ʾal-FAYYUMMI (SAʿADIA GAON, 892-942) was the author of the most important medieval theological and philosophical work, "*Kitab al-Amanat,*" or *Book of Philosophical Doctrines and Beliefs* (933 in Bagdad). The tenth chapter of this work contains a full paragraph devoted to music. In it, SAʿADIA investigates the influence of music upon the human mind; his treatment, the first of its kind, had wide repercussions everywhere in the Jewish world especially at a time when the admissibility of music in secular life, and even in the sacred service was hotly debated.[27]

SAʿADIA wrote his book in Arabic; his text is preserved in a number of copies along with Hebrew translations having many variants. This made it difficult for scholars to collate from these sources an authentic interpretation of the author's ideas. More recent research has succeeded in establishing that SAʿADIA's approach to musical art centered around its rhythmic and not its melodic aspect, as was the general consensus up to that time.

At any rate, SAʿADIA's treatise is an important milestone in the history of Jewish music, because it paved the way for a number of other medieval musical treatises, in which the theory and philosophy of music are further developed. These works will be scrutinized in one of the following chapters.

It is vital to mention, at least cursorily, SAʿADIA's great merits as an expounder of the Bible, an activity which earned him recognition as "perhaps the greatest Bible commentator of all times."[28]

2

The Musical Instruments of
Post-Biblical Jewry

AN OUTLINE OF THE MUSICAL PRACTICE OF THE JEWS IN THE EARLY
centuries of the Diaspora would be incomplete without adding
a short survey of the musical instruments used by them during
that time. "Musical instruments are bound by a thousand threads
to the sum of human activity and thinking. Their history is the
history of the human spirit."[1]

Our knowledge about the music instruments used by Diaspora Jewry comes from the rabbinical writings, including the
Mishnah, the *Talmudim,* the *Midrash,* etc. All these instruments
are treated extensively, from the historical as well as from the
artistic points of view in this author's *Music in Ancient Israel.*
The following brief survey should give us at least a glimpse into
this significant branch of the music practice of post-Talmudic
Jewry.

To what extent the Hebrews in the first centuries after the
destruction of their national existence still used the instruments
of Biblical times cannot be ascertained. Assumedly, however, a
considerable number of these instruments may have been preserved; but in the troubled times music teaching and music practice in general slowly fell into desuetude, which brought about
their unavoidable neglect, leading to the gradual deterioration,
and eventually to the abandonment of the Biblical instruments.
The rabbinical prohibitions of music-making after the national
tragedy—though not abolishing entirely the practice of music—
certainly discouraged the making of new instruments, and the
surviving Biblical *kinnorot, nebalim,* as well as the *ḥalilim* and

the other delicate species of string—and woodwind—instruments were condemned to a slow but inexorable death.

However, in the course of the centuries the never ceasing need of the Jewish people for music and, by implication, for musical instruments, created new types and new species of these. Jewish musicians either modeled them after the Biblical prototypes, or improved and developed them into new variants, or, finally, imported from the surrounding nations entirely different instruments. How they acquired the new arsenal of musical instruments is not divulged by the rabbinical writers. We learn only the names of the instruments, and sometimes are given scant information about their external characteristics. For the rest, we must rely upon analogies and deductions, in order to compare them with similar instruments of those nations among whom the Jews lived.

In our above-mentioned study dealing with the instruments of Ancient Israel, we described and analyzed twenty-eight terms; of these we identified eighteen as having been terms for the existing instruments of the Hebrews; the others were interpretations, assumptions, or hypotheses of Biblical expounders with vague probability of having been instruments of the Hebrews. Yet, since some renowned Biblical scholars ascribed to them the meaning of instruments, we had to investigate them critically, in order to formulate our conclusions about the validity of such scholarly assumptions.

In post-Biblical literature there also exist more reliable records on the subject in question. With a few exceptions, where the terminology is veiled or ambiguous, all the instruments mentioned in the rabbinical writings were actual instruments, used by the Hebrews. These were described by the *soferim* of the post-Biblical books, as well as a person not versed in musical matters was able to utilize them.

In the category of the stringed instruments, the rabbinic writers mention four: *pandura, ḥinga, baṭon* (or *baṭnon*), and the *ʾadrabolin* (or in another spelling *ʾardabalis*). This last term is doubtful, since it could possibly have been mistaken for a wind instrument, the *barbolin*.

The *pandura* was, according to a Talmudic statement an instrument used to accompany the singing of the shepherds.[2] It might have been a three-stringed lute, having a small body and a long neck, as we see them depicted partly in Assyrian, but mainly in Egyptian antiquities. The word seems to have been derived from the Sumerian *pan-tur,* meaning "bow-small," or "small-bow." Since such an instrument does not resemble a bow, its Sumerian origin is doubtful. It is more probable that it originated in Western Asia, where a string instrument named *fandur* or *fandir* had been used. It was shaped like a bottle, and had three or four strings which were played either with the fingers or with a plectrum. The confusion about this instrument was caused by an obviously erroneous statement of ISIDORE of SEVILLA (sixth century c.e.), who maintained that the *pandura* was named after its "inventor," Pan. He based his assertion upon a manifestly misunderstood verse of Virgil, in which the Latin poet refers to the Pan's pipe, a wind instrument, while the *pandura* was, according to the testimony of the Talmud, a string instrument.

The Talmud does not furnish any explanation why Jewish shepherds did not use any of the ancient Hebrew stringed instruments for their pastime, such as *kinnor, nebel,* or *'asor.* The reasons appear obvious: Biblical instruments might have fallen into obsolescence after the national disaster; they were no longer made, and the surviving ones may have deteriorated to a point where they were no longer usable. Furthermore, the *pandura,* with its smaller size and reduced number of strings, was much more convenient to carry, and easier to learn, while the *kinnor* and *nebel,* with more strings, required greater skill in playing and maintenance, evidently beyond the abilities of simple shepherds. Therefore, despite the *pandura's* reduced sonority in the open air, the Talmudic report about it as the favorite instrument of the shepherds has a definite credibility.

The *ḥinga* is mentioned in a fantastic tale of the Talmud, which narrates a fight between mortals and demons.[3] To exorcise these demons (sixty of them!), a *ḥinga* was suspended on a tree, to the accompaniment of which some magic formulas were sung to chase away the demons. Thus, the name *ḥinga* is here used in the meaning of a musical instrument, but of what particular kind can only be surmised.

The term, however, has two other meanings, according to modern scholars:[4] (1) a circle, dancing, chorus, feast, and (2) the dancing place in the vineyards. Since none of these meanings can be applied to the Talmudic story, we have to assume that the word *hinga* in this case indeed signifies a musical instrument. This conjecture is corroborated by the fact that *Targum Onkelos* to Gen. 31:27 renders *kinnor* as *hinga,* although in Gen. 4:21 the same word *kinnor* is translated by *Onkelos* as *kinnora.* Additional confusion is caused by another translation of the *Targum* to 1 Kings 1:40, where *hinga* is used for the Biblical *halil.* Furthermore, the *Targum* to the Psalms translates the heading of Ps. 5, *'el ha-nehilot,* as *'al hingin,* meaning "with flutes," and in other *Targumim* (*e.g.* to Exod. 32:19; Judg. 11:34) *hinga* is used for the Biblical *meholot,* "dances."

It is well known how arbitrarily the translators of the *Targumim* handled the names of the music instruments. In the above mentioned case, the fight of men with demons, there appears little doubt that, notwithstanding its other meanings, the term denotes some kind of a stringed instrument, perhaps a lute or possibly the *baton.*

The name *baton* (or *batnon*), mentioned in the *Mishnah,*[5] may be derived from the Hebrew noun *beten,* meaning "belly," or an "empty" or "hollow" object. It is probable, therefore, that *baton* refers either to the bulging form of the instrument, or to the indication that it had to be played at waist level, in contrast to other string instruments which were held in front of the breast.

Our only knowledge about this instrument stems from a late commentator of the *Mishnah,* 'OBADIAH of BERTINORO (fifteenth century), who declares that the *baton* was a large guitar (which he calls *zithra* in his commentary), hung over the player's body or carried in front.

Neither the Egyptians nor the Assyrians had zithers or zither-like instruments. Israel's neighbor, the Phoenicians, however, knew such a type. Two of them are depicted on a carved ivory pyxis of the eighth century B.C.E. On these reliefs the backs of the zithers cannot be seen, so it is not possible to verify whether they are flat or bulging.[6] Whether such an instrument had been used by the ancient Hebrews cannot be ascertained; there is no mention of it in the Bible, the Apocrypha, nor in the early rabbinical literature. It is also doubtful whether the Mishnaic reference means a zither or a somewhat similar instrument. According to the etymology of the word it more probably denotes a belly-shaped guitar or lute.

In modern Hebrew *baṭnon* is the name of a very large *kinnor* with a heavy sound, consequently a double-bass.[7]

Much confusion remains about two Aramaic names of instruments mentioned in the *Midrash*. As a commentary to Gen. 4:21, the *Midrash* interprets the Biblical *kinnor* as *ʾadrabolin,* meaning "organ players," and the *ʿugab* as *barbolin* (spelled also *korablin* or *karkalin*), "flautists."[8] (The English rendition belongs to the translator of the Soncino Press). In another passage of the *Midrash* both words are mentioned together, but in a completely different meaning. Here, *ʾadrabolin* is again translated as "organs," (or "organplayers"), but *korablin* as "cymbals." "Organs," or "organplayers" certainly is not the correct translation for the Biblical *kinnor,* just as "cymbals" cannot be considered the exact rendering of the instrument named *korablin.* This latter word is evidently the Aramaic adaptation (or corruption) of the Greek *choraulēs,* "flute player"; the English interpretation would at least render justice to the original meaning of it, as well as of the Biblical *ʿugab.*

But how about *ʾadrabolin,* which in the Aramaic text stands for *kinnor?* In the rabbinical writings *ʾadrabolin* has many other spellings, such as *ʾardabalis, ʾadrikolin, hardulis.* This last variant in particular strongly suggests that it was the Aramaic corruption of the Greek *hydraulis,* the water-organ.

The existing confusion is further aggravated by RASHI's commentary to *Midrash,* Genesis L:9, in which he defines both words as *mine zemer,* "instruments for the song." If it could be assumed that the *korbalin,* the *ʿugab,* might have been used on certain occasions as accompanying the song, the same cannot be valid for the *hydraulis,* a rather clumsy and loud instrument at that epoch.

The erroneous Midrashic juxtaposition of the two names of instruments, which in the Bible stand for two different categories, is one of those frequent misconceptions of the rabbinical scribes not versed in musical matters, which we encounter so often in their writings. The English translators should have taken care to refrain from repeating this error and to indicate, at least in a note, that their interpretation of the Midrashic ʾadrabolin does not convey the exact meaning of the term.

As a synonym for the Biblical names ḥalil and ʿugab the Talmudic literature uses the term ʿabub. According to R. PAPPA, the three words designate the same instrument, the pipe (or oboe).[9] ʿAbub is related to the name of the Akkadian (Semitic) imbubu, an instrument of the pipe family, brought to Syria, where the Israelites may have taken it over.

There is a rabbinical legend that states "there was an ʿabub in the sanctuary, which was smooth (i.e., it had a pleasant sound), made of reed, and dated from the time of Moses. At the king's command it was overlaid with gold, but its sound was no longer sweet. They removed the overlay and its sound became sweet as it was before."[10] If there really was among the instruments of the cult one dating back to Moses' time, the Biblical chroniclers would have hardly missed the opportunity to refer to so venerable an item. It is clearly one of those pious legends so frequently encountered in the rabbinical literature.

The Mishnah says that there were ʿabubim entirely of metal, differing acoustically from those of reed by their stronger sound.[11] In his commentary to this passage, MAIMONIDES says that the ʿabub was a pipe of reed with a mouthpiece of metal or reed. It is not easy to figure out how a reed instrument could have had a mouthpiece of metal.

In the later period of the Second Temple the soft ʿugab might have been permanently supplanted by the more vigorous sound of the Syrian ʿabub.

Of widespread notoriety, in antiquity, were the Syrian ʿabub-playing girls, who were renowned not so much by their artistry, but by their immoral life. Roman poets report that the ambubajae, the flute girls, lived in the basement of the Roman circus which, accordingly, was surnamed ambubajarum collegia. Here their pipe playing was used merely as a pretense for their ignoble trade. It is highly probable that such Syrian flute girls had found their way to Israel as well.

No instrument supposedly known to the Israelites has created so many contradictory reports and opinions as the *magrephah*. The various statements and descriptions of it in the rabbinical writings are so fragmentary and confusing that it is nearly impossible to gain a clear idea about this instrument from them.

It is not even evident whether the *magrephah* existed as a musical instrument in the Temple. Some sages are affirmative, others deny this explicitly. Furthermore, the terminology of the rabbinical writers varies greatly about the character, the shape, and size of the *magrephah*. Some identify it as the Greek *hydraulis*, the water-organ, others hold that it was quite a different instrument. None of the rabbinical sages who in the Talmud discuss the existence or nonexistence of such an instrument in the Temple lived in the time where the sanctuary still stood; consequently, their testimony is not based on their own observations but on hearsay.

Some of the rabbinical statements and descriptions of the instrument would conform with the assumption that the *magrephah* and the *hydraulis* were one and the same instrument. Others are contradictory. They invoke liturgical and musical arguments against the assumption which held that such a clumsy and loud instrument was used in the Temple. This certainly would have "interfered unfavorably with the sweetness of the singing," described in the Talmud.[12]

It is striking that neither the Apocrypha nor the writings of Josephus and Philo or their contemporaries contain the slightest allusion to such an instrument. It would seem that the implements of the sacred service, and especially its musical part, should have been well known at least to the two Jewish historians, both of whom lived during the last decades of the Third (Herod's) Temple. Their complete silence on this point is all the more significant as we learn from the Talmud that the sound of the instrument in question was extremely powerful, and this could have hardly remained unnoticed by the Jewish writers.

A further complication arises from the fact that in two different chapters of the rabbinical literature, the word *magrephah* refers to completely different objects. Apart from its meaning as a musical instrument, the Talmud says that it was a shovel made of brass which was used for removing the ashes and cinders from the altar. Rashi suggests that "there are possibly two sorts of *magrephot,* one for the ashes and one for music.[13] Furthermore, he has a third explanation of the term, identifying the *magrephah* with "a set of bells."[14]

According to a rabbinical description, the *magrephah* had "ten holes, and every hole emitted ten different sounds."[15] The Palestinian Talmud contains a verbatim discussion about the *magrephah* by two learned rabbis, RAB and SAMUEL, one of whom said that the instrument had ten holes, each producing one hundred different sounds; the other that it had one hundred holes, each emitting ten sounds, amounting in both cases to one thousand different sounds.[16] A famous rabbi, NAHMAN bar ISAAC, felt induced to utter a warning that this was an obvious exaggeration. It is commonly known that the rabbinical writers, in retrospect, frequently attributed grandiose and exalted qualities to the institutions of the Temple. This might have been such a case.

The Talmud says that the *magrephah* was cast or thrown (to the floor?), thereby producing a sound that was so loud that, according to one rabbinical statement[17] "no one could hear the voice of his neighbor in Jerusalem because of the sound of the *magrephah,*" and it was added in the same passage that "from Jericho they could hear the sound of the *magrephah.*"[18] Here are two irreconcilable statements. Should the *magrephah* have been a musical instrument, it would have been unthinkable to throw or cast it without inflicting serious damage to its many delicate parts. If, on the other hand, it was a shovel to clean the altar from the slags, it could not have produced a sound powerful enough as claimed in the *Mishnah.*

There is one point on which the rabbinical descriptions concur, namely, that the instrument (or whatever it might have been) had a handle. This was probably the main reason why the *magrephah* has been identified with a shovel.

Modern commentators are inclined to interpret the *magrephah* as a kind of signal instrument, a drum, a gong, a tympanum, or something similar. Among the contemporary explanations that of JOSEPH YASSER deserves particular consideration. According to his theory, the *magrephah* was a pipe-work, not an organ of any kind serving musical purposes, but a noise-making signal instrument, consisting of a great number of small, shrill pipes, activated pneumatically and sounding simultaneously. YASSER thinks that the "throwing" or "casting" of the instrument might have involved the back-and-forth swinging of the handle which pumped the air for the pipes and which, incidentally, may conceivably have been shaped like a shovel.[19]

From such a mass of contradictory statements it is difficult to pick a kernel of historical truth or even a remote probability. Nevertheless, a few facts emerge as explanations for the radically divided opinions of the rabbis about the *magrephah*.

Manifestly, Hellenistic Jewry must have known the Greek *hydraulis*, the water-organ, or its equivalent, the primitive pneumatic organ. If we follow YASSER's theory, the *magrephah*, having been a sheer noise-making contrivance, might have been more acceptable to the Temple authorities than an instrument for the accompaniment of the song. Furthermore, nothing opposes the assumption that the *magrephah*, in the meaning of a shovel, was one of the cleaning implements in the Temple service.

This assumption is apt to be reconciled with the rabbinical statement that there never existed a *magrephah*, i.e., a Greek water-organ, in the sanctuary. As for its powerful sound, this may be one of the frequent exaggerations of rabbinical scribes, which is even shattered by the *Mishnaic* text itself.

As for the use of the *hydraulis* by the Jews outside the sanctuary, there are reasons to believe that this may have occurred at secular occasions. There are a few references in the *Midrashim* to the effect that players of water-organs (*ʾadrablin-hydraulis*) had been employed at festivities.[20] To be sure, the *Midrash* does not make clear whether such itinerant organ-players were Jewish or non-Jewish. But probably the latter was the case, since it is known that Gentile musicians were frequently employed at Jewish weddings, especially on the Sabbath when playing of instruments was forbidden to the Jews.

The name of a medieval instrument, *kalameyles*, serves RASHI as an explanation of the Biblical *halil*. It is evident that the two instruments, one of the Biblical epoch, and the other in France of RASHI's time (1040-1105) could not have been identical. RASHI's term is nothing else than the medieval French *chalamele* (the later *chalumeau*), an oboe-like instrument, mentioned in the Talmud in a Hebraized form.

Under the heading of percussion, shaking and rattling instruments, the rabbinical literature shows a great variety. These instruments seem to have been, basically at least, similar to the corresponding instruments of Biblical times, but evidently in more developed forms, shapes, and sonorities, owing to the higher technical skill of the artisans, and also due to the influence of the more advanced instruments of the environment in which the Jews lived.

The *niktimon* (in another spelling *nikatmon*) seems to indicate the pegs on which the strings were fastened. Yet, several Talmudic writers interpret the word as the name of a musical instrument resembling the protruding arm of an object or a "wooden leg." In discussing the prescriptions for cleanliness, the *Mishnah* mentions *niktimon* repeatedly, without giving any indications about its specific characteristics. Into these many contradictory explanations SACHS sheds some light by employing the comparative method of the history of musical instruments. His interpretation of the *niktimon* comes close to a satisfactory explanation of the seemingly enigmatic word: "If this term does mean an instrument, it might refer to those Egyptian clappers of wood or ivory which were carved to form a human arm with the hand and which were exclusively played by women; or the boot-shaped clappers of the Greek".[21] Cautiously SACHS adds: "But this is nothing more than a suggestion." It is probable, however, that the word refers indeed to a kind of clappers, since the latter instrument is mentioned also at another place of the rabbinical literature.[22]

RASHI's commentary may be mentioned merely for the sake of curiosity. He defines *nikatmon* as a "sort of instrument for the song (*niggun*), made in the form of a wooden foot (or an artificial leg)".[23] A string instrument in this shape was not known in antiquity. A clapper, on the other hand, cannot be considered to be "an instrument for the song."

RASHI still gives other, nonmusical, interpretations of the term, which gives an explanation at least of the etymology of the word, but fails to provide an unequivocal answer to the question which instrument, if any, may be hidden under the term *niktimon* or *nikatmon*.

SACHS' interpretation comes closest to a satisfactory solution, and therefore it may be assumed with a certain probability that, if a musical instrument is meant by it, the term indicates clappers made of wood or bone.

An instrument named *ṭabla* is mentioned in several rabbinical writings. About its nature and character there are only vague and largely contradictory opinions.

The etymology of the word would indicate that it refers to a sort of drum, having had a square shape, since *tabla* in Greek designates "something square." In some Talmudic passages *ṭabla* is the generic word for musical instruments; in an early Greek translation, the word signifies "bells hung from a wooden frame." RASHI's commentary to the term follows the same idea; in another Talmudic passage he adds the explanation that the *ṭabla* was a set of "wedding bells" to be shaken. In the belief of the Orientals that the tinkling of bells would chase away evil spirits, it is very probable that the use of such an instrument at weddings was based upon this superstition.

The real form of the *ṭabla* is easily disclosed once we realize the purpose of the instrument. It was undoubtedly played at weddings to enhance the general rejoicing. This manifested itself mainly in dancing. We may safely follow the majority of the commentators who take the *ṭabla* as a hand drum (possibly square-shaped) with the same functions as those of the biblical *tof*. The instrument may have been bedecked in later times with all sorts of ornamental pendants, among them also little bells. This might have been the reason that the *ṭabla* was considered a bell or a bell-like instrument.

The word *'erus* (or *'irus*) is found in two passages of the *Mishnah*, indicating in both places a drumlike instrument. Nevertheless, the Talmudic commentators give the word distinctly different meanings. RASHI says it was "a bell with a single clapper"; in another place he suggests that it was "a knocking clapper." MAIMONIDES believes it to be a round tambourine. Several commentators have ventured the supposition that the *'erus* must have been a rather voluminous drum since, according to a rabbinical statement, the wailing woman would sit upon it at funerals. This, however, is an obvious mistake, because the drum referred to was not the *'erus* but the *rebi'it.*

We probably will come close to the truth by assuming that the *'erus* was a small, brightly adorned hand drum, used at weddings for the accompaniment of dancing and enhancing the general rejoicing. It may have been a more developed and more embellished form of the Biblical *tof.*

Another type of drum was the *tanbura* (or *tanburi*) which gave rise to all kinds of misinterpretations, since the words *'erus, tabla,* and *tanbura* are frequently interchanged in rabbinical literature to designate the small hand drum. Other terms for the hand drum are *rebubah,* in another spelling *rekubah,* with further variants *dekoba* and *dekuba,* and—evidently corrupted—*babuy)a.* All these words and their variants designate the small hand drum such as the *'erus.*

A larger type of drum was the *rebi'it,* used at funerals by the wailing women who, during the funeral oration, used to sit upon it. There is a striking assonance between this word and two other terms of the *Targumim* and the *Peshitta,* the Syriac version of the Bible. They are *rebi'in* of the former, and *rebiy'a* of the latter, both being renditions (in Aramaic and Syrian) of the Biblical *mena'an'im* (2 Sam. 6:5), all unanimously interpreted as sistra.

MAIMONIDES holds, however, that the *rebi'in* were two wooden sticks, struck together rhythmically, and thus representing a clapper instrument as depicted on Egyptian wall paintings. However, the passages of the *Mishnah* in which *rebi'it* is mentioned do not agree with the idea of concussion sticks. Sistrum would be a more appropriate interpretation; but for the use of sistra at Jewish funerals there are no references in rabbinical literature.

The *rebi'it* might have been a rather large, oblong drum with a deep tone. The hollow sound quality of such a drum may have blended better with the gloomy mood of the funeral ceremony than the lively tone of the *'erus,* or the shrill rattling of the sistrum.

As can be seen, the rabbinical writers indiscriminately employ the terms *'erus, tabla, tanbura, rebuba, dekoba* (or *koba*), *rebi'it,* to which the Aramaic and Syriac *rebiy'a* (*rebi'in*), *pelaga,* and *tuppa* may be added. All these terms designate hand drums which in all probability may be differentiated by their shape, size, and construction.

An instrument frequently mentioned in rabbinical literature is the *zog*. It is essentially similar to the Biblical *pa'amonim*, the little golden bells on the high priest's garment which in Talmudic times served varied purposes. They were widely used on doors, garments, even on the locks of the bearers, and hung on domestic animals. They were magic means of protecting the persons and the useful animals against the harmful influence of evil spirits and demons. The *Gemara* discusses extensively the prescriptions compulsory for men, women, and children for their protection when leaving the house on the Sabbath. Since all active anti-demoniac precautions exercised on weekdays were forbidden on the Sabbath, the hanging of bells upon oneself remained the only measure that automatically safeguarded the individual against the evil influences. The same belief applied to the use of bells on doors, to prevent a malevolent demon from sneaking into the house together with the entering person.

Thus, we see how ancient heathen superstitions survived in a veiled form even far into post-Biblical times.

The Aramaic word *karkash* (or *kashkash*, or *kishkush*), designating a clapper, is obviously an onomatopoeic word construction, as there are so many others among Hebrew sound-producing instruments. Despite its clear etymology, RASHI gives it another meaning, namely *tabla*, "wedding bells," that were shaken like the tambourine.

This explanation is an obvious anachronism, since instruments of the tambourine type (that is, round hand drums with small metal plates applied to their frames) are not attested prior to the thirteenth century.[25]

It may be assumed that *karkash* and *zog* referred to two different types of clappers. The latter represented the bell type, sounding by itself, that is, by the bodily movements of those who carried it, whereas the *karkash* must have been the clapper which had to be activated, *i.e.*, stricken always anew.

As the Talmud states, the leading goat had around his neck a bell, called in Aramaic *sharkukita*. The word is derived from the Hebrew verb *sharak*, "to hiss," "to whistle," which is also the original word for the instrument *mashrokita,* mentioned four times in the Book of Daniel. The peculiar thing about these two Aramaic words is that *mashrokita* indicates a wind instrument, whereas *sharkukita,* if the Talmud is correct, appears to refer to a shaking instrument. It is difficult to understand how both actions, the whistling of a pipe and the tinkling of a bell, could have been expressed imitatively by the same sibilant root.

The most logical explanation of the word is that of KRAUSS, who maintains that *sharkukita* might have been a flutelike instrument, or, more precisely, "the Pan's pipe." For this assumption there is even a vague corroboration in the Bible. Judg. 5:16 contains the expression *sherikot ʿadarim,* "the pipings for the flocks"; *sherikot* has the same root as the Aramaic *sharkukita.* This concurs very well with the Talmudic statement that the *sharkukita* was an instrument which had a specific function in the life of the shepherds.[26]

How long the "Talmudic" instruments remained in use of the dispersed Jews cannot be said with certainty. The Biblical instruments must have changed under the influence of the times, either being transformed into newer variants, or abandoned as obsolete and replaced by more advanced types. Thus, the instruments used by the Hebrews in the early Diaspora may have been superseded by better constructed and more attractively sounding instruments of the ascending Middle Ages. We have no documentary evidence that the Jews living in Germanic countries adopted the instruments of their host nations. In Latin countries, however, and particularly in the Islamic portion of the Iberian peninsula, there are abundant records in this regard. Moreover, it is in the Moorish world, the greatest and culturally most important Western settlement of the Jews, where the instrumentarium had become completely assimilated to that of the conquering Moslems and, later, to the more developed instruments of the Christian world.

3

The Jews in Spain—Sephardim

SEPHARAD IS MENTIONED IN THE BOOK OF ʿOBADIAH (1:20) AS THE name of a district in Asia Minor, where deported Jews were settled after the Babylonians captured Jerusalem in 586 B.C.E. Later it became a Hebrew term for Spain, and the Jews of Spanish or Portuguese origin were called Sephardim.

Jews have lived in the Iberian peninsula since the earliest times. The apostle PAUL desired to visit Hispania to propagate his teachings among the Jews of that Roman province. VESPASIAN, and later HADRIAN, who himself was a Spaniard (born in the Spanish town Italica), transported Jewish prisoners to Spain. Several passages of the Talmud and *Midrash* refer to Spain, and Jewish coins unearthed in ancient Taragona give evidence of early settlements of Jews in Spain.[1]

The Jews, who were treated on equal terms with the other inhabitants under the rule of the Visigoths, rapidly spread throughout the Iberian peninsula. They engaged in trade and agriculture, and often were given judicial offices of trust.[2] The first attempt to disturb the friendly relations that existed between Jews and Christians originated with the Council of Elvira (303-304). In the following centuries the Jews were alternately tolerated and persecuted.[3]

The Jews, either directly, or through their coreligionists in North Africa, encouraged the Mohammedans to invade Spain, and greeted them as their deliverers.

After the decisive battle of Jerez (711), in which African Jews fought valiantly on the side of the Mohammedans, the conquerors placed the cities of Cordoba, Malaga, Granada, Seville, and Toledo in charge of the Jewish inhabitants. The Jews were given complete religious freedom by the Arabs, who required of them only a small annual tribute.[4]

Following this conquest, a new era dawned for the Jews in the Iberian peninsula, for their number had been considerably augmented by the African Jews who had followed the conquerors.[5] To repopulate the land, the Arabs encouraged immigration; 50,000 Jews came from Africa and Asia; some towns, like Lucena, were inhabited almost entirely by Jews.[6] Southern Spain became an asylum for the oppressed Jews.[7] Freed from economic disabilities, the Jews of Moslem Spain spread into every field of agriculture and economic activities, soon prospered and with their regained well-being, their intellectual life thrived as before. Jewish knowledge, Jewish science, and also Jewish music gained new luster under these favorable living conditions. The Jews adopted the dress, language, and customs of the Arabs, and were hardly distinguishable from their Semitic cousins. Several Jews became court physicians, and one of these was made adviser to the greatest of the Caliphs of Cordova.[8]

The century of the reign of 'ABD 'AL-RAHMAN III (called 'AL-NASIR, 912-961) and his son 'AL-HAKIM, was one of undisturbed happiness for Spanish Jews, materially as well as religiously and intellectually. An unfortunate struggle for the succession to the throne, in which the Jews sided with 'AL-HAKIM, ended this golden era; the Jews were mercilessly expelled from the country (1013). For centuries, the Moslems continued to rule the Spanish lands, but nothing was done to relieve or improve the situation of the Jews. Moreover, after the defeat of the Moslems the Christian princes took over the country, and treated the Jews mercilessly. The Crusaders began their "holy war" in Toledo (1212) by robbing and butchering the Jews; only the intervention of armed groups of Christian knights prevented the total extinction of the Jews in Toledo.

During the reign of FERDINAND III (1199-1252) the Jews were compelled to wear a yellow badge. However, the Spanish kings availed themselves of Jewish money for their wars; in recompense, they granted some privileges to the Jews and even distributed land among them, in spite of the objections of the clergy. FERDINAND allowed them to erect a magnificent synagogue in Cordova.

The fate of the Jews improved still further under FERDINAND's son, ALFONSO X (1221-1284), who was scientific-minded and a gifted author. He maintained relations with the Jews even before his accession to the throne (1252). He commissioned three Jewish physicians, YUDAH ben MOSES COHEN of Toledo, and ABRAHAM and SAMUEL LEVI, to translate astronomical and astrological writings from Arabic into Spanish. ZAG (ISAAC) ibn SAID, *hazzan* of Toledo, compiled in May 1252 the famous astronomical tables called, after the king, the Alfonsine tables, which were later claimed by ABRAHAM ZACUTO (1450-1510) as his own, and which enabled Columbus to navigate to the New World. Ibn SAID in 1266 observed three eclipses of the moon; many of the astronomical works of this Rabbi ZAG (or ÇAG) are still preserved in Spanish translations in the Escurial. This renowned astronomer, we repeat, was by profession a *hazzan*. His astronomic works were written down, but the same advantage was not applicable to his musical works, since these could be transmitted only orally.

In 1264 ALFONSO still showered land and privileges upon the Jews, but soon after, under the pressure of the clergy, subjected them to the severest restrictions. They were not permitted to associate with Christians, live under the same roof, eat and drink with them. There also was a long list of other oppressive regulations, ordinances to wear a badge, or be subject to heavy fines or other punishments. In spite of all these restrictions and regulations, ALFONSO allowed the Jews to live peacefully in their *Judería;* he ordered that they were not to be disturbed in the exercise of their religion, that their synagogues and sacred implements should be respected, and—most unusual for a Christian king—that they should not be forced or bribed to embrace Christianity.

In great contrast to Alfonso's leniency, however, one of his literary works, *Libro de las Cantigas,* contains the fantastic and false legend that every year, on Good Friday the Jews crucified a Christian child. ALFONSO, called "the Wise," ordered that every Jew accused of such a crime be brought before him and, if convicted, slain.[9] How easy in those times for anyone to make such an accusation!

Matters became even worse. Toward the end of his life, (in 1280-81), ALFONSO commanded the execution of his most trusted

Jewish courtiers. What their crime might have been is not divulged by the chroniclers. DON ÇAG [Isaac] de la MALEHA, the most influential of them, was publicly hanged. In addition to this carnage, a number of Jewish communities, together with their elders, were herded and retained in prison for a long time.[10]

Thus, tyranny and savagery marks the end of the life of an enlightened ruler, whose reign started so auspiciously for the Jews.

In spite of such occasional setbacks, the Judaeo-Spanish settlement in time became so prosperous economically and advanced intellectually that it replaced Babylon as the cultural center of the Jewish world.

In the field of music, too, the Jews now entered upon a new phase. Until then, Jewish music and Jewish musicians were restricted to their own community, confining their activity mainly to the needs of the sacred service. Jewish popular music, as far as it existed under the precarious living conditions of the first centuries of Western Diaspora, had not been able to develop freely. It was too much under the influence of the outside world, under the irresistible forces of an alien popular art. Thus, Jewish popular music during these centuries was simply the reflection of the secular music of countries in which the Jews lived.

In the earlier Eastern settlements, in Babylonia, in North Africa, even in the Iberian peninsula before the Arabs took possession of it, Jewish song was mainly under the influence of Oriental musical practice. This changed after the Arabian conquest of Spain. The Jews adapted Arabian customs to their own needs, and increasingly adopted Arabian music.

Whereas formerly Jewish music was governed by modal melodies, free flowing without a rigid rhythmical pattern, this changed radically under Arabian influence. The Arabs' predilection for bodily motions while singing created a new type of song with strong rhythmic features; the freely flowing melodic line was squeezed into a definite rhythmic design, enabling Arab singers and dancers to continue a given rhythm for longer periods. It was unavoidable that Jewish song became enticed by this "innovation," and that Jewish singers followed the new trend, first in their secular melodies, soon, however, in their synagogue songs as well. This process of "Arabization" was not restricted to Jews in Spain. By the tenth century, in all the settlements where Jews lived together with Arabs, in Syria, North Africa, even in Babylonia, Arabian rhythmic tunes penetrated the synagogue service. "Hence, rhythmical song among the Jews of the Orient—and in Spain—became synonymous with Arab music."[11]

The Arabian, however, was not the only influence the Jews were subjected to. They adopted Spanish *romances,* as well as tunes and dances of the streets. Furthermore they let themselves be influenced by Italian, Turkish, and other Levantine ditties which were sung everywhere. Thus, Jewish music passed through an irresistible trend of imitation, a veritable musical mimicry, which infiltrated the Jewish home and, eventually, the synagogue itself. Here, the *hazzanim* were the principal agents for the corruption of the ancient synagogue tradition. This abuse was bound to create strong opposition on the part of the puritanic guardians of the synagogue song. We will presently see how this worked out in practice.

As soon as the Mozarabian Christians introduced in their liturgy the plain song, the intonation of the Sephardim succumbed to this new influence. Plain song flourished in the Christian Church until about the thirteenth century and, accordingly, we find in the Sephardic chants which survived this epoch mainly short phrases often repeated, just as they occur in Persian-Arabic melodic designs. Especially their congregational chants usually have a Moorish flavor.[12]

Soon, the practice of adopting tunes from Arabic music disrupted the unity of Sephardic synagogue songs. Moreover, when the religious poems (*piyyutim*) inundated the liturgy, the need of melodies for them compelled the *hazzanim* first to borrow Arabic and other secular tunes for the poems, and later compose music for them in the same vein.

There was an additional influence upon the music of the Jews in Spain, exerted by the artful songs of the noble troubadours and their counterparts in Iberian lands, the *juglares, jongleurs,* and *segrels,* the popular entertainers of those times. (To the interrelation of the troubadours' art and Jewish musical practice an entire chapter of this study will be devoted.)

The Rabbinical Controversy About Music

In spite of the importance of music during all the centuries in Jewish life, a controversy raged unabatedly whether music should be permitted or abolished in secular life, or even in the sacred liturgy. Time and again communities submitted this question to rabbinical authorities. The responses given by them would fill an entire volume, without clarifying the basic question: music or no music? The most outstanding rabbi of the times, MAIMONIDES (1135-1204), devoted an entire responsum to this problem. Before him, however, there were a host of other sages who grappled with this query; all of them were unsuccessful in establishing uniform rules, to impose their opinions upon world's Jewry. It is illuminating to show, in great outlines at least, how this question, for centuries, has intrigued sages and communities alike.[13]

What was the law concerning music in the early centuries of the Diaspora? We know that after the national catastrophe that befell Judaism with the destruction of their Sanctuary in Jerusalem, the Jews, following the rabbinical prohibitions and as a token of mourning, "voluntarily" refrained from listening to and practicing "loud music," that is, music in public. This is stated at least in our rabbinical sources. This self-imposed restriction was by no means as "voluntary" as the sources make us believe. Because, had it been carried out literally, it would have meant the end of Jewish music altogether. That Jewish music survived, nevertheless, is the proof that this restriction was far from being universally effective. Already in *Amoraic* times (third to fifth centuries c.e.) the prohibition of musical activities found little favor among the population. Especially in Babylonia the rabbinical edicts were almost completely ignored. Living far from the scene of the national tragedy, the Babylonian Jews could not share the emotional jolt of their Palestinian brothers who bore the immediate impact of the catastrophe and preserved longer the bitter memory of the sad event.

The *Amoraim* did what they could to curb music, especially at banquets, where it might lead to unseemly frivolity. One practice was that of using women as the singers and musicians at banquets, as was usual in the Orient. "In short, the rabbis were bent on counteracting the odious consequences of wine, women, and song."[14] It is also understandable that for many centuries the rabbis attempted to abolish at least the most glaring abuses of music-making. Such an argument that was used to frighten men and discourage their singing was clumsy indeed: "He who sings secular songs with women will be metamorphosed after death into oxen."[15] Obviously this menace had little effect in curbing their urge for singing.

Some rabbis maintained that the prohibition applied only to instrumental music, and that singing was permissible. About this question an inquiry was sent to the Exilarch MAR 'UKBA in Babylon. He responded unequivocally that the rabbis proscribed both kinds of musical entertainment. His opinion is the more surprising since in Babylonia the prohibition of music had never been severely enforced. Besides, it is known that the inauguration of a newly elected Exilarch invariably took place with rich musical deployment, as mentioned earlier.

R. HAI GAON (939-1038) advanced two opinions concerning music. To the scholars of Canas (a town in North Africa) he wrote that anyone who drinks wine at a place where instrumental music is being played, and especially in the company of non-Jews, is subject to excommunication. In this opinion crime and punishment are so glaringly disproportionate that it is highly questionable whether it was ever put into effect.

In his responsum to the scholars of Kairwan (another North African town), R. HAI showed more understanding for human nature. At banquets and weddings he did not object to the singing of hymns in God's praise, but forbade absolutely the singing of Arabic love songs. He also frowned upon women performers and dancers, as this might lead to lewdness.

In a brief responsum, another Gaon, R. HANANEL ben HUSHIEL (990-1050), maintained that the prohibition refers merely to listening to non-Hebrew songs, accompanied or not, but applies equally to a *ḥazzan* singing Arabic songs.

In spite of all legal prohibitions, Arabic songs must have been extremely popular among the people, for an inquiry was sent to R. ALFASI concerning a reader of prayers (*hazzan ha-keneset*), who used to chant airs borrowed from the Moslems. In his responsum, ALFASI declared that if the precentor (*sheliah zibbur*) persisted in this way, he should be dismissed.[16] At the same time we learn that a certain early Spanish Jew, ABEN SACHEL (12 cent.), wrote songs for dancing, a procedure which did not remain isolated among Spanish Jews.

None of the laws nor rigid rabbinical edicts concerning music were able to suppress the human instincts and love of music, and therefore singing and playing of instruments continued unabatedly. This created vigorous opposition among law-abiding scholars, and so this question was submitted to MAIMONIDES (1135-1204), the greatest rabbinical authority of that time.

In his responsum he goes into great detail concerning the rabbinical pronouncements on the subject.[17] But he approaches the question also from an ethical and philosophical point of view. He was aware that music exercised an ennobling influence upon the individual. The law, however, was intended for the benefit of many; therefore music, except in connection with prayer, was to be banned because it was wanton and voluptuous, and carried with it a sensuous thrill, especially when the songs were performed by women at banquets. Therefore, MAIMONIDES would prohibit not only Arabic but also Hebrew songs, if their content were such as to lead to excitement and debauchery.

MAIMONIDES' responsum dealt mainly with music in liturgy. From his opinion it is clear that it was not the music per se that he opposed, but the admittance of certain secular melodies as well as the exaggerated use of *piyyutim* in the synagogal service. Music of a religious character is permitted. The only decisive criterion of music's value is its religious-ethical essence. To draw from his conclusion that he was "extremely antagonistic to all poetry and music," as IDELSOHN maintained,[18] seems far-fetched. True, there were voices raised against the use of *piyyutim* in the service as early as the 11th century, as we know from HANANEL ben HUSHIEL (d.1050) and HAI GAON (d.1038). Yet, in the following century, YAAKOB ben MEÏR (d.1171) had allowed their use.

With secular music, MAIMONIDES dealt in another responsum which unlike the first, was written in Arabic, utilizing Hebrew script.[19] He maintained that secular music is to be prohibited, because it arouses lust and wickedness. But he realized also that, with all his opposition to frivolous melodies, the existing custom could not be completely ignored. What prevailed among the Jews in Spain, was the same as in Egypt, where the responsum was written. Therefore, MAIMONIDES could not simply condemn an art that had become part and parcel of the social life of the Jews. All he intended to achieve was to rationalize it.

MAIMONIDES' general attitude to music was influenced by the Arabic writers before him, such as ḤUNAIN ibn ISḤAḲ (d.873), ʾAL-FARABI (d.950), IBN SINA (d.1037), ʾAL GHAZALI (d.1111), and IBN BAJJA (d.1138). These writers dealt more or less extentensively with music in its practical and theoretical aspects, as well as in its moral sense.

Prior to MAIMONIDES, the illustrious IBN GABIROL (1021-1069), argued that it was not merely listening to music that was forbidden, it was listening to those indecent ideas that might be contained in a song. This was also the guiding principle leading to MAIMONIDES' views about music.

The strict view adopted by MAIMONIDES went as far as was possible toward the abolition of music. Yet, he considered not merely the legal aspect of the question, but treated also the moral side of it. Since in the ancient Orient music was performed largely by women, such songs were often too prone to kindle the passions. Moslem jurists, too, wrote many responsa prohibiting music, but their views did not influence the Arabs to any considerable extent, because music played an important part in their life, just as it did in the life of the Jews.

MAIMONIDES' responsum on music seemed to have exercised little influence upon the attitude of later authorities. Some European rabbis subsequent to MAIMONIDES were much more liberal, evidently due to the changed social conditions under which they lived. Thus, R. JOEL ben ELIEZER ha-LEVI, a German rabbi of the twelfth to thirteenth century, permitted Jews to hire Gentiles on the Sabbath to play instrumental music at wedding parties, for there could be no wedding without music, and its prohibition on the Sabbath may be disregarded at the celebration of a wedding which is a religious duty. We know of liberal rabbis in the Provence in the thirteenth century who permitted the playing of stringed instruments on the Sabbath on the ground that the prohibition of the Talmud applies to handclapping and the striking the thighs only, these gestures being concomitant to dancing; consequently, this edict was, in reality, only a prohibition of dancing, not music.

It is evident, therefore, that the practice of music, and especially of singing, continued unrestrictedly, not only in Spain where the opinion of MAIMONIDES had its greatest weight, but also in the Jewish settlements in East and West. A striking example is the case of ISRAEL NAJARA (or NAGARA), who was poet, composer, and *ḥazzan* (1555-1628). For some of his poems he composed his own melodies, but wrote most of them according to the rhythm of popular Arabic, Turkish, and Spanish tunes. In the preface to his *Zemirot Israel* (published in Venice, 1597) he said that his aim in composing his *piyyutim* was to turn the Jewish youth from profane songs. His poems were highly praised by R. LEON MODENA, who composed a song in his honor, which was printed at the beginning of NAJARA's *"'Olat Shabbat,"* the second part of his *"Zemirot."* Some of his poems were written in Aramaic, the best known of them is *"Yah Ribbon 'Olam"*, a Sabbath hymn recited and sung in all countries and printed in most Jewish prayerbooks.

The Social Situation of the Jews in Spain

Meanwhile, the Jews in the Iberian peninsula carried on an existence in which joyous and gloomy periods alternated with a dismaying regularity. During times of a lull in the hostilities, the Jews, due to their industry, became affluent and wealthy, and their knowledge and ability won them influence and high offices. As soon as they prospered, however, they provoked the envy of their Christian surroundings and the enmity of the clergy. The kings, especially those of Aragon, regarded the Jews as their property; in this respect the Jews in Spain were not much better off than the slaves of antiquity, who were the personal property of their owners. The kings spoke of "their" Jews, of "their"

Juderías; by this royal "sympathy" the situation of the Jews was in some way alleviated, but only as far as the Jews, or their money, could be put to good use.

Jews were considered mere chattels. PEDRO II of Aragon (1174-1213) transferred "his" Jews from Zaragoza with their families, descendants and property to the Order of the Knights of St. John, Queen SANCHA, in her will (1208), bequeathed the Jews from Huesca, Zaragoza, Calatayud, Alagon and Daroca to the Convent of Sigena,[20] with the added stipulation (in 1210) that the convent could not exchange these Jews.[21]

Jews were not permitted to emigrate. With every fugitive Jew, the kings lost a piece of their property, the feudal lords a piece of their prey, and the townships a piece of their income.[22]

The further history of the Jews in Spain stands under the sign of "paying." They paid taxes, they paid "encabezamiento," or poll tax, and they were burdened with numerous other taxes. Whenever the kings of Aragon or Castile stayed in a city in which a Jewish community existed, the Jews were required to provide the royal household with beds and other furniture. This could be avoided, however, by the paying of a specified sum. On the occasion of a royal visit to a city inhabited by Jews they paid a tribute to the royal guard. In addition to all these taxes the Jews paid a coronation tax, pasture tax, tithes on houses for the bishops and their households, special customs duties, bridge tolls, etc.

In those times the Jews of Catalonia and Aragon were called "coffres y tesoro del rey," not only because they were tax collectors and administrators of the finance (al-faquini, bajuli, repositarii, dispensatores), but mainly because, through all kinds of voluntary and not so voluntary contributions, they made up the chief source of income for the royal houses.

Despite all these contributions of the Jews to the royal treasuries, anti-Jewish enactments followed one after another, only to be topped by massacres. There was one in Valladolid in 1366, another, much more serious, in Sevilla in 1391, followed by similar acts in Cordova, Valencia, Lerida, Barcelona, and other places. Thousands of Jews had perished, many of their communities had been annihilated; but the country itself was the main sufferer. The instigator of this butchery—which even as late as in the nineteenth century was described as a *"guerra sacra contra los Judíos."* or, according to another "interpretation," as a social eruption—was JUSEF the Archdeacon of Ecija who later was honored as a saint on account of "his piety." In all of Castile the agitators and perpetrators of these inhuman crimes remained unpunished.

Following the bloody excesses of 1391 the popular hatred of the Jews led to the forcible conversion of the Jews to Christianity. The Inquisition closely watched the converted Jews, issued many edicts forbidding Christian neophytes, as well as Jews, to study the Talmud or read anti-Christian writings. Jews had to avoid pronouncing the names of Jesus, Mary, or of the saints. They could not build new synagogues or repair old ones. In addition, Jews were denied all rights of self-jurisdiction, nor might they proceed against their accusers. Public offices were forbidden them, nor might they practice any handicraft, or act as brokers, physicians, apothecaries, or druggists. They could neither bake or sell *mazzot,* or to give them away; nor dispose of meat which they were prohibited from eating. They were excluded from all intercourse with Christians, and could not disinherit their baptized children. Besides, all Jews over twelve of both sexes were required to wear a badge at all times. Thrice a year they had to listen to a Christian sermon on Christ, the Messiah.[23]

The persecutions, the laws of exclusion, the humiliations inflicted upon the Jews, and the many conversions among them not only reduced their influence, but along with them suffered the entire kingdom of Spain. Commerce and industry came to a standstill, the soil was not cultivated, the finances were disturbed. In Aragon entire Jewish communities had been destroyed, and many were reduced to poverty, losing more than half of their members.

In mentioning this very brief outline of the history of the Jews in Spain in the fourteenth and fifteenth century, it is not our aim to recall the endless martyrdom of the Jewish people. However, it is necessary to show the atmosphere in which this oppressed and persecuted people was nevertheless able to bring forth great poets, thinkers, physicians, scholars, and musicians. Whenever a short pause in the persecutions occurred, the unbroken Jewish spirit manifested itself almost immediately. Their accumulated energies—physical as well as intellectual—erupted with elemental force, for the creativeness of the race overcame all obstacles in asserting itself.

The "golden age" of Jewry in Spain, as long as it lasted, was a beautiful dream. It was not so golden after all. It was merely an interruption, a lull, in the perpetual war of the Christian world against a people whose industriousness, learning, commercial ability, and human dignity provoked envy, jealousy, and latent as well as undisguised hostility. At any moment of history it could, and did, erupt into open persecution and degenerate into violence and massacre. To be sure, in their peaceful period of existence in Spain, the Jews could walk erect, and could exercise their religion freely. They were not hindered in their civil rights, could amass fortunes and give their children a good education.

But what kind of human liberty could this have been that, which, at a moment's notice, or, on the change of a king, or due to the fanaticism of a pope or a bishop, could turn into bloody excesses with the complete loss of liberty so much valued by this proud and productive people? However much the Jews in Spain enjoyed their human rights, they were constantly aware of the fact that possible disaster continually hung over their heads like a Damocles' sword. How was it possible that with this threat to their destiny, even their lives, their intellectual energies brought forth scholars, philosophers, scientists, and poets, whose works have lasting values and are still admired after centuries? Their poets in particular created immortal works of art, which are read today with the same enjoyment as at the time of their creation.

Jewish poets sang "The Lord's song in a strange land," not as the Psalmist complained (Ps. 137), but with a joyous heart, with hope and reliance upon the future.

One of the first great singers of that era was SOLOMON ibn GABIROL (1021-1069), whom HEINRICH HEINE described as "a nightingale singing in the darkness of the Gothic medieval night." Even more famous was YUDAH HALEVI (c. 1066-1145), whose poetry breathes fervor, piety, and love of God and man. His poems reach their highest beauty when they express his longing for Zion. He wrote numerous love songs which he was wont to perform himself with musical accompaniment: a real medieval troubadour. In the Yemen prayerbook[24] many of his wedding odes are included; scores of his hymns adorn our contemporary prayerbooks. His "Ode to Zion" was considered by GOETHE as one of the greatest poems in world literature.

MOSES ibn EZRA (c. 1070-1139), famous for his penitential songs, "was nevertheless the author of Hebrew love songs worthy of the most light-hearted troubadours."[25] After his death, YUDAH HALEVI referred to him as

> "The fount of wisdom, in whose mouth I find
>> The place of gold, the mine of purest ore."[26]

One of his poems, 'El Nora 'Alilah ("God, that doest wondrously") is incorporated in our prayerbooks in the Neilah Service (closing prayers of the Day of Atonement) and is sung to a Sephardic tune in all Sephardic and most Ashkenazic synagogues.

His brother, ABRAHAM ibn EZRA (1092-1167), though excelling in poetry, became famous mainly for his Biblical commentaries. "He has been called the father of commentators and for a long time had no rival in this field."[27]

The prayerbook became the treasure house of medieval Jewish poetry. This was the glorious period of the piyyutim. In this epoch were written such Jewish hymns as "'Adon 'Olam" and "'Adonay Melek" by unknown authors, the Sabbath hymn "Leka Dodi" by SOLOMON 'ALKABIZ, and countless more that survived all the centuries and remained outstanding pieces of Jewish liturgy.

These and many others had been the medieval folk bards in Jewish history. They exerted the same influence upon Jewish life, Jewish poetry, and Jewish ethics as the medieval "troubadours" did upon their Christian audiences. Just as the troubadours had been poets and singers of noble ancestry, the Jewish poet-singers may be considered as belonging to an aristocracy of the spirit. They may also be considered to be the true counterparts of the Christian troubadours.

Besides this intellectual "aristocracy," there was in Iberian lands a class of Jewish entertainers, among the juglares (as the French jongleurs were called in Spain) whose exploits and social status will be the subject of the next chapter of our study.

After their expulsion from Spain and Portugal, a multitude of Jewish exiles migrated to North Africa, the Balkans, and Turkey, taking with them their ancient spiritual heritage together with a deeply impressed hispanic culture. An important part of this culture was manifest in their love for the popular Spanish ballads, or *romances,* which they preserved faithfully in oral tradition with remarkable vigor up until the early decades of the present century and which have suffered a continual decline henceforth. Although the texts of these ballads have maintained the archaic Castilian language dating back to fifteenth-century Spain, if not earlier, it is still quite difficult to ascertain, at the present time, which of the melodies of the ballads did stem from the Iberian musical tradition.

A Spanish captain, DOMINIQUE de TORAL, who traveled the Mediterranean, related that, upon his arrival in Aleppo in 1643, he found more than eight hundred houses in which Jews lived, and among them he found avid readers of such masters of the artful *romance* as LOPE da VEGA (1562-1635) and LUIS de GONGORA (1561-1627), who flourished long after the expulsion of the Jews from Spain.[25] This is but one example from the vast number of early post-exile documents which attests to the fact that the Spanish *Romancero* had established strong roots in the Near East. Sixteenth- and seventeenth-century collections of metrical and rhymed liturgical hymns (*piyyutim*) written in Hebrew characters played an important role in alluding to a representative number of Spanish ballads—upon which they were modeled— in their elaborate incipits. It was through this very practice of *contrafacta* that a good portion of the music was preserved.[29]

However, the incipits, besides indicating to which *romance* melody a particular *piyyut* was to be sung, also referred to popular Greek, Turkish, and Arabic melodies which were adopted in the new lands of emigration. These collections of *piyyutim* were found scattered all over the Mediterranean region and were considered as important for *romancero* sources as were the *cancioneros* and *vihuelista* collections of fifteenth- and sixteenth-century Spain. Two noteworthy collections of liturgical poems, called *juncas,* were still entoned up to relatively recent times in the Portuguese Temple of Adrianopolis. These poems, composed by

ISRAEL NAJARA (1555-1628), or those by MAGULA, were inserted in the Sabbath morning liturgy of the Adrianopolis Synagogue. The well-known Turkish Sephardic scholar ABRAHAM DANON identified the *romances* among their incipits.[30]

Also found in the musical heritage of the Sephardim were *endechas*, or dirges, sung for funerals and periods of mourning, especially during the week preceding Tisha b'Ab. Numerous collections of these, also in Hebrew characters, were published in Constantinople, Salonica, Sofia, and even in Jerusalem (Illustration No. 1).

ISRAEL J. KATZ has undertaken a thorough investigation of the Judeo-Spanish *Romancero*, and has recorded on tape the oral tradition of Sephardim residing in North Africa and Israel. In a preliminary study, KATZ pointed out two musical style traditions of the Sephardic ballads, a Moroccan and Turkish—and possibly three with Greek—located at opposite ends of the Mediterranean basin.[31]

From this preliminary study, we quote a ballad in the Turkish style, "*Irme kero, la mi madre*," which is very popular among the Balkan Sephardim. (Mus. ex. No. 1.)

Mus. ex. No. 1

"La chosa del desesperado"

(Translation: "Oh mother, I shall go wandering through the fields.")

Ballad in the Turkish style, recorded in Jerusalem (1960). After Israel J. Katz, Toward a Musical Study of Judaeo-Spanish Romances. *In:* Western Folklore *(April, 1962), vol. XXI, No. 2, p. 86.*

4

Jewish Troubadours and Jongleurs
in France

IN HIS BRILLIANT ESSAY ON THE JONGLEURS IN FRANCE,[1] EDMOND
FARAL poses the rhetorical question: "What is a jongleur?" His
answer is quite substantial:

> A jongleur is a multiple being: a musician, a poet, an actor, a
> buffoon; he is a kind of supervisor of the entertainment at the
> royal princely courts; he is a tramp who roams the highways and
> gives performances in the villages; he is a fiddler who, after a day's
> march, sings heroic ballads for pilgrims; he is a charlatan who en-
> tertains the people at crossroads; he is the author and actor of
> "plays" performed on festival days after the church services; he is
> the dancing master who incites and leads the young people in
> dancing; he is the drummer, the trumpet and horn player who
> directs the order of the processions; he is the raconteur, the singer
> who adorns the festivities, the weddings, the carousals; the acrobat
> who dances on his hands, who juggles with knives, who jumps
> through hoops, who eats fire, falls backwards and dislocates his
> limbs; the prestidigitator who shows off and is an actor; the buffoon
> who jokes and brags loutishly; the jongleur is all this and more;
> having given this long definition we have not yet told everything.
> One could ask, in addition: Is the jongleur all these at the same
> time? Or is the jongleur only a poet, a charlatan, or a musician?
> And furthermore: for which epoch is this definition valid?; Does it
> cover the entire period of the Middle Ages? Or is it to be applied
> to a particular moment in history?

Searching for a simple formula to give answer to these and
some additional questions, FARAL opines that the jongleur may

best be defined as a class whose vocation was to entertain the people.

The profession of the jongleur made its appearance in the ninth century. This is the time when the term is first mentioned in existing medieval records. The word is derived from the Latin *jocular* and *joculator* (jester, joker), which, as time went by, entered the (old) French language transformed to *jogler* and *jogleor*, and in Spanish as *juglar*. It is certain that the profession of the jongleur did not appear suddenly in the epoch in which it was first recorded in the literature. There must have been a long evolution leading from the Greek and Roman jesters to the jongleur. Furthermore, the jongleurs may be considered as the successors of the ancient folk-bards who entertained their audience by singing heroic ballads. Some historians of literature have established a kinship between the jongleur and the *scôpes* of Germanic countries. They were, like the jongleurs, poets who performed their epic songs with musical accompaniment. *Scôpes* is a term of Celtic and Anglo-Saxon origin; this type of folk-bard was called a *Spielmann* in Germany.

The European jongleur can look back upon a long historic development. From the *ithiphallēs* of Sykion, the *dikelistēs* of Sparta, the *ethelontēs* of Thebes, one can draw a straight line in the history of popular entertainment which leads to the Roman *mimus* and *histrio*, all these representing actors and jesters. Until the ninth century all popular entertainers had been called *mimes*. In popular parlance jongleur and mime had the same meaning. Their survival and success during these centuries is attested by the fact that the philosophers in classical antiquity and, later, the Church authorities usually looked askance at this class of merry-makers.

Prior to Carolingian times, ninth-century authors, poets, and musicians, termed as mimes, had spread over Europe. They became the most revitalizing element in all countries where, under the iron rule of the Church, the populace was put on a meager ration of entertainment. As a consequence, the people lavished its affection upon the only class that could bestow them some joy. It was in France, and especially in the southern part of it, in sunny Provence, where the jongleurs' activity reached its peak.

From Charlemagne's epoch on, their profession became an officially recognized factor in the social and courtly life of the French
people. But in the North, in Gaul, and also in England, beginning
with the eighth century, these popular entertainers were increasing in number. They crossed the Rhine into Germany, where the
populace still clung to their *Spielmann,* so that the jongleurs
could not take deep roots. Nevertheless, they left their imprint
upon German taste, morals, and influenced Teutonic art, habits,
and social culture.

The Church looked upon the jongleurs and their rapid expansion through civilized Europe with ever-increasing hostility. Ecclesiastical authorities hurled interdictions, edicts, bans, and all
kinds of prohibitions against them—for the most part ineffective.
The more the Church stressed the idea that the jongleurs constituted a public danger, the more the people clung to their beloved
jesters and continued to patronize them publicly and privately.

The public performances of the jongleurs usually took place
on the church premises after the services. And once they gained
a foothold on the church porches, it became the inevitable sequel
that they entered the church itself. Later we find them as musicians, actors, and even dancers, in, or loosely connected, with the
divine service. The bishops, the councils, and finally, the popes,
made a loud hue and cry against this profanation; but these repeated vociferations remained without result. Eventually, realiz-
ing that all protests were in vain, the Church authorities condoned their intrusion into the confines of the sanctuary and tried
to make the best of it.

But there soon arose a more acute danger. As time went by,
the profession of the jongleurs became attractive to individuals
of the most diverse strata of society. Fascinated by the pleasant
and free-wheeling life of the jongleurs, a goodly number of people
gave up their erstwhile occupations and took to the road, alone
or in company with already established professionals. Members
of the low clergy, artisans, merchants, and all kinds of bourgeois
craftsmen embraced the glittering profession of the itinerant
"artists." This, in the long run, constituted a real nuisance to the
Church and endangered public morality. Soon, these jongleurs
were called "vagrant clerics," or simply "vagrants." They invented

a patron saint named Golias, after whom they called themselves Goliards.

Once the legend was created, it grew by itself. They gave Golias the title "bishop"; people tried to "discover" some facts of his life, and if this was not possible, they devised these facts themselves. An obscure scribe pretended that Golias was the author of the poems of an imaginary *archipoeta* of Cologne. His followers established his character according to their own ideas foisted upon him and they lived a life which, in their imagination, was that of this artificially created saint.

The thirteenth century became the golden age of the jongleurs, especially in France and in the Iberian peninsula. They became a public power; they were beloved and respected. They amused the lowly as well as ladies of high society; they spread delight around them and were honored. They were also feared, since their word had undeniable influence upon the people. Thus, they could achieve anything they wanted. At the height of their influence they clothed themselves in lavish white and grey robes.

Several French kings, following a line of austerity prescribed by the Church, were hostile to the jongleurs. Louis the Pious (814-840) had admitted them to his court, but made it a point never to attend their performances. Gradually, however, the resistance of the ruling class against them diminished. At the beginning of the thirteenth century we find accounts for jongleurs at all courts and in all countries.

Louis IX, called the Saint (1226-1270), was a special protector of the jongleurs. Even in Spain, the jongleurs (*juglares*, as they were called in Iberia) were invited to the princely Courts, where their performances were greatly enjoyed.

Through a professional guild the jongleurs established for themselves a particular organization that guided their lives during the centuries of their existence.

Once the functions of the early medieval folk-bards were superseded by the new class of the jongleurs, this had split up into different categories according to the social strata from which it emerged. If a jongleur was a nobleman, he was called *troubadour* or *trouvère* (spelled *trobaire* in the Provence). He composed his own poems (hence the name from the French *trouver*, "to find"), although he was not necessarily his own performer. If he was a poor singer, he called upon a *chanteor*; if his playing left something to be desired, he employed an *istrumenteor*. He found many in both categories among itinerant musicians, who were flooding all countries. Nevertheless, in the late Middle Ages the troubadours were still called jongleurs.

Another category of poet-singers was the *menestrel* or *ménétrier*, the minstrel (a word derived from the Latin *ministeralis* or *ministrellus*). These were permanently attached to a royal Court or to that of some nobleman. As time went by, the minstrel assumed an intermediary role between the aristocratic troubadour and the plebeian jongleur. The troubadour did not ask, nor accept any recompense for displaying his art; the *menestrel*, however, even if he was sometimes of a noble lineage, made his living by the favors he received for his services.

Finally, there was the class of the jongleurs proper, who were of a lowly, bourgeois origin and were entirely dependent on what they earned by their roving profession. Many of them derived an additional income from being artisans, traders, and merchants.

Jongleur was the late French term, replacing the older *joglar* and *jogleor* for the itinerant musicians. In the Iberian peninsula, as already mentioned, they were called *joglares* or *juglares*, the mimes *remendadores*, and the troubadours *segrers* or *segrels*. These latter ones, however, had not the same social status as the French troubadours, for frequently they did not belong to the nobility and accepted remuneration for their services. They represented, therefore, more or less, an intermediary group akin to the French *ménéstrier*. Their main artistic quality, the only one required from them, was to sing well, the same quality the jongleurs had to possess. Sometimes both terms, *segrel* and *juglar*, were used interchangeably.

The description of the jongleur's profession would be incomplete without referring to a sub-species, that of the *jongleresse*, the female jongleur. Old miniatures show that jongleurs, especially those who were successful in their profession, employed singing and dancing girls. For several centuries a favorite piece of the jongleurs' repertoire had been "The Dance of Salome," which was performed by women.

RICHARD of CORNWALL saw, in 1241, Saracene jongleresses dancing and singing at the court of FREDERICK II. The princess ELIZABETH, granddaughter of King ANDREAS of Hungary, was sent to the Wartburg in 1211, as betrothed to the Landgrave LUDWIG of THURINGIA; to accompany her, the King sent a jongleresse named ALHEIT, in order to help her forget the loss of her country of origin. (ELIZABETH was canonized on account of her saintly life.) WENCESLAUS, King of Bohemia, was a well-known protector of the minnesingers (the counterparts of the troubadours in Germanic lands). He had at his court a favorite jongleresse of the name of AGNES, who was well versed in singing and playing the harp and occupied a high place in the royal household.

A fresco in the Cathedral of Brunswick (Germany) shows a dancing girl in the apparel of a jongleresse, accompanied by a *viala player*; another jongleresse is seen seated at the table with a young nobleman who seems to be making amorous advances to her.

Evidently enough, the jongleurs took their place in the lowest as well as in the highest strata of the population. In civilized Europe they spread joy on the one hand, while constituting a public danger on the other.

As the status of the jongleurs gained in importance, it was not fit for a person of high standing to simply invite an occasional itinerant jongleur into his house. It became customary, and even was considered a social obligation to maintain in his entourage an entire troupe of jongleurs. This was an expensive luxury, while at the same time, it was proof of an individual's standing in society. Kings and princes spent large sums to sustain a group of jongleurs as befit their rank. Not only in Latin countries, but elsewhere in Europe, the company of jongleurs in one's abode was considered the mark of high nobility. WILLIAM of LONGCHAMP, chancellor of England and regent of the kingdom during the absence of King RICHARD the LION-HEARTED, brought a band of jongleurs from France who entertained him at his leisure.

The generosities doled out to a relatively small number of jongleurs did not alleviate the economic situation of their majority, but rather indicated that these performers were not considered social outcasts wherever they went. The remuneration a jongleur received for his services varied anywhere from a rich reward to leaving a festivity empty-handed. Very often, if a nobleman would not remunerate the jongleur from his own pocket, he gave him a letter of recommendation to a friend or relative, praising the talent of the jongleur and asking that he be received with favor at the other place. It was a cheap way to evade one's direct obligations, but the jongleurs seem to have been satisfied with this procedure. The jongleur RUTEBEUF, who flourished in Paris in the thirteenth century, left us a poem which describes drastically his colleague's disappointment in the miserliness of a certain nobleman. (See p. 94)

As the jongleurs became more and more class-conscious, they organized themselves into guilds and fraternities. Still, only a privileged few belonged to these professional organizations, and these few had been just the ones, who being well-to-do and sometimes even rich, least needed the protection of the guilds. The great majority of the jongleurs were and remained unprotected and had to rely upon the good will of their "employers," which was far from adequate. Such fraternities were established in Arras, in Fécamp, in Amiens, and many other places. Whether they had ways and means to protect their members against abuses of the nobility is not known. Yet these guilds had other merits which distinguish them in the history of music. They organized in their respective towns important music festivals, called "puys de musique,"[2] with singers, instrumentalists and choral groups participating. A winner was always chosen for such musical contests who was declared "King of the Puy," and was awarded a crown.

In a broader sense, the influence of these musical contests is incalculable for the development of musical culture in the Middle Ages. We have only to consider the environment created by this particular activity of the jongleurs in order to understand the important role they played in the social, intellectual and artistic life of the civilized nations of Europe from the tenth to the thirteenth centuries.

Now we come to the important question: how did the Jews fit

into this picture? The answer is virtually obvious if we realize how great the attraction of the jongleurs was upon the people.

It most certainly affected the Jewish society as well. The Jews in the Diaspora never gave up in their musical practice; and being by nature particularly gifted for musical art, the result was that quite a number of them were tempted by an outwardly resplendent profession which seemed to match so closely their natural inclinations.

It is not surprising to find Jewish names among the jongleurs. The relative scarcity of such names in historical records should not be taken as a proof that there might have been only a few Jewish jongleurs. Rather, the scarcity of Jewish names may be explained by the fact that the few who were mentioned were undoubtedly jongleurs who gained admission at some princely court, or whose names were obtained by some civil legal document. If we consider these relatively few names as being merely a cross-section of existing conditions, we are closer to the truth with regard to the real number of Jewish musicians who embraced the profession of a jongleur. At any rate, the historical facts of the existence of Jewish jongleurs are a clear indication that Jews participated actively in the musical culture of the Gentile world and that, when given the opportunity and incentive, Jewish musicians and singers participated in all domains of intellectual and artistic activity, striving to equal their Gentile competitors, often successfully.

JEAN de NOSTRADAMUS in 1575 published an anthology of the most famous poet-singers of the Provence with some biographical notes, which are the main source of the life and work of the troubadours and jongleurs in Southern France. Among them are several jongleurs with the name of ELIAS. Now, the French form of this name is ELIE; it is therefore peculiar that ELIAS should be the name of quite a number of French jongleurs. There is, of course, no positive proof that these were Jews; it is merely a surmise that this might have been the case.

There lived, for instance, ELIAS de BARJOL (1200-1230), son of a merchant from the district of Brignolet, department Var. It is said of him that he was for a long time attached to the court of a nobleman.[3] Although he is designated in our sources as a *"gentilhomme,"* this does not mean that he was of noble ancestry. Otherwise he would have been called a troubadour. Aristocratic troubadours have always the title of "seigneur," "Sieur," "comte," "chevalier," "vicomte," or simply *"issue de noble passe"* ("of noble descent"). Whereas the jongleurs of bourgeois lineage were generally called *"gentilhomme,"* or, if they were former clerics, *"chanoyne,"* or else, referring to his real profession, *"jurisconsulte,"* or to that of his father, f.i. *"fils d'un pelletier,"* ("son of a furrier"). About ELIAS de BARJOL the chronicler states that he was a man of spirit and of pleasant ideas, besides being a good singer. ELIAS was the author of a poem in which he reported the victories of the Count of Provence (1150). Another of his poetic works was a ballad entitled "The Wars of the Baussenes," which was praised for its beautiful and elegant style. Furthermore, he left us a collection of love songs, entitled "The Largesses of Love."[4]

Another jongleur of this name was ELIAS CAIREL, from the district of Sarlat, in the Dordogne (fl. about 1220-1230). Two other jongleurs were also named ELIAS, without a surname. JEAN de NOSTRADAMUS mentions some other jongleurs by this name: ELIAS FONSALDA and ELIAS RUDELH, both from the district of Bergerac in the Dordogne, ELIAS d'UZES, ELIAS d'USSEL, surnamed CORREZE, and ELIAS de SOLIER (fl. 1464).

Whether these ELIASES were really Jews cannot be proved. Maybe they were converts, like a jongleur whose name was ISRAEL le BIENHEUREUX (d. 1014). His conversion procured him a carefree position, since he is recorded as the precentor of the church of Dorat, in the District of Haut-Vienne.[5] Like so many converts, he was eager to forget his Jewish past, and this no doubt was his incentive to write the *Life of Jesus Christ*; he also was the author of a Bible in verse form. Neither of these are preserved.

Then, a name crops up among the French jongleurs which we will find frequently among the Jewish juglares of Spain, the name BONAFOS. A French jongleur, with a slight variant of this name, BONAFE, was the companion of the famous provençal troubadour BLACATZ. He could have been either the *chanteor* or the *istrumenteor* of this errant knight. Owing to their close partnership, BONAFE was allowed to collaborate on one of the lengthy poems of BLACATZ; he furnished two stanzas to it. The other jongleur, his name spelled like that of his Spanish colleagues, BONAFOS, was the companion of another famous troubadour of the Provence, named CAVAIRE. Presumably the same relationship existed between the two as in the aforementioned case; he also contributed to his master's poem, this time only one stanza. The home of BONAFOS seems to have been the Auvergne, but he probably lived with his partner in Aurillac; he states in his poem that he did not like the people of this district—a curious example of regional jealousies in the poem of a Jewish jongleur!

The same name BONAFOS among French jongleurs and Spanish *juglares* indicates that this Jewish family must have split up early in the Middle Ages, one branch settling in the Provence, the other in Spain.

While we can only venture to guess that the above-mentioned ELIASES were of Jewish origin, we have conclusive information about two jongleurs who were Jewish beyond a doubt. One is ISAAC GORNI, who flourished late in the thirteenth century in the Provence. He is erroneously called "troubadour,"[6] since being a Jew he could not belong to the privileged class of the singers of noble descent. We know about him from a *Diwan* (a collection of poems) which is preserved. In one of his poems he expressed confidence that his songs brought comfort for many grieved hearts, but complained bitterly about the lot of the wandering musician, the ridicule and disdain heaped upon him and the hard living conditions he was subjected to.[7] GORNI shared the fate of most Jewish jongleurs: he was forgotten, which is all the more astounding since his collection of poems has survived.

The other Jewish jongleur, living presumably in northern France, is known in the history of the French medieval literature as CHARLOT le JUIF; his life and fate was recorded by one of his colleagues, the successful jongleur RUTEBEUF, who flourished in the thirteenth century and, at the end of his career, settled in Paris where to all appearances he became very popular and acquired considerable wealth.

We may assume that, at least at the start of his activity as a jongleur, RUTEBEUF knew misery which, in a sort of autobiography, he described vividly.

Among his literary output there is a fabliau (as the medieval

epic poems with rhymes were called in France), which tells of
the misadventures of another jongleur, CHARLOT le JUIF. Whether
this was a real living person, or existed merely in the fancy of the
poet, cannot be determined beyond doubt. There are, however,
strong reasons for the assumption that this CHARLOT was a real
person, whose unfortunate life served RUTEBEUF as a pretext to
narrate his own miserable youth.[8]

The preamble of this fabliau shows that CHARLOT entertained
at weddings to earn his living. He seems to have been very
witty, the people liked his jokes and enjoyed his narratives. Like
other jongleurs, he lived on his earnings and was dependent for
this on the generosity of his sponsors. He was in the service of
several noblemen, among them ALPHONSE, Count of Poitiers,
brother of King LOUIS the SAINT (1226-1270). It appears that
he was, at least for some time, at the court of this king, as evidenced by a petition he addressed to the king, written in the
florid style of the time, to make appeal to the liberality of the
monarch. His petition may have gotten some results for CHARLOT.
Toward the end of his days, looking back on his life, CHARLOT
admits freely that he had always lived on handouts from others.
if nothing else, this "retrospect" is a clear indication that CHARLOT
might have been a real person, since RUTEBEUF was, as hinted
above, during the greater part of his life well-established in Paris,
where he was virtually free from any material cares.

In RUTEBEUF's poem the misfortunes of CHARLOT are impres-
sively described. CHARLOT complains about the miserliness of his
sponsors' gifts; they were oftentimes insufficient to provide for
his daily needs. His misery follows him everywhere, and RUTE-
BEUF characterizes him as a pitiable figure. Like other jongleurs,
he was a beggar; besides, he was addicted to gambling; as he says
himself, the dice ruined him (again a statement which does not
tally with the well-to-do RUTEBEUF). Often he returns to his
home empty-handed. On one occasion, after a festivity, CHARLOT,
instead of being paid by the nobleman he entertained, received
from him a letter of recommendation to a friend, a certain
GUILLAUME. We have already discussed the usage of letters of
recommendation in lieu of payment to a jongleur. For remuneration, GUILLAUME gave CHARLOT a miserable skin of a hare, which

was wretched pay even to poor CHARLOT. He attempted to get revenge for this treatment, but being luckless, even this vengeance backfired.[9]

These facts as related by RUTEBEUF are significant for our subject, since they give us insight into the fate of a Jewish jongleur at those times.

We have already mentioned the fact that clergy, artisans, merchants and others gave up their professions to become jongleurs, because they were fascinated by the "show business" aspect of this profession. For the same reason, the Jewish jongleurs clung to this insecure existence, for despite all the misery it entailed, compared to life in the secluded areas of the *Judería,* and the crowded cramped quarters of the city, there was glamour in the outdoor life, as well as a certain liberty which a civic occupation could not afford them. They gladly endured the hardships of being itinerant musicians because they liked to entertain, and were eager to earn the applause of the masses for whom their performances were the only recreation available. But the main reason was certainly the inborn love of music; only as jongleurs could Jewish musicians in those times exercise freely and untrammeled by other obstacles a profession which they considered to be their vocation.

As an example, we quote here a stanza of RUTEBEUF's fabliau in the original medieval French. It comes in the middle of the poem, entitled *"De Charlot le Juif qui chia en la pel dou lievre,"* translated roughly "About Charlot the Jew who fouled his rabbitskin."[10]

The passage comes at the end of the description of a wedding feast at which jongleurs from all parts had gathered unbidden to amuse the guests in the hope of recompense. Just before our text opens everyone is getting ready to go home. The jongleurs wanted either to be taken along to a manor where they would be fed in return for their entertainment or to receive some monetary remuneration.

> Li menestreil, trestuit huezei,
> S'en vindrent droit à l'espouzei;

N'uns n'i fu de parler laniers:
"Donnez nos maistres ou deniers,
Font ils, qu'il est drois et raison,
S'ira chascuns en sa maison."

Translation:

Booted for their journey
The minstrels came straight to the celebrants.
None was afraid of speaking out:
They say, "for it is only right and reasonable
If everyone's going home."[11]

5

Jewish Juglares in The Iberian Peninsula

IN HIS ANTHOLOGY JEAN DE NOSTRADAMUS GIVES AN INTERPRETATION
of the term *juglar* or *joglar,* the Spanish equivalent of the French
jongleur. As he says, almost all of the Provençal poets had been
joglars, men who earned their living by their poems and songs.
The greatest favor a princess could bestow upon a Provençal
poet was to call him *mon juglar.* Whereas the term *juglar* was an
honorary title, its variant *jangloux* had a derogatory meaning.[12]

Except in a few cases, the existence of Jewish jongleurs in
France could only be surmised. In Spain, however, there is documentary evidence about a number of Jewish *juglares.* Among the
best known of them, was Rabbi SANTOB de CARRION (fl. fourteenth
century), who is recorded in Jewish historiography as a "troubadour" at the court of DON PEDRO of Castile. This is an obvious
misnomer, since being a Jew, he could not have been a troubadour; this term as we know was restricted to singers of a noble
lineage. SANTOB is the Spanish phonetic adaptation of the Hebrew
name SHEM TOB, frequently used in medieval times.

The Book of Rabbi de Santob or *Rabbi Don Santob* is a valuable
document for early Spanish literature (preserved in the National
Library at Madrid). The purpose of it is to give moral counsel
to the new king PEDRO called "the Cruel" (1334-1369) whom the
poem repeatedly requests not to underestimate its author because
he is a Jew.

The book written in 1350 has an uncommonly easy and flowing
style. "After a longer introduction than is needful," says TICKNOR,
"the moral counsel begins with the 54th stanza and continues
through the rest of the work which, in its general tone, is not
unlike other didactic poetry of the period, although it is written

97

with more ease and more poetical spirit. Indeed, it is little to say that few rabbis of any country have given us such quaint and pleasant verses as contained in several parts of the curious counsels of the Jew of Carrion."[13]

SANTOB's *Book of Maxims* still enjoyed considerable reputation in the fifteenth century for its elegant style and high ethical content.[14]

In a Moorish world, and especially in princely courts, the Jewish *juglares* were definitely in the minority.

But already, early records mention a Jew, ISMAËL, player of the rota (a string instrument), and his wife among the twenty-seven *juglares* at the court of SANCHO IV of Castile (1257-1295). Thirteen of them were Moorish, and these two were Jewish. Yet the Archpriest of Hita, JUAN RUIZ, considered the Jewish women singers equal to the Moorish girls; and in fact, all the large festivals of the Spanish towns where Christian churches coexisted with synagogues and mosques had been attended by *juglares* and *juglaresas* of all three religions. An early example of such a festival, in which the three religions participated, was the solemn reception of ALFONSO VII (1104-1157) in Toledo in 1139. All the townspeople came out to meet him, Christians, Saracens and Jews, with drums, lutes, rotas, and all kinds of musicians, each singing the praise of the king in his own language. There is a poetic commentary for this event: a Judaeo-Spanish *romance*, in which the reception in honor of the Catholic king's daughter, betrothed to King DON MANUEL of Portugal, is described.

"Out came to meet me the three religions in their best, The Christians with their crosses, the Moors in their own garb, The Jews with the *vihuelas*, making the city resound."[15]

Among other favorites of the Spanish kings, the existing records mention repeatedly BONAFOS and his son SENTO [SHEM TOB], Jewish *juglares* of Pamplona. They were rewarded by King CARLOS II of Navarre (1332-1387) with houses, farms and several other gifts.

A document, dated April 24, 1386, records a royal donation in Tudela: "We made, a long time ago, a donation of the above mentioned houses situated in the *Judería* of Pamplona, to BONAFOS and his son SENTO, Jewish *juglares*, living now in the above-

mentioned city of Pamplona, who had been away from our kingdom for about three years."[16]

Besides real estate and money, wheat was the usual gift to
juglares. The King of Navarre, CARLOS II, ordered in Pamplona
(July 8, 1365), "to be given and delivered at once to BONAFOS,
Jewish *juglar,* four bushels of wheat, according to Pamplona
measure. We have given this wheat to him as a special favor, as
a provision for his home." The receipt of this donation, preserved
in the archives of Pamplona, was written by BONAFOS himself and
stamped by his own seal. It says: "Know ye all that I, BONAFOS,
Jewish *juglar,* acknowledge the receipt . . . from you, BARTHO-
LOMEO d'ARRE, tax collector of the community of Pamplona, of
four bushels of wheat, royal measure, which His Majesty graciously donated me as a provision for my home. By this donation,
I consider myself well paid, and as a proof of it, I give this letter
stamped with my seal."[17]

The *juglar* BONAFOS figures in quite a number of other official
documents. There are records of tax privileges for him (August
9th, 1364), also for another *juglar,* JACOB EVENAYON, *judio de
Pamplona, compaynero de* BONAFOS, *nuestro juglar* (Jew of
Pamplona, companion of BONAFOS, our *juglar*).

BONAFOS seems to have been cheated out of his parents' and
sister's heritage. His protector, CARLOS II of Navarre, gave order
on October 22, 1365, to the Master YENEGO DERDORÇAYA, licentiate
of the arts, to investigate the claim of the *juglar* BONAFOS.[18]

As a reward for his services, CARLOS II transferred to SAMUEL
ALFAQUI of Pamplona a house in the *Judería* of this town that was
formerly owned by BONAFOS and his son SENTO. Furthermore,
there is a record of a payment of 100 *maravedis* (silver pieces) to
BONAFOS, *el joven judío* (the young Jew), anno 1381.

Whether this BONAFOS, who enjoyed so many favors and privileges by the king was a member of the aristocratic Spanish
family of BONAFOS, is not known. This clan, together with other
families of the Jewish oligarchy of Spain, the NASI, PROFET,
CAVALLERIA, RAVALYA, PORTELLO, and others, were "each in
possession of patents, rights and privileges which not only conferred to them valuable holdings, lands and revenues, but a
special status in law in relation to taxes and to the courts of

justice. Walking with princes and standing before kings, these favored sons were the natural champions of their people's cause."[19]

As is prevalent, a wealthy Jewish family usually possesses its "poor relatives." This might well have been the case in Spain, since it cannot be assumed that a member of this aristocratic family would embrace the vagrant profession of a *juglar*. Yet even this "poor" branch of the family, or at least one of its members, made good, since BONAFOS and his son SENTO had been knighted by the king. The receipt of a donation on this occasion, preserved in the archives of Pamplona, was signed in Hebrew.[20]

In the accounts of the tax collector of Pamplona there is another document (1367) stating that a house close to [the church?] Santa Maria belongs to BONAFOS, *juglar judio,* and his son JENTO (SENTO misspelled), by virtue of a donation by the king.[21]

PEDRO IV (1319-1387) admitted IÇACH BONAFOS, *magistrum cortinarum* (master of the courtiers) and his son among his *familiares*—his retinue (July 10, 1374).[22]

There are quite a number of other members of the BONAFOS family whose names are preserved in ancient records. Several of them held important functions at the royal courts: BONAFOS ben YUDA, who was *baile* of the King of Aragon (1192), SALOMON BONAFOS, who held the same office at the court of the King of Catalonia (1233), and another BONAFOS who also was a royal *baile* (1208).

Some famous members of this family are BONAFOS VIDAL, a renowned Talmudist of Barcelona (end of the thirteenth century) and BONAFOS (or BONAFOUX) MENAHEM ben ABRAHAM of Perpignan (end of the fourteenth century), philosopher and author of an important book *Sefer ha-Gedarim* (Book of Definitions).[23] It is a Hebrew dictionary of philosophical and scientific terms, written at the end of the fourteenth century, but published two centuries later, at Salonica in 1567. Curiously enough, this comprehensive scholarly work contains one single musical item, *neimah,* "melody."[24]

The name BONAFOS is mentioned in numerous other documents from the years 1195, 1227, and quite frequently in the fourteenth century (1346, 1353, 1367, 1370).[25] These are only the names of such who had some official business with secular authorities. There must have been many more of this widely spread family, possibly also musicians among them, the names of whom are not preserved.

Among the *juglares* we find the names of two sons of the noted physician, SAMUEL ALFAQUI of Pamplona.[26]

The joyous Purim festival was celebrated everywhere in the Diaspora with music and dance. This was not different in Spain, and there are records that Jewish musicians played at this festival in the town of Villafranca. This must have been an infringement of an existing city ordinance, since the musicians were fined for such a transgression. We are not informed whether they appealed to the crown for the suspension of the penalty, or whether some influential Jewish functionary at the court intervened on their behalf. At any rate, the result was that JAIME II of Aragon (1264-1327) ordered that there should be no penalty imposed upon the Jews of Villafranca, named SOLOMON de BESERS and his sons, and VITALIS FERRARI, and VITALONUS BERTEELAY [BARZILLAI] who played at the Purim festival, *"ut moris est judeorum,"* according to the customs of the Jews.[27] It was probably on such a joyous occasion that Jewish *juglares* showed their skill as lion tamers,[28] as a counterpart to Jewish toreadors, mentioned in the archives of the city of Segovia.

About another Jewish musician we are informed from a record of the purser of the Infant JUAN of 1352: "I also donate to YUSSEF AXIVIL, a Jew from Borja, 20 *maravedis*, which His Highness the Infant graciously ordered to be given to him as a reward for his playing the string instrument called *viala* [*i.e.* the *vihuela*] with a bow, as he [evidently the Infant] walked on the road to the city of Oscha."[29]

A Jewish musician, SAÇON SALOMON, *ministerius instrumentorum de corda* (minstrel, *i.e.*, leader, of the string instruments) had been exiled for some reason. The crime must not have been very serious, since the Queen VIOLANTE repealed the exile in Zaragoza on March 2, 1391.[30] The same SALOMON figures in 1391 and also in 1400 as *ministrer* (minstrel) *de casa del senyor rey*. Therefore, he must have been an outstanding musician at the king's court.[31] In a further document from the year 1392, his name appears as "SASSON, the Jew, player of the *laut* (*laúd*=lute) of the Court of the King, our Lord."[32]

The minstrel of the Queen SIBILE, JOHANAN BARUCH, *judeu*, is repeatedly mentioned in official documents. On July 19, 1382, he gets permission to marry a second wife. In another record of the year 1390 he is carried as *ministrer destroments de corda da casa de la senyora reyna* (leader of the string instruments of the court of our Lady the Queen).

At times we learn in a roundabout way about the prominence of a Jewish musician. JUÇEF de EÇIJA was chief tax collector of the King of Castile and, although not a musician himself, showed much interest for music. This was the reason that the King ALFONSO IV of Aragon (1299-1336) requested him to ask the King of Castile to send him two Jewish *juglares* who played for him in a reunion at Tarazona (Valencia, Oct. 19, 1329).[33] If a monarch asked for specific musicians, it may be assumed that they were excellent.

Jews in Spain were also renowned for their skill as instrumentalists. For instance, we have records of a famous composer, ISHAK ben SIMEON, a Cordovan Jew. It is said of him that he had displayed great talent in composing melodies of different schools and styles, besides being a good singer and player of instruments.[34] He was the author of many appealing songs about wine and the lute.

Already in early Mohammedan Spain, long before the country had been reconquered by the Christians, Jewish musicians played an important role at the courts of Moorish Sultans. We know of one such a musician by the name of ʾAL-MANSUR, who first was attached to the court of ʾAL-HAKAM I and, upon his death (822), to that of ʾABD-ʾAL-RAHMAN (912-961). He was evidently a confidant of the sultan, since he was the carrier of important messages to and from high placed persons. As our sources show further, the sultan followed his advice in important state affairs.[35]

In 1648 the Sultan IBRAHIM employed Jewish fiddlers and dancers. At a royal banquet at Adrianople, during the reign of the Sultan MAHOMET IV (1675) Jewish minstrels and dancers, passing from tent to tent, entertained the guests.

Jewish and Moorish *juglares* were often ordered to display their skill for the entertainment of the Christian populace. In 1480, on Corpus Christi Day, they were ordered to exhibit in public their "national" dances.[36] Why this spectacle had to be done on this particular holiday is not divulged by the records.

The excellence of Moorish and Jewish music must have exerted an irresistible attraction for the Christians. They not only frequented places where Moorish and Jewish musicians could be heard, but they did not refrain from hiring such musicians even for services in their Christian churches, a fact which was considered as bordering on the scandalous. The Council of Valladolid, in 1322, stated in the Canon XXII, *De Judeis et Saracenis,* that it was a blasphemy for Christians to permit the presence of Jews and Saracens in the sacred services of the Christian liturgy. In the same Canon, the *vigiliae nocturnes* were prohibited, on the ground that the presence of "infidels" led to an unseemly noise, "because they make a tumult with their voices as with all kinds of instruments."[37]

King MARTIN (1374-1409) "admits ABRAHAM MAYOR [MEÏR], the Jew, public and sworn guardian, on account of his good and accomplished services in the above mentioned guardian's office, as well as in performing the function as minstrel (leader) of the stringed instruments, together with his two sons, to his minstrels, retinue and members of his household. Given at Zaragoza, June 5, 1399."[38]

Jewish musicians, like other *juglares,* had quarrels with each other, perhaps due to professional jealousy, or possibly concerning a beautiful lady who might have preferred one to the other. On one such occasion a certain BARZALAY, a Jewish *juglar,* was killed at a dance in Calatayud by another *Jehudanus* (Jew) of Caluo. BARZALAY must have been a favorite of King JAIME II, because in a rescript given at Barchinono, dated November 8, 1315, the king inquired about BARZALAY's condition and wanted to know who started the quarrel and whether the killing occurred in self-defense.[39]

In view of the deep involvement of the Jews in the musical life of Spain, it would be surprising not to find Jews as professional dancers, a field in which they were also outstanding especially later, in the Italian Renaissance. Indeed, we encounter in Spain very early, in the fourteenth century, the name of a Jewish dancing master, Rabbi HACEN ben SALOMO. It is said of him that he was called upon to teach Christians a choral dance around the altar at Saragossa, in the Church of St. Bartholomew, in the year 1313.[40] We do not know anything about his life, and activities, nor do we know whether he was in the service of a court or nobleman, as was usual at those times. The mere fact that he was asked to teach Christians dancing, and in a church, warrants the assumption that he might have been an outstanding dancing instructor in his time.

It was an ancient Oriental custom to hire wailing women for funerals. They are mentioned in the Bible, and the Talmud contains some pertinent information about this musical profession.[41] This Oriental custom was introduced into Spain by the Moors. It appears that Moorish wailing women performed their chants in such a fascinating manner that this was considered a dangerous musical attraction for the Christians. Therefore, the Council of Valladolid prohibited Christians to approach any of the places where the Moors celebrated their weddings and their funerals.[42]

It is significant that Jewish women were also employed among the *endicheras*, as the wailing women were called in Spain. One of the ordinances of the city of Seville, in the time of ALFONSO XI (1337-1347) states: "If a knight or a burgher dies, the funeral wailing (*llanto*) should not be extended over the funeral ceremony itself, and Moorish or Jewish women should not be hired for the lamentations (*para fazer llanto*)."[43]

In a document from the year 1344, there is an item among the expenses for the funeral of the Jewish lady DOÑA MAYOR [MEÏR] PONCE: *a las judías endicheras 15 mrs* (to the Jewish wailing women 15 *maravedis*).[44]

Juan de Valladolid

In 1319 at Toledo, a solemn reception took place at the Court of ALFONSO IV of Aragon (1299-1336), in which JUAN de VAL-

LADOLID played a prominent part and was honored as a great poet. He was a typical representative of the itinerant *juglares*, singing *romances* and entertaining the populace. In this epoch JUAN acquired an uncontested fame and popularity in low as well as in high circles. He was a converted Jew, son of the town crier of Valladolid. According to the testimony, evidently prejudiced, of one of his competitors, the *juglar* MONTORO, JUAN's father was the executioner of VALLADOLID and his mother a servant girl in an inn.

According to other sources, JUAN was probably born in 1283 at Alcalá de Henares, a town near Madrid; and since this place was the seat of Archbishop Ximenez' famous university, he may have studied there. This tallies with the fact that he entered the clergy and eventually became the Archipriest of Hita, a position in the low clergy corresponding closely to present day's rural dean. We further learn about JUAN that between the years 1337 and 1350 he was imprisoned in Toledo by the Cardinal-Archbishop GILDE ALBONAZ for some unexplained offence against ecclesiastical morals. These offenses might not be so "unexplained" if we take a good look at his love poems, written while he was still an ecclesiastic and which abound in qualities of lasciviousness and sensuality.[45]

Although JUAN was not called a *juglar* (the term was already obsolete at that time), he was quite similar to the court *juglares*, the ancient Galician or Provençal poet-singers. He wandered tirelessly from one castle to another, always taunted, even vilified by his competitors on account of his Jewish ancestry. Furthermore, his colleagues were envious of him not only because of the gifts showered on him by his patrons, but also because being courageous enough to write a kind of poetry which, as they claimed, was not compatible with his lower social status.

Around 1320, we find JUAN POETA (as he was called in the princely courts) in the service of the MARQUÈS de VILLENA. There he provoked the ire of the aforementioned *juglar* ANTON de MONTORO, who was a tailor in civilian life, and who was and remained JUAN's enemy during his lifetime. MONTORO addressed a poem to the city fathers of Cordova, in which he chided them for having lost their good sense when they granted 300 *maravedis* to this "poetaster." It is incredible, said MONTORO, that the city fathers,

being so enlightened, would consider JUAN de VALLADOLID a
"poet," after he plagiarized other poets' verses and was no more
than a *juglar* practicing the "blind man's" art (a pejorative expression characterizing low-class poetry), and performing *fazañas*
(old-time street ballads).[46]

From MONTORO's verses we may infer that, prior to becoming
an acknowledged court poet, JUAN had been a simple folk-singer
of *romances* in the popular vein. On learning that JUAN was in
Sevilla, MONTORO sent his own poems to the Archbishop of
Sevilla in order to prevent the bestowing of any gifts to his rival
JUAN, whom he characterized as a common "haggler of the old-
timers' exploits." All his poems reflect the unadulterated enmity
of the tailor of Cordova against JUAN. In one of MONTORO's poems
a nobleman (real or imaginary), GOMEZ MANRIQUE, "in the name
of the tailor," (i.e., MONTORO), begs the MARQUÈS of VILLENA not
to tolerate in his house JUAN POETA, "that fat and curly toad, who
makes his living by stealing other people's poems" and who
prospers by "borrowed poems wrought of scrap-iron." In his
unconcealed envy, MONTORO resorted to all kinds of calumnies to
dissuade the Queen and the clergy of Cordova from bestowing
gifts upon JUAN. And when, despite all these intrigues, the city
fathers of Cordova felt induced to confer a large donation to
JUAN, MONTORO tried to redicule the award by declaring that this
was done not to honor JUAN as a poet, but because he was a poor
man.

Like other *juglares,* JUAN traveled from court to court in Navarre
and Aragon. He also lived for some time in Italy, where he
gained access to princely courts by all kinds of fake credentials,
pretending to be one of the courtiers of King JUAN of Aragon and
Navarre, or introducing himself as being in the service of King
FERDINAND of NAPLES. In his further travels in Italy JUAN abandoned his royal credentials; instead he invoked a singular
qualification: to be able to chase away clouds. It is well known
to what degree even cultured and educated persons were influenced by astrology and magic in Italy during the early Renaissance. In these courts he was generally called "ZOAN de VAGLIA-
DOLID, popular poet of Spain," and was praised for improvising
Spanish poems and composing sonnets, which are considered the
oldest examples of Spanish poetry in Northern Italy.

JUAN POETA left to posterity, among lesser poems, his great work, *El libro de buen amor* (publ. in 1343), a curious mixture of literary value, crudeness, even ribaldry, mostly in the style of cheap street *romances* of the time. The love adventures that abound in this and his other poems amused and shocked his contemporaries, whether they were read by the public at large or by his superior clergymen. He presented these amorous escapades as his own love affairs; but of all his courtships not one seemed to have been successful. In one of his poems he described how he tried to soften the heart of his lady-love by sending her poems, *trovas* and *cantares*, in great profusion, with no result at all. It may be assumed that he poured his disappointments and frustrations into his poems.

Furthermore, in his *Libro de buen amor* he vents his anger at the clergy; he describes how "clerics and laymen, friars and nuns, ladies and *juglares* went out to meet Don Amor (the god of love)." This procession presents us with a most humorous and bizarre assembly of clerics, of *juglares,* and ladies of questionable repute, almost of a gargantuan jocularity. It is not surprising, therefore, that the clergy was outraged by such erotic extravaganzas of one of its members and tried to muffle, at least temporarily, JUAN's muse by putting him behind prison bars.

Despite all its coarseness and occasional vulgarity, *El libro de buen amor* is considered by historians of literature as the *Comedia Humana* of the fourteenth century and the comic epopee of Spain of the Middle Ages.

For our subject, JUAN's poem has a double significance. First, he states in it:

"Depués fiz muchas cantigas de danca é troteras
Para judías, et moras, e para entenderas,
Para en instrumentos de comunales maneras;
El cantar que non sabes, óilo á cantaderas." (verse 1513)[47]

"Then I wrote many dance and street songs
For Jewish and Moorish girls, and for women who
    carry love messages [*i.e.,* procurers],
For all instruments, in an uncouth manner;
For what you do not know, listen to any singing girl."

Here we have contemporary evidence for Jewish *juglaresas,* who played an important role along with the Jewish *juglares.*

A matter of further importance for us lies in the fact that JUAN's poem divulges the coeval instrumentarium used by the *juglares,* Christian, Moorish, and Jewish. It is without doubt a rather complete listing of the musical instruments of Spain from the twelfth to fourteenth centuries. We shall discuss presently this feature with regard to JUAN's poem.

About the French *troubadours* and *jongleurs* there are an ample number of historical sources; the same is true about the Christian *juglares* of the Iberian peninsula. Their lives and accomplishments are recorded; their literary output is either preserved in extant manuscripts, or mentioned and described in works of their contemporaries or in later times by literary historians.

Concerning Jewish *juglares* we possess only scant data. We quoted above some documents in which their names are mentioned, or in which donations or other favors by princely sponsors were recorded. Yet these few extant items are of utmost importance to us, because they show that Jewish *juglares* worked at the same level as their Christian or Moorish counterparts, with whom they vied in popularity, and were to enjoy the fruits of their profession, in spite of the handicaps which Jewish musicians certainly encountered in a generally hostile environment. The little that we learned about them from these records gives us reason to assume that they lived and worked like their Christian and Moorish counterparts, sharing the fate of the ordinary *juglares* and—as far as their material welfare was concerned—they were in general content with their lot.

The Musical Instruments of the Juglares

Our knowledge about Jewish *juglares* is greatly enhanced by pictorial documents, dealing with the activity of Christian and Moorish *juglares.* If we look at the general working conditions of the members of this profession, we gain a clear insight into that of the Jewish *juglares.*

In the Escorial near Madrid there is a valuable manuscript from the thirteenth century entitled "*Cantigas de Santa María*," attributed to ALFONSO X, called *El Sabio* ("the Wise," 1252-1284), king of Castile and Leon, already mentioned in an earlier chapter. This manuscript is illuminated by numerous miniatures in vivid colors, depicting the courtly life of the Spanish kings and noblemen. Another richly illustrated manuscript from the time of ALFONSO III, King of Portugal (1248-1279), with the title "*Cancionero de Ajuda*," contains sixteen miniatures. Four of these show a single *juglar* each, accompanied by an *istrumenteor*; the remaining dozen have *juglaresas* or *soldaderas* as their subject. Other instruments are depicted in another illuminated codex called "*Beato de Liébana*," preserved in the Spanish National Library.

From these miniatures we have made an appropriate selection, which will afford us a good idea about the musical practice of the *juglares*, which must have been identical for Christians, Moors and Jews alike.

We see in these miniatures the most frequently employed instruments of that epoch, among them such string instruments as:

1. The ordinary *vihuela*, played with a bow (Illustration No. 2);

2. A bass species of it, the *gran vihuela*, played with a large bow (Illustration No. 3);

3. The *rabel*, the precursor of today's violin, played with a bow (Illustration No. 4);

4. The *laúd* (the Arabian *úd*), today's lute, a large guitar with a bulging body, having nine strings, plucked with the fingers (Illustration No. 4);

5. A smaller guitar with seven strings, with a seemingly flat body like that of the present-day guitars (Illustration No. 5);

6. The *arpa*, harp, the shape of which is similar to today's Irish harp (Illustration No. 6);

7. The *cedra* or *citola*, seemingly a zither according to the

etymology of the word, but it has more the appearance of the modern mandolin and was played, like today's instrument, with a plectrum (Illustration No. 8);

8. The *canón* (the Arabian *kanún*), a medieval species of the psaltery or zither of the ancients, having many strings stretched above a flat body with three, four, or more resonance holes; the instrument was played with a plectrum. In our pictures there are four different species of this instrument (there might have been even more variants): one in a triangular shape (Illustration No. 11); a square-shaped one (Illustration No. 7); one in the shape of a trapezoid (Illustration No. 9); and one with a straight upper part and a curved lower part (Illustration No. 11). Illustration No. 11 shows three different types of *canóns*, in addition to the *vihuela* and the *dulzaina* (a clarinet-like instrument);

9. The *sinfonia* (*zanfoña* in medieval spelling), later called the hurdy-gurdy, activated by cranking a cylinder to which hooks or nails were attached and which pinched the metal strings, by pressing the keys of a keyboard on the side of the instrument (Illustration No. 10).

Certainly, there were other instruments known at that epoch, such as the *albogue*, a kind of double flute with an attached resonance body; the *albogón*, a large type of horn, either of wood, tin, or brass; the *bagpipe*, with one chanter and two drones; and among the percussion instruments, the *pandera*, the hand-drum with one skin; the *tamborete*, a drum in the shape of an hour-glass, with skins on both ends; and the *crótalos*, clappers. All the percussion instruments were usually played by the *juglaresas* and *soldaderas*. We know of many more that are not depicted in any of the three manuscripts mentioned above. JUAN de VALLADOLID, in his *Libro de buen amor*, enumerates quite a few more species. In verses 1227-1234 of his poem he mentions nineteen string, nine wind, and six percussion instruments, all of them having been played by the *juglares* of his time. Whether all these had been played by Jewish *juglares* as well, can only be surmised. It seems that the miniatures show the most commonly used instruments; thus we have at least a good insight into the instrumentarium of the itinerant musicians of that epoch.

The artisans who manufactured these instruments must have been of high professional caliber. Certain Spanish cities in these centuries were famous for building fine instruments that were superior to anything produced elsewhere. Sevilla, in particular, was the center of this industry and had a sizable export trade of musical instruments.[48]

6

Jewish Music Under
Arabian Influence

EVEN BEFORE THE DESTRUCTION OF THE SECOND TEMPLE, THE LITUR-
gical service shifted more and more to the synagogue. As time
passed, the synagogue became the seat of Jewish worship for a
number of practical reasons. The precincts of the Temple could
not hold the considerably increased population of Jerusalem,
which necessitated the creation of numerous neighborhood pray-
ing and study houses. One Talmudic source reports that Jerusalem
had at its destruction 394 synagogues, another source states 480.[1]
Although these figures are greatly exaggerated, it is certain that
there were at that time a goodly number of synagogues in Jerusalem. There was even a synagogue in the Temple itself, in the
Court of Squared Stones (*lishkat ha-gasit*), where the priests assembled occasionally for prayers and benedictions. The *Mishnah*
reports that following the daily morning sacrifice, after the prepa-
rations had been made for the offerings, the priests left the sacrificial animals lying on the altar and proceeded to this court to
recite the *Shem'a* and the Benedictions,[2] after which the sacrificial
act continued. The Levites also offered prayers in this synagogue
situated in the Temple Court.[3]

To understand the importance of the synagogue in Jewish worship, it must be stressed that no other medium than music and
singing was more effective in creating the "communion of the soul
with God," which is so characteristic of the synagogue. The religious leaders of the people must have recognized this soon enough
once they did not object to the transplantation of the music from
the Temple to the Synagogue.

With the destruction of the sanctuary by the Romans, the Jewish religion and all its established customs, including singing, would have been in extreme danger of being dissipated, had not the synagogue become the institution that succeeded in maintaining the tradition. "Unlike the Temple, a synagogue could not be destroyed by an enemy. With the burning of the Temple, its entire sacrificial system was obliterated. The destruction of any number of synagogue buildings entailed no change in the established liturgy or mode of worship. The Jews assembled anywhere in public or private were the real *synagōgē* which could conduct regular service like that held in the largest and most gorgeous structure."[4]

Centuries later, St. AUGUSTINE had acknowledged admiringly: "The Jews, although vanquished by the Romans, have not been destroyed. All the nations subjugated by the Romans adopted the laws of the Romans; this nation has been vanquished and, nevertheless, retained its laws and, inasmuch as it pertains to the worship of God, has preserved the ancestral customs and ritual."[5]

It is obvious, therefore, that in the Diaspora singing constituted an essential part of the synagogue service. It was the substitute for the sacrificial cult of the Temple. The end of the Temple ritual with its animal sacrifices would have constituted a serious crisis for any other religion, but in Judaism it did not in the least affect the continuity of worship. Once the Jews accepted the loss of their sanctuary, the synagogue satisfied their religious needs. Instead of the Temple at Jerusalem, the synagogue became for the Jews the place, wherever it was located, where God could be worshipped and where the individual as well as the congregation could pour out their religious fervor before the Eternal. The ritual underwent some changes, but the character of the service remained unaltered. The one essential modification was that the animal sacrifice was replaced by a spiritual sacrifice, a sacrifice which represented a sounding devotion, and was performed in song.

Owing to the great spiritual and practical importance of liturgical music, especially singing with its "ethico-modal" development in the Diaspora, there exists abundant information about all this in rabbinical responsa, and the philosophical treatises of the time. Unfortunately, we lack information concerning secular and folk music in the social life of the Jews.

When the national homeland of the Israelites ceased to exist, their folk music suffered, because it no longer had the necessary soil upon which it could be nurtured. To replenish this loss with newly created folk music under the hardships of the Dispersion and in a foreign environment would have been a formidable undertaking. But a people cannot, over a period of time, exist without having a sufficient stock of its own folk music. It can be assumed, therefore, that the Jews might have taken over popular tunes and dances from the peoples among whom they lived, such as the Babylonians, Syrians, and Arabians. It thus stands to reason that the Jews had to rely extensively on these newly-introduced melodies because their own music had only a few Jewish features; it contained mostly borrowed elements.

This change might have taken place in a well-nigh radical fashion, once the Jews came under the influence of the Arabian culture. The highly developed Arabian music must have had the strongest predominance upon the Hebrew minority, not merely upon the male population but, following the Arabian example, also upon women, and especially young maidens.

We will understand better the musical implications of the social life of the Jews in this epoch if we place them alongside the musical culture of the Arabian environment.[6]

Before the advent of Islam, the women in Arabian social life were not yet separated from men and enjoyed as much liberty as men. Particularly in music, women took a leading role in all family or tribal festivities. In the household of every Arab of standing there were singing-girls (ḳaināt or kiyān). How much the singing-girls had become an integral part of Arabian social life may be judged from the early life of Muhammad himself. He had with him "all the instruments and appurtenances of pleasure, and singing-girls, the latter performing on musical instruments, singing near every water where a halt was made." At the courts of the tribal chiefs there were a number of singing-girls, sometimes ten or more; such singers were also employed in taverns for the entertainment of the visitors; they accompanied themselves on the jank, the Arabian harp. About the character of the singing of these girls we learn that "before the Islam, music was little else than unpretentious psalming [chanting], varied and embroidered by the singer, according to the taste, emotion, or effect desired. These variations were prolonged interminably on a syllable, word, or hemistich in such a way that the singing of a *cantilena* of two or three verses might be prolonged for hours." This was done according to the Oriental system of *makamat*.[7] This practice was already highly developed among the Arabs of pre-Islamic days, as it was among the Hebrews in Ancient Israel; like with that of the Jews, "music and song were with the Arabs from the lullaby at the cradle to the elegy at the bier."[8]

The pre-Islamic period in Arab life, called by them the Days of Ignorance, coincided with the first centuries of the Jewish Diaspora. After the invincible flood-tide of the newly born Islamic religion the musical usage of olden times was carried into all the conquered lands, along with the instruments, the dances and the singing-girls, so highly valued by the Arabs.

Therefore, it is not surprising, that Jewish social life was greatly influenced by Arabic culture already in the first centuries of Jewish dispersion, wherever Jews came into contact with the Arabs. Moreover, as soon as the Arab conquerors took over the Western settlement of the Jews in Spain, the domination of Arabian music upon the Jews must have become overwhelming. Inasmuch as Arabian and Jewish music were both branches of the same Oriental music culture, there were many affinities between the two. These similarities, though modified and diversified by the ancient tradition of the Jews, a tradition which, in spite of changes of fortune, still glimmered under the ashes, prevented Jewish music from becoming totally subjugated by Arabic domination. However powerful the influence of the Arabian upon the Jewish secular music may have been, the latter was saved by one characteristic aspect of Jewish life: the family.

At all times the family was the cornerstone of Jewish morals, ethics, and social life. The sanctity of the home, the honor due parents, the veneration of the old, the loving care of the children were the basic tenets of Judaism. Even in Spain, this was no different. The more or less voluntary enforcement of living in close groups and in confined quarters prevented the loosening of Jew-

ish family ties and made the individual aware of his personal
and moral behavior. Even if one member broke up the close
bonds of the family by leaving it to become an itinerant *juglar,*
this would not affect the coherence of family life itself. And just
as the family was the guarantee for the future survival of the
Jewish people, so it was due to the family that Jewish secular
music regained its former importance and acquired in Spanish
lands a new meaning.

To understand this, we have to compare the social implications
of Arabian and Jewish musical practice. In Arabian music the
love-song, as performed by favorite singing-girls, was the focus
of musical attraction. In Jewish usage love songs were denounced
as un-Jewish, not merely by severe preachers, but by the elders
of the families. Such songs were looked upon as indecent and
lustful and harmful for family morals. In particular, songs praising
the beauty of a woman were considered undecorous, strictly contrasting with Arabian usage. The same austere principles governed the courtship and the attitude of betrothed people to each
other. Amorous wooing, embracing and flirtations were frowned
upon. In Jewish society such delicate attentions of early love
were not approved of.

In married life, too, there were many restrictions regarding the
behavior between the spouses, all of them regulating the moral
aspect of the family. Despite all such restraint, music flourished
in family life, but it was basically different from the sensual
Arabian model. The music of the Jewish family was mostly of a
religious, or semireligious, character. It centered in the *zemirot,*
table songs which were sung during and after the Friday evening
meal by the entire family. (About *zemirot* more will be said in
a subsequent chapter.)

But the wedding was the occasion in public life where music
and singing were most abundantly performed. As in ancient times,
likewise in the Diaspora, the wedding took place with rich musical display. Special chants were usually offered in the synagogue
to salute the bridegroom when he entered the sanctuary. The
bride was honored by appropriate songs, praising her beauty and
charm. Dances were offered in her homage. Dancing was permitted at weddings and other joyous occasions, but only woman

with woman, or man with man. The participants in the bridal cortège from the synagogue to the bride's home sang religious hymns, as well as popular songs which at those days were current in the streets. The aim of all this musical display was to enhance the joy of the festivity.

The influence which Arabian social life exerted upon the Jews was considerably increased by a branch of Arabian music practice in which the Jews participated in an ever-increasing number: the profession of the *juglares*. It entailed widespread repercussions not only for the social and economic status of the Jewish musician, but also for the family life itself. It was a Jewish tradition of long standing that the son followed his father's profession, unless he devoted himself exclusively to scholarship, in which case he in all probability ended in the rabbinical fold. Now it happened in Spain, and in increasing numbers, that the son did not follow in his father's footsteps, but chose a profession entirely outside the Jewish domain, a profession which he considered his vocation. In liberating himself from the bonds of traditional family life, a decisive transformation had taken place in the mentality of the Jew in general, and in that of the Jewish artist in particular. Up to now, the Jew's life, and also his profession, had been restricted by laws, rules, edicts, regulations of all kinds, issued by secular authorities, kings, princes, clergy, nobility, civic officials; his life's way was predetermined for him almost from the cradle to the grave; he was bound to spend his whole life in the same local (unless one of the frequent expulsions occurred); he could embrace only a minute number of professions, not knowing when a benevolent prince would rob him even of this slim chance; he was milked by royal, clerical and civic authorities; he had to pay, whether he was able to do so or not, for all the whims of the rulers, their wars, their amusements, their luxuries. Now there was a God-sent opportunity to free himself from all the shackles of a precarious existence, live free and unhampered, go into the wide world, bring joy to the masses, earn recognition as an artist, be his own master after centuries of an enforced existence which was suspiciously close to serfdom. It was indeed an unprecedented development not only in the profession of the Jewish musician, but even more so in Jewish family life.

Curiously enough, contemporary Jewish records are silent about this new profession in Jewish existence. There is documentary evidence of almost all civilian trades and occupations. In Avila, for instance, there were fifty families whose occupations were mainly those of small shopkeepers and artisans, among them blacksmiths and dyers. Among the fifty-five Jewish families in Segovia twenty-three were weavers, shoemakers, tailors, furriers, blacksmiths, saddlers, potters, and even one toreador. In Talavera there were three silversmiths, two shopkeepers, a few physicians and farmers, the rest were artisans like in other communities. In Saragossa the Jewish *draperos* (cloth merchants) enjoyed high social standing, second only to that of the courtiers. In Avila the Jews also had land under cultivation and owned small herds of sheep and cattle. Many of the merchants and artisans, in addition to their business or handicraft, devoted part of their time to the cultivation, by their own labor, of a field or vineyard they owned in the environs of the city, and from whose produce they drew their livelihood.[9] Nowhere is the Jewish musical profession mentioned, let alone that of a *juglar*. It seems that the itinerant musician was not eligible to be counted among the burghers of a Jewish community.

Nevertheless, not only historically, but from a sociological point of view, the Jewish *juglar* is an important steppingstone in Jewish cultural life. It was in Spain that, after many centuries of interruption, the Jewish free-lance artist was reborn. We know that this category of secular musicians already flourished in Ancient Israel. Their art had its roots in the people and served the people. Neither birth, nor the fact of belonging to a class, or a guild were decisive requirements in Biblical times for becoming a musician, but rather the aptitude and talent. Secular music became in Ancient Israel a free-lance profession, for the first time in the history of human civilization. After many centuries of stagnation, this historical, artistical and sociological phenomenon repeated itself in Spain. It was brought about by the Jewish *juglar*. His enthusiasm for music was his inspiration, his talent was the measure of his success, the public acclaim his reward. However much the Jews might have been despised in general, the Jewish *juglar*, as an entertainer of the masses, was usually exempt from the contempt that fell upon his people. This might have been the most potent reason why many Jewish musicians embraced this profession, in which they felt free, could wander around unmolested, earn their living by an artistic activity which afforded the self-respect and inner satisfaction they could not have gained in any other profession in those days. Even where a Jewish *juglar* was in the service of a court or a nobleman, he was still a freelance artist, who enjoyed the advantages of the profession, and at the same time, accepted all the risks and occasional hardships which this kind of life entailed.

Thus we witness in medieval Christian Spain a unique phenomenon: the Jewish musician asserting himself in a generally hostile environment, looked after and being successful despite severe odds and hard competition, and constituting a driving force in Jewish musical culture. This force was sustained and shaped the popular music of the Jews in future centuries.

Jewish Writers on Music Between the Twelfth and Fourteenth Centuries

During all these centuries the Jewry of the other Western settlements confined itself mainly to theological studies, following the strict orthodoxy of rabbinical thought. According to this school of Jewish learning, music was embodied in the notion of synagogal chant, excluding other aspects of tonal art, particularly instrumental and folk music. By this rigid approach the development of Jewish music in Central European countries was considerably delayed, while in the Arab sphere it kept in step with the expanding musical culture of the Moslem world.

In the early centuries of Islamic learning, music—theoretical as well as practical—had been investigated by numerous Arabic writers. They continued the science of music where the Greeks left off. Arab translators revived the works of Aristotle, Aristoxenos, Euclid, Nikomachos, and Ptolemy and based their own musical theories on these fertile sources.

Greek learning, however, was not the only means open to Arabic writers for establishing their musical theories. Curiously enough, they borrowed certain elements from the Old Testament.

The Arabian authority on music, for instance, 'AL-MAS'UDI (d. 956) adopted the Biblical legend about the origin of music and of musical instruments. Not content, however, with the Biblical story, he amplified and garnished it in a manner that makes his narrative fantastic and amusing at the same time. This is what he states about the birth of music in his most important work, *Book of the Golden Prairies and of the Mines of Precious Stones:*

> Tubal, son of Lamech, invented the drums and the tabrets; Dilal [Zillah], daughter of Lamech [invented] the *māzaf* (harp); the kinsfolk of Lot the *tonbour* (mandoline), with which to charm the young boys. Shepherd peoples, such as the Kurds, devised a kind of wind instrument which they blew to reassemble their dispersed flocks. Later the Persians built the flute, which corresponds to the lute [*sic!*]; the *dou-neï* (double-flute), which corresponds to the mandolin; the *sournaï* (oboe) which corresponds to the drum; and the *djenk* [corresponding] to the *sandj* (sambuca, harp). They accompanied their songs with the lute and the *djenk*, instruments which were familiar among them; they devised the modulations, the rhythms and the divisions, and the *royal modes*. There are seven such modes.[10]

In this narrative 'AL-MAS'UDI mingles legend with reality, fantasy with facts. Nevertheless, his book contains much valuable information about early Arabian music which shows that its author's fame in the history of Arabian music was well merited.

'AL-MAS'UDI and quite a number of other Arab savants, such as IBN 'ABD RABBIHI (d. 940), 'AL-KINDI (d.c. 874), and HUNAIN IBN ISHAK (809-873), to mention only a few, were instrumental in creating the Arabian musical science.

It is common knowledge that the Jews participated actively in all branches of Arabic learning, guided by and mostly imitating the accomplishments of Arabic scholars. No wonder, therefore, that the Arabic preoccupation with musical theory stimulated Jewish writers and philosophers to enter also this new field of human knowledge as well. We saw that SA'ADIAH GAON (892-942) paved the way for this segment of Jewish learning (*supra* p. 53). A number of other Judaeo-Arabic writers, inspired by SA'ADIAH's example, treated music in their philosophical writings as belonging to the four "sciences" in the Middle Ages: Arithmetic, Geometry, Astronomy, and Music. Among them, such early writers should be mentioned as YIZHAK ibn SULAIMAN (ISAAC ISRAELI), a prominent Jewish philosopher (c. 842-932), who considered music as one of the most important subjects to be studied by Jewish scholars; then the Karaite NISSIM ben NOAH (ninth century), DAVID 'ALMOKAMMEZ (tenth century), and BAHYA ibn PAKUDA (eleventh century). Their occasional excursions into musical science should not be considered as significant contributions to this field of knowledge and therefore this does not qualify them as Jewish scholars for the development of musical theory.

There was, however, in these early times, a Jewish savant in Moorish Spain who was famous as a mathematician and astronomer and who, in addition, was learned in the science of music. He was 'ABU'L-FADL ibn YUSUF ibn HASDAY, the scion of an old Jewish family of Saragossa in Andalusia. The dates of his birth and death are unknown; the only indication about his life is that in 1066 he was a young man.[11]

Whether a fragment in Arabic, but in Hebrew letters, from a musical treatise by IBN 'AL-'AKFANI has a Jewish author or is merely a copy by a Jew of the Arabic original, cannot be ascertained. There are also among the Hebrew manuscripts of the Berlin Library (Ms. Or. Oct. 350) some which are still unidentified. These do not contribute much to Jewish musical science and mentioned only for the sake of completeness.

Inasmuch as Jewish musical creativity entered the field of practical music as well, we have a number of facts to substantiate this point. We know of a wandering minstrel, ABRAHAM ben HALFON (fl. c. 1000), who can legitimately be considered a forerunner of the later flourishing art of the French jongleurs and the Spanish juglares. He is the first of Jewish itinerant musicians whose name was preserved. In Cordova, there originated a school particularly among the pupils of MENAHEM ben SARUK, which attempted to introduce metrical forms into Jewish poetry in order to make it more readily adaptable for musical settings. The chief adherent of this new art form was SHMUEL ibn NAGRELA, called HANAGID of Granada (fl. 1020-1055). The poet-musicians of this epoch, together with another known representative of this art,

JOSEPH the SCRIBE (fl. 1042), might constitute the transition for the upcoming great writers of *piyyutim*, among them SOLOMON ibn GABIROL (c. 1020-1058), MOSES ibn ESRA (c. 1070-1139), who was the author of an important treatise about poetry, his brother ABRAHAM ibn ESRA (c. 1086-1167), and the most outstanding among them, YEHUDAH HALEVI (c. 1066-1145).

MOSES ibm ESRA left to posterity a critical essay on metrical Hebrew poetry, after having scrutinized about sixty Hebrew-Andalusian poets, the output of whom span a period of two centuries. The fact that so many Jewish poets flourished prior to MOSES ibn ESRA, is conclusive evidence of the Jewish participation in the art of poetry.

Other famous poet-singers of this epoch were MESHULLAM ben KALONYMOS of Mainz (nine-tenth cent.), the renowned *hazzan* of Worms. MEÏR ben YIẒHAK (end of the eleventh century), YOM-TOB of YORK (d. 1189), and the illustrious Rabbi MEÏR of ROTHEN-BURG (c. 1220-1293). (Concerning his tragic fate see note 22 of chapter 2.)

Jewish writings on music during this period were mirrored upon the then developed Arabian science of music. Even MAI-MONIDES, who made a slight excursion into music theory, in a treatise about mathematics, based his views upon an essay in the Arabic encyclopedia of ʾABUʾL-ZALTH UMAYA (Sevilla, 1068-1124) which, in turn, is based upon ʾAL-FARABIʾs earlier theories on music. Because this treatise was preserved solely in a Hebrew manuscript, we have reason to believe that its author was a Jew.

Furthermore, there is, in the Bibliothèque Nationale of Paris, a Hebrew manuscript by YEHUDAH ben ISAAC (first half of the twelfth cent.). The original of this treatise was written in Latin—there is no other known version but this Hebrew manuscript. (Incidentally, its author should not be identified with YEHUDA JONA ben ISAAC, whose role in the creation of GIULIO BARTOLOCCIʾs *Bibliotheca Magna Rabbinica* (publ. in Rome, 1675-1693) will be shown later. (See p. 208, note 10). YEHUDAʾs treatise deals mainly with the acoustical measurements of instruments and other theoretical matters.

Among the representatives of the approaching *Ars Nova*, LEVI ben GERSHOM of Avignon (1288-1344) must be mentioned, whose collaboration with PHILIP de VITRY, the learned bishop of Meaux (1290-1361) will be discussed presently (See p. 127).

The first Jewish scholar who not only continued the uncertain path taken by these early writers, but gave a comprehensive delineation of the musical science of his time, was a disciple of MAIMONIDES, YUSSUF (JOSEPH) ibn ʾAKNIN. Neither his essay, however, nor those of the other authors named below may be considered to be well organized treatises on musical art or science. The musical items which are scattered among general philosophical or ethical topics, do not represent dissertations on music in the strict sense of the word. Nevertheless they are valuable contributions to the history of Jewish philosophy between the twelfth and fourteenth centuries, and as such they deserve to be dealt with succinctly in a survey of the intellectual accomplishments of the Jews in this period.[12]

JOSEPH ben YUDAII IBN ʾAKNIN (c. 1160-1226), in his essay "Tabb-al-nufus" (Recreation of the Soul) correctly states that the practice of music should precede the theory. Thus, theoretical speculation cannot be well-grounded without former practical knowledge, a postulate which is still valid today.

YEHUDA HALEVI's works also contain some occasional remarks about music. But they are based mainly on the writings of the Arabic scholars ʾAL-FARABI (d. 950) and IBN SINA (AVICENNA) (d. 1037), whose works are considered only of a minor importance for Jewish musical science.

YEHUDA ben SOLOMON AL-ḤARIZI, a contemporary of IBN ʾAKNIN, developed a short curriculum, in which music occupies a modest part.

The same rather limited importance of music in general learning is apparent in YEHUDA ben SAMUEL ben ʾABBAS' book Yaʾir Natib (Illumination of the Path).

More emphasis on music, as science as well as practical art, is expressed in SHEM-TOB ben YOSEF ibn FALAḴERA's (1225-1295) book Reshit Ḥokma (Introduction to Science) written in his youth (about 1250). The second part of it, dealing with the Number of Sciences is almost a literal translation of an essay of the Arabic scholar ʾAL-FARABI (d. 950). In the didactic novel, Ha-Mebaḳḳesh (The Seeker), written in his more mature age

(1264), FALAKERA goes somewhat deeper into music, but he still subordinates it to that of Biblical and rabbinical studies and the worldly science of mathematics.

The cabalistic writer ABRAHAM bar YIZHAK of Granada (fourteenth century) classified the sciences of his time methodically. He based his system upon a Talmudic passage,[13] in which the six orders of the *Mishnah* were defined. As to the framework of his classification, he refers to the verse in Isaiah 33:6: "And the stability of thy times shall be a strength of salvation—wisdom and knowledge and the fear of the Lord is his treasure." Following the trend of cabalistic thinking, ABRAHAM interprets this verse in an esoteric sense: stability stands for Arithmetic; strength for Geometry; wisdom for Ethics; knowledge for Astronomy; the fear of the Lord for Metaphysics; and salvation for Music. For this latter interpretation he uses the Biblical verse of 2 Kings 3:15, in which the affinity between prophecy and music becomes evident: "But now bring me a minstrel," asks Elisha. "And it came to pass, when the minstrel played, that the hand of the Lord came upon him."

In his large essay, ABRAHAM divides the science of music theory into five lengthy sections. The first deals with the elements required for musical science. The second treats the methods to be used for composing melodies and the different categories of them. The third has as its subject the musical instruments. The fourth analyzes the melodic and rhythmic patterns of music. In the fifth section he discusses the ways and means of writing beautiful melodies. In addition, and in support of his theories, he quotes a great number of Biblical verses and Talmudic passages.

All in all, this is a remarkable attempt at establishing a comprehensive syllabus of the musical science of his days.

ISAAC ben ABRAHAM ibn LATIF (c. 1220-1290), a philosopher and cabalist, in the fifteenth chapter of his *Ginze ha-Melek* (The King's Treasurehouse), establishes the relationship between music and the esoteric principle of the "Harmony of Spheres," the theory of the cosmic harmony. It consists in the movements of the seven planets and the all-comprehending eighth sphere, which corresponds to the eighth modes in music. He concludes therefore that there is a profound analogy between the science of astronomy and music.

Incidentally, PHILO, among the early Jewish philosophers, had been an adherent to the same idea. According to him, the heavens are the prototype of all musical instruments; he compares the seven strings of the lyre with the seven planets. MAIMONIDES, on the contrary, rejected entirely the theory of cosmic harmony.

In Spanish intellectual life, an important role was assumed by the ABULAFIA family, a dynasty of healers, philosophers, musicians, and cabalists. (Incidentally, ABULAFIA in Arabic means "father of health"). Some of its most famous members were ABULAFIA MEÏR ben TODROS HALEVI (b. Burgos 1170, d. Toledo 1244), who was a great Talmudic scholar (*RaMaH*), ABULAFIA TODROS ben JOSEPH (b. Burgos 1224, d. Toledo 1283), a noted Talmudist and cabalist, a.o.

Among the members of the family who distinguished themselves also in the field of music, MOSES ABULAFIA (or 'ABU 'AMRUM MUSA ben JOSEPH) a physician and musician deserves a special mention (d. 1283). He wrote a treatise on music, *Hokmat ha-Musikah*, in which he deals, however, exclusively with the mathematical aspect of music.[14]

A close interplay between cabalistic thought and music is exposed in the writings of another member of the distinguished ABULAFIA family, who acquired fame not only among his contemporaries, but as long as the Cabala was the guiding force of Jewish mysticism. This was ABRAHAM ben SAMUEL ABULAFIA, about whose life and literary activity we are informed almost exclusively by his own writings. He was born in Saragossa in 1240 and died in Barcelona c. 1292. His youth was spent in Tudela, in the province of Navarre. His father was his main teacher, who taught him the Bible and its commentaries, as well as the *Mishnah* and Talmud. This was the normal curriculum for every youngster belonging to a distinguished Jewish family in those times. But ABRAHAM especially mentions among his teachers the precentor of his town, BARUCH TOGARMI, who initiated him into the true meaning of the *Sefer Yezirah* (The Book of the Creation), the oldest cabalistic work, extant in a longer and shorter version. That BARUCH might have given his pupil an insight not merely into the Cabala, but also into the domain of musical science and practice is evident from some pertinent statements in his writings about music as an art.

ABULAFIA's speculations led him to the creation of a peculiar discipline which he calls *Hokmath ha-Zeruf, i.e. Science of the Combination of Letters.* He describes it as a methodical guide to meditation with the aid of the Hebrew letters and their configurations.

As he explains it, the purpose of this discipline is to stimulate, with the aid of meditation, a new state of consciousness; he defines this state as an harmonious movement of pure thought, and compares it with music. The systematic practice of meditation as taught by him, produces a sensation closely akin to that of listening to musical harmonies. The science of combination, as he conceives it, is a music of pure thought, in which the alphabet takes the place of the musical scale. The whole system, as he expounds it, shows a fairly close resemblance to musical principles, applied by him not to sounds but to thought in meditation.

In one of his unpublished writings he establishes an even closer interrelation between the science of combinations of letters and musical phenomena. He says:

> Know that the method of *Zeruf* can be compared to music; for the ear hears sounds from various combinations; in accordance with the character of the melody and instrument. Also, two different instruments can form a combination, and if the sounds combine, the listener's ear registers a pleasant sensation in acknowledging their difference. The strings touched by the right or left hand move, and the sound is sweet to the ear. And from the ear the sensation travels to the heart, and from the heart to the spleen (the center of emotion), and enjoyment of the different melodies produces ever new delight. It is impossible to produce it except through the combination of sounds, and the same is true of the combination of letters.[15]

As ABULAFIA sees it, the musician's inspiration is akin to the ecstasy of the mystics. Just as the musician expresses in wordless sounds "the world once again," and ascends to endless heights and descends to endless depths, so the mystic. To him, the closed doors of the soul open in the music of pure thought and in the ecstasy of the deepest harmonies which originate in the movement of the letters of the great Name, they throw open the way to God.[16] This is quite a remarkable combination, in medieval times, of the esthetics of music as pure sound and mysticism as pure philosophical concept.

ISAIAH ben ISAAC ben NATHAN, a physician of the fourteenth century, wrote a commentary on AVICENNA's "*)Al-kanun*," in which he states that "the task of music is the composition of *laḥanim*. The elements of which the *laḥanim* consists are twofold: the individual tones, and the structure or shape [of the melody]. The first one is the matter, the second is the form of the complete tune," a view about the creative procedure of a composer which, incidentally, remained valid throughout the ages.

While all these efforts of Jewish writers did not further the theory of music in a substantial way, it was a Jewish scholar who made a breakthrough in this respect. LEVI ben GERSHOM in Avignon, (GERSONIDES, RALBAG, or LEO HEBRAEUS, as he was called) (1288-1344) was the author of a treatise written in Latin, *De Numeris Harmonicis* (1343), which advanced musical science considerably. He wrote it at the request of PHILIP de VITRY (1290-1361), bishop of Meaux, an outstanding theoretician and composer of the time, who initiated the *ars nova* movement in France. With all its importance for establishing the foundation of VITRY's system of rhythmic division and notation, GERSONIDES' treatise cannot be considered as having furthered *Jewish* musical theory in particular. But its significance lies in the fact that a renowned Christian theorist and composer had to enlist the aid and cooperation of a Jewish scholar in order to formulate and develop his bold and advanced theories.

In addition, another medieval Jewish music theorist should be mentioned—the Italian-born SERAḤYA ben ISAAC, who wrote about musical science. However, as he did not belong to the Judaeo-Spanish environment, he is mentioned here primarily as an additional exponent of Jewish musical science.

From the above brief synopsis of Jewish writings on music in the course of two centuries (twelfth-fourteenth), it becomes evident that, as in other fields of philosophy and the sciences, Jews were active in the domain of music theory as well. Even though they did not advance this discipline to a pronounced degree, their efforts constitute an important link to the musical science of later times. As to their creative accomplishments in this field, there are unfortunately very few existing documents containing musical examples of that period. While this grave lacuna constitutes a serious handicap in our appreciation of their musical creativity, we have ample evidence bearing out those Jewish accomplishments in other areas of human knowledge.

אינדיג׳אס די תשעה באב

מדינה פֿרינה וננקחם לחטן

וננו איסטה איל טוֹאין רייֹ וננו איסטנה קי נו קאֿ-
מאֿלֿת קייטי דוקֿטוריס לו רייֹין דוקֿטוריס די גֿלֿאֿדֿי
פֿאֿמֿה . קייטי וכו׳

אֿאֿינֿדֿה וננֿקֿה פֿור צ׳יֿיר איל דוקֿטוֹל די וננֿם
וננֿגֿה פֿאֿוֿוֿת . אֿאֿינֿדֿה וכו׳

קייטי וננֿלֿאֿם לי קאֿגֿאֿבֿֿייֿוֿם פֿול איל קֿאֿוֿנֿיֿוֿ די
שֿאֿלֿאֿם . קייטי וכו׳

קֿאֿוֿנֿיֿוֿ די קיֿמֿי דיֿאֿם דיֿאֿם חין קייטי לֿוֿם אֿיֿיֿגֿאֿלֿֿת .
קֿאֿוֿנֿיֿוֿ וכו׳

 אֿה אֿיֿנֿטֿרֿאֿדֿה דילֿה פֿוֿחֿיֿרֿעֿת נֿה וֿוֿנֿה קי אֿריֿ-
צֿיֿנֿטֿאֿלֿֿת נֿה אֿיֿנֿטֿרֿלֿאֿדֿה

נֿה וֿוֿנֿה נֿה וננֿם אֿיֿוֿנֿוֿחֿה נֿה קי איל ריי אֿיֿגֿבֿֿי-
כֿיֿאֿלֿֿת נֿה וֿוֿנֿה

לֿייֿם צֿיֿנֿו איל דוקֿטוֹל די גֿלֿאֿבֿֿדֿי פֿאֿוֿוֿת .
לֿייֿם צֿינו

אֿיֿ קֿיֿנֿטֿוֿקֿי אֿם נֿה לֿה קֿאֿבֿֿיֿסֿיֿרֿה איל פֿוֿלֿכֿו נֿי אֿטֿיֿנֿֿ-
טֿאֿלֿֿת אֿקֿיֿנֿֿטֿוֿסֿי

קי דיֿזֿם איל טֿוֿאֿין דוקֿטוֹל איסֿטֿי וֿוֿאֿל קֿי איל
דייֿו לֿי דֿאֿלֿֿת קֿי דיֿזֿם

וֿוֿל וֿוֿי פֿֿלֿיֿסֿי איל טֿוֿאֿין רייֿ פֿֿאֿלֿֿה איל דייֿו נֿו
איס נֿאֿלֿֿת . וֿוֿאֿל

Galician-Portuguese juglar *playing the* vihuela *with a bow. Singer with* pandero. *(Canc. de Ajuda).*

Large vihuelas *played with bows. Tenth century. (Beato de Liébana).*

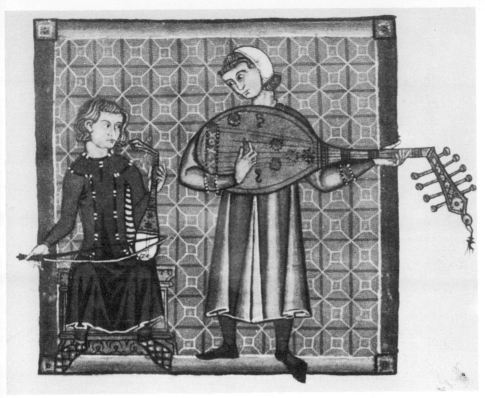

Juglares *with* rabel *and lute. (Cant. de Santa María).*

Castilian juglar *singing, accompanied by a Moorish* juglar. *(Cant. de Santa María).*

Galician-Portuguese troubadour with a juglar *playing the harp. (Canc. de Ajuda).*

Juglares *playing the* canon. *(Cant. de Santa María).*

Juglares *playing the* cedra *and* citola. *(Cant. de Santa María)*.

Dance of the soldadera, *accompanied by a psaltery. (Canc. de Ajuda).*

Juglares *of the thirteenth century, playing the* sinfonía; *one of them a* cleric. (Cant. de Santa María).

Alfonso X *exhorts his singers and musicians to honor the Virgin with songs, accompanied by dances. (Cant. de Santa María).*

Disputation between Jews and Christians. From Seelenwurzgarten
(Ulm, 1483).

The first printed pictures of Jews. (After Lee M. Friedman). In: HUCA, vol. XXIII, part 2 (1950–51), pp. 433–448.

7

The Jews in Central Europe—Ashkenazim

THE NAME *Ashkenaz* APPEARS FIRST IN GENESIS 10:3, AS A GREAT-grandson of Noah; in Jeremiah 51:27, it is the name of a kingdom in western Asia; among early rabbinical writers it was the name for Germany, later *Ashkenazim* became a synonym for the Jews of Germany and France, afterwards it also included those of Poland, Russia, Austria-Hungary, and Bohemia.

History reports Jewish colonies along the Rhine already in times of the Roman Empire. Many of these colonies had Latin names, like Magentia (Mainz), Colonia Agrippina (Cologne), Augusta Trevirorum (Trier), etc. In all these, and in other places in the western part of Germany, there were sizable Jewish contingencies. It was natural, therefore, that these early settlements had a magnetic attraction for Jewish emigrants from the east. At the time of CHARLEMAGNE (742-814) there already existed several fair-sized Jewish communities in the Germanic parts of the empire.

While maintaining discriminatory laws against them, the emperor protected the Jews as useful and enterprising craftsmen, merchants, doctors and financiers, and even employed a Jew as his personal physician. Under his protection Jews prospered everywhere in his realm. At those times they were the actual agents of international trade; "almost all international commerce was in their hands."[1] They maintained cargo ships that sailed from Germanic ports to all important trade centers of England, France, and Italy, as well as the Mediterranean, and to far reaching ports of the Orient.

Their commercial expansion went hand in hand with their intellectual and spiritual development. CHARLEMAGNE was intent on furthering the spiritual welfare of his prosperous and well-paying Jewish communities. In the eighth century he invited the famous Italian rabbi Moses ben Kalonymos and his son Meshullam from Lucca to settle in Mainz. He encouraged a Jewish sage from Bagdad, R. Machir, to come to France for the purpose of teaching in the city of Narbonne, southern France.[2] From that time on Jewish learning, based on the Babylonian tradition, was transplanted to Germany and France. Another scholar who migrated from France to Germany was R. Simon bar ʾAbban (eleventh century).

R. Machir's case was not unique. Other understanding rulers, following Charlemagne's example, invited learned rabbis from the Orient to Germany and France during the tenth and eleventh centuries. Even Jewish communities sought out such rabbinical sages to establish educational institutions in their cities. These rabbis brought with them their Oriental ritual; thus, prior to 1000 C.E. there was almost no difference between the Jewish rituals of the French and German communities.[3]

At that epoch, the Church looked favorably on the commercial activity of the Jews, since it contributed greatly to the development of urban life of the early medieval towns. The wealth of the Jewish merchants "trickled down" to the rest of the population, a factor in which the clergy took an increasing interest. This was the time of the planning and building of the great cathedrals of Christendom in the West. Where would they take the necessary money if not from the burghers of the cities; their welfare was considerably augmented by Jewish commerce; hence the interest of the Church was maintained by the thriving Jewish population.

During the period of the Crusades these erstwhile favorable living conditions of the Jews underwent a tragic change. Nowhere else had the Jews suffered more hardships, persecutions and atrocities, which were first condoned, then encouraged, and finally instigated by the Church. Up to this time, the Church had shown a certain understanding and toleration of the Jews, if for no other reason than their being the most useful source for filling their coffers.

Prior to the Crusades the living conditions of the Jews in Germany and France were satisfactory from the material point of view. This induced them to strengthen their spiritual life. In addition to their own renowned religious leaders, many of whom acquired fame, they also invited outstanding scholars from Italy and elsewhere, in order to elevate their Jewish communities into recognized centers of learning. As mentioned above, R. Moses ben Kalonymos settled with his family in Mainz, and gradually made this city an abode of Jewish scholarship celebrated far beyond the limits of Germany.

Their material welfare secured, at least temporarily, and with the decline and, later, the expulsion of the Sephardim from Spain, the Ashkenazim rose to a dominant position in European Jewry. Moreover, with their migration to the East and their settlement in Poland, Russia, Bessarabia and other Slavonic countries, the Ashkenazic Jews became the overwhelming majority of the Jews not only in Europe, but in all other countries where Jews existed in compact groups.

In the European Middle Ages Latin was the language of the Church, as well as the international language of scholarship and science. In Germanic lands, the populace spoke the Middle-High German; based upon which the Jewish settlers developed their own tongue, a specific type of German dialect with numerous inclusions of Hebrew words and phrases. As time passed by, this dialect became known as a particular Judaeo-German idiom, the "Yiddish," and was adopted as the lingua franca by the Jews in all Eastern European countries. In France, the Jews adopted the vernacular. Rashi, for instance, who lived at Troyes in France, tried to explain to his Franch compatriots some Biblical and Talmudic musical instruments and has employed the French terms of his time for their equivalents. Thus, we find in his commentaries French words (written in Hebrew letters, of course) such as *kalameyles* ("chalumeau," for *ḥalil*), *ṭanbura* (for *tof*), *zimbanu* (for *zelzelim*), *vadil* (for *magrephah*), *ʾeskaliṭa* (for little bells), *ʾeskada* (for clappers), etc.

The education of the average German in those days was on a rather low level. It is significant, therefore, that burghers and members of the clergy frequently visited the local rabbi for the purpose of "picking up some crumbs of learning," and that many of them came to the synagogue just to listen for hours to the liturgical singing.

The higher ecclesiastics considered this situation dangerous to the souls of the faithful, and consequently found it necessary to prohibit such "unchristian peregrinations."[4] Such a step is understandable from their point of view, since it is known that Gentiles attended synagogue services en masse, because such opportunities to hear good music were then very rare indeed.

In the early centuries of the Middle Ages the music of the Germanic people must have been rather unartistic, according to contemporary records and statements, for instance those of Emperor JULIAN (332-363), JOHANNES DIACONUS (seventh century), and others. Even as late as the sixteenth century, "the German people were very little educated in singing."[5] LUTHER, in his oration of praise on music, describes the Germans' singing of his chorales as a "chaotic, wild screaming of asses."[6] It can therefore be assumed that it was the Jews who succeeded in teaching the Germans a more artistic manner of singing, at least in the beginning of their coexistence. The creation of ecclesiastical singing schools altered this situation. In the churches, the singing, performed by trained clerics, became gradually more attractive, while the singing of the Jews remained Oriental in its character, and did not show much improvement. Thus, the singing of the Christians soon surpassed that of the Jews in style and elaboration, that is harmony and polyphony. As a matter of fact, the very hostility of the Church against the intercourse between Christians and Jews may have contributed to putting an end to the temporary supremacy of Jewish singing over that of the Germans. Now the reverse had come about: Jewish singing was influenced by ecclesiastical practices and had to take a back seat during the European Middle Ages, at least until the Renaissance in Italy, where Jewish singing and Jewish singers came to the forefront.

Nevertheless, it is generally known that Christian clerics in medieval times studied assiduously the Hebrew language and literature, and were instructed by the Jews in the ethics of the Jewish religion and also in singing. This practice seems to have reached such proportions that the Archbishop ODO of Cologne had to issue in 1197 a prohibition against it. Regardless of this prohibition, the "literary Judaizing" of Christian laymen and clerics continued, whereupon the clerical authorities interfered repeatedly with decrees against such "sacrileges." When the famous German grammarian, JOHANNES REUCHLIN (1455-1521), introduced "officially" the Hebrew language as a legitimate subject of scholarly studies (see later), some German theologians were eager to devote themselves to this study, which led the monks of Cologne to preach publicly against it.[7]

Just as Christians tried to make use of Jewish learning and musical practice, there were also increasing tendencies among the Jews themselves to introduce Church hymns and tunes into the synagogue service. It will be shown later in our study how the *hazzanim* had been the chief promoters of such procedures. There are also records concerning Jews who studied the Christian liturgical books, especially the Christian hymnals. JOSEPH HAHN, a rabbi and *hazzan* at Frankfurt a.M. in the seventeenth century, complained about the practice of Jewish families who used in their homes on Sabbath eve as *zemirot,* certain Christian tunes. They attempted to justify this procedure on the ground that these Church tunes were "borrowed," i.e., "stolen," from the Temple of Jerusalem. This idea was drastically expressed by the famous Jewish poet IMMANUEL of ROME who, quoting the Biblical verse (Gen. 40:15), applied it to music in saying: "What does the art music say to the Christians? 'Indeed, stolen was I out of the land of the Hebrews.'"

Even pious rabbis yielded sometimes to the seduction of Christian chant. It is reported for instance, that R. SIMEON the GREAT (eleventh century) heard a melody in his dream, the tune of "Magdala," which he retained as a hymn for himself, because it was supposed to be similar to the songs of the angels.[8] No wonder, therefore, that from the Jewish side a vigorous protest arose against Christian and other extraneous musical influences. This procedure at times became quite bizarre. Jews were forbidden to teach a priest or a Christian layman a song of the synagogue.[9] It was even strictly prohibited for a Christian nurse to sing a Church song as a lullaby to a Jewish child.[10]

However, this mutual distrust and all the prohibitive actions of the clergy did not deter the Christian laymen, and even dukes with their courts, as late as the fifteenth century, to attend services in synagogues; the music presented there was too much an attraction for Gentiles during a period which lacked of readily accessible musical performances. During all these centuries Christians and Jews who were not blinded by religious fanaticism exercised quite normal relations with each other, in spite of the restrictions imposed by both sides. All this was due to the excellence of both the music of the Synagogue and that of the Church.

Despite all the rabbinical opposition, it was inevitable that foreign elements crept into synagogue music—Spanish and Arabic motives into that of the Sephardim, and bits of German folksongs into that of the Ashkenazim. The German folk song, in particular, with its strong emphasis on rhythmical patterns and expressive melodies, had a powerful impact upon the formation of the synagogue songs of German congregations. In fact the most beautiful synagogue melodies owe their origin to this musical exchange in Germanic countries, especially in the Rhineland. Some of these tunes acquired the halo of "sacred melodies." Later generations of Jews, not knowing that they were partly German folksongs grafted upon Jewish melodies, called them *Missinai* melodies, *i.e.*, "received on Mt. Sinai," thus attributing to them divine origin. Such songs were numerous in the ancient settlements of Worms, Mainz, Speyer and other communities of southwest Germany, the places that for several centuries had been the centers of Jewish learning.

In Spain, as we have seen, the activity of the *juglares* left its imprint upon the Sephardic sacred song, while in France and Germany the art of the troubadours and minnesingers influenced the creative efforts of the Ashkenazim who were eager to adapt their synagogue songs to the enticing music of the environment. It is not surprising, therefore, that most of the *ḥazzanim* in the period from the tenth to the fourteenth centuries, including those rabbis who also functioned as *ḥazzanim,* wrote liturgical texts and also "composed" melodies for them, as well as any layman could do. About this musical practice more will be said in one of the following chapters.

By such blending of the elements of the Oriental-Semitic Jewish song with German folk tunes, a new type of song was created which, over the centuries, became the genuine expression of the German Jew. "Here for the first time since the Hellenistic period two conflicting elements met and were merged and moulded into one."[11]

It is desirable to discuss at this point, a few terminological expressions concerning the tonal basis that has gradually come into use among the Ashkenazim and are fully retained to this day.

Derived from the motive-born Biblical cantillation, the Ashkenazic *hazzanim* still avail themselves of the old terms, already familiar to us, and ordinarily in the plural, such as: *ne'imoth, ta'amim, neginoth* and *tropes* (sing. *ne'ima, ta'am, neginah, trope*). The individual choice of these terms under various circumstances depends largely on the particular purposes (liturgical, historical, theoretical, practical, etc.) for which they are intended. The expression "tropes" seems to have become, during the current century, a sort of popular and almost colloquial term, especially among the East European Ashkenazim, for both the graphic signs and musical configuration of the Scriptural motives.

Outside of Biblical cantillation, the *hazzanim* in Germanic regions apply the term *Steiger* (scale) as a modal designation, together with its innate melodic line, to be used for prayer recitations. In France and other Latin countries the Romance word *Gust* (after the Latin *gustus* = taste) is used for modal indications in chanting the prayers, whereas in Eastern Europe the sacred Hebrew melody (and partly its implied scalar mode), the rendition of which differs so markedly from that of other music, is called *Scarbove*, erroneously believed to be a Slavonic-Yiddish corruption of the Latin *sacra*. In fact, the origin of the term is the Polish *skarb*, "treasure," and *Scarbove* means "from the treasure," *i.e.*, an "authentic" melody.[12]

8

Süsskind of Trimberg—A Jewish Minnesinger

FOLLOWING THE ABOVE GENERAL SURVEY OF THE SOCIAL AND MUSICAL conditions prevalent among the Ashkenazim in the European Diaspora, let us now focus our attention upon an individual occurrence in Germanic lands, which may constitute a parallel to the activity of Jewish musicians and singers in Latin countries. It has been shown how Jewish musical talent and initiative made a breakthrough in France and the Iberian peninsula, creating, in a Christian world, a class of Jewish professionals in music who were, for those times at least, unusual and even anomalous. This was not just an artistic, but also a sociological phenomenon, treated as such earlier in our study.

It would have been surprising had the creative drive of the Jews, so predominant in all walks of life, not prevailed in Germanic countries. Yet prevail it did, for there are reliable historical records describing a German-Jewish minnesinger.

JOSEF KASTEIN, in his book about SÜSSKIND VON TRIMBERG, adds the subtitle *A Tragedy of Homelessness* when summing up the fate of this Jewish minnesinger. This fate, this life was little short of tragic—the existence of a Jewish troubadour in the midst of a Christian world of knighthood, in which the Jew was barely tolerated, but in most instances disdained and persecuted. What could possibly have motivated this Jewish poet and singer, living in a feudal society where balladeering was restricted to the noble knights of yore, to follow his heart's desire and choose a profession for which he was predestined neither by origin nor faith?

About Süsskind's private life little is known—almost all that

136

exists in the historical records is more or less legend. He was born in Trimberg, a hamlet near Schweinfurt, in Bavaria, about 1200. Like his co-professionals of noble lineage, he traveled, lute in hand, from castle to castle, entertaining the gentlemen and ladies of noble birth with poetry and song. He derived his livelihood from handouts. That these were, in most cases, meager, is attested to by his own recorded complaints about the stinginess of the feudal barons, a circumstance which prompted him eventually to give up this profession in total disgust over the lack of appreciation for his art, and to devote his poetry solely to religious subjects and introspection.

From medieval German times a collection of songs has been preserved, the MANASSE CODEX, named after its probable collector RÜDIGER MANASSE of Zurich. (The manuscript is kept in Heidelberg.) This collection contains poems and songs by various poets, and of special importance are the pictures showing many of its poets. The collection contains examples of poets both good and mediocre, singers who were knights and singers who were burghers, writers of talent, and writers lacking talent, minnesingers and moralists.

In the midst of this variegated collection can be found a few songs by a poet who, even if his name were not mentioned, could be recognized as someone apart in type and character by the accompanying illustration.

Here, on an elevated stool, the episcopal staff in hand, sits a clerical dignitary. Another cleric and a novice priest stand by him. The dignitary points, with inviting gesture, at the man standing at the right of the picture, looking toward the three, who appear to be his audience. His eyebrows are straight and horizontal, while those of the others are curved. His long, ermine-lined coat, trimmed with a fur collar, is similar to the one worn by the clerical dignitary. His undergarment is red, the topcoat purple. His hair is long, as is the hair of his audience. Yet he is the only one whose face is bearded, and also the only one to wear a flat saucer-shaped hat with a high steeple-type crown ending in a ball tip. His hands display an expressive gesture. (See Frontispiece.)

All these details individualize him clearly in the framework of his time; long beard, pointed hat, characteristic garb, violent gesture typifying his peculiarity of origin—all in all: a Jew. To top it off, the inscription confirming it: Süsskint, the Jew of Trimperg.

This name Süsskind, unimaginable for a non-Jew, was quite frequent among the Jews of that time. "Sweet child"—this sums up all the exaggerated tenderness which Jews bestowed upon their children at a period when tenderness existed only in the sanctity of the home, not in the outside world.

His domicile: the hamlet Trimberg, on the river Saale, near Würzburg, a town where fate meted out to Jews at the end of the thirteenth century had not yet been forgotten. How can we fix the year with any certainty? From the statement by Süsskind that now he would again put on "the Jewish dress of old." And while mentioning hat, coat and beard, he omits reference to a Jewish insignia. Therefore he speaks of a time when the law of the Lateran Council of 1215 had not yet been put into effect, so this could be no later than the end of the thirteenth century.

He made his living by writing verses, composing melodies thereto, and traveling about to perform at courts and castles. The profession in those times, was an honorable though not always a lucrative one.

Was there no other way open to him to earn a livelihood for himself and his family? A theory exists that he may have been a physician by profession, and certain arguments can be found in favor of this. One stanza of a poem describes a mixture of salves expertly concocted, as only a doctor or druggist could. Another argument: the audiences of the day recognized two categories of Jews with which they were used to deal and to whom they were reasonably well accustomed: the Jewish financier and the Jewish physician. The Jewish healer, whose genius had been established in the early years of Diaspora, could not be displaced in the German world, even though the Church tried strenuously to instill hatred in the people and opposition against the Jew. All this did not prevent even archbishops from keeping a personal Jewish physician. As for Süsskind, whether he had been a doctor or not previously, he did not practice this profession, but devoted himself to a life of a wandering balladeer, and was so devoted to this life that there was for him no way back into any former existence, whatever it may have been. He desired and wanted to be a poet and singer, surely not because of any material advantages, for there were few. What is it that spells the difference between a mediocre trade and an inspired profession? A person's calling, an avocation.

There can be no explanation for SÜSSKIND's choosing this profession except one: an inner force shaping his will, for he wrote poetry and sang songs not because he wanted to, but because he was *compelled* to.

He was no minnesinger, nor had he ever sung of love. The classical minnesong, or courtly love song, was monopolized by the members of knighthood. SÜSSKIND belongs to the category of the poets of proverbs. In this domain, to judge from the twelve poems he left behind, he did creditable and respectable work.

Of the twelve poems, six have been proved authentic, the other six are doubtful, according to the judgment of literary historians. These poems, written in a German known as *"mittelhochdeutsch"* (Middle-High German), show traces of a way of thought differing vastly from that of the noble Christian minnesingers. While these balladeers sang primarily of worldly things, such as tender love, glorification of womanhood, heroism in battle, patriotism, and the like, SÜSSKIND's poems are of a philosophical and introspective nature. They originate from Biblical, even Talmudic trend of thought, and show great familiarity with the contents of the Jewish prayerbook. The phraseology and style of his poetry is so profound that in German literature SÜSSKIND is mentioned on equal terms with the greatest minnesingers of the Middle Ages, such as WALTER von der VOGELWEIDE, HARTMANN von AUE, GOTTFRIED von STRASSBURG, and others of renown.

Just as in France and Spain, so also in Germanic lands an artistically gifted Jew was able to overcome and burst the confining bonds imposed on him by his origin and faith. He could strive, in other words, against all obstacles to succeed in a profession for which, by natural inclinations and social circumstances, he was not fitted.

The illustration of SÜSSKIND depicts him wearing the typical round hat with rounded spire tip, which was required to be worn by Jews during the European medieval period, thus giving unmistakable proof of his being a Jew. This type of hat can be seen in numerous coeval pictures showing Jews (Illustrations Nos. 12, 13, and 14). Furthermore, Süsskind's picture in the MANASSE-CODEX bears, on its upper margin, the title inscription "SÜSSKINT DER JUDE VON TRIMPERG," written in the illustrator's hand.

In spite of these apparently irrefutable facts, Süsskind's Jewish origin has of late been subjected to doubt. Several years ago there appeared, in an American periodical, a long dissertation attempting to disprove that this German balladeer had been a Jew.[13] According to this treatise there never had been a Jewish minnesinger in a Christian medieval Germany, and everything ever written to that effect was pure fantasy. Even his name, it is claimed, was in no way Jewish, for in those times it existed in abundance among Gentiles.

However, neither in old chronicles nor in the anthologies or official documents does this name Süsskind ever appear in reference to Germans. It is typically Jewish as are the pet names which Jewish parents give their children, such as Süss (cf. Süss von OPPENHEIM), GLÜCKEL (von HAMELN), LEBELE (HERZCHEN)—"*Leb*" signifying "heart" in Hebrew—or "*Herz*" in German (cf. the famous rabbi and cantor at Frankfurt a. Main, HERZ TREVES), and others. It is inconceivable that a German Christian family could have named their offspring SÜSSKIND. If nothing else, the pointed hat in itself remains the irrefutable proof of Süsskind's religion. (Illustrations Nos. 12, 13, and 14).

The author of this article, RAPHAEL STRAUSS, lists arguments refuting Süsskind's Jewish origin, but refuses to list those which might tend to prove it. There is a document, for example, kept today in the archives of the City of Würzburg, which contains the registration of a real estate sale dating back to 1216. According to this document, "the Jew SÜSSKINT, of St. Aegidien and Dietrich Hospital, purchased, with permission granted by the Prior OTTO, a piece of land with the condition that the buyer has to build and entertain a subterranean waterduct."[15] The bill of sale further names *testes Judaei* (the witness for the Jew): CALEMAN, LIEBERMAN von GRUNEVELT, BONIFAU, SCONEMAN and ABRAHAM, all evidently Jews. Later on, in the year 1225, a dispute arose over this waterduct, which was mediated and settled by the same

Prior OTTO, and this document again refers to *judaeum* SUẒKINT, SÜSSKINT, the Jew.[15]

RAPHAEL STRAUSS evidently missed the inscription on the illustration, or else saw only a reproduction thereof, which did not include this heading. Actually several historical works have published SÜSSKIND's picture without this significant and explanatory inscription.[16] STRAUSS also completely ignores the fact that the pointed hat was the infallible sign of a Jew. He lists no single proof of his theory, only suppositions, negations, critical sophistries, meaningless phrases. But he does say: "A few rather doubtful books have been written on this rather insignificant poet, containing many allegations on the poet and his time based on nothing other than the author's esthetic feeling—poetry itself with some flavor of learning." He castigates severely KASTEIN's book, which he calls "a curious mixture of learning, fancy and rigmarole." Finally he makes a somewhat contradictory confession: "The poet's Jewish descent, although not proved, cannot be called a mere legend. It is more than that. On the other hand, it is by no means a confirmed historical fact, and therefore it is unacceptable for scholarship. Preferably it should be called a myth handed down from one writer to the other, based on mere tradition."

There has been preserved one religious poem by SÜSSKIND, a prayer of quiet and deep affirmation of faith. It bears a striking resemblance with Biblical poetry, as for example with the 24th Psalm, the prayer recited nightly by pious Jews, and with a prophecy of Isaiah. It cannot be ascertained that this similarity is proof in itself, for Biblical content and knowledge thereof was a requisite for every wandering poet and singer. Nevertheless, this definite resemblance appears to confirm the existing assumption concerning SÜSSKIND's origin.

In his old age SÜSSKIND began to hold the mirror up to a world differing so vastly from that of his own provenance through poems exalting what he considered to be true nobility and genuine morals. It is quite conceivable, even probable, that his criticism practiced in the world about him, made him even less popular, and that he no longer may have been received with honors and open arms. As his audience dwindled, he was no longer invited to entertain them. People were fed up with him, and doors remained shut to his face. And so Süsskind von Trimberg intoned his swan song.

> Why should I wander sadly,
>   My harp within my hand,
> O'er mountain, hill and valley?
>   What praise do I command?

> Full well they know the singer
>   Belongs to race accursed;
> Sweet *Minne* [love] doth no longer
>   Reward me as at first.

> Be silent, then, my lyre,
>   We sing 'fore lords in vain
> I'll leave the minstrels' choir
>   And roam a Jew again.

> My staff and hat I'll grasp, then,
>   And on my breast full low,
> By Jewish custom olden
>   My grizzled beard shall grow.

> My days I'll pass in quiet,—
>   Those left to me on earth—
> Nor sing for those who not yet
>   Have learned a poet's worth.[17] (Illustration No. 15)

Thus Süsskind of Trimberg shed his knightly garb, and went back into the life of a Jew. It is not known how he was received there, and what became of him subsequently. A none too reliable tradition states that he fell on hard times in his old age and that his children forsook him. It is alleged that he was alone when he died. Be that as it may, we can conclude, even without these reports, that someone who had left his own world so far behind, and was not permitted to speak freely in his new chosen surroundings, was bound to return home with a painful inner wound and a deep hurt.

We may state in conclusion that there can be no doubt whatsoever about Süsskind's Jewish origin. His entire life was the epitome of Jewish talent asserting itself successfully in hostile surroundings; his fate is the typical fate of the misunderstood artist, his artistry proof that the Jew can triumph intellectually not only at periods where conditions favor his development, such as in the Islamic and Christian Spain, but even where obstacles are put in his way, and true talent remains his sole weapon in the battle for existence.

Thus Süsskind of Trimberg stands before posterity, the tragic figure of Jewish talent unappreciated, full of courage and fight, but misunderstood by his contemporaries.

9

The Locheim Songbook

WHETHER THE PHENOMENON OF SÜSSKIND WAS A UNIQUE AND ISO-
lated occurrence in Germany, or whether it was duplicated by
another German itinerant bard, is a matter of conjecture. Yet
there are strong reasons to believe that this might have been the
case. Such an assumption is based upon a literary and musical
discovery at the turn of the 19th century, which created a considerable stir in the scholarly world.

We refer to the *Locheimer Liederbuch* (Locheimer Songbook)
which, although not in itself a monument to Jewish music, is of
the greatest interest to the scope of our present study.

This book is a handwritten collection of forty-eight vocal compositions, set for two and three voices, and gathered by an
unknown scribe of music of the 15th century. Opinions have for
a long time been divided whether this scribe may have copied
these songs for his own use, possibly as an amateur singer, or in
the employ of some music lover, or music collector.

The songbook first was scientifically analyzed and described by
FRIEDRICH WILHELM ARNOLD (1810-1864).[18] ARNOLD was the first
to set down a most detailed history, a veritable Odyssey, of this
manuscript, as it went from hand to hand before its significance
was even realized. Thereafter he established a positive fact, later
confirmed historically beyond any doubt, that this manuscript
constitutes the earliest milestone of written polyphonic singing
in Germany and therefore is of the greatest value for musical
scholarship.

This manuscript is particularly important to us because it contains below song No. 16 at the bottom of page 17, a dedication
by the scribe in German language yet in Hebrew letters, written
right to left, which reads:

"Der allerliebsten Barbara, meinem treuen liebsten Gemaken"
(To the most beloved Barbara, my faithful and dearest spouse).

One line higher, at the right of the page, where the Hebraic letters start, there is an additional short dedication, in German lettering: *"Ir zu lieb,"* i.e., "To please her." (Illustration No. 16.)

ARNOLD proceeds to examine who might have been the possible author or scribe of this manuscript. Certain dates contained in the texts give a clue that 1450 may have been the year of origin of this collection. In ARNOLD's words:

> Since no Christian person living in or about 1450 understood Hebrew, a language which REUCHLIN, having learnt it from Jews, first included in his philological studies fifty years later, there can be little doubt that the writer of the first thirty-six songs was a Jew. Further proof appears to be that he uses the ʿAyyin as an *e* in German, while in the written language it is a consonant. Furthermore we can assume with certainty that this Jewish scribe was no mere employee, for as such he would never have dared to scribble Hebraic letters upon the songbook of a noble Junker at a time when severe pogroms had driven the Jews out of Augsburg, and when such scribbling would have been considered cabalistic Godlessness. . . . The loose, almost incoherent setting of the songs seems to indicate that many of them were set to paper from memory, or after a singer's performance.
>
> If we conclude that no hired scribe produced the songbook, then it follows that this Jewish scribe was also its owner, one WÖLFLEIN VON LOCHAMEN, as indicated in writing. The first name WOLF to this day has remained common among the Jews, and the surname LOCHAM discloses its derivation from a south Bavarian hamlet still known to us as Lochem, but now spelled Locheim. The Jew apparently assumed the name of his birthplace, as was generally practiced in those times due to the lack of indigenous-sounding surnames."

ARNOLD then lists peculiarities of the then spoken German dialect as proof thereof, and concludes:

> We must assume that our 'WÖLFLE von LOCHEM,' as he might still today be called in that region's dialect, was a song-happy Jewish individual who, for his own predilection gathered together a

songbook into which, from time to time, he entered songs he liked, just as they came to him, a songbook which might have served as a sort of guest book. . . . This theory is supported by the entire aspect of the handwriting to its most insignificant details.

It appears that German scholarship could never admit that the oldest monument of polyphonic German song originated with a Jewish writer, For this reason the editor of the periodical, the renowned musicologist FRIEDRICH CHRYSANDER, felt it was up to him to come to the rescue of German honor. In his postscript to ARNOLD's article (signed also by another German musicologist, JOHANN FRIEDRICH BELLERMAN) he performs a veritable scientific sleight of hand when he writes:

The assertion voiced with such certainty by ARNOLD that the writer and owner of the songbook, WÖLFLEIN von LOCHAMEN, had been a Jew, appears to us thoroughly unfounded inasmuch as it is based solely on a few hebraic letters which spell out a German name and a German thought. The mere fact that someone can write down hebraic letters does not signify that he is a Jew, but merely that he may have studied Hebrew writing, possibly the Hebrew tongue. The claim that in 1450 Christians were not yet cognizant of Hebrew is most difficult to substantiate. Long before that time there existed rabbinical schools in Regensburg, Mainz, and other German townships, however for Jews only; nevertheless the possibility must be considered that Gentiles, spurred on by the awakening of scientific endeavor and the zeal of that century to collect scripts of all kinds, to copy them and start libraries, may have studied directly (or indirectly) in those schools. . . . JOHANN REUCHLIN, born about 1450, was however the first to create a Hebrew grammar, but almost at the same time the theologians of his period began to pursue their hebraic studies with such dedication that the Cologne monks preached against this phase of learning, and sarcastically proclaimed to the public that a new language had been discovered, by the use of which one would turn into a Jew. ARNOLD's theory is best disproved by the inner character of the manuscript. The songs express German mind and Christian ideas throughout, such as could scarcely have been the utterance of a Jew living at that time. Nothing was more remote to persecuted and oppressed Jewry of that day than acceptance of German muse and German music, and expression thereof. The name WÖLFLEIN von LOCHAMEN consequently must have belonged to a German nobleman, the locality-defining surname tends to prove that he resided either in a castle or in a monastery of a religious order.[19]

And with this pregnant statement German honor has been allegedly vindicated.

In the present-day German encyclopedias the Jewish origin of the songbook's author is discreetly left unmentioned and WÖLF-LEIN von LOCHAMEN has become a Nürnberg patrician and "indubitably" the owner of the book.

However, the one indisputable fact that proves that the writer of the songbook was a Jew, is the short German sentence above the line in Hebrew, a sentence which appeared insignificant to the sleuths. Any German writer would most certainly have begun the line *at the left margin*; WÖLFLEIN began his new line *at the right*, as any Jew would have instinctively begun his.

We therefore have no reason whatsoever to doubt that the evidence established so clearly and logically by ARNOLD, can with all reasonable certainty convince us that the writer and owner of the song collection had been the Jew WÖLFLEIN, from the township of LOCHEIM.

There remains but one enigma: what forces could have motivated a Jew of the European Middle Ages, who was not a professional musician, to assemble for himself a *polyphonic* songbook? In such an outlandish tiny Bavarian village he surely had no immediate use for a many-voiced songbook. If indeed he was "song-happy," the term ARNOLD uses, a single voice lead sheet of the melodies would have been sufficient for his own use. Now, from where did he obtain the three-part harmony? It could be argued that the harmonizations could have originated or were copied from a similar collection of a professional musician and, taking this one step further, that WÖLFLEIN himself was the *composer* of the songs, a theory for which there is scant support.

Mus. ex. No. 2

No. 18. Ein vrouleen edel von naturen.

Transcription in modern notation of p. 20 of the Locheimer Songbook.
In: Jahrbücher für Musikwissenschaft (1876), p. 121.

Why then a collection of polyphonic songs? Such songs could *only* have belonged to a professional. Could it be that WÖLFLEIN used them, in the capacity as a wandering minstrel? If this is the case, he must certainly be included among the category of Jewish minnesingers, as the second important exponent of this art in Germany.

It is definitely in the realm of possibility that this assumption may point toward this being a fact, for how else could a Jew, not practicing the musical profession, living in a faraway little hamlet, compile for himself a *harmonized* song book for which, according to human reckoning, he had no conceivable use.

Since we can in no wise, at present, substantiate and prove this line of reasoning, the why and wherefore of the LOCHEIM SONG-BOOK, for a time at least, will remain an insoluble enigma.

10

The Oldest Written Sources of
Jewish Music

ACCORDING TO OUR PRESENT KNOWLEDGE, THE OLDEST WRITTEN
source of Jewish music is a manuscript discovered about 1920 by
ELKAN NATHAN ADLER in the Genizah of the old synagogue at
Fustat, near Cairo.[1] It is a melodized fragment of a *piyyut,* the
acrostics of which point to 'AMR ibn SAHAL as the poet, a *paytan*
who lived in the twelfth century. The date assigned to the manuscript is either the end of the twelfth or the beginning of the
thirteenth century. The poem is a "Eulogy of Moses"; on the *verso*
of the manuscript there is a quotation from Isaiah 60:1 (Illustration No. 24a and 24b). Both poem and quotation are provided
with staffless neumes which resemble the medieval Lombardic
notation. In the present manuscript these neumes proceed from
right to left in conformity with Hebrew writing. The neumes of
the quotation from Isaiah are less elaborate than those of the
recto; the melody indicated by the neumes is very similar to that
of the *Haftarah.*

The *Catalogue Adler* contains a detailed description of the
manuscript together with a transcription of the neumes in modern notation (Mus. ex. No. 3).

This transcription was made by the Benedictine Fathers of
Quarr Abbey on the Isle of Wight, who are known as experts in
deciphering early medieval neumes. Therefore, within certain
technical limitations, they should be seriously considered, while
figuring out an accurate transcription of this ancient melody.
However, ERIC WERNER considers this transcription "highly
dubious."[2]

Mus. ex. No. 3

Transcription in modern notation of the neumes of the manuscript Adler, made by the Benedictine Fathers of Quarr Abbey.

In deciphering early medieval neumes, there is always a leeway open to personal interpretation. Thus, in his desire to obtain as authentic a transcription of this melody as possible, ARTHUR M. FRIEDLANDER, of the Royal Asiatic Society in London, submitted the document for this purpose to Mr. ABDY WILLIAMS, a specialist on the subject of medieval neumes. WILLIAMS, in turn, consulted DOM ANDRE MOCQUEREAU of the Benedictine Fathers at Solesmes, the eminent authorities on Gregorian music. With the help and advice of these two scholars, FRIEDLANDER made his own transcription,[3] reproduced here:

Mus. ex. No. 4

ka-mo - šeh: ? ? ? ? el

ha - E - lo-[him] 'a - da - - thi ḳu-mi ki

bo ọ - rekh u - - kh° - bhod A -

do - nai 'a - la - yikh za - raḥ:

Transcription in modern notation of the neumes of the manuscript Adler, made by Dom. André Mocquerau.

The difference between the two is mainly of rhythmic nature. FRIEDLANDER has attempted to squeeze the melody into the barlines of our metrical system, a procedure which is problematic for any melodic structure of an epoch in which this device was unknown. However, whether we make use of the barlines or not, at least the basic character of the melody in the two versions is not altered.

This transcription as well does not meet with WERNER's approval. While he considers it, as a whole, "meritorious," he does not think that it is "entirely successful."[4]

Then WERNER made his own transcription. By this, he maintains that DOM MOCQUERAU "read the notes well, but did not interpret correctly the Hebrew clef." Yet WERNER does not say which "Hebrew clef" this might have been. Furthermore, WERNER made his transcription "for the purpose of popular [phonographic] records."[5] He felt induced to add to his version of the melody an organ accompaniment, a questionable procedure by which he admits himself, "the character of the piece is somewhat altered."[6] Moreover, he extended the melody beyond the point where the neumes of the original manuscript terminates, arbitrarily adding a kind of "Coda," evidently in order to end "musically" the melody for the purpose of his recording. He also expressed the hope that "the transcription will provide a fairly faithful picture of the piece"[7]

In his attempt to analyze and evaluate this document, WERNER

Mus. ex. No. 5 (The last line of this Mus. ex. is Werner's addition.)[7]

[Hymne auf den Tod Moses'] [Hymn on the Death of Moses]

Paraphrase of Text: Who will accompany
him, God's prophet, on his heavy way? When he climbs
Mount Horeb . . ., who will be with me? . . .
"Arise and shine; for your light has come,
And the glory of the Lord has risen upon you."

*Eric Werner's transcription of the neumes of the manuscript Adler.
In: Anthology of Music, p. 9 (Köln a. Rh., 1961). Courtesy of Arno
Volk Verlag, Köln a. Rh.*

made two basic errors. First, he stated that the manuscript was of Palestinian origin. Later on he asserted that it originated in Ravenna or thereabouts (even though it was found in Cairo). Furthermore, he maintained that the neumes are Italian in type (which is correct), while the Hebrew script shows Byzantine influence (which is not). Yet, the paper of the document is "of the type commonly used in Genizah manuscripts of the twelfth century—thick, slightly tan, and quite evidently of Egyptian provenience,"[8] while the Hebrew script shows predominantly Eastern paleographic features.

HANOCH AVENARY made a thorough study of this oldest known specimen of Jewish music and furnished his own version.

According to AVENARY, the medieval Jewish author must have been familiar with European-Christian music and its notation (AVENARY thinks he might have been a refugee from persecutions during the time of the Crusades, settling in Cairo.)[10] The general appearance and style of the script conforms to that of the Italian neumes of the early twelfth century, or to that of Northern France of the latter part of that century.

The neumes placed above the initial five Hebrew lines of the text do not indicate as a possible clue the presumable "key" or "mode" for their proper musical reading. The manuscript having no staff lines, it appears that the medieval scribe made several mistakes by placing various neumes too low. In order to correct his error, it is probable that the neumator has affixed the Hebrew letter *daleth* (‫ד‬) at the right corner along the sixth line and continued in this same manner until the end of the page. Thus, he indicated with the daleth a clef for the reading of the neumes. AVENARY assumes that the pitch level indicated by that particular Hebrew letter corresponds to our conventional note D (*Re*). Following this clue, AVENARY deciphered and transcribed the neumes. Here is the result of this attempt at reproducing, in modern notation, the earliest piece of extant Jewish music. (Mus. ex. No. 6).

Apart from the musical transcription, AVENARY has also discovered that not only the concluding portion of this *piyyut* carries a Scriptural quotation, as mentioned at the beginning of the present chapter, but other such quotations are likewise inserted

Mus. ex. No. 6

Hanoch Avenary's transcription of the neumes of the manuscript Adler.

in each and every strophe of the poem. This will become fully
evident from the following English translation of its entire text
which indicates the exact Biblical references of these quotations:

1. Who stood on Mt. Horeb

Deut. 5:28   absorbing the content of "Stand with me,"
                   as Moshe.

2. Who in the desert lead my flock bringing

Numb. 21:17   forth water [by saying] "Rise, Well,"
                   as Moshe

	3. Who entreated me for mercy
Exod. 32:12	saying, "And repent of this evil,"
	as Moshe.
	4. Who visioned statutes for multitudes
Numb. 12:8	visioned "In revelation not in riddles,"
	as Moshe.
	5. Who taught my people diligently
Exod. 24:16	and was worthy of "And came into the cloud,"
	as Moshe.
	6. Who rose to the heavens for forty days,
Exod. 34:28	existed "Without bread and without water,"
	as Moshe.
	7. To the heavens he came to God.
Isaiah 60:1, 2	Know, my people, "that your light has come. The glory of God has shone upon you."

Even a cursory comparison of AVENARY's musical transcription with those of his three predecessors will reveal at once that it differs quite substantially from all of them, especially in the closing portion of the piece. AVENARY's version has two strong points to its credit: (1) He seems to have correctly identified a "key" which the original neumator intended to apply to the reading of the neumes, thus giving a sound basis for the deciphering; (2) he did not compress the rhythmic pattern of the neumes into modern rhythmical values, such as quarter and eighth notes. The only rhythmic interpretation made by AVENARY concerned the neume *virga*, being a slightly longer note and above which he placed a *tenuto* sign. The medieval performer (ordinarily a *ḥazzan*) might have applied as the rhythmization of the melody the inherent metrical and syntactical values of the words. AVENARY correctly avoided any rigid rhythmical pattern, leaving it to the individual taste of the performer.

More recently, through the research of two Jewish scholars, ALEXANDER SCHEIBER and NORMAN GOLB, light was shed on the author of the Adler manuscript. Furthermore, the fortunate dis-

Mus. ex. No. 7

Israel Adler's transcription of the neumes of the manuscript Adler. In:
Ariel *(Jerusalem, 1966), No. 15, pp. 32–33.*

covery in 1965 by NEHEMIAH ALLONY of a similar manuscript with
neumes at the University of Cambridge was the vindication of
AVENARY's assumption that the writer of the Adler manuscript
must have been a European refugee who settled in Egypt. The
Cambridge document shows the same paleographic features as
the Adler manuscript, giving proof that the writer of both docu-
ents, and in all probability also the composer of the melodies,
was indeed a European refugee, 'OBADIAH the Norman Proselyte.

About the life of 'OBADIAH we are quite well informed from
some autobiographical fragments that survived the ages, and also
by a letter of recommendation given to 'OBADIAH by the Rabbi
BARUCH ben ISAAC of Aleppo, to be produced "in all the Jewish
communities to which he may proceed."

As these sources indicate, 'OBADIAH was born in Oppido (now
Oppido Lucano) in Apulia in the third quarter of the eleventh
century (ca. 1070), and was the scion of a noble Norman family.
His name was originally Johannes or Giovan', which he himself
gives with a transliteration in Hebrew characters, as JHNS and
GV'N. His family destined him to become a priest, and for some
years he was educated in a monastery in southern Italy. There
he undoubtedly acquired the knowledge of the notation of music
by neumes. In September 1102 he was converted to Judaism,[11]
but whether his conversion took place in Europe or in the Near
East is not known. It is probable that the latter assumption is
correct, since we can follow—even though fragmentarily—his
travels in the Near East, in Babylonia, Syria, Mesopotamia and
the Holy Land until 1121. We know, furthermore, that he settled
for a time in Bagdad, where he was supported by the Jewish
community. It was there, evidently, that he learned to read and
write Hebrew, sitting in a classroom among schoolchildren.

In order to avoid 'OBADIAH's subjection to receiving alms, the community created a special office of a *gabbai* (collector of donations) for him, which every week solicited contributions for the benefit of the proselyte—a procedure not uncommon in Jewish congregations to support needy foreigners of high social standing.

In a later period of his life, he lived for some time in Aleppo, again supported by the Jewish community. Eventually, after 1121 he settled in Egypt, where the first of the two documents attributed to him, the manuscript Adler, was discovered in the Genizah of the Synagogue of Fustāt-Misr. He died about the middle of the twelfth century, probably before 1141, at the age of seventy.

'OBADIAH was a prolific writer. He composed fourteen tractates on the truths of the Jewish faith.[12] Modern research also reveals a *Megillah* (scroll) written by him, of which the manuscript Adler and the two Cambridge documents are supposed to be parts. Lately, ALEXANDER SCHEIBER discovered in the Genizah collection of Budapest another fragment of four pages which are similar to the Cambridge documents.

Moreover, in the Genizah collection at the Hebrew Union College Library, Cincinnati, there is also a fragment of a *Maḥsor* (prayerbook), written in 'OBADYAH's own hand, as he himself stated. The script of this fragment, written in square Oriental letters, is identical with those of the manuscript Elkan Adler and of the Cambridge discovery. (Illustration No. 19a and b) This proves beyond any doubt that 'OBADYAH was the scribe of these two last named documents.

What the reason of 'OBADYAH's conversion was, is not known. It may have been the outcome of a long process. S. D. GOITEIN thinks that 'OBADYAH was "obviously stirred by the cruel persecutions by the Crusaders of the Jewish communities of Western Europe."[13] Yet, such humanitarian sentiments were extremely rare in those times, and even more so among the clergy.[14] Therefore, GOITEIN's hypothesis does not have much credibility.

Another more plausible impulse for his conversion might have been prompted by the example of ANDREAS, Archbishop of Bari, who recognized the truth of the Torah. ANDREAS went to Constantinople (Byzanz), and there embraced Judaism. "At first he was persecuted by the Christians, . . . but afterwards the persecutors themselves followed his example and were converted to the Jew-ish faith."[15] The news of his conversion spread through Northern Italy to Rome, and caused even in Byzanz great consternation among Church dignitaries.

But the strongest motive for 'OBADIAH's conversion might have been a mystic occurrence about which his "Scroll" informs us. In the first year of his priesthood he had a dream: "He saw him-self officiating in the Basilica of Oppido, when a figure appeared at his right hand and called him by his name." Unfortunately, some pages of the Scroll, which might have contained the sequel of his dream and the appeal addressed to him are still missing. It is to be hoped that further discoveries might reveal more about his stirring experience, and hence the decisive impetus leading to his conversion.

The same mystery as regarding the motive for his conversion clouds the origin of the melodies which he employed for the two *piyyutim* selected as his lyrics. There are two hypotheses in this regard: 'OBADIAH was either the composer, or the notator of the melodies which he heard from European *hazzanim*, who escaped to the Near East during the early period of the Crusades. NORMAN GOLB intimates that these melodies show some affinities with Gregorian chants, which would not be surprising considering the fact that 'OBADIAH spent some years of his youth in a monastery.

It is surmised that 'OBADIAH might have made his living as a *hazzan*, or as an instructor of music (in this case of *hazzanut*) to other cantors, or both. This assumption is very plausible, since Oriental *hazzanim* ordinarily had no musical education and might have been eager to take advantage of such instruction by a quali-fied teacher. In fact, several cases are known in which immigrant Frenchmen held the office of *hazzanim* as well as instructors of music for them.[16]

AVENARY made his own transcription of the Cambridge docu-ment. His version is meritorious, particularly as he submits not only his own interpretation of the neumes, but brings the result-ing melodic strain into relationship with Moroccan, Italian and Ashkenazic recitative modes as well (Mus. ex. 8a and b). There is indeed a strong similarity between the second half of the third line of his transcription and the fragment of a Genizah tune, which appears to indicate the common origin of both. Thus, the source is revealed from which 'OBADIAH might have borrowed his melody. (Mus. ex. Nos. 8a, 8b.)

Mus. ex. No. 8a

Hanoch Avenary's transcription in modern notation of the Fragment Cambridge T.S. K 5/41.

Mus. ex. No. 8b

Comparison of the twelfth century recitative-mode employed by 'Obadiah with similar recitatives used in modern synagogues (Morocco, Leghorn, Ashkenazic). In: The Journal of Jewish Studies (London, 1966), vol. XIV, Nos. 3–4, pp. 87–104.

In two revealing studies, ISRAEL ADLER sheds some additional light upon ʿOBADIAH together with the two musical documents attributed to him.[17] Like AVENARY, ADLER made his own transcription of the medieval neumes, but arrived at a quite different solution. The reason for this divergence is that both interpreted differently the "clef," which is the solution to the deciphering of the neumes. As ADLER maintains, the extant transcriptions are based on erroneously selected "clefs." He concludes that the correct clef for the neumes of ʿOBADIAH should be based on *Fa*, and using this clef, he made his own transcription of the manuscript Elkan Adler as well as of the recently discovered Cambridge documents (Mus. ex. 9a and b)

AVENARY's and ADLER's transcriptions are rather similar, as far as the intervallic relations of the modern notations are concerned. The obvious difference is that, owing to the different clefs, AVENARY's melody starts on the note *A* (la), while ISRAEL ADLER's version of the manuscript Elkan Adler begins with the note *C* (do). ADLER's transcription of the Cambridge document begins with the note *D* (re) on recto, and with *G* (sol) on *verso*.

Although the investigation concerning the Cambridge discovery is still in its initial stages, we feel that the results, such as they are, of our present knowledge of the document, cannot be omitted from our study. Therefore we give, in Mus. ex. No. 9, ISRAEL ADLER's transcription in modern notations.

The text of the document constitutes a *piyyut*, the words of which are merely quotations from the Bible. In the recto,[18] the composer (or neumator) combined texts from Isaiah, the Proverbs and Psalms into one coherent sentence. Here follows the translation of this *piyyut*:

> verso 1. Blessed is the man that trusteth in the Lord, and whose trust the Lord is (Jer. 17:7).
> 2. Trust in the Lord with all thine heart; and lean not unto thine own understanding (Prov. 3:5).
> 3. In all thy ways acknowledge Him, and He will direct thy paths (Prov. 3:6).
> 4. Happy is the man that findeth wisdom, and the

man that obtaineth understanding (Prov. 3:13).
5. Behold, happy is the man whom God correcteth;
therefore despise not thou the chastening of the
Almighty (Job 5:17).

Mus. ex. No. 9

recto   6. And I shall know, and I shall know, what to say
in the gates [towns]; and what I shall say, and what
I shall say, what I shall answer, Thou teach me.

Ms. B (Cambridge T.S.K5/41)

RECTO

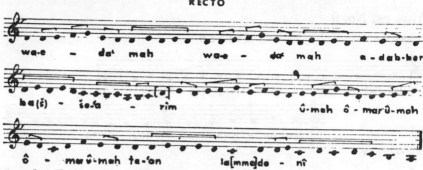

Israel Adler's transcription in modern notation of the Fragment Cambridge. T.S. K 5/41. In: Ariel (Jerusalem, 1966), No. 15, pp. 34–35.

A recent study of Avenary[19] clears up still existing doubts concerning these ancient relics. First, his statement is revealing that the Benedictine Fathers of Solesmes changed their opinion about the transcription of the neumes of the manuscript Adler, as published by Friedlander. By this, one of the controversies about the real meaning of the neumes has been eliminated.

Secondly, Avenary furnishes the definitive proof that 'Obadiah was the scribe of both, the Adler and the Cambridge documents. As mentioned above, the script of both is identical with that of the Mahsor-fragment (in the Hebrew Union College) written in his own hand. (Illustration No. 19a and b).

It is Avenary's opinion that "'Obadiah's notational practice appears to be rather avant-garde for a man who finished his studies at the latest in 1102."[20]

Furthermore, Avenary states: "With regard to this tune [the Cambridge document] one dare say that 'Obadiah has noted down a genuine Jewish melody that was common in his days."[21]

For the question where 'Obadiah might have picked up this melody, Avenary ventures the hypothesis that "if 'Obadiah did not become a proselyte in the Orient, he could have contacted the rabbis [or the hazzanim] of any of these towns (Melfi, La-

vello, Ascoli, Satriano Altamusa, Matera, etc.). Especially the town
of Venosa, where 'OBADIAH's musical education took place in the
Benedictine Abbey, harbored one of the oldest Jewish communities in the region."[22]

Finally, everything points to the assumption that 'OBADIAH
served in the Orient as a *hazzan* and teacher of music, as many
needy itinerants used to do.[23] At that time there was, especially
in the Orient "an urgent demand for ever new *piyyutim*, and of
the eagerness of the precentors to meet this desire."[24] This sheds
light upon the lyrics of 'OBADIAH's manuscripts, which afford
added insight into the dual capacity of 'OBADIAH as a poet and
composer.

In Spain a document was found originating from medieval
times, which contains an early notation of Jewish (or seemingly
Jewish) music. It is a vocal composition, written somewhere between 1450 and 1460 in Northern Spain, discovered by the Spanish
musicologist Monsignor HIGINIO ANGLÉS. The manuscript was
originally part of the *Chansonier of Sevilla* in the Biblioteca Co-
lombina, and it was there that Monsignor ANGLES saw it first. He
described it in the *Estudis Universitatis Catalana* in 1929 and
published several articles on it.[25] Using this material, ERIC WERNER
published the original in facsimile in 1945, and has written an
article about it in 1947, which contains a modern notation as well
as some conjectures about the presumable author and the hypo-
thetical purpose of the composition.[26]

Using the initial words of the cryptic text, WERNER called it a
"*Kedusha-Motet.*" It is set for three voices, Cantus, Tenor, and
Contratenor, and WERNER considers it "an elaborate contrapuntal
piece." He transcribed the individual parts, written in medieval
mensural notation, and assembled them into a score.

Here is the original and WERNER's transcription (Illustrations
20a and b and Mus. ex. No. 10).

This musical piece involves a number of problems. The difficulties begin with the text which is an incomprehensible mumbo-
jumbo of unidentifiable, evidently corrupted or purposely dis-
torted Hebrew, Spanish, Arabic, and possibly Ladino words. It
reads as follows: "Cados, cados, adonay cherubim, cados, si

Mus. ex. No. 10

The Ḳedushah-motet *(transcription in modern notation by Eric Werner). In:* Anthology of Music *(Köln a.Rh., 1961), p. 19. Courtesy of Arno Volk Verlag, Köln a.Rh.*

smyher, harumbrael, rausar maho, maho et ydrorum naiso soposo dislacherubim, a mealbul lumbi, lari discaho, cados, cados." There is also a marginal note in the manuscript: "4 nulame."

In an attempt to unscramble the hodge-podge of the few corrupted Hebrew words and the other unintelligible gibberish, WERNER hazards an opinion that this "composition" might have been written "by a Marranic composer for the secret meetings of the 'New Christians' during the High Holidays, which was virtually the only time when the Marranos dared to congregate. Possibly the text is camouflaged and only seemingly senseless"; it was, according to WERNER, well understood by the crypto-Jews.[27]

To WERNER's article Rabbi D. A. JESSURUN CARDOZO added a note in which he says that "it is most unlikely, if not impossible, that a Marrano in Spain would have taken this enormous risk to *write down* a Hebrew melody. Any visible or "concrete" proof of "Judaizing" would have been fatal. Writing down a Hebrew prayer or hymn by a Marrano would practically mean signing his own death warrant."[28]

This reasoning of an expert in the Sephardic tradition is apt to eliminate once and for all WERNER's hypothesis concerning a camouflaged ritual piece for a secret meeting of Marranos.[29] There is, however, another logical explanation for the appearance of this curious piece to be given presently.

We must now unravel a few problematic points concerning the music itself. According to WERNER, the Cantus is the ancient Ashkenazic tune of the preamble to the Kedusha for the High Holidays, therefore he calls the piece *"Kedusha-Motet."* We have checked with many experts (cantors and musicologists) about this Cantus; but none would endorse WERNER's contention. Furthermore, as ANGLÉS asserts, this manuscript originates in northern Spain in the middle of the fifteenth century. At that time Spanish Jews were familiar only with the Sephardic ritual and songs. It is highly improbable that a Jewish, or crypto-Jewish musician, who allegedly wrote this piece, could have been acquainted with an Ashkenazic melody for the High Holidays.

A further difficulty arises with the Tenor part, which is devoid of any musical significance. According to the general technique of vocal compositions at the period in question, the principal melody of a piece is carried by the Tenor; masses, cantatas, motets even are named after the melody or tune which constitutes the "Tenor" of the composition. Now, the Tenor of our *"Kedusha-Motet"* does not show any recognizable musical physiognomy of its own. Whether the melodic line is supplanted by a rhythmic design (the *shofar* signal, as WERNER thinks) is very doubtful, to say the least. We possess the rhythmical notation of *shofar* calls in two authentic medieval documents, one from the thirteenth, the other from the fourteenth century.[30] The Tenor part of our piece does not show any similarity to these ancient rhythmical patterns. Yet, even if we follow WERNER's interpretation, it is evident that the reproduction in the Tenor of *shofar* signals could only have been done by a Jew, who should therefore be considered the author of the piece as well; an assumption which must be discarded for reasons exposed by R. JESSURUN CARDOZO.

Finally, the Contratenor intones several times the beginning of the medieval Gregorian hymn: *"Alma Redemptoris Mater."*

As WERNER maintains, "the composer succeeded in combining these three tunes in a masterfully contrapuntal fashion." We can agree that it is a skillful combination of three different melodic lines, even if there might be some doubt about the Tenor as an "independent" tune. At any rate, the author, whoever he may have been (a convert, perchance) must have been a trained musician, perhaps a cleric, who attempted to ridicule in a musical fashion the Jewish religion. The piece is obviously one of the frequent pasticcios of the time, a musical parody, destined for the amusement of the masses—clerics, noblemen, and laymen alike. The persiflage of the Jewish religion, like this, must have had an appreciative audience and could count on the plaudits of the masses.

A similar anti-Semitic musical comedy (to be fully discussed and exemplified in a subsequent chapter) is ORAZIO VECCHI's *Amfiparnasso* composed in the sixteenth century. In this work not so much the Jewish religion as the speech, the manners and the business practices of the Jews are pilloried and caricaturized.[31]

A further musical relic from the Spanish peninsula has been

discovered in a richly illuminated Bible-Codex from about 1400. It was found in a synagogue at Cairo in or about 1936. The Polish art historian, ZOFJA AMEISENOVA, gives a detailed report about the wondrous destiny of this Bible, how it was discovered and, eventually, lost.[32] The Bible contained about sixty miniatures depicting Biblical scenes in the manner and the technique of the thirteenth-century Christian Bible illustrators. From these pictures AMEIZENOVA selected six, which are published together with her article and aptly described by the author.

One of these pictures has a particular significance for us; it is an illustration belonging to the Book of *Shir ha-Shirim* (Song of Songs). In this painting King David and a young shepherd are represented, both holding in their hands some kind of a music scroll; above them is a pole held by a young man; a band is wound around the pole; on this band there is a musical notation in the mensural notes of the time, and under this notation, which represents a melodic design, there are words in Hebrew: the first verses of the Song of Songs (Illustration No. 21). The melody as well as the words are interrupted by the double winding of the scroll around the pole. It remained a challenge to musicology to decipher this early document of Jewish sacred music. This task was undertaken and finally solved by the Hungarian musicologist BENCE SZABOLCSI.[33] As he states

> . . . the notation follows the well-known types of the 'Roman plain song' of the fourteenth century. . . . The two melody lines which proceed following the Hebrew writing, from right to left, are divided by the double winding of the scroll into six partly fragmentary sections; the melody, however, continues within these portions as well as do the words. Its closer scrutiny will convince anyone that the melody is an authentic, not an imaginary or arbitrary product. It represents, in other words, a living and actually sung tune, perhaps copied by the miniator from Hebrew liturgical manuals used at the time, or recorded with the aid of a musician.

SZABOLCSI's article contains a transcription of the six fragments in modern notation, first with the average note values of the original, then rhythmicized approximately within the bar lines of the contemporary Western musical system (Mus. ex. No. 11).

Mus. ex. No. 11

Transcription in modern notation of the music in the Cairuan Codex by Bence Szabolcsi. In: Semitic Studies in Memory of Immanuel Löw *(Budapest, 1947), pp. 131–133.*

As Szabolcsi comments, "a particularly close connection seems to exist between our melody and the music of certain mystery-plays of the fourteenth century; thus, with the characteristic tune of the dramatic *'Complaint of the three Marys'* in the *Processionale of Cividale,* known since the publication of Coussemaker (*Les drames liturgiques du moyen âge,* Rennes, 1860, p. 285) and based upon a Planctus sequence of the thirteenth century, these Middle-European offshoots of the Gregorian plain song are evidently parallel and cognate phenomena with the late Hebrew psalmody style."

Szabolcsi's merit is not lessened by the fact that his statement according to which this is "our first, most ancient musical document in notes," is now superseded by other and earlier relics. The manuscript discovered by Elkan Nathan Adler is certainly older. Nevertheless, the musical notation of the Cairuan Codex is, and will remain, one of the most valuable discoveries pertaining to the authentic synagogue melodies of the Spanish epoch under consideration.

Finally, a tune dating from the same period should be mentioned which, though outside the category of Jewish musical relics, has a certain dismal significance for the cultural history of the Jews. It is a ditty, sung by the Spanish populace after the "most Catholic" rulers, FERDINAND and ISABELLA, expelled the Jews from Spain in 1492. It is preserved in a book by FRANCISCO SALINAS (1515-1590), *De musica libri septem* (publ. in Salmantice, 1557), and reproduced in FELIPE PEDRELL's *Cancionero musical popular español.*[34] Here is the tune in modern notation:

Mus. ex. No. 12

Transcription in modern notation of an anti-Semitic Spanish ditty *(After Felipe Pedrell.* Cancionero musical popular español *(Boileau, n.d.), 2nd. ed.*

The words, literally translated, have the following meaning: "Go on, you Jews, pack up, since the Kings order you to cross the seas."

It is well known that European composers of the Middle Ages frequently availed themselves of a popular tune for the Tenor of a mass or another liturgical composition. Nevertheless, it is shocking to find this cruel and widely sung ditty used as the Tenor of a mass composed by JUAN de ANCHIETA, citizen of Azpeitia, choir master and cantor of the Catholic kings; also the music-master of the Infant DON JUAN and, incidentally, a relative of SAN IGNAZIO de LOYOLA. All these facts are faithfully reported in SALINA's book.

This anti-Semitic ditty, used as the Tenor of a Catholic Mass, affords us only a minor episode in the gruesome finale of the great Jewish national tragedy, and to the annihilation of a culture which, for centuries, brought to Spain progress, wealth and fame.

We could not leave this survey of the oldest *musical* relics of Jewish music, without dealing briefly with the recent discovery of the oldest Yiddish literary document, which—by implication— seems to have a definite connection with music, despite the fact that it does not contain any musical examples.

The discovery was made in 1953 by LEIB FUKS in the Cambridge University Library. The lucky discoverer gave, in a well documented essay,[35] besides a facsimile reproduction, the history, and the characteristics—linguistic, ethnological, and others —of this unique document. To begin with, he shows that in fourteenth-century Egypt there was a Yiddish speaking community which produced its own literature.[36] It was in this environment that the *Codex C.Y.* (as he calls it) was written by a Yiddish *shpilman*, who gathered together poems in one volume *for professional reasons*.[37] It was written (or copied) by the same hand; possibly some of the poems were his own, for some others he gave the name of an author (or scribe), such as Isaac or Abraham. One of the poems is dated November 9, 1382, which makes it probable that the entire collection was written in that year.

As a matter of fact, the language of the *Codex C.Y.* is not Yiddish, but Middle-High German, an idiom the Jews of that epoch spoke wherever they lived. They were aware of the particularity of their language, which they called *leshonenu*, "our language." FUKS characterizes it as "Old Yiddish," the time of which he places between 1250 and 1500. The time of origin of the *Codex C.Y.* indicates that the Jewish community of Egypt consisted mainly of European Jews, who escaped from the ravages of the Crusades and found a temporary refuge in Egypt.

Is this Yiddish *shpilman* (maybe several of them?) in Medieval Egypt a counterpart of SÜSSKIND of TRIMBERG and (possibly) of WÖLFLEIN of LOCHEM in Germanic lands? It might very well be possible.

Undoubtedly, the poems of the *Codex C.Y.* were *sung* by the *shpilman,* who compiled them for his own use. No other justification for this collection of Yiddish poems would be logical.

The *Codex C.Y.,* although we do not know the author's (or scribe's) name, is, nevertheless, an eloquent testimony of the never-ceasing urge of the Jewish people for music, which manifested itself wherever they lived, in both good as well in bad circumstances.

11

Shaping Forces of Jewish Music in the European Diaspora

THREE FACETS OF JEWISH MUSICAL PRACTICE WERE SHAPED AND received their appropriate form in the course of Europe's medieval period. The first was synagogal music, whose course followed three channels: the formulation of the synagogal prayer modes; the orientalization, or rather ornamental "Arabization" of the melody; and the crystallization of the synagogal prayer recitations. The second facet was the creation and development of a system of written signs, the *ta'amim*, to direct the general melodic line of the cantillation. These signs, a crude forerunner of Western musical notation, grew out largely from the technique of cheironomy, the hand signs originally indicating to the singers the fluctuation of the melodic line. The third and final facet was the creation of a specific genre of Jewish songs, the *zemirot*, table songs partly religious, partly secular in character, in which the entire family participated.

In the synagogue song, the scalar pattern of the melody, shaped under Arabic influence in the Sephardic realm, and under the impact of the German folksong in the Ashkenazic fold, acquired a specific physiognomy for each of the two trends. These scalar patterns were later called "modes," and ever since have dominated exclusively Jewish melodic creation. The term *modos* is of Greek origin; in the music theory of the Hellenes it meant a certain and always variable succession of whole and half steps.

Jewish musical science adopted for shaping the melody the principle of the Greek system as a basis for some stereotyped melodic formulas. Therefore, Jewish modes in the full sense of

174

the term represent a sort of combination of scalar patterns with the melodic formulas based upon them. At this point, however, we are concerned solely with their scalar, not melodic aspect.

All Jewish liturgical modes are divided into two distinct categories: (1) cantillation modes (or Biblical modes) used for chanting the various portions of the Scriptures, and (2) the prayer modes, used for the musical recitations of the various extra-Biblical texts.

Of the first category, the most important "Pentateuch mode" is founded upon two tetrachords e-f-g-a + b-c-d-e and is identical with the ancient Greek *Dorian* mode. This, generally, is the basis for the Oriental and Sephardic Jewish melodic formulas. The Pentateuch mode of the Ashkenazim is different, its two tetrachords constituting the scale f-g-a-bb + c-d-e-f, which is the ancient *Lydian* mode of the Greeks. Despite the diatonic appearance of this scale, however, the actual Ashkenazic Biblical motives based upon it contain a sizable amount of intervallic patterns characteristic of the semitoneless pentatonic scale.[1]

Almost as important in the field of Biblical cantillation is the "Mode of the Prophets," which likewise has a bi-tetrachordal construction, but one that produces the scale d-e-f-g + a-b-c-d. This is identical with the ancient Greek *Phrygian* mode, which was eventually renamed by the medieval Church the *first Gregorian* mode. In many instances, however, the note *b* in the upper tetrachord is flatted in actual cantillation, thereby transforming the first Gregorian mode into the second (plagal).

There exist three principal forms of the prayer modes: (1) the *'Adonay-Malach mode,* c-d-e-f-g-a-bb-c; (2) the *Magen-'Abot mode,* d-e-f-g-a-bb-c-d; and (3) the *'Ahavah-Rabba mode,* e-f-g♯-a-b-c-d-e. In the last named mode, the *permanent* interval of an augmented second between the notes f-g♯ lends a distinct Oriental color to the melodies based upon it. This color is sometimes still further enhanced by the *occasional* raising of the penultimate note in actual practice, which creates another augmented second c-d♯ within this mode, thereby making it akin to the so-called *Gypsy Scale* and the Arabic *Hedjaz-Kar.*[2]

An augmented second f-g♯ also occurs in a prayer mode of far lesser importance, namely the *'Av-harachamim mode,* which can be conveniently expressed by the notes d-e-f-g♯-a-b-c-d, similarly to those of the *Ukrainian Dorian mode*.[3] According to some observations, this Jewish mode, too, tolerates an *occasional* raising of the penultimate note, but usually in conjunction with a simultaneous lowering of its sixth degree (this optional *b*-flat is a familiar trait in the *Prophetic mode* mentioned above). Such double chromatization not only leads automatically to the appearance of another augmented second (b♭-c♯) in the *'Av-harachamim mode*, but also places both these identical and characteristic intervals within a closer distance to each other and thus brings about an almost extreme Oriental coloration of the involved Jewish melodies. This intensely orientalized prayer mode (d-e-f-g♯-a-b♭-c♯-d) is said to be nicknamed in certain quarters—rather exaggerated, it seems—as the *Jewish scale*.

There also exist many other modes of a somewhat secondary importance in the two above-mentioned categories of the Jewish musical system. Such are, for instance, the cantillation modes for the Biblical books of Ruth, Esther, Ecclesiastes, Lamentations, Job, Proverbs, the Psalms, and the prayer modes known by the Hebrew names of *Seliha, Tahnun, Tefillah, Tal-*and-*Geshem, Yozer*, etc. Many of these have their Ashkenazic and Sephardic variants; and by their motivic formulas rather than scalar construction these modes have contributed, in various degree, to the shaping of the Jewish melos.

Among the Sephardim, the modal diversity is not as obvious as in the Ashkenazic tradition. The reason is rooted in the difference between the ritual of the Ashkenazim and Sephardim. While in the Ashkenazic rite the *hazzan* was the leading force for shaping the music, in the Sephardic liturgy more stress was laid upon the participation of the congregants, which gave the chant a simpler, more uniform rendering. The peninsular tradition ended with the expulsion of the Jews from Spain in 1492, to be revived in a modified, Europeanized form in the Jewish settlements in the Netherlands.

In Germanic countries JACOB ben MOSES MÖLLN in Mainz (1356-1427) and his disciples established the final regulation of the synagogue practice of the Ashkenazim, especially as to the music of the ritual. When in later centuries the Jews peregrinated to the eastern part of Europe, the *ḥazzanim* came under the influence of the Slavonic secular songs of their new environment, just as formerly the Sephardic song was shaped under Arabic influence.

The second important step in the formation of medieval Jewish musical practice was the final development of the *ta'amim* which were definitely stabilized in the tenth century in the so-called Tiberian system. This subject was discussed briefly earlier in our study (see p. 49); a more elaborate treatment would be beyond the scope of this book. There exist, however, a number of valuable treatises on this subject, where additional information may be gained.*

Zemirot

The third important factor for shaping the musical practice of the Diaspora Jewry had its origin outside the synagogue, in the Jewish home. It was the creation, or, more precisely, the crystallization, of a specific Jewish musical genre, the *zemirot*, table songs, used during and after the meal of the Eve of Sabbath, as well as during many other occasions.

The *zemirot* were considered a genuine creation of the Western communities. Yet such table songs were known much earlier in the Eastern settlements. Evidently the migrating Eastern rabbis brought the custom with them to Spain and Germany. There are records dating from as early as 870 c.e. which acknowledge the existence of table songs. From the *Book of Genealogies*, which narrates the family history of ʾAHIMAZ (publ. 1504), we read about ʾAARON the MYSTIC of Bagdad:

> As we were sitting at the table of the scholars in study with the head of the Academy, the teachers of the Law exclaimed: "Let us give praise, in pleasant and fervent song, with love and devotion to Him that is adored by myriads" . . . . then I began reverently to give praise in psalm and song to Him . . . there sat one of the elders in meditation, intently listening to my chanting.[4]

* See the author's *Bibliography of Jewish Music*, Nos. 1931–2155.

Though these were not *zemirot* in the proper meaning of the word, this "pleasant and fervent song" anticipates the mood and ethos of the table songs for domestic use.

While the Ashkenazim called *zemirot* the Hebrew hymns chanted in the intimacy of the family, the Sephardim applied the term to the psalms sung in the *Shaharit* (the early portion of the morning service). Early in the history of Ancient Israel, domestic table songs were a regular feature, although they were not called by this name. They were temporarily discontinued as a sign of mourning for the lost Sanctuary;[5] but evidently the prohibition of singing was never taken too literally, especially if the songs were devotional in character, as was the case of the table songs. Even then, some zealous rabbis insisted on abstention from such intimate melodies,[6] with not much result, however, as was already shown. Later, under the spell of the Cabala, the ancient custom was revived. The belief in the presence of heavenly guests at the Sabbath eve meal gave a powerful impetus to the singing of devotional Sabbath hymns.[7]

As to the melodies of such hymns, the heads of the families, being the leaders of the singing, were laymen who could only be expected to repeat the tunes they heard either in the world outside, or in the synagogue from their *hazzanim*. Of course, the florid chant of the *hazzan* could not be duplicated, nor even approximated, by members of the family, especially children. Yet, under the influence of that which the head of the household heard in the streets and in the synagogue, the pattern of *zemirot* took shape. This has eventually crystallized into a folksong type of melody which survived for centuries, retaining their original characteristics, if not their original tunes, even until our days. Such *zemirot* as *Shalom ʿAleychem, Ẓur mishelo ʾohalnu, Yah ribbon ʿolam,* though visibly under later East European influence, are nevertheless supposed to have originated in South German Ashkenazic communities. With the passing of time, the Ashkenazic melodies took on a chorale-like character akin to Church hymns, while the Sephardic tunes retained their more Oriental inflection.

Not all *zemirot* were of a devotional character. Particularly in Spain, under the spell of Moorish tunes, secular songs, both in

Hebrew and in the vernacular, found their way into the Jewish family. Among them were praises of wine and love, lullabies, wedding hymns and dance songs, all in a more or less accentuated rhythmic pattern, which had its repercussions even upon the synagogue songs. It is well known that the Arabs, in their secular music, employed certain rhythmic formulas which were supported and enlivened by bodily motions. To this came the unavoidable sequel whereby such rhythmical elements soon penetrated into the Jewish practice. By the tenth century Arabic tunes could be found in the synagogue services of Babylonia, Syria, Morocco, but mainly in Spain. Hence, the rhythmical song among the Jews of the Orient, and especially in Iberia, became synonymous with Arabic music.[8]

Under the influence of the lively rhythmicized Moorish tunes, the synagogue melodies in Spain were subjected to a slow but thorough transformation from the former Oriental, freely flowing melodic line into a square-shaped rhythmic design, thereby imparting new character to synagogue songs. This period was one of emasculation and de-Hebraization for synagogue music.[9]

As in former times, the rabbis castigated such procedures, and again with no practical result, since the pleasure of singing these lively tunes was too enticing to be eradicated by rabbinic disapproval. This type of sensuous song survived the centuries, for we find them much later in German communities. There, however, they became decorous in character and did not transgress the ethics established by religious precepts. They were merry, without containing anything which would be taken for licentiousness.

In Spain, on the other hand, if the melodies for the *zemirot* were not actually taken over from Arabic tunes, the Jewish writers of the lyrics "composed" their own melodies. Sephardic tradition is particularly rich in *zemirot* concluding the Sabbath, such as *Hamabdil, Bemoza'e Menuhah,* etc.

The most fertile of all writers of the *zemirot* was ISRAEL ben MOSES NAGARA (or NAJARA, 1555-1628), who composed no less than 650 hymns. He wrote his verses to pre-selected folk melodies and ditty tunes of the Levant. His collection, *Zemirot Israel*, was published at Safed in 1587; in 1599-1600 followed a second, enlarged edition, 'Olat Shabbat, published this time in Venice, and this soon became the most popular songbook among all the Oriental communities. In his collections the texts of the zemirot are arranged according to the memorized and unrecorded melodies he used, while the original Arabic, Turkish, Spanish, Greek, and Italian titles of the tunes are printed above the Hebrew verses. Most of these orally transmitted melodies have fallen into oblivion, so that we have only a vague idea how NAGARA's zemirot might have sounded.

Generally, melodies of zemirot have a short life; they scarcely survive a few generations. Meanwhile variants crop up, followed by other variants, obscuring the original melody, until it becomes almost unrecognizable; finally, another, more recent and more popular melody supplants the old one. The evolution of today's zemirot is certainly no different than what occurred in much earlier times.

As time went by the music of the zemirot surpassed the text in importance. In increasing numbers the paytanim wrote their poems according to the rhythm of a certain tune; others simply retained the melody without change and put a new text to it. Even some rabbis, in their zeal to prevent their congregants from singing words of questionable morals, would supply religious texts, keeping the melodies intact. This, in some instances, went so far as to imitate the sounds of the vowels of the original, secular texts. (See p. 239).

Just as in Spain, where the Arabic influence prevailed in shaping the zemirot, so in Central Europe the Gentile music, in its two extreme manifestations, Church hymns and street songs, was instrumental in creating an entirely different type of family songs. These songs developed to a point where "the Jewish table songs were the bridge between the human and the divine, where they were at once serious and jocular, and where they were at the same time prayers and merry glees."[10] On Friday evenings, especially in Germanic countries with their long winter nights, "the family would remain for hours round the table, singing zemirot led by the head of the household, the boys joining in vigorously. The girls sang choruses of their own, and husband and wife sometimes inaugurated the Sabbath with a duet sung to musical accompaniment."[11] The *zemirot* which needed instrumental accompaniment were sung before the Sabbath started; after the commencement of the Sabbath, generally no instruments were used (for exceptions see later).

There have been many attempts to establish literary parallels between ancient poems for graces and *zemirot*. These attempts have remained inconclusive, for the Hebrew table songs are a unique blend of the sacred and the secular. Many other nations had their table and drinking songs, which differ fundamentally in character and ethos from the Hebrew *zemirot*. So, for instance, HORACE's drinking song *Nunc est bibendum* is sometimes put in parallel with a *zemirah,* also some of the graces in the Christian *Hymnarium* which, in the eleventh century, was incorporated into the *Breviary*. All these parallels are inept. Medieval ascetism was not favorable to Christian table songs. Nevertheless, in the *Didascalia* or *Apostolic Constitution* there is a "Prayer for Dinner Time" (VII, 49). The curious fact about the *Didascalia* is that it was originally a Jewish Manual for proselytes, which, after some modifications, was adopted by the Early Church. This "Prayer" might be, therefore, an ancient abbreviation of the Jewish grace (or benediction) for *gerim* (converts).[12]

ALBINUS FLACCUS ALCUIN, a monk of Canterbury, and afterwards abbot of St. Martin at Tours (d. 804), wrote several poetic graces which have some affinities with *zemirot*. There are many more examples throughout the entire Middle Ages, up to the present time, of Christian table songs; with all their seeming similarities, they are lacking the "unique combination of adoration of God with genial appreciation of good cheer," which is the essence of Hebrew table songs.[13] The added touch of ecstasy, infused into the *zemirot* by medieval Mystics, vibrates even today in these songs, which are the products of the Jewish genius.

The day of Sabbath was always a time of joy for the Jews; the music used on Sabbath eve in the family circle served the purpose of making it a day of delight. This had particular significance in Germanic lands, where the persecutions of the Jews increased constantly, aggravating the miseries of everyday life until it became almost unbearable. The Jews took their refuge in the peace of the Sabbath; the only means of escape was their song.

The *zemirot* were, therefore, an important psychological factor for giving them some respite from the weekday tribulations and for keeping alive their longing and messianic hope for a better future. Thus, *zemirot* in Germanic countries meant more than simply enjoying music and singing; it was the retreat of the Jews from life's realities into an imaginary land of peace and bliss. This might also be the explanation for the fact that the most joyous *zemirot* were created in the darkest hours of Jewish existence.

The Cabala with its mystic ideas had a great impetus for the increase in the creation of *zemirot*. The Cabalists of the sixteenth century stressed particularly the power of song to enhance the devotion and to arrive at some mystic union with the Creator. The Sabbath song *Lekah Dodi*, which welcomes the Sabbath as the personified bride of Jewry, was a typical product of the Cabalistic trend. Its author, SOLOMON ha-LEVI ʾALḳABIẓ (see later), was especially encouraged by his teacher ISAAC LURIA (1544-1572) to compose this poem. LURIA himself was the author of such famous cabalistic songs as "ʿAzammer bi-Shevahin," "ʿAtkinu Seudatah," and others, which later became very popular among the Ḥasidim.

In subsequent centuries the East European Jews wrote numerous table songs in their own peculiar jargon; Ḥasidic music, especially, is rich in *zemirot*, both with and without words. About this type of inspirational hymn, more will be said later.

In a later period the diminutive appellation *zemerl* was introduced into the Yiddish vernacular denoting a secular tune or—if devotional—a nonliturgical melody.

Not all the borrowed secular melodies were adapted without changes for the *zemirot*; sometimes a modification was introduced under the influence of the traditional *nussaḥ* (prayer mode) which gave the erstwhile popular song a certain Jewish inflection. Eventually, by such changes, the original tune was almost eclipsed, and what remained was considered, by later generations, a genuine Jewish creation.

12

Early Synagogue Hymns

LIKE THE DEVELOPMENT OF THE ZEMIROT, THE CRYSTALLIZATION OF specific synagogue hymns was a slow process, subject to many extraneous influences, changes, and adaptations until at last a temporary final form was achieved.

The introduction of religious hymns (*piyyutim*) into the ritual appears to have been the reaction to the restrictions imposed by the Emperor JUSTINIAN I in 553 upon the Jews of the Byzantine Empire. This repressive act caused the Jews to create poetry that would enrich their religious services. This included appropriate hymns for holidays, and soon were likewise employed for the Sabbath day's service.

Among the earliest *paytanim* (poets), whose hymns are preserved, were JOSE ben JOSE (sixth century), YANAI (ca. 700), and, already in Arabic times, ELEAZAR KALIR (eighth century).

A pupil of SAʿADIAH GAON, DUNASH ben LABRAT (940-950), composed Hebrew poems in quantitative meter; this endeavor was short-lived, since Hebrew versification does not lend itself appropriately to the use of long and short syllables.

Whereas in many cases it is difficult to establish the exact time when a certain synagogue hymn came into being, it is sometimes possible to come close to it.

"ʾAdon ʿOlam," for instance, was written in the eleventh century by SOLOMON ibn GABIROL; "ʾAta hu" and "ʾEin kamoka" by MESHULLAM ben KALONYMOS (ca. 1100); "Yigdal" by DANIEL ben YUDAH (thirteenth century); the "Selihot" (penitential prayers) go even further back, allegedly to the sixth century; but since no names of poets or composers are known, this cannot be proven conclusively.

183

We possess, however, concrete data about a number of hymns, texts as well as music, which have survived and constitute even in our days the strong pillars of the varied Jewish religious services.

1. 'Alenu (Adoration). According to the ancient tradition, the text of it was written in the third century in Babylonia for the Musaf (additional service) of the High Holidays. It is recorded historically that Jews sang this hymn during the persecutions of the earlier Crusades, when they were forced to embrace Christianity, but instead they often preferred to be killed or burned. As on other occasions, dying martyrs sang the 'Alenu. There is a contemporary report about the mass execution in Blois, France, of Jews accused of ritual murder, who were burned on the stake in May 1171. EPHRAIM ben JACOB (1132-ca. 1200), a German Talmudist and poet, kept a Book of Historical Records, in which he mentions an eye-witness who wrote in a letter to R. JACOB of ORLEANS that "as the flames mounted high the martyrs (thirty-four men and seventeen women) began to sing in unison a melody

Mus. ex. No. 13

'Alenu (After Idelsohn, p. 148).

that began softly but ended in a full voice. The Christian people came and asked us: 'What kind of song is this, for we have never heard such a sweet melody?' We know it well," continued the letter writer, "for it was the song *'Alenu.*"[2]

The rabbi and cantor HERZ TREVES of Frankfurt a.M. (1470-1550) established the practice for the High Holidays, at which *'Alenu* should be recited softly by the congregation, while the *hazzan* sang the melody, a procedure which might have been very impressive.

The oldest written form of this hymn can be found in the manuscript volume of AHRON BEER, *hazzan* in Berlin, who notated it about 1765(?). Several European *hazzanim* wrote it down with some melodic variants, still its basic motives remained unchanged.

2. *Ha-Melek* (*The King*). This melody is part of the early morning service (*Shaharit*). According to sixteenth century sources this regulation was established in Worms by R. MEÏR of ROTHENBURG (1215-1293). However, it was not adopted everywhere; in 1300 it was still unknown in several German districts.

The following musical example is from a collection of Löw SÄNGER, *hazzan* of Munich (1840). Because of the relatively recent date of this notation its authenticity as an "old" synagogal song is rather doubtful.

Mus. ex. No. 14

Ha-melek *(After Idelsohn, p. 148).*

3. ʾAvot *(The Fathers, i.e., The Patriarchs).* R. Meïr of Roth-enburg is said to have introduced this melody into the ʿAmidah (the prayers recited while standing, "Silent Devotion"). Soon it

Mus. ex. No. 15

ʾAvot *(After Idelsohn, p. 149).*

took roots in the ritual and was already considered "traditional" in the seventeenth century.

The earliest notation of it can be found in the manuscript collection of AHRON BEER.

4. *Kaddish* (*Sanctification*), has quite a number of musical settings, the most important ones being those for the Sabbath and for the Three Festivals. Besides, there are many variants, such as the *Half Kaddish*, the *Full Kaddish*, and other altered forms employed for the various holidays as well. The following musical examples are taken from a manuscript volume of JOSEPH S. GOLDSTEIN, who was "bass singer" in Oberlauringen bei Schweinfurt on the Main, and who collected synagogal melodies which are stylistically typical for the end of the eighteenth century.

Mus. ex. No. 16

Kaddish I, II (After Idelsohn, pp. 151–152).

5. _Bar'chu (Blessing)_ is an integral part of every Jewish service. Its origin can be traced to the eleventh century; the _hazzan_ in Mainz ELIEZER ben MESHULLAM, surnamed "the Great," is said to have sung it in the Sabbath service "in a long tune," which probably meant the use of rich ornamentations. The report, however, that "for each occasion a special tune was invented," should not be taken literally; it rather seems to indicate that the _hazzanim_ used a kernel of a melody upon which they developed lengthy and diversified improvisations.

6. On the Ninth of ʾAb, the day of the destruction of the Temple, the elegy _ʾEli Ziyyon_ is sung. Although this tune is sometimes considered genuinely "Jewish," it is found in a German-Catholic Church hymnal printed in 1642; furthermore, it is similar (a) to a Spanish melody of the seventeenth century, and also (b) to a Slovakian folksong.

Mus. ex. No. 17

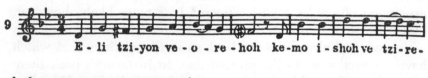

'Eli Ziyyon *(After Idelsohn, p. 168).*

17 a

The same tune discovered as a Spanish folksong of the seventeenth century. *(Ibid., p. 173).*

The same tune discovered as a Czechoslovakian folksong. (Ibid., p. 173).

17 b

IDELSOHN held that this melody originated in Spain and, in all likelihood, was carried to Central Europe by pilgrims and picked up among others by Jewish singers.[3] It is more likely, however, that it is one of those internationally known "migrating" melodies which we find already as far back as medieval times and which have survived even to the present day. In IDELSOHN's book there is a comparative table showing one such melody (pp. 222-225).

7. A special place among the traditional melodies is occupied by the *Kol Nidre*, the opening chant of the Yom Kippur Eve service. Both the text and melody have a colorful history. The words are Aramaic, but in some medieval prayerbooks a Hebrew version was used. The hypothesis that the *Kol Nidre* was introduced into the ritual for the sake of the Spanish Marranos, forcibly converted to Christianity, is erroneous, although the formula of dispensation from enforced vows and oaths might have been used in Spain by these pseudo-Christians. Already in the Gaonic period the prayer was part of the Yom Kippur ritual, but since its author is unknown, the exact time of its creation cannot be established.

The melody is one of the most famous in Jewish liturgy, but it has suffered from the many variants, changes, additions and embellishments applied to it through the centuries. While the basic motives, the opening portion as well as some of the middle parts, are very similar in all existing arrangements, there is probably no synagogue in which the melody is chanted in exactly the same manner, unless one of the modern printed versions of it is used; and even then, the individual taste of the *hazzanim* frequently causes drastic changes.

It is believed that the *Kol Nidre* melody dates from somewhere around the eleventh century, or even earlier and that the singing school of St. Gall had some influence in shaping it. St. GALL, who lived 550-645 c.e., was the founder of the Swiss-German monastery which in time developed a famous school of music and became a repository for the Church chant. It is rather far-fetched, however, to assume that this Christian singing school might have had any part in the shaping of the *Kol Nidre* melody or, for that matter, any other synagogue song.

As early as in the eleventh century the *Kol Nidre* was sung

three times as part of the opening liturgy on the eve of *Yom
Kippur*; a custom which has remained until our days. In olden
times the *hazzanim* used to begin it with a soft voice, increasing
in intensity with each repetition so that by the third time it was
sung with full voice. R. JACOB LEVI MÖLLN (1356-1427) used to
avail himself of different melodies for the repetitions, prolonging
the singing until nightfall, so that latecomers would participate
in this solemn pronunciamento. In our days the melody of the
Kol Nidre is kept identical all three times, except for some occasional embellishments by the *hazzanim* in the repetitions.

There are only a few basic motives in the *Kol Nidre* which
would claim to be "traditional," i.e., authentic. Here, the additions
and variations of the *hazzanim* have caused it great harm. The
moving simplicity of the melody is almost completely obscured
by the overabundance of "embellishments." There were numerous attempts at trying to separate the chaff from the grain;
the consensus is that probably no other synagogue melody contains so many grafted elements.

During Europe's Dark Ages the closing phrase of the *'Alenu*
was sometimes substituted for the last strain of the *Kol Nidre*. It
was assumed that this was done in remembrance of the martyrs
of Blois who, in 1171, were burned at the stake (see above). This
custom did not take roots in the liturgy; the fate of the martyrs
remained only as a haunting reminiscence without having been
anchored in the *Yom Kippur* ceremony.[4]

The oldest notated form of the melody is in AHRON BEER's
manuscript collection. There is an early notation of it from the
year 1720, and a later one from 1783. The following musical example (No. 18) is the later notation.

Mus. ex. No. **18**

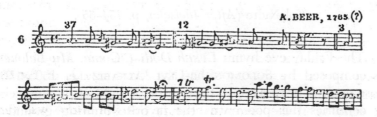

A. BEER, 1783 (?)

Kol Nidre (*After Idelsohn, p. 154–55*).

8. The Friday eve hymn *Lekah Dodi* ("*Come, My Beloved*") was composed by SOLOMON ha-LEVI 'ALḲABIẒ (c. 1505-1560), whose name is preserved in the acrostic of eight of its nine verses. For centuries this poem was the favorite hunting ground for

Jewish composers, Eastern and Western, professionals and amateurs, serious tunesmiths and folk bards. There was probably no
ḥazzan who did not try at least one musical setting to it. IDELSOHN
figured that there are about 2,000 musical settings to the poem.[5]
This is merely a guess, since no human effort or science could
ever hope to count the plethora of melodies, in print and, more
so, in manuscript, which were continuously pouring upon the
lyrics. In the Sephardic rite there is supposed to be one setting
which can be traced back to an ancient Moorish chant, and is
still sung in Sephardic synagogues.

Mus. ex. No. 19

LEKAH DODI (Moorish Chant)

Lekah Dodi *(Moorish Chant). (After F. L. Cohen, In:* J.E., VII, *pp.*
676–677.

   This melody, according to F. L. COHEN, is much older than the
text of *Lekah Dodi.*[6] COHEN gathers this from the rubric of old

prayerbooks, directing *Lekah Dodi* "to be sung to the melody of *'Shubi Nefshi li-Menuḥayeki'*, a composition of JUDAH ha-LEVI, who died nearly five centuries before 'ALḲABIẒ." This seems to be a remarkable occurrence indeed, because it shows the evolution and transformation of certain synagogue songs under the influence of purely external circumstances.

Among BENEDETTO MARCELLO's Hebrew intonations there is one of *Lekah Dodi* (No. VII), as he heard it sung by the Ashkenazic Jews of the Venetian ghetto. F. L. COHEN transcribed this melody, altering arbitrarily MARCELLO's double-time ($\frac{2}{2}$) signature into a triple-time signature ($\frac{3}{2}$), by which procedure the joyous character of this Sabbath hymn is perceptibly altered.[7]

Mus. ex. No. 20

Lekah Dodi *as notated by Benedetto Marcello (1724–1727)*.

In order to restore MARCELLO's double-time signature and to bring the intonation closer to the rhythmical, square-shaped pattern of the Ashkenazic synagogue melodies, we ventured to employ a different rhythmization. At the same time we were able to correct an obvious error committed by F. L. COHEN at the end of his transcription. It will be seen how this rhythmization, with its groups of sixteenth-notes, approaches the rhythmic pattern of the above quoted Moorish chant.

This modification was undertaken merely to show how a rhythmical change may bring the melody closer to the Ashkenazic pattern and, at the same time, impart to the seemingly elegiac

Mus. ex. No. 21

Lekah Dodi *rhythmically changed.*

melody of MARCELLO the character of a joyous hymn, as unmistakably conceived by the poet.

Of all the countless tunesmiths whose inspiration was kindled
by the poem of 'ALḲABIẒ, one composer must be singled out, who
without a doubt was the most prolific of them all in this respect.
He wrote no less than twelve melodies for one voice, a duet for
two voices, a setting for four-part male chorus and, in a separate
collection of twenty-five synagogue songs, several additional melodies for one voice to the same text. This composer was the *ḥazzan*
ISAAC JUDA EBERSCHT of the town of Offenbach on the Main
(1778-1850), the father of the famous operetta composer JACQUES
OFFENBACH.[8]

9. The ḤANUKKAH hymn *Maoz Ẓur* ("Rock of Ages") is in its
present form the synthesis of two German tunes; one is the
German folksong, *"So weiss ich eins was mich erfreut, das plüm-
lein auff preyter heyde,"* the melody which MARTIN LUTHER
adapted to his chorale-text, *"Nun freut euch lieben Christen
gmein,"* written in 1524; the other is a German battle hymn
known by the name of *"Benzenauer,"* composed in 1504, which
was very popular in Germany in the sixteenth century.[9] These
two German tunes might have penetrated into the ghetto and
here some enterprising *ḥazzan* must have fused them into one
tune which he used for the celebration of the Maccabean victory.

He borrowed the first four measures of Luther and, for the
middle part, he adopted the second half of the *"Benzenauer."* In
this composite form it was first sung in the family circle for the
kindling of the Ḥanukkah lights. Owing to its uplifting melodic
characteristics, however, it was soon introduced into the *Ḥanukkah* service in the synagogue.

Mus. ex. No. 22

The Ḥanukkah hymn Maos Ẓur (After Idelsohn, p. 168).

Mus. ex. No. 23

The origin of the Ḥanukkah hymn Maos Ẓur (After Idelsohn, p. 173).

Before this melody became popular, there may have been others set to the poem of *Maos Zur*. A reference dating back as far as 1450 states that the *paytan* BARUCH (BENEDICT) ARVILLER, in the introduction to his hymn *")Elohim hillalnu kol ha-yom"* made the comment: "To the tune (*b'niggun*) of *Maos-Zur Yeshuati*, I have composed this for . . . Ḥanukkah, in the year (5)210 /1450/."[10]

In the seventeenth century we know of several other compositions of *Maos Zur*. In 1606, R. ABRAHAM SAMUEL BACHRACH, one of the pupils of MAḤARIL of Prague, composed the Ḥanukkah hymn *"Shadai salli um'zudati, leko domin tehillah,"* which is simply a paraphrase of *Maos Zur*, to be sung to its tune.[11] In the year 1696, YUDAH LEIB ZLICHUBAR, in the preface of his poem *"Yah go'ali, zuri,)eli,"* states in Yiddish: "This hymn is to be sung to the tune in which many people sing *Maos Zur* on Ḥanukkah."[12]

In the ghetto of Venice, the Ashkenazim used to sing a different tune, which was notated and published by BENEDETTO MARCELLO in his *Estro poetico-armonico* (Venice, 1724-1727). (See mus. ex. 45, No. 4.) However, the version used by LUTHER for his chorale, together with the *"Benzenauer,"* because of its popular character and uplifting spirit, is today generally sung at Ḥanukkah celebrations.

HANOCH AVENARY made a thorough study of the origin of this melody, which definitely points to Central Europe.[13] He discovered in several Cantionales of the fifteenth and sixteenth century strains of this melody, particularly the initial phrase which is identical in all of them. These Cantionales are:

(1) *Cantional Franush* (1505, p. 121), preserved in the Krajske Vlastivedne Museum, in Hradei Kralova (Czechoslovakia). (See: Dobreslav Orel, *Cancional Franushov* (Prague, 1922), p. 43).

(2) *Cantional Neumarkt*, a manuscript of the year 1474 (Codex No. 58, p. 210 b). In the Archives of the Duchy of Vrazlav (Breslau).

(3) *Cantional Zwickau* (Codex No. 119, pp. 70a-71a). A photographic reproduction of it can be found at the Department of Musicology, University Jena (Germany).

In conclusion, AVENARY refers to the well-known fact that church music of the fifteenth and sixteenth centuries, particularly the Protestant chorales, were frequently adapted to, or taken over from, German folk songs. This also must have been the case of the *Maos Ẓur* melody. LUTHER may have heard it in the countries of Bohemia or its neighboring regions, and employed it as the melody for his chorale.

These and a number of other "authentic" synagogue songs are believed to have originated in the European Middle Ages. However, since their earliest musical notation (except the songs notated by MARCELLO) is found originally in some eighteenth-century manuscripts, their exact age is questionable.

For some *piyyutim* we have more reliable information as far as their time of origin is concerned. Thus, *Shalom ʿAleychem* is known to have been introduced by the Cabalists and is therefore no more than three hundred years old; *Yah Ribbon ʿOlam* was written by ISRAEL NAJARA and despite its Aramaic text has gained widespread popularity throughout the Jewish world; *Yom zeh meḥubod*, a poem also by NAJARA, was printed already in 1545; *ʾElijahu ha-Navi* was sung as early as the eleventh century by all Jewish communities.

According to Jewish belief, there are many more "traditional" melodies, even if the exact time of their creation cannot be ascertained. However, it is a curious fact that some songs which were considered traditional in the eighteenth century were not yet traditional in the seventeenth century. Furthermore, the nineteenth century looked upon some melodies as "traditional" which were not designated as such a century earlier. It is evident that the distinction of being traditional rests, for a melody, upon a very loose definition. Here, not only is the time element involved, but there is also an ever-changing esthetic evaluation. Even liturgical modifications have influenced such decisions, as well as the individual approach of the *ḥazzan*, whose sole judgment establishes in most cases the supposedly "final" criteria of the sanctity, i.e., "tradition" of a melody. It will be shown presently how the medieval *ḥazzanim* abused their functions as arbiters of synagogal music.

With the increased migrations of German Jews to the East, a new type of Ashkenazim developed. In time the Polish, Lithuanian, and Ukrainian Jews created not only their own religious, social, economic and cultural world, but also their own musical atmosphere, which was basically different from that of the "original" German and French Ashkenazim. Moreover, with the Ḥasidic movement a new type of song has been created, to which a subsequent chapter will be devoted.

Before we proceed with a survey of the incunabula of Jewish music, which delve into the musical meaning of the Jewish accents (ta'amim), it is essential that we first review a number of manuscripts, in which Jews have expressed themselves in a poetico-musical language. Although no musical documents are preserved prior to the fifteenth century, we are fortunate in that recent discoveries in the field of poetry have given us insights concerning the unfaltering urge of the Jew to express himself musically.

The earliest known of these relics is an anthology of poems, of epic and folksong character, compiled by a wandering Jewish minstrel around the year 1382. No other information about this minstrel has survived. This anthology, written in the German-Jewish idiom, employing Hebrew letters, contains such disparate items as the German Gudrun-epos, Jewish prayers, rhymed fables, an even an epic poem about Abraham.[14] The melodies of such wandering minstrels were undoubtedly familiar to Jewish audiences, and were evidently sung well into the seventeenth century. (It may be interesting to compare this minstrel with WÖLFLEIN of LOCHEIM, who himself may have been a wandering *shpilman;* see p. 149.)

During the fourteenth and fifteenth centuries there were a number of Yiddish song collections, labeled by the rabbis *"törichte Bücher"* ("foolish books"). These collections dealt with secular subjects, among which was the story of the knight *"Ditrich fun Bern,"* and others. The melodies of such secular poems not only penetrated the synagogue but even Talmudic schools. For instance, the halakic song *"Hilkheta k'man"* (fifteenth century), was sung *"be-niggun"* (to the melody) of *"Herzog Ernst."* Another song, *")Ahavath ha-kesef"* (the desire [love] for money") was sung *be-niggun "Hoch rief der Wächter."* Even religious songs sung in Yiddish penetrated the synagogue, a practice which enraged MAHARIL (JACOB MOSES HALEVI, 1355-1427) and caused him to raise his voice against such abuses.[15] There were numerous rabbinical prohibitions against these abusive practices, which attest to the wide distribution of such secular melodies among the Jews.

Where did the Jews learn these tunes? They must have heard them sung by the Christians among whom they lived and adapted them for their own use. This was evidently easy in view of the close linguistic relationship which existed between the German vernacular and Yiddish, as spoken at that time.

One such Yiddish collection enjoyed immense popularity: the *Shemuel-Book of Moshe Esrim Wearba*.[16] It was already acclaimed in the fifteenth century, and the melody of it was certainly well known to *kol Yisrael* ("all Israel"), as indicated in the preface of the foremost edition of Augsburg (1544). Literary historians assume that it was the work of a Yiddish *shpilman*. However, this *shpilman* could not have been an ordinary wandering minstrel, who sang and played for all festive occasions, like the *badḥanim* of later centuries. There are certain intellectual qualities in this book, which indicate that its author was an educated person. It appears that he was knowledgeable in the Bible, and to some extent in rabbinical literature. In addition, he was familiar with German folklore. With these facts in mind, it is surmised that the unknown author of the *Shemuel-Buch* was a learned man, or possibly an itinerant preacher.[17]

One melody, which was particularly ascribed to the *Shemuel-Buch*, and for which no notation exists, was claimed to be very popular among the Jews in those times, and was used for the singing of a number of secular poems. How this melody could be linked to the German *"Hildebrandston,"* having furthermore alleged elements of German folksongs as well as Christian church melodies, is merely an overly gross speculation.[18]

Among other similar epic poems was a Yiddish version of the Book of Daniel, the *Daniel-Buch* (printed in Basel 1557). In its preface is found the indication to sing it in *"weis un dôn"* ("in the mode and tune") of the *Shemuel-Buch*.

Several similar Biblical epics in Yiddish are preserved, e.g., the *Melochim-Buch*, an adaptation of the Books of Kings I and II, with some textual additions taken from Chronicles II. Its author, like that of the *Shemuel-Buch,* must also have been an educated person, knowledgable in the Biblical commentaries of RASHI (1040–1105), REDAḲ (R. DAVID ḲIMḤI, 1160–1235), and RALBAG (R. LEVI ben GERSHOM, 1288–1344). He paraphrased several Talmudic passages and—like the author of the *Shemuel-Buch*—was familiar with German epic literature of that epoch. Its author is also unknown, though he may have been likewise a wandering intellectual, a *shpilman* of a higher order. A number of them left Germany during the fourteenth and fifteenth centuries, on account of the plague which ravaged Germanic lands, and settled in Italy. They transferred their religious institutions to their new homeland, carrying with them the Yiddish idiom, which they practiced assiduously in their communication with the stream of new refugees from Germany. This explains how a number of Yiddish literary products survived in Italy, while those of Germanic lands were undoubtedly destroyed.

Nothing is known about the presumable melody of the *Melochim-Buch,* like that of the *Shemuel-Buch;* we can only assume that there was a prescribed tune for it. Perhaps the *Melochim-Buch* was not as popular as the *Shemuel-Buch,* since its melody is not alluded to so often as that of the *Shemuel-Buch.*

We are better informed about the melody of another Yiddish epic poem, the *Baba-Buch,* translated in 1507 from the Italian by ELIAS LEVITA, or 'ELIYAH BAḤUR (i.e., "bachelor," as he signed himself, 1469–1549). Born in the hamlet of Ipsheim, near Neustadt, he emigrated as a young man to Italy, where he became a famous lexicographer and grammarian. Besides his grammatical works in Hebrew, among the *Sefer Masoret ha-Masoret* (The Tradition of the Tradition), he earned great recognition in the field of Yiddish literature. He adapted two Italian chevalieresque novels into Yiddish and introduced the Italian *ottava rima* into Yiddish poetry. The two novels were *Paris un Viena,* and the *Baba-Buch,* the latter dealing with the adventures of the Italian knight BABA d'ANTONA.[19]

LEVITA was at times referred to as "the last Yiddish troubadour," an epithet which truly cannot be applied to him, because— as we explained earlier, a Jew never could become a troubadour.

In medieval times, this profession was reserved exclusively to knights of noble lineage.

The melody of the *Baba-Buch* was widely diffused. There are a number of references about it in Yiddish literature. The introduction of the *Baba-Buch* contains a note of the translator (LEVITA), saying:

> Aber der *niggun* der darauf wird gehen,
> Den kann ich nit geben zu verstehen,
> Denn einer kann *Musiga* (*sic*) oder *tulpah*(?)
> So wollt ich ihn wohl haben geholfen.
> Aber ich sing' es mit einem *welschen* Gesang,
> Kann er drauf machen ein bessern,
> So hab er dank.

> (About the *niggun* which goes with it,
> I cannot explain it.
> If one knows music or *tulpah* [an
>   incomprehensible term],
> I could have helped him.
> But I sing it to an *Italian* tune,
> And if somebody can make a better one,
> He should be thanked for it.)

Evidently, "somebody" really found a "better" melody, otherwise it would not have gained such a widespread popularity. The new melody survived until the seventeenth century, at which time this melody was sung to a poem for a highly "official" occasion. It was the song celebrating the wedding of the Austrian Emperor JOSEPH I (reign. 1705–1711). The title of it was "Ein schön *Freuden-Lied* zur Hochzeit des römischen Kaisers JOSEPH und Kaiserin Prinzessin AMALIA WILHELMINE, etc.," with the indication: *Melodie: Baba-Buch*.[20]

The Ashkenazim of Germany adopted also the *"Bruder-Veits-Ton,"* and—among others—the *"Stüblein-Weise,"* which is notated in the *Locheim Songbook*, discussed above (see p. 142).

STEINSCHNEIDER, in his *Bodleian Catalogue*, quotes numerous other songs (poems), whose authors have referred to specific melodies, such as: *"Ach Gott wie bin ich ein verirrter Mann"* (Cat.

Bodl. 3625); *"Es frie (?) sich auf ein junger Markgraf"* (C.B. 3627); a bridal song to the tune of *"Ich hab mir vor Allen, Nach meinen Gefallen, Ganz auserkoren, Und hochgeboren"* (C.B. 3643); another bridal song to the melody of *"Gut Schabbes"* (C.B. 3681); a song about some important events in Hamburg, Melodie: *"Ein Mahl dass ich zu Lust bekam"* (C.B. 3636); a *ķinah* (dirge) about the great *sreifah* (conflagration) in Frankfurt a.M. (Jan. 15, 1711), to be sung to the melody of *Haman in the "Ahaschwerosch-Spiel"* (publ. in Frankfurt a.M. 1708, see p. 370), (C.B. 3647); the *"Shlomo Melech Lied,"* to the melody of the *Shemuel-Buch* (C.B. 3695); and others (Nos. 3644, 3650, 3688, 3687, 3695, etc.).

On August 22, 1614, VINCENZ FETTMILCH led a group of bandits through the *Judengasse* of Frankfurt a.M., where he chased all the Jews from the ghetto and plundered their homes. In February, 1616, an imperial commissioner escorted them back in a solemn procession, with blaring trumpets and kettle-drums. About these events, ELCHANAN HELEN ben ABRAHAM composed a Hebrew poem with some inserted German stanzas, entitled *"Megillah Vintz—Vintz-Hans-Lied,"* which was to be sung to the melody of *"Die Schlacht von Pavia"* (The Battle of Pavia). This poem was printed first in 1616 and reprinted many times thereafter.[21]

The treasure trove of tunes serving as model melodies for Yiddish poems must have been infinitely larger, since those quoted by STEINSCHNEIDER represent only poems which were preserved in print, the melodies of which remained unrecorded. There is, however, an indication which hints at the origin of some of the tunes which were popular among the Jews. The *Bodleian Catalogue* mentions *"Fünf schöne Lieder"* (Five beautiful songs, C.B. 3671), carrying the following indications as for the tunes to be used:

1. *Ich hab mein Lust ins weite Feld*
2. *Der grimmig Tod*
3. *Herzlich tut mich verlangen*
4. *Sollt ich denn nit klagen*
5. *sine melod.*

Among these, Nos. 1 and 2 could have been German folksongs, while 3 and 4 Protestant chorales (in fact, JOHANN SEBASTIAN BACH used the text of No. 3 for eleven of his chorales).

Furthermore, a number of poems, part German and part Yiddish, were preserved either in individually printed sheets, or in manuscript collections and anthologies. Two such anthologies comprised that of MENAḤEM OLDENDORF (1517), and that of EISIK WALLICH (second half of the seventeenth century). Most of the poems indicate the tunes to which they are to be sung, some of them refer to Jewish songs, some to Christian melodies, and the remainder to German folksongs.

Finally, we must refer to the epic poem " *'Akedath Jizḥak*" (The Sacrifice of Isaac), which was widely circulated among the Jews in Germanic lands. The earliest known manuscript of it is dated 1574, and it was repeatedly printed in the seventeenth century. The poem starts: *"Jüdischer Stamm von rechter Art, der von Abraham Abinu geboren ward"* (Jewish tribe of noble kind, which was begot by our Father Abraham). The melody of this poem must have been very popular, since among the relatively few preserved poems there are three times references to it.[22] While the names of most of the poets are preserved in acrostics, it is unfortunate that the music of the poems did not survive.

13

Jewish Musical Publications and Unpublished Manuscripts between the Sixteenth and Eighteenth Centuries

WE HAVE SEEN HOW THE JEWISH MUSICAL SYSTEM IN SPAIN GREW from modest beginnings and how the work of coeval Jewish writers on this subject failed to have any repercussions upon the further development of general musical theory.

This was different in countries where the Ashkenazim lived. In Germany, about the year 1500, there had suddenly risen an interest in Hebrew language and Hebrew philosophy. The language of the Bible was elevated to a new science and admitted as a subject of learning to many universities and other scholarly institutions. Within a short time, the participation of non-Jews in this new field of learning took on such proportions that the clergy had to raise its voice against the "sacrilege" connected with the study of Hebrew.[1]

One of the most ardent participants of the new science was the Catholic priest and scholar JOHANNES BÖSCHENSTEIN (1472–1540).[2] He taught Hebrew in various Christian institutions in Germany, had many Jewish friends and evidently attended synagogue services, where he took interest in the Biblical cantillation of the Jews. With his inquisitive mind he tried to formulate rules for chanting and, probably with the aid of his Jewish friends, established these rules in writing. As BÖSCHENSTEIN had a substantial musical training, he fixed, for the first time in musical notation, the exact meaning of the Hebrew accents found in the Scriptural text.[3] Before him, AARON ben MOSHEH ben ASHER, in

Tiberias (around 900), attempted to explain in words the rules of Biblical cantillation and its modal aspects. His treatise, *Diḳduḳe ha-ta'amim,* first published 1515 in Venice, is preserved in several copies. Although it might have been written before his time, it is generally attributed to him. His erudite explanation was in vain, because the tonality of Jewish music connot be defined theoretically without the aid of musical notation. This also applies to similar attempts made by other learned Jewish grammarians of later centuries, among them YEHUDAH HAYYUY, KALONYMOS ben DAVID,[4] SIMON DURAN ben ZEMAH,[5] and also the ubiquitous ABRAHAM ben DAVID PORTALEONE who, as we shall see, dabbled in all the sciences of his days.[6] All these attempts remained fruitless.

BÖSCHENSTEIN was the first to succeed, because he realized that the musical meaning of the *ta'amim* could not be explained without the aid of musical examples. He prepared his notation for the Hebrew Grammar of JOHANNES REUCHLIN (1455-1522), printed in Hagenau 1518. (Illustration 30.) REUCHLIN's book reproduces the musical equivalent of the accents on staves of five lines, printed from right to left, in mensural notes, with the Hebrew names of the accents under each musical example.[7] His notation is of utmost value for Jewish musical science and has remained almost unchanged to the present day. It is one of the chief sources for a knowledge of the musical meaning of the medieval accents.

REUCHLIN as well as BÖSCHENSTEIN not only left us their musical transcriptions of the Biblical accents, but both attempted to note down even more extensive portions of Jewish synagogue chants. REUCHLIN's notation (1518) of an Ashkenazic Pentateuch melody was incorporated in an organ composition by one of his pupils, CHRISTOPH SCHILLING.[8] And, in BÖSCHENSTEIN's hand, there is in the Bavarian State Library at Munich a notation of the Pentateuch and Psalm modes (Cod. Hebr. 401).[9]

The beginning of the sixteenth century witnessed the awakening of humanism in Central Europe and of the growing *rapprochement* between Christian and Jewish scholars. Among the Jewish writers of importance, JOHANAN ALLEMANO deserves mention. He was the friend as well as the "teacher" of the famous cabalist PICO della MIRANDOLA (1450–1533). During these times, the rela-

Mus. ex. No. 24a

The Pentateuch accents in Reuchlin's De accentibus . . . (Hagenau,
1518).

tionship between Jewish and Christian writers as "teachers" and
"pupils" should not be taken in the literal sense. It was more by
an exchange of ideas and by discussions that this cross-fertiliza-
tion took place. Thus, WIDMANSTADT, a pupil of REUCHLIN and

Mus. ex. No. 24b

Reuchlin's Pentateuch accents in modern notation.

a friend of AEGIDIUS of VITERBO, spoke with great admiration of his "teachers" DAVID ben YAḤYA ben JOSEPH of Lisbon (1465–1543) and of BARUCH of BENEVENTUM. This last-named scholar was the first to introduce the *Zohar*, with the aid of AEGIDIUS, among Christian writers. AEGIDIUS was the pupil of ELIAS LEVITA, the Hebrew grammarian and lexicographer of note, who made also important contributions in the field of Yiddish literature (see p. 201). REUCHLIN himself was a pupil of JACOB YEḤIEL LOANZ, a "physician in ordinary" to the Emperor FREDERICK III (1415–1493), and of ʿOBADIAH SFORNO at Rome (1498).

Jewish scholars contributed to JOHANN BUXTORF's *Bibliotheca Rabbinica* (1613), to JOHANN CHRISTOPH WOLF's *Bibliotheca Hebraica* (1715–33, 4 vols.), and mainly to GIULIO BARTOLOCCI's *Bibliotheca Magna Rabbinica* (1675–1693, 4 vols.), whose entire material was indebted to the research of his teacher, a converted Jew, YEHUDA JONA ben ISAAC (1588–1668).[10]

STEINSCHNEIDER cites many other examples for mutual endeavors of Jewish and Christian authors, and further states that "for centuries, the Biblical scholars and students of Hebrew literature, from REUCHLIN to the Professors DELITZSCH and EWALD, were, like JEROME, directly or indirectly pupils of Jews."[11]

Prior to BÖSCHENSTEIN's pioneering attempt, Jewish music has been printed to JOHANNES FOENISECA's *Grammatica Hebraica*, published in Augsburg in 1515 (mus. ex. No. 25). This is the earliest known example of Jewish music in print.

After BÖSCHENSTEIN, other attempts were made to reproduce the *ta'amim* in musical notation. The most important ones are by the following authors:

SEBASTIAN MÜNSTER (1489-1552), in his *Sefer ha-ta'amim* (*Accentum Hebraicorum brevis expositio*). This is an excerpt from ELIA LEVITA's treatise *Tob Ta'am*, first published in Venice in 1538, second edition in Basel in 1539 (mus. ex. No. 26).

JOHANNES VALENSIS (sixteenth century), *Opus de prosodia Hebraeorum* (Paris, 1545). This work contains, in its Appendix,

Mus. ex. No. 25

The earliest known printed notation of Hebrew music. In: Johannes Foeniseca, Grammatica Hebraica (Augsburg, 1515), p. 2.

Mus. ex. No. 26

INSTITVTIO HEBRAEA
est luna filius diei suæ.

Sextus תְּלִישָׁא קְטַנָּה id est,triplex
paruum,qui & תַּלְשָׁא uocatur.

Septimus שׁוֹפֵר מוּנַח id est,cornu
repositũ,& potest ubiq; poni. Hic quo-
que uocatur שׁוֹפֵר עִלּוּי quando mox
præcedit regem zarka, aut æthnahtha,
aut zakeph caton. Quãdo autem alios
reges præcedit , uocatur schophar munah.

Octauus שׁוֹפֵר מַהְפַּךְ id est, cornu reuersiuũ,& poni solet in secun.& ul.

Nonus est שׁוֹפֵר עִלּוּי id est,cornu
eleuatum . uocaturq; etiam alio nomine יֶשֶׁר & potest ubiq; poni.

Vltimus uocat שׁוֹפֵר מְבַרְבֵּל id est,
cornu sustinens,& ponit in fine. Húc di-
cunt figurari sicut uersum mahpach cũ
duplici mercha. Ex his itaq; ministris,
semper aliqs uel aliqui præcedũt reges,
cõmunius tñ munah. Verum de his sa-
tis.

eis. Quod si qs plenius de eis cupiat in-
formari,ille legat Capnionis prosodiã.

Sequuntur nunc musicorum accen-
tuum melodiæ,ne quid desit curiositati.

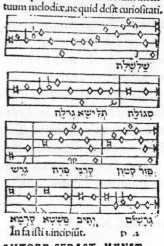

In fa isti ...incipiũt. p. 2

INSTITVTIO HEBRAEA

AVTORE SEBAST. MVNST.

Variant inter has melodias nõnul-
læ ab illis , quas Capnion in sua signa-
uit prosodia , nempe quas ego
ipse ab עִבְרִיִּים בַּהֲגִים
non semel cantilla-
ri audiui.

p 3 Versr

The Hebrew accents. In: Sebastian Münster, Sefer ha-ta῾amin *(Basel, 1539).*

Mus. ex. No. 27

The Hebrew Accents. In: Johannes Vallensis, Opus de prosodia Hebraeorum *(Paris, 1545).*

Mus. ex. No. 28

The Hebrew accents. In: Athanasius Kircher, Musurgia universalis Rome, 1650).

the musical notation of the *regum ac ministrorum* (the Kings and the Ministers) of the Hebrew accents (mus. ex. No. 27).

ATHANASIUS KIRCHER (1602–1680), in his *Musurgia Universalis, sive ars magna Consoni et Dissoni* (Rome, 1650, 2 vols.), reproduced the Sephardic tradition of the Pentateuch chant (mus. ex. No. 28).

JULIUS BARTOLOCCI (1613–1687), in his short essay *De Hebraeorum musica brevis dissertatio,* has given us, among other things, the musical notation of the Biblical accents used by the German, Spanish and Italian Jews of his time. These were published in his *Bibliotheca Magna Rabbinica* (Rome, 1675–1693), vol. IV, pp. 429-31, 434-41.[12]

We may note in passing that Vol. 2 of the same opus contains another chapter devoted to Jewish music. *"De Psalmorum libro, Psalmis et Musicis Instrumentis Hebraeorum, Rabbinorum Sententiae,"* in which all the rabbinical sources concerning Hebrew music and musical instruments are enumerated.

The Preface of the Bible published by ERNEST DANIEL JABLONSKI in Berlin (1699) contains a transcription of the Pentateuch and Prophet modes, according to the Sephardic tradition, made by the physician DAVID PINNA of Amsterdam.[13] (See Idelsohn, *Thesaurus,* Vol. V, ex. 302.)

In addition to the printed musical notations of the Biblical *ta'amim,* which appeared initially in the early sixteenth century and continued to our own days with all sorts of variants, improvements and deviations, other melodic material of the Ashkenazim began to appear in print from the middle of the seventeenth century.

Thus, JOHANN STEFAN RITTANGEL published in 1644 a *Haggadah* for *Pesaḥ* which contains two melodies for soprano with bass.[14]

BARUCH ben MOSHEH of PROSNITZ, a converted Jew (better known under his baptized name FRIEDRICH ALBERT CHRISTIANI) was the author of another *Haggadah,* published in 1677, in which three Passover songs are included in mensural notation.[15] It is significant that at the end of his life this convert returned to the fold of Judaism.

ABRAHAM CACERES furnished two liturgical songs to IMMANUEL

Mus. ex. No. 29

עַל נִגּוּן זֶה חִבֵּר הַמְחַבֵּר הַפִּזְמוֹן שֶׁל שַׁבָּת וּמִילָה וּתְפִילִין מַלְאָכְתּוֹ הַכִּוּנוּ כְּכָתַב עַל יַד מִי שַׁבְּקִי בְּחָכְמָה זוּ יוֹתֵר
בְּמֶּנּוּ וְהוּא אִישׁ תָּם וְיָשָׁר כ׳ אַבְרָהָם קָאסִירִס מֵעִיר חָאת לְחֶזְקַת הַגְּבִיר כ׳ יְהוּדָא מַאוּרְבִּינוֹ יִצְ״וּ אוֹהֵב חָכְמָה זוּ :

Music in Emmanuel Ḥay Ricchi's Sefer hon ʾashir *(Amsterdam, 1731),
p. 4. The single Hebrew letters below the music refer to the corresponding lines of Ricchi's poem on the following page. The second
poem contains, in an acrostichon, the author's name.*

ḤAY RICCHI's "*Sefer Hon 'Ashir* (Amsterdam, 1731). To these RICCHI added appropriate texts. These are Judaeo-Portuguese melodies in a rather awkward notation, which do not expand our knowledge of the Sephardic tradition (Mus. ex. 29).

For the propagation of their religious tenets, the Reformation and Counterreformation made ample use of a most potent medium for community singing, by publishing numerous songbooks. Jews had to wait some time for a printed songbook of their own. The first of this kind came into being in Fürth (1727) under the title *Simḥat ha-Nefesh* (*The Delight of the Soul*) (Illustrations No. 31, 32). It contains thirteen poems of the Judaeo-German writer ELCHANAN-HENLE KIRCHHAN, poems that have partly religious and partly ethical contents and are written in a didactic vein, without genuine poetic spirit. The aim of these poems was to prevent the author's coreligionists from singing vulgar German tunes for liturgical purposes, a practice which became evidently too strongly ingrained in synagogue singing. He adopted German melodies of the post-Baroque idiom of his time, or may have composed some himself, imitating that particular style. KIRCHHAN stresses the fact that the tunes were written down by an expert musician.

The songs were destined for the following liturgical occasions: (1) Friday evening, (2) Sabbath morning, (3) Sabbath evening, (4) New Moon, (5) High Holidays, (6) Tabernacles, (7) Ḥanukkah, (8) Purim, (9) Passover, (10) Shabuot, (11) Circumcision, (12) Bridal song, and (13) Daily song. Irrespective of its purely musical value, the importance of the book as the first Jewish songster warrants its inclusion in our study since it contains melodies in modern notation (Mus. ex. No. 30) (after Idelsohn).

The musical settings of these songs as well as the contents of their texts are rather uninspired. Congregational singing among the Jews must have been on a rather low level if KIRCHHAN considered his songster an improvement in this respect. The situation among the French Ashkenazim could not have been much better either, since most of their synagogue melodies were old French or Provençal folksongs.[16]

KIRCHHAN's songbook is the only printed publication of Jewish

Mus. ex. No. 30

The tunes in modern notation of Kirchan's Simḥat ha-Nefesh.

music in the eighteenth century, a regrettably inadequate output
as compared to the multitude of similar songsters of the Christian
world during the same period. Nevertheless, it is the first gentle
stirring of Jewish musical initiative, however subdued and handicapped by ghetto walls it may have been. This situation was
radically changed by the Emancipation. In the nineteenth century a great many German-Jewish songsters were published, following the reform movement with its repercussions upon Jewish
life, ritual and music. The full story of this development, however,
is outside the scope of our investigations. It has its own rich
literature, from which relevant information may be obtained
about the transformations caused by the German reform.

If printed synagogue melodies in the eighteenth century were
restricted to those in KIRCHHAN's book, we are more fortunate to
have a number of compilations in manuscript, from which we may
gain a good knowledge about the liturgical music practice of
that epoch.

The oldest handwritten collection of synagogue songs dates
from 1744, and contains 302 items, all written in the style of the
pre-classical era; the texts are missing, but most of the melodies
have Hebrew titles, thus indicating at least in which parts of the
service they were used. Around 1930 the original manuscript
was in the possession of ARNO NADEL (Berlin), who called it the
Hannoverian Compendium, and gave a detailed description of
it,[17] with the reproduction of some musical examples. (Mus. ex.
No. 31.)

To begin with, the melodies of this collection are of a definitely
instrumental character. Furthermore, they are headed by terms
such as "Sarabande," "Aria," "Minuet," "Italian Aria"— all names
of the various movements of the instrumental "Suite" or "Partita"
of the seventeenth–eighteenth centuries. NADEL poses the obvious
question: "How is it possible that such instrumentally smacking
tunes could be intoned by the Cantor?" He gives an explanation,
and a rather embarrassing one, namely that these tunes were
overtures or finales to the synagogue songs proper, "chiefly rendered by the human voice." Now, the counterquestion is: what
might have induced the unknown scribe of this "Compendium"
to notate the secondary portions of the synagogue melodies, the

preludes and postludes, and leave out the "body" of the sacred songs? It would be more logical to assume that this collection represents *real* synagogue songs, the style of which was completely assimilated to the music of the existing environment. NADEL himself acknowledges this when he says that "we must be grateful to find in this magnificent collection *genuine ancient Hebrew tunes*." Where he errs is that these are *not* Hebrew tunes, but melodies which were either taken over from secular sources, or purposely devised imitations of tunes from the surrounding milieu. By this, the "Compendium" is at best a forerunner of the nineteenth-century trend of assimilation of synagogue music to the style and technique of the time.

Mus. ex. No. 31

Ḳaddish *for the High Festivals. From the* Hannoverian Compendium (*After Arno Nadel*).

There are a number of other synagogue songs, hymns and melodies preserved in more or less authentic notations. In general they represent a true picture of the trend to adapt and adopt anything that appealed to the ears of a *ḥazzan*. Even while closed up within the ghetto walls and forced to live a relatively isolated life, the *ḥazzanim*, responsible for the quality of the music performed at sacred services, had to follow as closely as possible the currents of the musical styles of the surrounding world.

For this reason it is impossible for us to apply exact criteria
for the "antiquity" of Jewish melodies. Unfortunately, we do not
possess any notated examples of synagogue melodies prior to the
seventeenth century, save for the few, considered "traditional,"
which must be approached with utmost caution.

The Ashkenazic *hazzanim* began laying the groundwork for the
compilation of synagogue melodies to liturgical texts in the early
seventeenth century. This mostly for their own use and, of course,
with no historical interest to preserve the musical heritage of the
Jewish sacred music. The earliest of such collections known to us
is that of ABRAHAM SAGRI (fl. c. 1581), *hazzan* of the Ashkenazic
congregation in Casale Monferrato. He eventually transmitted
the compiled synagogue melodies to his disciple and successor
DAVID FINZI, who later became a *hazzan* in Modena. Of this collection only one item, the Psalm mode, has survived.[18]

The eighteenth century brought us other important sources for
our knowledge of Jewish music, or what was considered "Jewish"
at those times. EDUARD BIRNBAUM (1855–1920), Cantor at Königsberg (Germany), an indefatigable collector of Jewish musical
items (literature and music, printed and in manuscript), left to
posterity a collection, unique in its multifarious contents. After
his death, the collection was acquired by the Hebrew Union
College in Cincinnati.[19] Among the many invaluable manuscripts
of Jewish music there is a huge thesaurus of synagogue songs of
the eighteenth century in several volumes, compiled by AHRON
BEER (1738–1821), Cantor in Berlin from 1765 to 1821. The manuscripts bore the date 1782 (1785?), at which time the collection
was probably finished.

BEER was an avid compiler of compositions, sacred and secular,
written by many of his contemporaries. His collection contains
over 1200 pieces, marked with the dates of the compositions and,
in many cases, with the name of the composer. Among others, it
contains the oldest written form of *Kol Nidre*, dated 1720, and
another version of it marked 1783, both of which have already
been referred to. Other religious compositions, especially for the
High Holidays, preserved in this volume show no discernible
differences from their present form. It may be assumed, therefore,

that at least these traditional songs were already known, though only orally, in the seventeenth century.

Another volume by BEER, written neatly in his own hand in 1791, is a collection of 447 synagogue compositions, probably for his own use, arranged for the entire cycle of the year, for all Sabbath, High Holidays, and minor festival services. The tunes throughout this volume are all for a single voice, sometimes marked "singer," or "bass."[20]

Through the names of the composers which BEER has provided for each item we learn the existence of several synagogue composers about whom there are no other records. Among them there is a *ḥazzan* by the name of MOSHE PAN, whose name is prefaced by the title Rabbi; this might very well have been professional blandishment from BEER to a fellow singer. More appropriate is his calling MOSHE PAN *"Ha-meshorer Gadol"* (The Great Singer), by which epithet PAN's real profession is revealed. He must have been a prolific composer of synagogue songs, as evidenced by the 144 items in BEER's collection.

IDELSOHN succeeded in shedding some light upon this composer by proving that the name PAN is the Jewish pronunciation of a place called Peine near Hildesheim in Germany; the archives of this city contain indeed the names of several MOSHE PEINES, who were citizens there.[21]

In addition, BEER's collection contains 51 items by a rabbi-*ḥazzan*-composer YIZḤAḲ ḤAZZAN of Glogau, who was the teacher of another famous *ḥazzan*, ISRAEL LÖWY (1773–1832). LÖWY was the first to organize a group of synagogue singers with whom he toured European countries. He was known as various times by the names of ISRAEL GLOGAU, ISRAEL FÜRTH, ISRAEL MAINZ, and ISRAEL STRASSBURG, according to the places where he held cantorial offices and composed the songs which made his name famous during his lifetime. He must have possessed a beautiful voice, and was so renowned in Bavaria that the reigning duke invited him to sing the tenor part of Haydn's *Creation,* a rare distinction for a Jewish cantor.

Twelve items in BEER's collection are by MEYER LEON (c. 1740-1800), whom BEER calls "LEON singer of England." He was the composer of the well-known *"Leoni-Yigdal"* still sung in today's synagogues, and even in Christian churches to an altered text. About his life and achievements IDELSOHN's book contains pertinent information.[22]

The second part of BEER's collection was started by him in 1765 and was partially written about 1790–1799 by the "bass" singer JOSEPH GOLDSTEIN, who incorporated sixteen pieces of his own. According to the catalogue of this second volume, it contains 1,200 items and, among others, compositions of otherwise little known *hazzan*-composers such as ABRAHAM SINGER (2 pieces), WOLF BASS (1), LÖB WOLF (11), YEKASIEL MESHORER (4), YUDA SCHATZ (2), YEKEL SINGER (1), and SHOLOM FRIEDE (16).

Most of the synagogal pieces collected by GOLDSTEIN bear no specific Jewish characteristics and they lack an individual physiognomy. These pieces are but weak imitations of the "sentimental style" (*Empfindsamkeit*), which dominated the music of the pre-classical period. They are nevertheless valuable testimonies for the fact, already hinted at above, that despite all seclusion in the ghetto, despite the enforced segregation of the Jews from the current vogues of the ever-expanding European intellectual life, the music of the environment penetrated the ghetto walls. There it found receptive minds and ears and helped to stir, however gently, Jewish creativity that burst into full bloom as soon as the eighteenth century Emancipation liberated the Jewish mind from the shackles in which it was held through the ages.

The eighteenth century, though not prolific as far as Jewish creativity in music is concerned, indicated at least the direction which Jewish music had to take in order to compete successfully with the freely developed musical culture of other European nations. As soon as the Emancipation released the hitherto hidden capacities of European Jewry, we witness a sudden and unexpected upsurge of Jewish creative forces in all branches of intellectual life, literature, science, arts and music.

Thus ended the almost two millennia of Jewish struggle in the Diaspora for self-assertion in the musical field, a struggle in which musically less gifted nations would have hopelessly succumbed.

With the crumbling of the ghetto walls around 1800 C.E., the epoch which we have specifically labeled as the Middle Ages of Jewish Music history, had come to its completion and the Modern Era erupted, giving rebirth to Jewish musical creativity.

The story of this rebirth and that which followed in the nineteenth and twentieth centuries are outside the scope of the present study; it is left to competent scholars to give account of this modern miracle.

14

The Ḥazzan

NO OTHER PROFESSION, CRAFT, OR INTELLECTUAL ACTIVITY, NOR THE piety and devotion of the rabbis, nor the learning of the great scholars, nor the inspirational power of the poets, has exerted so much influence upon Jewish musical life as has the activity of the *ḥazzan*. The liturgy and the ritualistic practices would have been dull and colorless without him. In the domain of entertainment he was the indispensable provider for the emotional needs of the people; he brought sunshine into the drab existence of his co-religionists.

It can be stated unequivocally that Jewish music owes its existence, its survival to the unremitting activity of the *ḥazzanim*. In describing and analyzing the musical practice of the Diaspora Jewry, the *ḥazzan* deserves a thorough study of both his life and work in order to appreciate the role assigned to him by destiny to save Jewish music from decay and extinction.

Nowadays the title *ḥazzan* evokes the image of a singing synagogue official, one who leads the prayers with his sonorous chanting and who, in some places, is also in charge of teaching Hebrew to the children, as well as preparing them for the *bar miẓvah* ceremony. In the synagogue hierarchy of our time he is subordinate only to the rabbi, the spiritual leader of the congregation.

Not so in ancient times. It took an evolution of centuries to transform the erstwhile functions of the *ḥazzan* as they are practiced today. The word *ḥazzan* is of Assyrian origin; in that language the term *Ḥazanu* meant "overseer." In the El-Amarna tablets found in Upper Egypt in 1887-88, there is mention of Egyptian governors, called *ḥazzanuti* (the plural of *ḥazzan*) who were stationed in the conquered cities.[1] Assyrians, Egyptians and other peoples of Antiquity also had temple functionaries called *hazzanim,* but who held purely administrative offices.

In the rabbinic literature *hazzan* denotes a number of different functionaries, such as: (1) an overseers of a city;[2] (2) the inspector of a court of justice at whose order the sessions opened;[3] (3) the official who executed judgment on those who acted against the laws;[4] (4) the overseer in charge of the Temple utensils;[5] (5) in a later period the superintendent of the synagogue; his title was then *Ḥazzan bet ha-keneset.* His functions were: (a) to take from the Holy Ark the scrolls of the Torah and return them;[6] (b) to announce with trumpet- or *shofar*-blasts the beginning of the Sabbath and the holidays, this duty to be performed from the highest place in the city, such as the roof of the Temple or of the synagogue; (c) to tend the lamps of the sanctuary, especially the *ner tamid,* the eternal light, burning above the Ark;[7] (d) to receive and accompany the pilgrims who would bring in the first fruits to the Sanctuary.[8] The Talmud mentions often the *shamash* (beadle) whose office at that time was identical with that of the *hazzan ha-keneset.*

As a complementary sideline to his duties, the *hazzan* taught the children to read,[9] and sometimes assisted the schoolmaster in his task. Furthermore, he had to read aloud in a speech-song manner passages from the Torah whenever asked by the congregation. It was this latter function which became the real turning point in the career of the *hazzan,* and ultimately led him to the permanent status of a musical interpreter. Meanwhile, in the way of an organic evolution, the *hazzan*'s duties developed to a more responsible position, mainly leading prayers in the services. In fact, in smaller communities the *hazzan*'s duties comprised those of a preacher, judge, schoolmaster, reader of the Torah with appropriate cantillation, and chanter of prayers.

Among the earliest precentors of the Christian Church of whom we possess historical records were converted Jews, who came to Rome in the fourth century. In Roman catacombs (e.g., that of St. Calixtus) several tombstones have been found, which bear inscriptions of early Christian cantors. Among them was the name of JONATHAN, changed to the Latin DEUSDEDIT, which is the translation of the Hebrew name. His epitaph reads:

> *Hic levitarum primus in ordine vivens*
> *Davitici cantor carminis ipse fuit.*
> (A Levite of the first order of life,
> He was cantor of David's songs.)
>
> (Transl. by E. Werner)

Another of these early converts was RUBEN, who adopted the name of REDEMPTUS. He must have had an exceptionally fine voice, as his epitaph described him:[11]

> *. . . Redemptus*
> *Levitam subito rapuit sibi regia coeli.*
> *Dulcia nectareo promebat mella canore,*
> *Prophetam celebrans placido modulamine senem. . . .*
> (Redemptus, the Levite, soon rapt away
> By the Kingdom of Heaven.
> In nectar-like melody he produced songs sweet as honey,
> When he, in lovely strains, celebrated the ancient prophet.)
>
> (Transl. by E. Werner)

The term "ancient prophet" refers to King David, whom the Early Church considered a prophet.

The Talmud lists the multiple functions with which the *hazzanim* were charged in the early Diaspora. To illustrate this: the inhabitants of the community of Simonias asked the Patriarch JUDAH to send them a man who could serve as a preacher, judge, sexton (*hazzan*), schoolmaster, teacher of the traditional law, and whatever else they needed. This long list contains all sorts of congregational duties, except chanting, which at this time evidently did not belong to the *hazzan's* functions. The patriarch succeeded to find such a universal genius in the person of a certain LEVI ben SISI.[12] Whether this prodigy of efficiency turned out to the satisfaction of the community is not divulged by the Talmud.

The florid melodious intonation, which required a certain vocal agility, existed, as the cantillation of the Scriptures shows, even before the musical direction of the services was entrusted

to the *ḥazzan*. The records show that this intonation was transmitted from the Babylonian Jewish communities to European
settlements in the seventh century C.E. There it developed rapidly,
being considered as the old Jewish tradition of expressing devotion; more than anything else this vocal technique led to the
later complaints against the abuses of the *ḥazzanim* in the sacred
service. In the Sephardic ritual, the increased share of the congregation in reciting the prayers tended to restrict the excessive
employment of the *ḥazzan* in the service and checked his vocal
display.

As time went by, the *ḥazzan's* social and religious status was
elevated considerably, especially when he was considered to be
the *sheliaḥ zibbur*, the representative of the congregation in
prayer and, even more important, the intermediary between the
congregation and God. In the Gaonic period, when the knowledge
of Biblical Hebrew declined, singing was a natural substitute
for the predominantly didactic character of synagogue worship.
The musical function of the *ḥazzan* assumed a steadily increasing
precedence over his other duties. In later periods the *ḥazzanim*
did not confine themselves to the mere recitation of traditional
prayers, but began to compose new prayers and even set them
to music. Thus the office of the *ḥazzan* rose to an important position in the synagogue service.

In earlier times, the qualification of a *ḥazzan*, apart from his
vocal merits, were not too high. It sufficed that he had some
knowledge of Hebrew, the Biblical text and of the liturgy, but
these were qualities which any well educated member of the
congregation undoubtedly possessed. As for his outward manner,
he was supposed to have a pleasing appearance, wear a long
beard and, of course, he had to be married in order to avoid
reproaches which in later times were frequently raised about the
questionable behavior of some of the *ḥazzanim*. In this respect
MAIMONIDES showed a rare human understanding in holding that
a *ḥazzan* should be tolerated even "when he might have a reputation not wholly spotless, provided he was living at the time of
his appointment a life normally free from reproach."

We possess evidence that there were even female *ḥazzanim*.
In some synagogues, as for example in Worms, the female wor-

shippers had a separate building for their services, connected with the main house merely by a gallery. In such cases it was preferable to have female precentors to conduct independent services for the women. Medieval records from the thirteenth century mention in Worms and Nüremberg such female *hazzanim*, "bearing the picturesque names of URANIA and RICHENZA."[13] They were called in Yiddish *sogern* (Germ. *Sagerin*).

The artistic qualities of the *hazzan's* performance were stressed very early in synagogue worship. YEHUDA HADASSI (middle of the twelfth century), for instance, maintained that the congregants were more receptive if the *hazzan* had a beautiful voice, since his song was meant to purify their hearts and ennoble their minds. And YEHUDA ben SAMUEL he-HASSID of Regensburg (d. 1217), in his book *Sefer Hasidim*, gives the following definition of the purpose of singing, and at the same time admonishes the *hazzanim*: "If you cannot concentrate in prayer, search for melodies, and if you pray choose a tune you like. Then your heart will feel what your tongue speaks; for it is the song that makes your heart respond."[14]

As the musical aspect of the *hazzan's* functions grew in scope, this part of the liturgical service required a more elaborate treatment. In some later centuries and in larger congregations the single voice of the *hazzan* did not satisfy the needs of the community. He was, therefore, accommodated with musical assistants; first a singer with a lower voice, appropriately called "Bass," and subsequently a singer for the treble, usually a boy. In the *Mahsor Leipzig* (fourteenth century), preserved in the University Library of that city (V, 1102), there is a beautiful illustration, depicting the officiating *hazzan* surrounded by his "bass" and "singer." (Illustration No. 25). This sort of participation in the synagogue that forbade instrumental accompaniment generally sufficed for the somewhat expanded rendition of the musical part of the service. Only in larger and more affluent communities was the number of vocal assistants enlarged so as to form a choir.

For the High Holidays an exceptionally qualified *hazzan* was required whose life had to be irreproachable and who was expected to be outstanding in the expressive delivery of the prayers.

Some congregations, especially those of small townships, encountered difficulties in finding such a person. This led some rabbis already in the eighth and ninth century c.e. to rule that youths of seventeen or eighteen and, in case of insurmountable obstacles, even boys of thirteen were eligible for the office of the *ḥazzan*.

The hiring of a *ḥazzan* was done by the majority vote of all residents of the Jewish community. Those who had children of school age had the decisive influence in the voting procedure, but as most families had children, the voters encompassed practically the entire congregation. The candidate had to account for his upbringing and had to submit documentary evidence of his past conduct. Communities often had unpleasant experiences with vagrant *ḥazzanim* and consequently congregations were cautious of newcomers. Despite precautionary measures, however, it occasionally happened that morally unworthy *ḥazzanim* obtained a position, and it was subsequently difficult to dismiss them.

In addition to their qualifications as leaders of congregational singing and schoolmasters, the *ḥazzanim* at least until 1800 (but in Eastern Europe until recently) had to be efficient in ritual slaughtering.

Among the conditions mentioned in the early rabbinic literature for hiring a *ḥazzan* one, and the most important, is completely missing—the familiarity of a candidate with the traditional chant —the *nussaḥ*. In this respect, too, many congregations, after hiring a *ḥazzan* without an appropriate try-out, experienced great disappointment.

Originally, the *ḥazzan* received no regular wages. He was given free living quarters, mostly in the synagogue building or close by, and depended for his livelihood on more or less voluntary gifts (food, wine, oil, etc.) from the well-to-do members of the community. It is possible that he supplemented his wages by some trade or skill as an artisan. As the functions of the *ḥazzan* became more and more numerous and time-consuming the office developed into a full-time occupation for which the *ḥazzan* had to receive a salary. His wages came from three sources, one-third paid by pupils (or their families), one-third by taxation of the wealthy, and one-third a fixed sum assessed equally on all heads of families.

As early as the time of HAI-GAON (939-1038) the *ḥazzan* had received a salary which was determined by judgment of his abilities. Furthermore he was exempt from communal taxes. This, however, had not been achieved without opposition. A controversy was aroused about the question whether the *ḥazzan* should be included among the functionaries of the religious service who enjoyed tax-exempt privileges. In the eleventh century a strong opposition arose concerning the payment of the *ḥazzan*. The reason might have been professional jealousy on the part of other synagogue officials, since the functions of the *ḥazzan* gradually grew in importance, and possibly because of his popularity with the congregation. Eventually, however, the good sense of the communities seems to have won the upper hand, since the opposition to his remuneration was dropped.

R. PROFIAT DURAN (fourteenth century) asserted that in Islamic countries the leaders of prayer were exempt from taxation, whereas in Christian countries they were liable to pay. Whether this helped to promote the *ḥazzan*'s case is not certain, since this seems to have been a generalization. Records show that in different countries the question of the *ḥazzan*'s payment was handled individually.

The removal of a *ḥazzan* from office depended in most cases upon the will of those who paid the highest taxes in the congregation. As a humanitarian measure it was an accepted rule that the *ḥazzan* should not be discharged immediately, or even upon short notice, at the request of a few members of the community who took a dislike to him. Inasmuch as the *ḥazzan* was selected and hired by the majority vote of the congregation, his discharge was also to be effectuated by all, or the majority, of its members.

One of the main reasons for the dismissal of a *ḥazzan* was proof or even suspicion of unchastity. It was generally accepted that the *ḥazzan* was more a musician, an artist, than a minister of the sacred service, and as such he was looked upon as subject to an artistic disposition, with all the frailties seemingly associated with it. The comparative infrequency with which the *ḥazzan* was uspected in regard to his moral fibre is testimony to the fact that only a minute segment of the order might have been guilty of neglect of the necessary restraint in their moral lives. The historically recorded number of learned *ḥazzanim* who were noted for the piety and purity of their lives exceed by far the occasional sinners who had to pay with the loss of their jobs for their lack of chastity.[15]

An old *ḥazzan* who lost his voice could be dismissed, but generally some arrangement was made for his maintenance. A blameless *ḥazzan* could not be removed simply because another had a more pleasant voice; however, a second *ḥazzan* might be hired, if the community so decided.

In the early Diaspora the office of the *ḥazzan* was held in high esteem. As the records show, scholars of high repute frequently took over the functions of leading the prayer, an activity which necessarily entailed the chanting of the sacred text. Among them were outstanding rabbis, such as ELIEZER ben MESHULLAM "the Great," in Mainz (eleventh century). R. MEÏR of Rothenburg (1215-1293), and others. The most famous of them was R. JACOB MÖLLN, called MAHARIL (born in Mainz, c. 1356, died in Worms 1427). He was instrumental in reforming and ennobling the synagogue song. At the desire of his congregation he took over the chanting of the prayers at festivals, especially on the High Holidays. He must have had a fine voice, since his rendition of the songs stirred the audiences wherever he led the prayers. He traveled through Germany and inspired everywhere devotion, uplifting the spirit of his audiences. He was convinced that the tradition of Jewish music could be saved by clinging to and preserving the old melodies. Since he was the greatest rabbinical authority of his time, his word was accepted and his example emulated by all rabbis and *ḥazzanim* who had come in contact with him. Thus, through his exalted personality, he was able to save the traditionally entrenched ritual of the synagogue and its music by sanctioning the old tunes. His manner of chanting was preserved posthumously by his disciples, who attempted to describe this manner in the *Sefer Maharil* (first publ. in 1556).

Among other famous rabbis officiating as *ḥazzanim*, ABRAHAM

HAZZAN of GERONA (called GERONDI, died 1263), who acquired fame as a writer of devotional hymns, deserves to be mentioned Early historical records show that the term *hazzan* had been adopted as the family name by an Oriental rabbinical family; the chosen name was evidently derived from the office of *hazzan* held by several of the ancestors of the family.[16] We know of several famous members of this family throughout the period of Diaspora and up until the eighteenth and nineteenth centuries Some of them were: ELEAZAR ha-HAZZAN, who lived in Speyer at the end of the eleventh century; GERONDI (see above) in the thirteenth century; MOSES ben ABRAHAM HAZZAN (fifteenth century); ABRAHAM ben JUDAH, *hazzan* at Kremenetz in Volhynia (sixteenth century); and JOSEPH ben ELIJAH HAZZAN, rabbi in Smyrna and Jerusalem (seventeenth century).

It is significant that most of the members of this family were not only distinguished rabbis and experts in the art of the *hazzanut,* but also renowned writers of synagogal poetry and other important literary works.

The attitude of the early *hazzan* toward his vocation and his professional pride in being a dispenser of joy for the masses is shown by a little anecdote related by IMMANUEL of ROME, the famous thirteenth century poet. In his work *"Mahbarot"* he tells us that he was travelling with one of his friends, a wealthy man, when they met several poor people, all of whom complained about their miserable life. Among them there was a *hazzan* whose misfortune must have been extremely hard, for he lamented bitterly about it. IMMANUEL asked him if he would like to exchange his lot with that of his rich friend and, of course, the *hazzan* jumped eagerly at this opportunity. But when he was told that he had to exchange his voice for the voice of the rich man, the *hazzan* grew indignant, declaring that his voice was his proudest possession, that with it he could conquer the hearts of the people, and that no terrestrial wealth could compensate him for the loss of this heavenly blessing.

In Germanic countries, and in later centuries, the *hazzan* was called *Vorbeter* or *Vorsänger* ("leader of the prayers, or of the song"), in English-speaking countries "precentor," in France and Italy *chantre* and *cantor,* respectively; this last term was eventually adopted as a designation for the *ḥazzan* in European countries and in America.

In the earlier period synagogue music was far from rich and subtle in ornamentation; volume of sound rather than delicacy was mostly required from the *ḥazzan*. This was natural, since the singers of those times probably had little, if any, vocal training and therefore were forced to make up for the lack of a cultured voice by volume alone.

The old Jewish custom whereby congregants arrived late and at irregular intervals for the services must have caused a great annoyance to the cantor. Those in the congregation who arrived early would have finished their prayers and engaged in lively conversation, while the others, coming at later time, would recite their prayers loudly, all giving rise to a babel of sound in the synagogue. Thus it became regular procedure, at least for the daily services, that while the *ḥazzan* performed his chants, much conversation and loud reading went on in the congregation with utmost disregard for the precentor's singing.

From what sources did the *ḥazzanim* gather their music throughout the entire period of the Diaspora? In the early centuries, especially in the late Talmudic times, scant oral tradition of the synagogal chant must have been alive. In Tannaitic times ancient melodies were probably still remembered; in a transformed and adapted form they might have been the substance of the *ḥazzanic* repertoire. In the long run this must have proved insufficient, consequently the *ḥazzanim* were compelled to search for additional material. Under Oriental influence they began to improvise, and then either to compose music for their songs or, what was simpler, to adopt for synagogue use whatever they found available in their own environment, such as popular airs, ditties, and also church songs (for the church in those times was the only producer of art music).

The early *ḥazzanim* had no musical education whatsoever, and consequently their taste concerning matters of music might conceivably have been on a low level. From this, certain conclusions can be drawn to show the extent of foreign musical elements which infiltrated the liturgical service. As early as the ninth century we already possess records of complaints on this point made against *hazzanim*, and undoubtedly such complaints occurred even much earlier. Especially when the *piyyutim* were to be set to music by the *hazzanim*, and introduced into the synagogue, most of the cantors faced insurmountable tasks. These cantors who were not trained musicians subsequently turned to the melodies purloined from the Church, from taverns, from the streets, and adapted them for liturgical use. This process so corrupted synagogue music that not even centuries of "cleansing" could eradicate the sins of the past. Historical records abound in indications that this or that *piyyut* had to be sung to the melody (*la-ḥan*) of a well-known Arabic, Turkish, or Spanish song or *romance*.

The chief supplier of rhythmical music for metrical poetry was the *hazzan*. His was the task of providing his congregation with new melodies. The weekday services, because of the brief time allotted to them, permitted no poetical and musical embellishments on a large scale. On Sabbaths and holidays, on the other hand, the people were free from work; on these days it became the duty of the *hazzan* to entertain them and to display his twofold role as a poet and singer. The *hazzanim*, from the tenth down to the thirteenth century performed practically the same functions as the ancient folk bards, the Arabic "singers" (*shuar*) and, with certain limitations, as the French troubadours, the Spanish *juglares*, and the German minnesingers.

YEHUDA ḤARISI, a Sephardic scholar and poet, who visited Mossul (Mesopotamia) at the beginning of the thirteenth century, left a satiric description of the "art" of the *hazzan* over there, enumerating all his grammatical mistakes in his prayers as well as in his poetry; relating how the *hazzan*, self-satisfied with his artistic performance, exhausted himself and the congregation and wasted so much time for his "art" that no time was left for the ritual proper. When ḤARISI called the attention of the *hazzan* and his admirers to the mischief, they declared that his poetry and his songs were more important than the prayers themselves.[17]

Opposition to this exaggerated emphasis on the poetry of the *hazzanim* was inevitable. In fact, already early in the eleventh century we hear the opposition of such great men as HAY GAON, himself a poet, of Isaac Alfasi, and Yehuda of Barcelona against too much use of poetry and Arabic melodies in the synagogue.

The famous preacher of Mantua, Yehudah Moscato, in his sermon about music (publ. 1589, see p. 287), uttered the serious complaint: "What shall we say and how shall we justify ourselves as regards some of the synagogue cantors of our day, who chant the holy prayers to the tunes of popular songs of the multitude, and thus, while they are discoursing on holy themes, think of the original ignoble and licentious associations!"[18]

Matters got worse by the vanity of the *hazzanim*, whose least concern was the sacred service, and whose only desire was to impress their audiences with their "virtuosity." They inserted into the prayers all kinds of vocal interludes, improvised coloratura passages, made use of other artifices like trills, slurs, portamenti, in order to offer the worshippers "vocal fireworks." Every complaint on this score was of no avail; the rabbis, wishing to maintain the dignity of the divine service, fulminated in numerous responsa and severe edicts, with little or no result. These abuses survived the centuries and cropped up in our times in Eastern Europe, where the local *hazzanim* followed the trend preached by the medieval *hazzan:* the brilliant vocal interpretation being more important than the dignity of the liturgy.

However, we must seek the deeper reasons for this state of affairs. In the life of the Diaspora the synagogue was the only place where the Jew could enjoy music. It so happened that the admiring congregation prompted, and even requested, that the officiant forget the text-matter and replace it with the song-manner (or mannerism). The result was that the *hazzanim* developed the technical intricacy of synagogal singing by the utilization of florid ornamentation which their audiences, out of touch with any music but the folk music of their day, enjoyed thoroughly.

The borrowed or adapted tunes were taken into the synagogue to make up for the lack of available melodies, which the rapidly increasing neo-Hebraic hymns needed.

Not all the airs which appeared like folk songs, however, were actually and directly borrowed; many of them were composed by those *hazzanim* who happened to be familiar with this craft. But even so, they were close imitations of the popular melody of the day; it goes without saying that they lacked any Jewish characteristics or even a faint likeness to older traditional elements. ABRAHAM IBN EZRA (in his commentary on Psalm 8) refers to the introduction of such alien airs in the eleventh century. According to SAMUEL ARCHEVOLTI, the sixteenth-century author, the practice was a general one in the days of YEHUDAH ha-LEVI, who lived in the early part of the twelfth century. ISRAEL NAJARA, rabbi of Gaza (1555-1628) published six hundred fifty Hebrew lyrics, most of them written to fit the melodies of Arabic, Turkish, Greek, Spanish and Italian songs selected by himself.

It is small consolation that this procedure was not restricted to the synagogue. Prominent Christian musicians of the time, who wrote for the church, have often chosen a secular melody as the *"cantus firmus"* of a mass. One of the most famous among such extra-liturgical melodies was the French popular air *"L'homme armé,"* upon which over thirty church masses were written by various composers between the fifteenth and seventeenth centuries. These works used to be called accordingly *"Messe sur l'homme armé."* Below we reproduce the French air referred to together with a fragment of the mass by GUILLAUME DUFAY (d. 1474), in which it serves as the *"cantus firmus."* (Mus. ex. No. 32 a, b.)

Following this is the synagogal song *Mizmor Shir* in the Sephardic tradition, which has been peculiarly influenced by the opening portion of the *"L'homme armé"* melody. (Cf. the first, second and fourth staves of the reproduced score of *Mizmor Shir.*) (Mus. ex. No. 33.)

Mus. ex. No. 32 a

66. Guillaume Dufay

a. L'Homme armé

The melody of L'Homme armé.

Mus. ex. No. 32 b

b. Kyrie I   Missa L'Homme armé

Part of the Missa l'Homme armé *by Guillaume Dufay. (After A. T. Davison and W. Apel,* Historical Anthology of Music *(Cambridge, Mass. 1966), p. 71.*

What sort of metmorphoses synagogue songs are sometimes subjected to becomes evident from the melody of LEKAH DODI, the lyrics of which were composed by SOLOMON ʾALḴABIẒ (ca. 1503–1580). The *Jewish Encyclopedia*[18] contains three different melodies on the text, all these adopted from popular tunes, one Moorish of the tenth century, one Polish of the sixteenth, and one German of the seventeenth century (see p. 193).

The *ḥazzanim* tried to bring up the music of worship to an up-to-date status. They later used Protestant hymns and chorales in which a slight change in the original German wording results in a complete change of the meaning. For instance, HEINRICH ISAAK's song *"Innsbruck, ich muss dich lassen"* (Innsbruck, I must leave thee) (1440) became the Jewish song "O World, I soon must leave thee." In Jewish practice a slight change in phonetics would justify the utilization of an air for devotional purposes. Thus, to the tune of the Spanish *romance "En Toda la Tramontaña"* was written *"Shir Todah le-ʾElohim Tanah";* and to another Spanish song, *"Muerame mi Alma, ai! Muerame"* an ingenious *ḥazzan* wrote *"Meromi ʿal Mah ʿAm Rab Homah."* A slight correspondence in the meaning of the Spanish and Hebrew initial words was

Mus. ex. No. 33   MIZMOR SHIR.

Mizmor Shir (After Aguilar, Emanuel Abraham and David Aaron De Șola, *The Ancient Melodies of the Liturgy of the Spanish and Portuguese Jews* ... (Oxford University Press, 1931), p. 6.

considered adequate connection, as when the verses *"El he-Harim Essa ʿEni"* are set to the air of *"A las Montañas Mi Alma! a las Montañas Me Iré,"* or *"Mar li Mar Mar Mar"* to the Turkish ditty *"Krodas Yar, Yar, Yar,"* in the latter instance, furthermore, the word *dost* ("friend" in Turkish") ending each line, is translated by the Hebrew *dodi* ("bride") in a similar position. Curious incongruities arose when a Hebrew hymn *"Shem Nora"* used the tune of the Spanish *"Señora"*; or *"Guri, guri"* that of *"Giuri, giuri"*; and *"Yaʿalat ha-mor"* was set to the melody of *"Perdone mi amor."* Few of such adaptations entered the liturgy itself, although some can be traced as, for instance, the beautiful tune of ABRAHAM ḤAZZAN of GERONA's fine hymn commencing *"Aḥot Ketannah,"* which was composed on the lines of a popular Levantine song, "The Little Maid."

Among other secular airs of European peoples adapted by Jews to sacred use may be mentioned: *"Permetid Bella Amaryllis,"* *"Tres Colores in Una,"* *"Temprano Naces Almendro,"* *"El Vaquero de la Morayna,"* *"Fasi Abassi Silvana,"* *"Les Trois Rois,"* *"Les Filles de Tarascon,"* *"Porque No Mi Hablas,"* *"Partistas Amiga,"* *"Pues Vos Me Feristes,"* *"En Los Campos di Alvansa,"* *"Blümlein auf breiter Heide,"* *"Dietrich von Bern,"* *"Pavierweise,"* *"Un Poggio Tiene la Contessa,"* *"Gulianita,"* *"Doliente Estaba Allessandri,"* and even, in the last century, such melodies for the KADDISH as *"La Marseillaise,"* or actually "The Girl I left Behind Me," or for ʾADONAY MELEK on New Year's Day an aria from *"La Traviata."* While another *ḥazzan* (WOLF SHESTAPOL) adopted a part of an aria from "La Traviata" for ʾ*Adonay Zekoronu* (Psalm 115:12-18).[20a] There were certainly many more adaptations of this kind, but the above will suffice for our purposes.

Many complaints were uttered, for instance, about the incorrect pronunciation of the Hebrew text. Furthermore, the immoderate raising of the voice of the *ḥazzanim* was a constant source of criticism. The manner of singing of the majority of the *ḥazzanim* has been called "a pilpul set to music," a bad habit which was carried over from the early Middle Ages to the seventeenth century and which constituted as well the ingrained singing practice of the Polish, German, Austrian, Hungarian and Rumanian *ḥazzanim*. In some cases, the standards of religious life were lowered not only by such musical abuses, but even more so by the unworthy behavior of the synagogue singers. It often happened that the service was interrupted by quarrels between the *hazzan* and his singers who tried to iron out their differences in plain view and hearing of the congregation, and not merely with words, but frequently with acts of violence. It happened once on the Day of Atonement that the *hazzan* had to be removed from his pulpit by the police. It is a small consolation that in the same epoch similar conditions were also prevalent in the Catholic Church.[21]

In the seventeenth century, R. MOSES MINZ, at the request of his community in Bamberg, wrote an opnion[22] concerning the rules of conduct for a *hazzan*. This opinion presupposes the existence of an ideal *hazzan* who, in reality, could never comprise in his total being all the qualifications outlined in this responsum.

A pamphlet, *Reshit Bikkurim*, by HANOCH b. ABRAHAM b. YEHIEL (written about 1650, published in 1708) enumerates a long list of charges against the *hazzanim*. One such charge draws attention to the irritating habit whereby *hazzanim* put their hands on the chin or throat while singing, evidently for the purpose of increasing the vocal vibrato or facilitating the trilling, or producing high and shrill tones. This artifice was generally employed by Oriental peoples. One may find such a visual reproduction upon an ancient Assyrian bas-relief, which was discovered at Kuyundchik. It depicts a solemn reception, with singing and playing musicians, of the victorious Assyrian King ASHUR-IDANNI-PAL. A female singer is shown with her hand pressed against her throat, in a similar manner to that which the Jewish *hazzanim* of later times used. At the beginning of the eighteenth century this practice was still very much in vogue.

In a guide for *hazzanim* written by the *hazzan* SOLOMON LIPSCHÜTZ, "*Te'udat Shelomoh*" (published 1718 in Offenbach), all these abuses were mentioned and reprehended without having altered appreciably the existing conditions.

It is noteworthy that such abuses did not prevail to any extent in Sephardic congregations. First of all, the reverence of the cantors for the tradition prevented such stylistic vocal deviations from occurring. Secondly, the existence of printed collections of *piyyutim* with their designated melodies furnished the backbone for congregational singing. Therefore the cantor did not have to perform beyond the established norms, because cantor and congregation functioned as a well organized assembly whose purpose was to uphold the dignity of the service.

A special kind of *piyyutim* were the *pizmonim,* poems in responsorial form, with a *ritornello* sung by the congregation, or by the chorus if there was one. This practice was frequently employed by the Sephardim.

It should be mentioned that in Iberian lands Christian noblemen, from the king to the knights, along with the ladies of the courts, showed surprising interest in the singing of the *ḥazzan* and attended frequently synagogue services, much to the chagrin of the congregation.[23]

Into an entirely different category belong the *ḥazzanim* of Italy in the Renaissance, the brilliant LEON MODENA, the versatile MENAḤEM LUZZATO, and the famous *ḥazzan*-composer SALOMONE ROSSI EBREO, as he called himself. About all these and others more will be said in a later chapter in which the musical achievements of the Jews in Renaissance Italy will be surveyed.

In the centuries troubled by repeated expulsions and almost continuous persecutions, Jewish community life became disrupted and, in some localities, was threatened by complete extinction. Under such conditions many congregations refrained from engaging permanent *ḥazzanim.* However, since the need for *ḥazzanim* still prevailed, a new type developed among them, the itinerant *ḥazzan.* The festivals and Holidays for which the professional *ḥazzan* was indispensable were relatively few, and consequently these itinerant *ḥazzanim,* to make a livelihood, undertook private appearances, accepted guest engagements for single services, and arranged secular concert-like performances. In these peripheral activities, all the mannerisms and bad habits, all the inveterate reprehensible customs, as well as the artistic vanities of such wandering singers came to the fore. Their comparison with the medieval *jongleurs* and minstrels is obvious, the only difference being that these *ḥazzanim,* with all their shortcomings, were still considered, in some way, to be the fitting exponents of the liturgy.

Owing to the prevailing political and cultural disturbances through the centuries, and also to the peculiar circumstances caused by the new way of living of those itinerant music-makers, the *hazzanim*, little by little, abandoned all their activities not directly connected with music. They considered themselves to be outstanding virtuosos and as such, restricted themselves to singing and "composing," *i.e.*, providing dazzling tunes for their audiences.

In the larger communities where the *hazzan* was released from all other duties to devote himself to music alone, he was honored with the title "*Shtot Hazzan*" (city *hazzan*).

In the fifteenth and sixteenth centuries the German Jews were subjected to atrocious persecutions. Toiling and striving during the week, they desired to have a brighter atmosphere on the Sabbath and on festivals; in their never ending desire to enjoy music they wanted, on these days, to hear attractive popular songs to help them to forget their tribulations. The people, especially the less educated, urged the *hazzanim* to satisfy their craving for music, despite the continuous protests of the rabbis. The traditional synagogue songs in their austerity were insufficient relief for the weekday's drudgery. The congregants demanded performances of popular tunes like the ones heard in the outside world, and they asked the *hazzan* to adapt such songs to religious texts. Needless to say, the *hazzan* consented gladly in view of the paucity of other songs. The rabbis and the better educated members of the congregations protested vehemently against such abuses, but to no avail. The desire of the congregations on the one hand, and the need of the *hazzan* to expand his repertoire with attractive songs on the other, resulted in the introduction into the liturgy of ditties, love songs, and all kinds of trivial tunes already popular in the streets, in wineshops and all public places. Nothing was too inviolable, not even church melodies, in the quest for filling up their musical stock with new hits.

This was an age in which all the faults of the past came to the fore, the neglect of the sacred text, bad pronunciation of the Hebrew, questionable behavior on the pulpit, and the overemphasis in showmanship. In such circumstances the manner, not the matter, was the decisive factor. Emotional and novel effects, often of a ludicrous character, captivated and fascinated the congregations. This was rather to be expected if we consider that the synagogue was the only meeting place and—at the same time—the center of entertainment for the Jews, especially before the Tanz-houses in the larger townships came into being. In those days not only the attitude of the *ḥazzanim,* but also that of the congregants, were highly reprehensible.

In the late seventeenth and eighteenth centuries, to avoid the constant persecutions in Eastern Europe, the Jews migrated in increasing numbers to the West, particularly to Germany and the Netherlands. At the same time, young *ḥazzanim* traveled about from congregation to congregation, bringing new melodies, and often also brought with them a choir, designated as *"meshorerim,"* songmakers. Their function was that of the youthful Levites standing below the platform of the singers in the Temple, to "give spice to the song," as we read in the Talmud.[24] The function of these *ḥazzanim* was not just a musical one; they also acted as an "oral newspaper," so to say, which carried the news from one district to another. The isolated Jewish congregations, starving for news, received them with open arms.

The *ḥazzan* now forced his voice to excess; his singing became an incoherent chant, full of repetitions, runs and slurs and embroideries. Meanwhile "singer" and "bass" stood at either side. By ear alone, improvising rather than following a prearranged harmony, they accompanied the *ḥazzan,* using at times such devices as the imitation of the bees and birds, the tones of the flute, the bassoon, or the now extinct serpent, which gave vent to an unbridled fancy of incoherent passages.[25] Such a form of concerted synagogue music still survived in our own century in Poland and Galicia and was still to be heard before the First World War in the ghettos of London and New York.

Fortunately for the dignity of the cantorial profession as well as for the ultimate destiny of the synagogal song, there were some Jewish communities in Germany which escaped the ravages inflicted by the Crusaders and later by raging mobs. In these localities the sanctity of the service and the integrity of the *ḥazzanim* could be maintained. These lucky towns preserved their *minḥag,* their old customs, and could thus become a standard for other communities which were less fortunate. In such cities as Frankfurt, Prague, Mainz, Worms, and others, rabbis and congregations established strict rules for upholding the purity of the liturgy and insisted upon the quality, personal as well as artistic, of the *hazzanim*. We find, indeed, in these places *hazzanim* of rabbinic learning and high ethical standards. As an example we may mention the *hazzan* of Frankfurt of the sixteenth century, ISAAC HAHN who, according to the testimony of his grandson (a famous writer of the seventeenth century), was appointed not owing to his sweet voice, but on account of his wisdom and piety.

Such cases became more and more numerous, and with the lapse of time, through the "purgatory" of the eighteenth-century cantorial reforms, led to the glorious epoch of the nineteenth century cantorial office, in which the *hazzan* ceased to be merely a singer, but became an artist, composer, scholar, a beacon of moral life and, after the rabbi, the leading personality of the congregation.

As a curiosum connected with the cantorial profession, it is worth mentioning that, due to ancient superstitious beliefs, the *hazzan*'s office at times involved personal dangers. In Yemen, for instance, according to the popular belief, the *hazzan*'s family had to suffer for any shortcomings of his official duties. The precentor, as an intermediary between the congregation and God, just as the high priest in ancient times, had the duty of rendering the prayers word for word, and letter for letter correctly. However, if he made the slightest linguistic mistake and failed to correct it immediately, his prayer, and at the same time the prayer of the entire congregation, would be rejected in heaven as defective. But in that case the precentor bore the sins of the congregation and would also be punished immediately. Hence many pious men were afraid to accept the office of *hazzan*, and they interpreted the mortality of their small children, which unfortunately was very high among them, as punishment for sins committed while they officiated as precentors.[26]

After the Emancipation the ancient practice of synagogue music was brought up to modern standards. With an ever increasing practical knowledge of music, the cantors were able to write down the traditional chants and tunes in modern notation.

Soon harmony and accompaniment were added to the ancient melodies. Unfortunately, these harmonizations, which employed style and technique of the late eighteenth and early nineteenth centuries spoiled the still surviving Oriental flavor of these songs, giving them the appearance of hybrid melodic strains that blended only superficially with the synagogue service. In this period of evolution, as we may call this transformation, the "old-time" *ḥazzan* gave way to the more sophisticated cantor, while his *meshorerim*, the former helpers of the *ḥazzan*, were supplanted by a choir of male or mixed voices. The choirs sang three or four part arrangements in the current style of the Christian church, and employed the accepted choral devices of the nineteenth century. It must be noted that, although the Ashkenazic and Sephardic traditional melodies have had largely a common origin, their characteristics developed along entirely different lines, resulting in a clear-cut division into an Ashkenazic (German and Polish) and Sephardic (mostly North African and Balkan) school of liturgical music. And of course, with these divisions emerge two different types of cantors.

With the "father of modern cantorate," SOLOMON SULZER (1804-1890) in Vienna, a new era of cantorial art and synagogue music was inaugurated. Inasmuch as his activity belongs to Jewish music history of the nineteenth century, we have to refrain from evaluating his far-reaching reforms, as this is outside the scope of our present study. It is worthwhile, however, to devote a few observations upon his immediate predecessors. These were the first to undertake, during the outgoing eighteenth century, the task of writing down, to the best of their abilities, the ancient melodies into Western musical notation—the oral tradition into modern musical language.

Previously (p. 191 et seq.), we have already given ample information about the earliest comprehensive collection of notated Jewish melodies assembled by AHRON BEER. This collection, together with some other treasures, is part of the BIRNBAUM LIBRARY, now at the Hebrew Union College in Cincinnati.

It is necessary to state at this juncture that in the preservation of ancient synagogal melodies some *ḥazzanim* of the outgoing eighteenth century have earned lasting merits. They inaugurated the movement of collecting and notating Jewish melodies, an activity which was methodically continued during the nineteenth

century. This had led eventually to such monumental achievements as BIRNBAUM's collection and IDELSOHN's *Thesaurus,* the
ten volumes of which are the richest repository of almost everything known about the Jewish melos at the turn of the twentieth
century.

Concerning the cantorial writers of the eighteenth century
mentioned by BEER as well as other famous *hazzanim* of the late
eighteenth and early nineteenth centuries, IDELSOHN's *Jewish
Music* contains invaluable information (pp. 217 ff).

What is important to our present survey is the fact that with
the single exception of the earlier mentioned ISRAEL LÖWY (or
LOVY) (1773-1832), the *hazzanim* of the eighteenth century did
not show any initiative to improve the liturgical chant. What they
did, and this was their only innovation, was to introduce measured melodies into the ritual—tunes in the style of the eighteenth-
century classical music, for three or four voices, or in the manner
of Christian church chorales. Through the use of measured melodies, alien to the spirit of Jewish song, synagogue melodies
became Westernized in style and did much to damage the extant
Oriental flavor of the traditional *nussah.*

Furthermore, this Westernization, which still dominates most
of today's Jewish services, caused the decline of the cantorial art,
based upon the ancient *nussah* and, at the same time, raised
infinitely the general *niveau* of synagogal music.

With the crumbling walls of the ghetto, signifying the end of
the Jewish Middle Ages, a new generation of *hazzanim* arose.
A new type of *hazzanim* came to the fore with a more intimate
knowledge of the artistic responsibilities of his profession, conscious of his duty toward the preservation of the *nussah.* Moreover, the *hazzan* of the new generation does not consider himself
merely as a singing virtuoso and entertainer of the congregation,
but rather as a leader and teacher whose most noble task is to
educate the worshippers for a better understanding of synagogal
art and to appreciate the traditional Jewish musical heritage.

At the same time a new trend became evident which pointed
toward the purification of the traditional *nussah* from the overgrowth of the long cantorial self-adulation. The *nussah* of the
nineteenth century had resumed an increasingly different aspect,

based on the purity of Biblical cantillation and prayer-chants, thereby leaving behind it an ever greater measure the misuse of centuries.

Thus, in the final analysis, the artistic conscience of today's *ḥazzanim,* coupled with their increased musical knowledge and their responsibility toward their sacred office, are the best promise for the future preservation and rejuvenation of the age-old cantorial art.

15

Jewish Musicians in the
Italian Renaissance*

IN THE HISTORY OF THE JEWISH PEOPLE, ONE MAY OBSERVE A FACT comparable to a perpetual *ritornello*, that wherever they lived in freedom, enjoying human rights, be it in their own national state in Israel, or in Babylonia, Spain, France, and later in the Netherlands, their untrammeled creative powers soared high and wide, bringing forth great poets, thinkers, writers and musicians.

This phenomenon, so obvious during their own national existence in Judah, manifested itself to an even greater degree in the Diaspora, where all kinds of obstacles had to be overcome, and lost time had to be made up with increased energy and valor.

It has already been shown how the Jews established themselves in the musical culture of Spain and how—little by little—they became active members of a musical organization the aim of which was the entertainment of wide strata of the population. It is to be assumed that, just as the French troubadours and *jongleurs* invaded other countries, fertilizing the music culture of these lands, the Spanish *juglares* also migrated into the neighboring provinces and there disseminated the art they practiced in their homeland. Direct proof of this are the peregrinations of JUAN de VALLADOLID who, at an advanced age, became a favorite entertainer at several Italian courts. Most likely there lived other *juglares* who tried their luck in Italy and spread musical entertainment there, as in Spain.

Without such musical fertilization it would be inconceivable

---

* For this chapter the author is greatly indebted to Cecil Roth's excellent monograph about the Jews in the Renaissance.

to find, in sixteenth-century Italy, a group of Jewish musicians suddenly emerging in towns where understanding and art-loving princes encouraged the settlement of Jewish intellectuals and of artists of all categories, among them musicians.

In the ensuing veritable rebirth of Jewish musical activity in Italy, the Jewish bankers, through their wealth and privileged social position, played an important role. They may have been the first to gather around them Jewish musicians, giving them opportunities not merely with regard to their livelihood, but also encouraging them in their creative efforts. How widespread the cultivation of music in these circles was at the beginning of the sixteenth century becomes evident from a report of the false Messiah DAVID REUBENI, who tells us that when he had a lengthy visit at the villa of the erudite and art-loving YEḤIEL NISSIM at Pisa in 1524, in the company of a number of distinguished patrician visitors, NISSIM's wife, Madonna DIAMANTE, with her daughter and several of her damsels, tried to solace his melancholy with music and dancing. Moreover, the town instrumentalists were engaged to perform at his host's house.[1]

As in all civilizations and at all times, a familiarity with music and especially the technique of mastering music instruments had to be acquired from teachers. There lived, in Italy, a number of musicians who gave instruction in their respective fields, some of whom were Jews. If only a few of their names are known, it is not because of their limited number, but because every good instrumentalist was supposed to be, in those days, a good teacher as well. Occasionally curious facts emerge with regard to music instruction, as when a Jewish pedagogue of the period, "in a letter to a favorite pupil, admonished him not to neglect to practice his playing on the lute and fife—but only at night, after his father had gone to bed."[2]

Dancing, as a concomitant to musical education for members of a Jewish family, was widely cultivated in Italy. The profession of dancing master was highly regarded and was lucrative because of the number of pupils from Jewish and Christian families. The teaching of dancing was a specific Jewish occupation in Renaissance Italy, due to their proficiency in this art form. The names of a number of outstanding Jewish dancing masters were handed down to posterity in the same manner as the names of famous rabbis, Talmudic scholars and poets. As early as the fifteenth century we hear of a Jew named MUSETTO (Little Moses), the esteemed dancing master of the children of MALATESTA V, duke of Pesaro. Another famous dancing master of that epoch was GIUSEPPE EBREO, whose "Partita crudele" (Cruel Parting) is incorporated in GUGLIELMO EBREO's manual for dancing.[3] In 1575 Pope GREGORY XIII (1572-1585) granted a special license to two Jews from Ancona for the teaching of dancing and singing.

The dance in the high society of Italy was an integral part of general education; it was a refined and complicated art, and those who taught it enjoyed full social equality with their employers who in many cases belonged to the highest nobility. The dancing masters, at least the most famous of them, were bent on publicizing their art also in books; there exist quite a number of practical manuals for dancing which, at that time, claimed to be "scientific" treatises. The most important among these is the "Trattato del'arte del ballo," the author of which is GUGLIELMO EBREO (William the Jew), of Pesaro.[4]

We know relatively little about his life other than that he was a pupil of DOMENICO da PIACENZA, the founder of a new school of dance. GUGLIELMO regarded himself as PIACENZA's most devout disciple and faithful imitator. He incorporated many of his dances in his own compilation. In his book (written ca. 1463) we learn that he must have been close to the brilliant circle surrounding the mid-15th-century court of the MEDICI in Florence. His book contains two dances composed (or choreographed) by LORENZO the MAGNIFICENT himself as a youth. A poem in praise of GUGLIELMO EBREO suggests that he was a familiar figure in other courts of Italy besides that of the MEDICI.[5]

For the marriage of CONSTANZO SFORZA with CAMILLA d'ARAGON in 1475, GUGLIELMO presented a divertimento with the assistance of numerous co-religionists. There were solemn processions by the Jews of Pesaro, in which splendid pageantry was displayed, and there were dances by one hundred twenty youths and maidens with rich musical accompaniment.[6]

There are indications to the effect that in his middle life GUGLIELMO converted to Christianity. Two of the few extant manuscript copies of his *Trattato* are anonymous; three bear his name; and one, with some additional chapters, is ascribed to a certain GIOVANNI AMBROGIO da PESARO. There is little doubt that the two persons were identical, since the same place of origin is given in both cases, and that in due course GUGLIELMO the Jew became known by the Christian name of GIOVANNI AMBROGIO.[7]

His career later brought him to the court of GALEAZZO MARIA SFORZA, Duke of Milan. In an illuminated codex of his *Trattato*, copied in 1463 for the Duke himself, there is a miniature "showing three dancers wtih their little fingers interlocked performing a *bassa danza* (the precursor of the *minuetto*), to the accompaniment of a harp. It may be that here we have in the central figure a portrait of GUGLIELMO himself" (Illustration No. 26). At this time he was still a Jew, his name being given as GUGLIELMO EBREO.[8]

Still later, the duchess BIANCA SFORZA sent him to Naples to visit her daughter IPPOLITA and act as dancing master for the royal children. After that, he is found at the court of FERRARA in 1481, where he became dancing master to the seven-year-old daughter of the ducal house, who became famous as ISABELLA d'ESTE, duchess of Mantua. At this point GUGLIELMO's name is lost of sight.[9]

In the last period of his life in Mantua, GUGLIELMO came into contact with the group of court musicians in the service of the art-loving GONZAGAS, among others with the most famous of them, SALOMONE ROSSI. Whether the two outstanding artists, one in dance, the other in music, collaborated on some project is a matter of conjecture. It is not impossible, however, that their art became enriched in the genial atmosphere of this artistic Mecca.

At the time of the Renaissance, just as in Biblical times, music and dancing were closely interlinked and were considered as branches of the same tree.[10] It can be assumed that when a dancing master composed a choreography, he usually composed its music as well. It is not positively known whether this was the case with the dance creations of GUGLIELMO; it can only be surmised that at times he also composed the music for his dances. If not, he could readily find, among his co-religionists, numerous talented musicians upon whom he could rely for furnishing him the necessary musical background. We have no knowledge of such associations; but the close connection of Jewish artists among themselves allows us to conclude that GUGLIELMO might have used the collaboration of Jewish musicians in Pesaro, Naples and Mantua.

Not only in Renaissance Italy, but in other countries as well, we encounter Jewish dancing masters. We know, for instance, of ISAAC d' ORLEANS, who was successful in this capacity in Paris during the sixteenth century.

A number of attempts have been made to reconstruct the choreography of GUGLIELMO's dances as he described them in his Codex.[11]

As for the music to these dances, "it is a question involved in even greater obscurity than the reconstruction of the actual dance steps and evolutions. . . . We can attempt nothing more than to give a survey of the problem as it now stands."[12]

"The Royal Library at Brussels is the possessor of a French collection of dances known as *Basses dances de la Bibliothèque de Bourgogne*, sometimes cited as *Basses dances de Marguerite d'Autriche*. It is a costly little manuscript, written on heavy black pages of small dimensions, in notes of gold and silver."[13] A number of outstanding scholars suggested methods for reading the notes in mensural notation, among them HUGO RIEMANN, FRIEDRICH BLUME, JOHANNES WOLF, WILLIBALD GURLITT, and others. None of them had as yet succeeded in arriving at a satisfactory solution, but they may have made practical suggestions toward solving the problem. And, as KINKELDEY thinks, "how Marguerite of Austria, Lorenzo the Magnificent, the lords and ladies of SFORZA, URBINO and ESTE really danced, will not remain a mystery forever." Furthermore, "there is reason to hope that some day we will recognize and become more intimately acquainted with the Lully or Rameau, or, if you will, with the Lanner and the Johann Strauss of that stately, highly artistic, life-and-luxury-loving period of the Renaissance."[14]

In the same century there were a number of instrumentalists of Jewish origin in Italy who occupied important positions and were renowned among the multitude of Gentile musicians. Some of their names are preserved for posterity. It must be noted that in those days an instrumentalist was by necessity a composer as well. The printing of music was then in its infancy; the only music available to the instrumentalist were manuscripts which he copied of other composers, a procedure that was cumbersome and not always bountiful, in some cases necessitating much travel. It was therefore more practical in the long run for an instrumentalist to be his own composer.

An outstanding Jewish lute player migrated from Germany and eventually settled in Florence. He seems to have been an itinerant musician, since he was looked upon as a low character by his contemporaries, which was considered usual when a man had no permanent domicile. In Florence he entered the service of the Medici, and, hoping for a better chance in his profession, he was converted to Catholicism, adopting the name of GIOVANNI MARIA, in honor of Cardinal GIOVANNI de MEDICI (later Pope LEO X). He obviously had a turbulent life and was implicated in a murder for which, in 1492, he was convicted and sentenced to death and his belongings were confiscated. Sensing his doom, he escaped from the city in time to avoid punishment. Next we find him at Urbino, then in Rome, in the service of the above-mentioned Cardinal GIOVANNI.

A few years later, we have knowledge of a singer and composer GIOVAN MARIA da CREMA, who supervised the musical education of the GONZAGA princes. Whether the two are identical is not certain. It is likely, however, that the latter was a different person, since it cannot be assumed that the GONZAGAS would have employed as a music master an individual implicated for a crime, however outstanding his artistic merits might have been.

In Rome, GIOVANNI MARIA was the favorite of his former patron, the music-loving Cardinal GIOVANNI de' MEDICI, who assembled around him a group of excellent musicians, whose performances afforded him a special delight. When in 1513 the Cardinal became Pope LEO X, the entire group enjoyed further privileges. GIOVANNI MARIA's son, CAMILLO, a musician like his father, also became a favorite of the Pope. GIOVANNI received a regular salary of 25 gold ducats, a payment which was secured from the revenues of the fortress-town Verocchio. GIOVANNI was made its

Castellan, with all its revenues and the title of Count (June 22, 1513).[15] This papal appointment brought about some objections by the inhabitants of the city. To enforce it, the Pope had to take firm steps to see that his instructions were obeyed.[16]

An urge for roving seems to have been in the blood of GIOVANNI MARIA, for he did not stay long even in this unique sinecure. After a time we find him in Venice, where his brother resided. There he entered the service of the Signoria, but, abandoning his lute on which he was a past master, he changed to the fife and became the Doge's *pifaro* (fife player). In spite of this, his artistry as a lute player was still remembered at the papal court. The Pope missed him in his entourage and, in May 1520, invited him back to Rome. Under the pretext of performing certain pieces of music, Pope LEO asked the Doge for GIOVANNI's return, which was granted for one year. When the year came to a close, the Pope procrastinated from month to month in releasing him. Apparently GIOVANNI meant too much to the Pope to let him go. In 1521 LEO died and GIOVANNI, instead of returning to Venice, sought employment in Mantua, supplied with letters of recommendation from a friend, the famous BALDASSARE CASTIGLIONE. Another such letter was from Cardinal GIULIO de' Medici (later Pope CLEMENT VII), who wrote of him: "I believe your Excellency knows how attached the late Pope of blessed memory was to the virtue and grace of Jo: MARIA the musician . . . who, accompanied by his art, served him until the last days of his life."[17] After a short while we find him again at the papal court, during the short reign of HADRIAN VI (1522-1523). On May 20, 1523, there was at the pontifical palace a great banquet with musical entertainment, at which "ZUAN MARIA," with three other lute players, gave an outstanding performance. Concerning the rest of his life nothing is known; he probably remained in papal service till the end of his days.

Outside of having been a virtuoso on at least two instruments, GIOVANNI was a prolific and highly recognized composer of the time, famous far beyond the boundaries of Italy. The Venetian ambassador to the court of HENRY VIII of England requested the Signoria, in 1515, that some of the compositions of GIOVANNI be sent to him to be performed at the English court. The German lute manufacturer and composer, HANS GERLE of Nüremberg (d. 1570) published in 1552 an anthology of lute compositions by the most famous lutists of the epoch, in which a collection of eight preambles and six dances of JOAN MARIA da CRESCA (evidently the *nom de plume* of GIOVANNI) are included. He also earned a reputation as a flute player. ANDREA CALMO, in his *"Lettere Piacevoli"* included a letter to him under the name: "M. ZUAN MARIA del CORNETTO, *kinsman of the Muses."*[18] In *"Orlandino"* of TEOFILO FOLENGO (IV, 27), GIOVANNI is praised highly as *"Cornetto Padoano* ZAN MARIA." In spite of his conversion to Christianity he continued to be known by his contemporaries as GIANMARIA GIUDEO, and several historians of the Renaissance did not even suspect that he had left his original Jewish faith.

CECIL ROTH corrects the erroneous belief, that the famous viola player of this period, GIACOMO SANSECONDO, who was painted by RAPHAEL, and a contemporary of GIOVANNI MARIA, was also a Jew. This view is based on a misreading of a passage in BURCKHARDT's *"Renaissance"*, in which he is mentioned immediately after GIOVANNI MARIA. The inference is false. BURCKHARDT and those who follow him err in stating that the reference to "GIOVAN MARIA da CORNETO" (sic) is to be found in the *"Orlandino."*[19]

Apart from the papal city and Venice, where Renaissance arts had been cultivated on a large scale, it was the ducal court of Mantua where the art-loving House of GONZAGA assembled around them a plethora of artists of all categories that made this provincial town a magnificent center of intellectual activities in sixteenth-century Italy. For the history of Jewish music, the period of Mantua's brilliancy is of particular significance, since the tolerant and broad-minded GONZAGAS not only permitted the settlement of Jews within the boundaries of their realm, but invited specially gifted Jews, writers, actors and musicians to adorn the illustrious gathering at their court. Thus, beginning with the first half of the sixteenth century, a whole group of Jewish singers, instrumentalists and composers lived and worked in Mantua, contributing greatly to the importance and glory of that court.

In the GONZAGA archives there is mention of a Jewish composer (probably also a singer and instrumentalist) DAVID da CIVITA (b. end of the sixteenth century). Nothing is known about his life except that in 1616 there was published in Venice a book of 17 madrigals for alto, basso and continuo, entitled *"Premitie Armoniche,"* (Harmonious First Fruits), which he, as his "most faithful and devoted servant," dedicated to the Duke of Mantua.

In the same archives there is further mention, in 1542, of a Jewish musician, ABRAMO dell' ARPA (Abraham of the Harp) (c. 1525-1566). In that year he participated in a dramatic production at the ducal court and was cast as the god Pan. He must have been such an outstanding musician that he was summoned to Vienna to teach music to the children of FERDINAND I of Austria (1503-1564). At that time (around 1560) there was at the Imperial Court another Jewish harp player, DANIEL LEVI. Whether ABRAMO's artistic temperament did not conform with the stiff etiquette of the court, or whether he was longing for the genial atmosphere of the intimate group of Mantua, he soon returned to that city, where he remained for the rest of his life, with only occasional interruptions. In 1555 he appeared in Rome under the name of "ABRAHAM, the Musician of Mantua," but shortly thereafter he returned to Mantua, where he got into trouble of some kind and was imprisoned in December, 1566. Apparently his crime was not serious, for he was soon released and again resumed his activities. By that time he was aging, which allows the assumption that he was born in the early sixteenth century. In his old age his nephew (or grandson?) ABRAMINO ("Little Abraham") dell'ARPA was his associate, and soon came into prominence in his own right. On one occasion (in 1587) the two collaborated in a sort of "Water music" entertainment, such as court musicians wrote for their princely employers in the following century. This festivity took place on a lake when Cardinal GAETANO of Bologna came to Mantua to baptize a newborn member of the ducal family. That year Duke GUGLIELMO, the faithful patron of ABRAMO, retired to Goito, a sick man. ABRAMINO accompanied him to comfort his last days with his playing.[20] This shows that the Dukes of Mantua, ardent music lovers during their life, did not want to dispense with it even while dying.

Even more versatile than ABRAMO and his nephew was the singer, lute-player, composer and teacher JACCHINO or ISACCHINO (Little ISAAC) MASSARANO. Added to all these talents, he pos-

A page of the Locheim Songbook, written by Wölflein von Locheim ca. 1450, with the dedication in Hebrew characters in the last line.

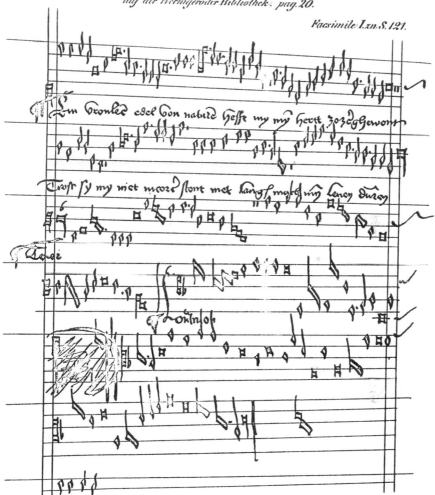

Facsimile of page 20 of the Locheimer songbook. Lyrics in Middle-High-German:

> Ein vroulein edel von naturen
> hefft my myn hertt zo zeer ghewont.
> Trost sy my niet in corter stont
> niet langer mach myn leuen duren.

Facsimile of the Manuscript Adler, in the Library of the Jewish Theological Seminary of America (New York).

מִי עֶלָהּ חוֹרֵב וַיַּעֲמִירוּ עֶגֶן קְשׁ...

כמשה : מִ... יְ... לִיךְ ...

... יָאֲרִי לְמשֶׁה : מִי

... שֶׁ... רָהָם חֵפֶל הַיְעֵל תַּעֲנִיוֹם

למשׁה : מִי כָה בָּאֵלִיךְ חֹק עֵדוֹת

בְּמִרְאָה וְלֹא בְחִידֹת ... שֶׁה : מִי זֹאת

Facsimile (recto and verso) of the Fragment Cincinnati ENA 4096 b.

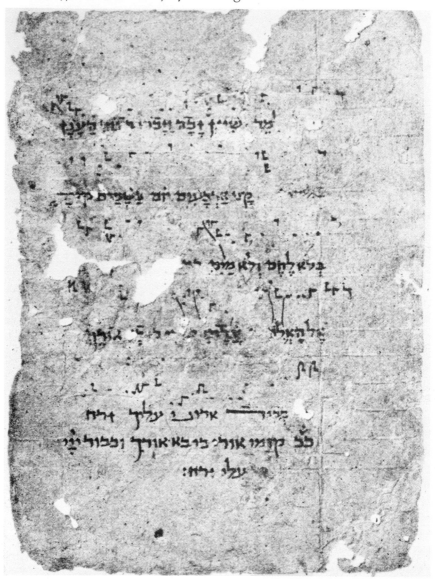

מי עַל הַר חוֹרֵב וַיַעֲמִידוֹ עַטְרָה קְשַׁ...

עֶגְלֵי כמשה: מִי ... אוֹ חַיִל ...

... אַשְׁרֵי כמשה: כִּי

... שֶׁ... וַעַל הֶעָ...תַּעֲלוּם

כמשה: מִי ... בְּאֵיתָן חֹק יְצִירוֹת

בַּבְּרָאוֹת ... וְלֹא כְּמִידוֹת כ.שה: מִי מָאֵל

sessed still another; he was an expert on choreography and as such he was commissioned to provide the dances for quite a number of important ballet productions of the Renaissance epoch. Among others he was selected to supervise the dances of GUARINI's *"Il Pastor Fido,"* a so-called "pastoral tragicomedy," the most famous play of that time. It was presented in 1591 on the stage of the ducal palace at Mantua. In the same year the poet MANFREDI entrusted him with the composition of the choreography of his new dramatic "sylvan" poem which, as he hoped, would be performed at the Mantuan court. In a letter addressed to *"Messer* ISACCHINO EBREO," he said that "he certainly did not require detailed instructions, but he was to pay particular attention to the choir's four *canzonette,* which were to be danced as well as sung."[21]

Whether MASSARANO acquired wealth through his musical or choreographic accomplishments, or whether he had other means of income cannot be ascertained. The fact is that, in 1594 he was capable of not only being host to the Duke and his entire court, but also entertained them in a lavish manner.[22] Such a social distinction was certainly no small honor accorded a Jewish musician, even in the enlightened atmosphere of Mantua.

The court of the GONZAGAS had, up to now, encouraged Jewish instrumentalists, composers and choreographers. The first famous singer since Biblical times was also noted in the annals of this court. MADAME EUROPA, as she was called, was the sister of SALOMONE ROSSI EBREO, the renowned composer, and possibly the daughter of AZARIAH de' ROSSI, the most outstanding literary figure of Renaissance Italy. She was prominent as one of the leading singers in MONTEVERDI's early opera, *L'Arianna,* which was presented in March 1608 in Mantua, on the occasion of the marriage of FRANCESCO GONZAGA, the Duke's son. The wedding festivities were of incredible luxury with no pains being spared to make the spectacle as perfect as money could pay. The actors exerted special efforts, studying and perfecting their roles for no less than six months prior to the performance.[23]

MONTEVERDI's opera represents a turning point in general operatic history. In it the composer revealed for the first time the emotional and dramatic value of musical discords, whereas his predecessors (PERI, CACCINI and others) used merely the style of inexpressive declamation for shaping their melodic lines. The highlight of the opera was the famous *"Lamento d'Arianna,"* a piece far ahead of its time, which is touching even today in its expressive beauty. We may imagine how the audience was enthralled by hearing the lament sung by MADAME EUROPA, and we understand such praises as that in a contemporary notice: "Understanding music to perfection, she sang to the great pleasure and greater surprise of the audience, her voice being so delicate and sweet, and her simplicity bringing tears to the eyes."[24]

The name EUROPA originates in all probability from an *intermezzo,* or musical interlude inserted between the acts of a play. In such an intermezzo, a singer whose name was not mentioned in the cast, took the role of *Europa;* she must have had such acclaim that she retained it as her stage-name. Her achievement in this role was probably the cause of her being cast in the leading part of MONTEVERDI's opera.

Musical talent was evidently hereditary in the ROSSI family. MADAME EUROPA's son, ANSELMO ("ASHER") de ROSSI was a successful composer himself. In a collection of *"Motets . . . written by various musicians, servants of the Lord Duke of Mantua"* (publ. in Venice 1618), there is a composition by ANSELMO for three voices entitled *"Aperi oculos meos"* (I opened my eyes). He must have written quite a number of other compositions, since his work was considered important enough to be included in an anthology of famous contemporary composers.

About his life nothing is known except for the fact that together with other members of the ROSSI family, ANGELO (identical with ANSELMO) and his sons GIUSEPPE and BONAIUTO, were in the service of the Dukes of Savoy at Turin. At this court, ANGELO achieved such success that he was taken over by the duke's half brother CARLO EMANUEL I, "the Great," under whose auspices the court of Turin began to acquire a brilliance which almost rivaled that of Mantua.[25] Here ANGELO had multiple functions; as a composer of the music to the ballets, as a player of the lute, as a music teacher of the princely children and of the pages about the court. His sons were accomplished guitar players; after their father's death they remained in the duke's service. GIUSEPPE stayed even until the second half of the seventeenth century.

As a special favor from his patron, and as a part of his remuneration, ANSELMO received a franchise to maintain a loan-bank at Rocconigi, near the country seat where the dukes spent their leisure. Thus he could be summoned at any time for musical entertainment. A curious, and probably unique, combination indeed in the life of a Jewish musician in the Renaissance: performer and moneylender at the same time. It seems that ANSELMO frequently displayed his talents in both capacities.

Another prolific Jewish composer of the Renaissance was ALLEGRO PORTO EBREO, as he called himself. His first name ALLEGRO is supposed to be the translation of the Jewish name SIMḤA (joy, gaiety). He belonged to one of Mantua's leading Jewish families, as proven by the fact that there was in the town a "Porto Synagogue," either built or maintained by this family. The existence of this synagogue is revealed by a *kinah* (dirge), written by MESHULLAM SULLAM ben ISAAC, on the occasion of a conflagration in the ghetto (June 19, 1610), in which the synagogue was destroyed, together with thirty-seven Torah scrolls (this *kinah* was printed in Mantua 1720).[26] A synagogue that possessed that many precious scrolls must certainly have been no modest house of worship. This sheds light upon the standing of the Porto family in Mantua.

Although it is logical to assume that the composer was a scion of this family, we do not know anything concerning his life. He was probably born between 1590 and 1595, and died around 1625. A brief reference to him is found in a collection of biographical notes about composers in the Vatican Library,[27] where he is referred to as *"Ebreo di età giovine"* (A Jew of young age), which may suggest the early death of PORTO.

The dedications of his printed works seem to indicate that PORTO spent some time in Germanic lands. In 1619 he dedicated a volume of madrigals to GIOVANNI SFORZA, *Conte di Porzia,* at the court of the Prince Elector of Bavaria. Two of the poems set to music by PORTO were written by the Count of SFORZA himself. Another volume of madrigals, published in 1625, is dedicated to the Emperor FERDINAND II (1578–1637), whose empress was the daughter of the Duke of Mantua (Illustrations Nos. 27 and 28).

The former collection "in the new style" was published in Venice (1619) under the title *Nuove musiche, a 3 voci, Lib. 2, col Basso Continuo per sonar con il Chitaron, Op. 4;* the second, also in Venice (1625), as *Madrigali a cinque voci, con Basso Continuo, e col Chitarrone.* Prior to this opus, PORTO published another set of madrigals, *Il primo Lib. di Madrigali a 5 voci, col Basso Continuo, e col Chitarrone stampato a di 14. Gennaro in Venezia l'anno 1622.* A further collection of his, madrigals for three voices "with some arias and romanesque dialogue," was published in the same year.

In his compositions PORTO follows the style and trend of his time: polyphonic vocal settings. In this respect his works do not differ in character from the works of other composers of the epoch; particularly, they are devoid of any specifically Jewish features.

An otherwise unknown musician at the Court of the GONZAGAS was DAVID SACERDOTE (the Italian translation of Cohen), about whom some light was thrown in a posthumous article by ALFRED EINSTEIN.[28]

Another Jewish musician of this period was BENEDETTO SESSIGLI, who was employed by the Court of Savoy. We do not know much about his life, except the anecdote describing his near-drowning during a water-entertainment held by the Duke in the park of his villa at Mirefiori, near Turin. While performing aboard the Duke's own barge, SESSIGLI lost his footing and fell into the water. Fortunately, he was fished out not much the worse, but at the Duke's expense his instrument had to be replaced.[29]

Whether SESSIGLI was also active as a composer is not known. No publications of his music have survived. However, in the last decades a large amount of research has been done in Italian archives, especially with regard to Renaissance composers, and it is possible that in time some works of this almost forgotten musician will turn up.

Jewish weddings in Italy, like those of Christian nobility, always were accompanied by a rich musical display.

One of the most important figures among Italian Renaissance musicians, and certainly the most outstanding Jewish composer before the dawn of the nineteenth century, was SALOMONE de ROSSI EBREO, as he called himself in his life, in the publications of his works and in the wordy dedications to his sponsors by which his published compositions were introduced. He sometimes signed himself SHLOMO MI-ha-ADUMIM, the translation of his Italian name into Hebrew. He was born in Mantua in or about 1565, and died there in 1628.

He came from an aristocratic Jewish family which allegedly could trace its ancestry back to King David. However, this appears to be no more than one of those pious legends which have cropped up in medieval times in relation to the genealogies of certain families. It is highly improbable that any Jewish family in the European Diaspora could have proven such a line of descent after so many centuries of migrations, turmoil and persecutions. It is certain, however, that SALOMONE's immediate ancestors played an important part in the intellectual life of the Italian Trecento and Quattrocento. Among them was the famous philosopher AZARIAH dei ROSSI (b. ca. 1514, d. in Mantua in 1578).

In the Mantuan archives it is stated that SALOMONE and his sister EUROPA were children of AZARIAH. This is clearly in error, since AZARIAH complained that he had no surviving son. However, SALOMONE might well have been his nephew.

ROSSI represents by reputation and ability a highly significant and characteristic feature of an age which divulged in the same family Hebraic and secular interests, synagogal inspiration and court activities. It is not often that the creative impulse in composition and instrumental virtuosity were so intimately intertwined with social adulation at the courtly level accorded ROSSI and his family.[30]

SALOMONE was originally a virtuoso player on the viol (the precursor of the violin); apparently he entered the ducal service at Mantua, together with his sister EUROPA, on the accession of Duke VINCENZO in 1587. Viol players at those times were mostly accomplished singers; or maybe the reverse was true, namely, that a Jewish singer had to be master of an instrument in order to be able to accompany himself, like the Levites in Ancient Israel? In any event, SALOMONE's rise at the court was meteoric. As he himself writes, he was taught composition by the musicians at the ducal court, among them, allegedly, MARC ANTONIO IN-GENIERI (d. 1603), who was also MONTEVERDI's teacher. This part of the statement, however, is not ROSSI's own, but originated from SAMUEL NAUMBOURG who, in 1876, was the first to publish several of ROSSI's works in a modern edition and in the form of a score. INGENIERI lived and taught in Verona, not in Mantua. ROSSI's teachers might have been other musicians living in Mantua, among them MONTEVERDI himself, who, from 1602 to 1613 was *"maestro di capella"* at the ducal court. Working with this great musician, ROSSI must have learned the craft of composition thoroughly. But the lion's share in ROSSI's musical education falls to FRANCESCO ROVIGO, a renowned composer himself, who lived in Mantua with-out being affiliated with the ducal court despite the fact that he was Jewish, or a converted Jew.[31] Soon ROSSI entered the creative field and in time became one of the leading composers of the Renaissance.

EINSTEIN ventures the hypothesis that there might have been two SALOMONE ROSSIS, an older and a younger one, father and son, or uncle and nephew, the younger of whom, our SALOMONE, may have been born between 1570 and 1580. He bases his assumption on a critical analysis of ROSSI's first published madrigals, in which he showed himself already an accomplished master who preceded MONTEVERDI by several years at least with his *madrigali con-certati*, the *accompanied* madrigals. True, MONTEVERDI published his first four books of madrigals for 5 voices between 1583 and 1603, but they were *a cappella*, for purely vocal performance.[32]

It appears that ROSSI had his own company of musicians (evi-dently all Jews), with whom he traveled about giving perform-ances in other cities.[33] Among them there might have been some of his relatives, like MATTEO ROSSI, a basso, ANSELMO (ANGELO) ROSSI, a lute player and composer. The writer BASTIANO de ROSSI, also in the service of the Mantuan court, seems to have had no musical talents and thus did not belong to SOLOMON's group of musicians. "When, in 1612, ALESSANDRO I, Prince of Mirandola and Concordia, was expecting a visit from his father-in-law, the

Duke of Modena, he sent to Mantua asking the State Counsellor to send him 'the Jew SALOMONE' and his company to give a concert in honor of the guests."[34]

Now there was a complication connected with this traveling company. The Jews were obliged to wear a badge inside and outside Mantua; Rossi and his musicians seem to have objected to being forced to wear this sign at a foreign court and at such a solemn occasion. Therefore, Duke VINCENZO, with the recorded words of "how dear to us is the service that SALOMONE ROSSI the Jew has performed for us for many years past by his virtue in music and playing," exempted ROSSI and the members of his group from having to wear the badge. This favor was conferred by successive rulers.[35]

In 1622 ROSSI was still in the service of the ducal court as a viol player, singer and composer, at a yearly salary of 383 lire (ducats?) and he continued to fulfill his functions until his death, about six years later (1628).

ROSSI's creative output consisted of a great number of vocal and instrumental compositions, most of them published during his lifetime, among which several were printed in many (up to seven) editions, a proof of how much the public at large appreciated them. Owing to the most diverse categories of his creative talent, EINSTEIN called him "a universal composer en miniature."[36] The Jewish synagogue service of his period was enriched by many of his liturgical compositions and, in addition, he collaborated with MONTEVERDI, MUZIO EFFREM and ALESSANDRO GUIVIZZANI in a remarkable dramatic composition, to which he contributed a sung and played balletto. Among the important Renaissance publications are his four collections of instrumental music (1607, 1608, 1613, and 1622), making him one of the outstanding pioneers in this field.[37]

ROSSI's first published compositions were not the madrigals which established his fame, but a collection of nineteen canzonette for three voices, printed in Venice in 1589 (this invalidates the assumption that he may have been born between 1570 and 1580; it is more likely that he was born around 1565, or even earlier). The canzonetta was a vocal composition less elaborate harmonically as well as contrapuntally, than the more sophisticated madrigal. A further volume of Rossi's *canzonette* was published in 1591.

For general music history, Rossi's outstanding achievements are the madrigals for 5 voices (publ. 1600, 1602, 1603, and 1622). Some of these volumes were repeatedly reprinted during his lifetime. Another vocal item of smaller design was a collection of 25 duos for two sopranos or two tenors (his Opus 13), which he called appropriately *"Madrigaletti"* (little madrigals); it was published at Venice in 1628. These chansons are the most enchanting duets of the Renaissance, true little masterpieces in form and treatment.

It is necessary, in this connection, to examine the choice of poets Rossi utilized for his vocal compositions. Here he showed himself to be a true man of the Renaissance. There are few contemporary composers who have so decidedly turned to the poets of their own time. EINSTEIN furnishes us a complete list of the poets of Rossi's compositions.[38]

Even more important than his vocal compositions were his instrumental works, in which he paved the way not only for the contrapuntal design in orchestral style, but even more so for harmonic innovations, considered "daring" at that time. Not before his first printed vocal works proved successful was he ready to publish his first collection of orchestral pieces, under the title *"Sinfonie e gagliarde a tre, quattro e cinque voci, per sonar due viole cuero doi cornetti e un chittarrone o altro istromenta da corpo"* (1607). Due to its marked success this collection was republished in 1608, 1622 and 1623. Another similar collection appeared in 1608, under the title *"Il secondo libro delle sinfonie e gagliarde,"* republished in 1623 as *"Sonate, gagliarde, brandi e correnti a due viole col basso per il Cembalo,"* succeeded in 1623 and 1638 by *"Il terzo libro de varie sonate, sinfonie, gagliarde, brandi e correnti, per sonar due viole da braccio e un chitarrone o altro simile stromenti"*; and finally by *"Il quarto libro de varie sonate, sinfonie, gagliarde, brandi, e correnti per sonar due violini et un chitarrone o altro stromenti simile"* (1622, 1642).

Some of the *gagliarde* carry titles which indicate that they were dedicated to sponsors or friends. Such headings are: *Gagliarda detta Venturino, Gagliarda detta Marchesino* (dedicated to the young crown prince), *Gagliarda detta La Massara* (dedicated to the Jewish singer and dancing master MASSARANO), and others.

Beyond these instrumental works, ROSSI contributed several pieces to composite volumes of the period, in which the works of various famous composers appeared in the form of an anthology. Such collections were, for example, the volumes "*Il Parnasso*," and "*Il Helicono*," both published in Antwerp in 1613 and 1614 respectively.

This was the era which saw the birth of the opera, the most revolutionary secular musical creation, which won for ROSSI's teacher, MONTEVERDI, lasting fame. Curiously enough, ROSSI was hesitant and made rather superficial approaches into the new dramatic form. In 1617 the Florentine, GIOVANNI BATTISTA ANDREINI, in Venice, produced a dramatic performance "*La Maddalena*," which he called a "sacred representation." Its music was furnished by the "most excellent composers" of that time, among them MONTEVERDI. To this "sacred opera" ROSSI contributed the concluding *balletto* for three singing voices, accompanied by three *viole de braccio* (violins), using as lyrics:

> *Spezziam pront' ò vecchiarelle*
> *Questo suolo*
> *Vago e solo*
> *Far d'augei predo più belle.*

The literal translation of it is:

> Let us sweep clean, oh little old ladies
> This ground,
> Beautiful and lonely.
> Make of birds more beautiful prey.

Freely interpreted, this is an invitation to dancing:

> Let's dance now, little old ladies.

HUGO RIEMANN calls him "undoubtedly the most important representative of the new style in the instrumental field . . . and the manner of his conception long remained a model for its

Mus. ex. No. 34

Balletto by Salomone Rossi Ebreo, to Giovanni Battista Andreini's
La Maddalena (1617).

simple form." Some historians consider him even the inventor of
the symphony in its modern sense; but this is certainly overesti-
mating Rossi's importance as an instrumental composer. The "in-
vention" of the symphony was the merit of the eighteenth-century
"Mannheim" school.

In his instrumental compositions Rossi was among the first to
apply the "monodic" principle, which was so far used mainly in
the new art form of the Opera. This principle consists in sustaining
the melody with a simple harmonic background, allowing the
singers *"cantare senza battuta,"* in a free musical declamation, as
it was termed in those days. This was in contrast to the polyphonic style, in which all parts were endowed with equal importance. This monodic design had a specific significance for
singers who were thereby able to elaborate upon their melodic
line, without disturbing the accompaniment. Later, especially in
the *opera buffa* of the seventeenth and eighteenth centuries, this
elaboration led to abuses of the singers, who took all kinds of
liberties with the composers' melodies in order to show off with
their vocal skill. What started as an important innovation was to
become, in the hands of conceited singers, a misuse against which
composers with artistic conscience fought in vain. The audiences
enjoyed the vocal fireworks of the singers, who considered their
vocal embellishments an inviolable privilege. It was not until the
reform of the Opera by Chr. W. GLUCK (1714–1787) that a
breach was made in this profanation of operatic art.

At the wedding festivities of the ducal court in Mantua, in 1608,
mentioned above, a drama by GIOVANNI BATTISTA GUARINI,
L'Idropica, was presented. To this play Rossi wrote an *intermezzo.* Another *intermezzo* from his pen was the opening piece to
MONTEVERDI's *L'Arianna,* which was performed for the first time
on the same occasion. Rossi's instrumental compositions contain
numerous *"sinfonie,"* (twenty in his first book, thirty in the second)."*Sinfonia"* at that time signified "overture," or opening instrumental music to a play, an opera, or a vocal concert work.
These pieces are not just independent compositions as they are
usually played in concerts, but always served as an introduction
or as an interlude for vocal chamber music, such as duets with
basso continuo, or for madrigals.[39] (Mus. ex. No. 35.)

Mus. ex. No. 35

Sinfonia Quinta by Salomone Rossi Ebreo from his *Il terzo libro de varie sonate* (1613) (After Paul Nettl, *Alte jüdische Spielleute und Musiker* (Prague, 1923), pp. 56–57.

In the third collection of his instrumental works, Rossi entitled one of his compositions "*Sonata prima, detta la Moderna*" (First Sonata, called the Modern). The title itself was novel and it is eminently justified if we consider how advanced, harmonically and structurally it was, compared to other music of the day. It had four movements, an innovation in itself. It also contained several "*sinfonie*," which served as connecting links between the movements.

Several decades later the principle of four movements for a chamber music work was generally adopted.

Rossi's importance as a composer and the esteem in which he was held is furthermore reflected by the names of the princely persons to whom he dedicated his works. During that epoch it was customary for an author to express his gratitude for favors received, or expected, or simply to impart some glamor to his work by dedicating it to a highly placed person, a nobleman, or to a member of a ruling house. The dedications were done generally in the form of a long-winded introduction and in the florid verbosity of the time, praising the sponsor's or benefactor's virtues as a patron or a protector of the arts. The dedication sometimes implied personal relations between the artist and his sponsor. In Rossi's case we may reasonably assume a genial relationship with the Dukes of Mantua, whom Rossi may have contacted daily. Still, it is difficult to believe that such exalted personages as the Duke of Modena, the Count of Sansecondo, the Prince of Guastalla, and others to whom Rossi dedicated his works would entertain more than a superficial, or at best condescending, attitude toward a Jewish musician.

Up to this point only the secular works of SALOMONE ROSSI have been discussed. However important and pioneering his activity in this field may have been, for the history of Jewish music it is eclipsed by his achievements in the field of synagogue music. In this respect his foremost merit consists in the fact that he introduced the spirit of the Renaissance into the sacred precincts of Jewish liturgy. To understand this, we must examine the state of the synagogal music in those days.

It has been repeatedly emphasized in our study that Jewish

religious and folk music has been influenced considerably by the national environment in which the various settlements had co-existed with the surrounding peoples. Babylonian Jewry was under the spell of Oriental musical practice; the music of the Spanish Jews was partly "assimilated" with that of the Moorish world; whereas Central European Jewry largely imitated, in the synagogue as well as in the home, German music, both in its secular (folksongs) and sacred aspects (church hymns and tunes). To this influence from without, was added the influence from within; the *hazzanic* "tradition" (if we may call it so), which consisted simply in borrowing from all available sources the material needed for the synagogal music service. The genuine tradition of the Temple and early synagogue music was preserved and continued as much as it was possible during the migrations along with the turbulent times. Still, with the exception of the Scriptural cantillation, most of it has been lost (or forgotten), because we find only faint traces of it in the synagogue music of the Diaspora. It is a curious fact, as modern research has established beyond doubt, that much of the early tradition was preserved more in the music of the early Church than in the Jewish synagogue itself. We can therefore state, without distorting the facts, that Jewish liturgical music in the Diaspora was in no small measure an amalgam of the most heterogeneous elements, styles and trends.

Such was the situation when SOLOMONE ROSSI, in a bold move, unprecedented in the history of Jewish music, undertook to *reform* synagogue music. Reform in this particular instance did not mean weeding out overgrowth, purifying the substance and, possibly, reestablishing the ancient tradition which, at that epoch, must have been largely lost anyway. The reform planned by ROSSI was more sweeping and far-reaching. It meant nothing less than rejuvenating the whole liturgical musical setup, which in practice amounted to composing entirely *new music* in the style of his time and introducing it into the synagogue.

It is generally accepted that ROSSI's reform amounted to a process of assimilation. However, just the contrary is true. ROSSI did not intend to adapt synagogue music to the trend of his time. His aim was to create an entirely new style for liturgical music.

He composed a whole set of pieces for Jewish worship, to be used in his own synagogue, hoping that his reform would be adopted and followed by broad-minded and enlightened rabbis and ḥazzanim in other Jewish congregations. His deep religious feeling revealed itself in these new works but in a musical language that was unusual, daring and thoroughly unorthodox. Therefore, it is not surprising that his reform provoked vehement opposition of the "conservatives," who took a stubborn stand not only against Rossi's radical changes, but against any changes in this field.

And yet Rossi's innovations were not entirely new. YEHUDA ARIEH (called LEONE) MODENA, one of the most universally gifted figures of the Renaissance, who was equally famous as a scholar, rabbi, singer and musician, was the first to introduce into the synagogue of Ferrara a choir of eight voices which he conducted himself in compositions (whether his own or of other composers is not known) "according to the relation of voices to each other," which means in the contrapuntal style of the period. His innovation was first met with strong opposition, but was upheld after the approval of a rabbinical assembly.

There were other synagogues in Renaissance Italy which committed various "sins" against the accepted tradition. The synagogue of Padua, for instance, employed, at the end of the sixteenth century, an organized Temple choir. BENẒIYYON ẒARFATI (d. 1610), who later became a rabbi at Venice, stated himself that he sang in this choir. ABRAHAM SEGRE, a ḥazzan in Casale Monferrato, a good musician with an adequate musical education, compiled a collection of synagogue melodies, some of his own, others "borrowed" for his disciple and successor JACOB FINZI (1582–1670).

The famous rabbi-poet-grammarian SAMUEL ARCHEVOLTI (1515–1611) was evidently a successful teacher. Among his Jewish and non-Jewish pupils two deserve a special mention. One of them was the Canon MARCO MARINI of Brescia, who wrote a Hebrew grammar (1580) and a Hebrew dictionary (1593), and even supervised a censored edition of the Talmud (1578–1581).[41] The other was the above-mentioned JACOB FINZI, who followed in the footsteps of his teacher ARCHEVOLTI, and wrote a grammatical treatise, Divre ʾAgur (The Words of Agur, cp. Prov. 30:1), published in Venice in 1605. In the preface of this work he mentions that he studied also with ABRAHAM (ben DAVID) PROVENZAL. What he might have learned from this teacher is not clear, because ABRAHAM was a physician. More light is thrown on this question, if we realize that ABRAHAM, together with his father, R. DAVID PROVENZAL, planned to establish a Jewish Academy (1566), in which religious and secular subjects, including philosophy, mathematics, rhetoric, etc. would be taught. Whether this plan has ever materialized is doubtful. At any rate, it must have existed only for a short time, because there are no records of its prolonged activity.[42]

But the greatest "sin" against the tradition was committed by the learned rabbi of Modena, ABRAHAM JOSEPH SOLOMON GRAZIANI, in the seventeenth century, who permitted the use of the organ in the synagogue, an unheard of practice in the Jewish liturgy. Possibly it was not so startlingly novel after all, since news might have reached Italy that in the Meisel Synagogue of Prague a similar "Christian" instrument had been established for the Friday eve services. When, on a certain occasion, a new Torah-scroll was dedicated in a neighboring community, LEONE MODENA wrote a special hymn "to be sung to music," that is, with instrumental accompaniment. Records show that, in the early seventeenth century, there existed in the Ferrara synagogue a youth choir of half a dozen voices which sang for a festive occasion.

In spite of all these precedents, ROSSI's reform tendencies met with stiff opposition and were considered un-Jewish. This is not surprising, since we know that Jewish pietists of all ages and in all countries were always dead set against changes, improvements and progress in the synagogue routine. We may imagine, therefore, how ROSSI's drastic reform movement may have adversely affected the zealous rabbis not only of their own, but other congregations as well, where the news of such a "sacrilege" transpired.

As could well be expected, LEONE MODENA supported ROSSI's reform to the hilt. With four of his rabbinical colleagues he wrote a responsum, or expert opinion, in which he demonstrated that, according to rabbinical law, there should be no objection to the use of music, new or old, in the synagogue service, since music of all categories is destined to glorify God. In spite of the moral support of such an outstanding personality, Rossi himself had difficulties in pushing through his reform even in his own congregation. He proceeded very carefully; he tried out all his synagogal pieces in his own services, and only when he was convinced that his music fulfilled his expectations he proceeded to release his synagogal works to the public. They were published in Venice in 1622-23 under the title *Ha-Shirim 'asher liShlomo* (Songs that are Solomon's), purposely associating his name with the Biblical Song of Songs. The collection comprised *"Hymns, songs and praises, brought together according to the science of playing and music, for 3, 4, 5, 6, 7 and 8 voices . . . to praise the Lord and to glorify His most high Name in all manner of holiness."* (Illustration No. 29.)

This time Rossi had dedicated his work not to a princely sponsor as the custom would have required, but to the head of one of the most prominent Jewish families of Mantua, Moses Sullam, the father-in-law of Sara Coppio Sullam, who acquired fame as a poetess and the most learned woman of the Renaissance period, and was also musically gifted (about her more later). Moses Sullam and his father were among Rossi's supporters from his earliest days and had contributed to his musical training; Moses was now one of those who urged Rossi to publish his synagogue compositions.

For his first published synagogal opus Rossi wrote an introduction in Hebrew, in the florid style of the time. In it he glorified his benefactor in a singular way. The word Sullam in Hebrew means "ladder." For anybody familiar with the Hebrew tongue it was easy to use this word for a clever pun: "The ladder (*sullam*) of your glory, like Jacob's ladder, rests on earth and his tip touches the heaven." It was certainly a flattery, while it corresponded to the style of such dedications of those days.

In this dedication there is an isolated remark which seems to indicate that Rossi was also active as a teacher of music: "Since God opened my ear . . . and has given me the grace to understand and to teach the science of music. . . ." Because his activity as a teacher of music was not corroborated by any coeval source, nor were pupils of his made known, this remark might refer to his activity as a choir leader in his synagogue, who rehearsed, i.e. "taught" his singers. However, this is merely a surmise.

To Rossi's preface, LEONE MODENA furnished, also in Hebrew, a lengthy foreword defending and justifying Rossi's reform. He emphasized that Rossi's musical rendering did not affect in the least the Hebrew words. A part of the foreword, addressed specifically to the opponents of the reform, reads:

> There are mong us certain people who fight against all that is new and against all progress; and these wish to proscribe the present useful innovation which their minds are incapable to understand. So I have thought to add here, as an important documentary evidence, a demand which was made of me on this same subject when I was rabbi of Ferrara. And also to make known my caustic reply, agreed to by all the Grand Rabbis of Venice. In this reply I showed the evidence from the Talmud itself that there can be no objection to the introduction of choral chant in the Temples. This should surely close the malevolent mouths of the detractors.

Not satisfied with this thrust upon Rossi's adversaries, LEONE MODENA, in addition, reprinted his "Responsum" referred to in the above quoted passage. This document of MODENA's was signed by four other Venetian rabbinical authorities.[43]

There is, furthermore, an epoch-making notice in this foreword: the warning that any reprint or sale of an "unauthorized" version of Rossi's sacred compositions was strictly prohibited. Up to that time anybody could reprint any work of an author or composer without penalty. The author's right in his work was for the first time legally stipulated in the Statute of Anne, Queen of England, in 1710. LEONE MODENA, in his preface to Rossi's work, established this right two centuries earlier. The only previous provision for a sort of copyright was that for the printers in Venice, established in 1491.

Besides taking up the cudgels for ROSSI, LEONE MODENA might have had a hidden personal interest in the publication. Among the half dozen hymns of the collection there was one for the wedding service, the lyrics of which were from his pen.

For two centuries after Rossi's death his works were almost

completely forgotten. They would still remain unnoticed were it not for the pioneering work done by SAMUEL NAUMBOURG (1815–1880), cantor of the Great Synagogue of Paris. In 1876 he published a sizable number of Rossi's synagogal compositions and some of his madrigals in modern transcription and in form of a score. The story of how Rossi's music was rediscovered is worth telling.

During one of his Italian trips, the musically inclined Baron EDMOND de ROTSCHILD came upon a batch of scattered parts of Rossi's vocal works which he brought to Paris. He urged NAUMBOURG to publish them, but since at Rossi's time only separate parts were printed, the isolated copies acquired by Baron de ROTSCHILD proved to be insufficient for publication. By a happy coincidence the Chief Rabbi of Mantua, MARCO MORTARA, learned of NAUMBOURG's plight. In the library of his synagogue there were bundles of ancient sacred music, among them an almost complete collection of Rossi's works, which R. MORTARA placed at NAUMBOURG's disposal. Furthermore, the Libary of Bologna owned two collections of Rossi's madrigals which the librarian, GAETANO GASPARI, lent to NAUMBOURG. VINCENT d'INDY, a young man at that time (born 1851), transcribed Rossi's vocal parts in modern notation. With his help NAUMBOURG published in 1876 the first modern edition of Rossi's music, thereby inaugurating a veritable rebirth of this composer's creations. The publication is not without errors, but in view of NAUMBOURG's pioneering achievement these are forgivable. Since then, musicology took an increased interest in Rossi's instrumental works; and in our times several were published for practical use. Still, the highest tribute for having been the first to promote the revival of Rossi's work goes to NAUMBOURG.

Rossi's synagogal opus contains thirty-three compositions which he wrote over a long period of years. The separate vocal parts were printed from left to right, like ordinary music; the Hebrew words, however, from right to left, not divided up into syllables so as to fit the musical text, but in complete lines.

Rossi selected the poems for his music from the liturgy: psalms, hymns, prayers for the Sabbath and the festivals, some were

Mus. ex. No. 36

Nọ 6. Adagio quasi un poco andante.

(see Chapter 12, Note 4). Theme of Beethoven's String Quartet in C♯ minor (Op. 131), sixth movement.

written for choir alone, some for solo and choir; yet all were rather unsophisticated and relatively easy to perform by trained singers. Completely missing in these compositions were items for congregational singing. Evidently Rossi's reform centered, like in Biblical times, in performances of a well-schooled body of singers, excluding any participation by the congregants.

It is the unanimous consensus of musical experts and laymen alike that Rossi's music lacks any traditional elements; there is not the slightest reminiscence of *nussaḥ*, cantillation, or of the Biblical accents (*taʿamim*), all of which are considered the life-blood of synagogal music by orthodox Jewry. This is certainly true. It is also true that Rossi's sacred works are pure Italian Renaissance music, conceived in the style of his epoch, but much less technically involved than his secular vocal works, which breathe the spirit of the standardized polyphonic idiom. It had been said about Rossi's synagogue compositions by his contemporaries, and more so by posterity, until our own days, that they were lacking any "Jewish" spirit and that they were unreligious and unfit for devotional purposes. Nothing could be further from the truth.

His synagogue compositions, just as his secular vocal works, were leaning toward the Phrygian mode, which was the basis of the ancient synagogue chant and largely that of the early Christian church. In this respect Rossi returned (voluntarily or otherwise) to the ancient tradition; despite the fact that he purposely avoided making use of the *nussaḥ* as it was generally practiced in his day, his creations cannot be regarded as un-Jewish.

We know that Rossi had a thorough Jewish education; without his Hebrew background he could not have assumed the functions of a *ḥazzan*. Furthermore, the use of the Hebrew texts in his compositions shows both in prosody and accentuation, the perfect familiarity with the Hebrew language. And as for the lack of synagogal inspiration, meaning the missing mood of the "Jewish melos," the reproaches of his critics are highly biased.

Admittedly he did not write music in the *"ḥazzanic"* manner, which stresses, and often exaggerates, the "emotional element." Rossi's reform abandoned all the worn-out devices of the *"ḥazzanic"* art in sensing correctly that they were artificial means to induce a talmi-religious feeling which was not identical with true devotion. His music is simple, unostentatious, *but not unreligious.* It bespeaks the musical idiom of its time, it makes use of the stylistic devices of the epoch; but it fits naturally into the liturgical service; and only those of his critics who are *a priori* antagonistic to any change, or any progress, could deny its sacred character, its justification in the synagogue, and its viability in the Jewish liturgy.

It is a genuine challenge to compare Rossi's attempted reform with the infinitely more successful musical reform of the nineteenth century. Far be it from us to question the merits of such reformers as SULZER, LEWANDOWSKI, NOWAKOWSKI, and others, in the shaping of the synagogue music of the Central European countries. Yet the question must be asked dispassionately: what is "Jewish" in such "war horses" of acknowledged synagogue music as for instance, SULZER's *"Ki mi Ẓiyyon,"* or LEWANDOWSKI's *"Mah tovu,"* or SCHORR's *"Ein kamoka,"* or in a host of other synagogue compositions which today are unshakable pillars of the repertoire of every synagogue, orthodox, conservative and reform, and which have the halo of Jewishness firmly established about them?

A simply comical claim upon the sanctity of tradition is SULZER's *Ha-yom t'amẓenu,* the hymn closing the *Rosh ha-Shanah* and *Yom Kippur* afternoon services. It is the German ditty:

> *Auf der grünen Wiese*
> *Hat er mich gefragt:*
> *Liebst du mich Luise?*
> *Hat er mir gesagt.*[44]

Mus. ex. No. 37

70. HAYOM T'AM'TZENU

Composed by
FR. VOLKERT
for the Schir Zion of
S. Sulzer
(1804-1890)

Hayom t'amẓenu *by Solomon Sulzer*, Schir Zion (1865), *vol. II, p. 301, No. 392.*

And how about that little gem *"En Keloheinu,"* the most un-Jewish of all Jewish liturgical hymns, which has become even a repertory piece in the synagogues of Israel at present? The author has heard it sung in the Sabbath morning service at the *Hechal Sh'lomo* Synagogue, the chief place of worship in Jerusalem, performed by the choir in a veritable gallop tempo that would almost fit into the finale of an Offenbach operetta.

IDELSOHN gives the genealogy of the piece with the aid of four versions, showing how it originated from a German Church Hymn, *"Grosser Gott wir loben dich,"* and went through several metamorphoses before arriving at its present, final, and authentic "Jewish" stage (Mus. ex. No. 38).[45]

We know, of course, that today's synagogue music of the Western world is the mirror image of the German nineteenth-century harmonic style, established by the composers at the beginning of the century but mainly by MENDELSSOHN and his followers. For over a century this was considered *authentic* Jewish synagogue music. Only in the last few decades, following the rebirth of the State of Israel and the resulting nationalistic trend in composition, has a new musical concept of "Jewishness" cropped up which holds promises for the future. But through the entire nineteenth and part of the twentieth century the assimilated Jewish music spoke the language of its time, a language as remote from Jewish-

Mus. ex. No. 38

En Kelohenu

The Origin of En Kelohenu *(After Idelsohn, p. 239).*

ness as Jerusalem from Athens. Nevertheless, routine, indolence of mind, and the objection to any change resulted in petrifying nineteenth century synagogue music, a trend that is very difficult to change today as it was in past centuries.

The older generation, then as now, clings to the music of their own time and refuses to accept as "Jewish" anything new. The people are supported in this by the *hazzanim*, who consider as "tradition" only that which they know, and reject everything that is new as un-Jewish.

The same conditions might have prevailed in Rossi's time. No wonder, therefore, that his attempt at a reform was doomed to failure from the start. He expressed the language of the times in his music; for Jewish liturgy this was unprecedented and, therefore, an unacceptable undertaking. Had he and his successors persisted more vigorously, his reform might have been successful, as it was two centuries later in Germany and France.

And yet, Rossi's synagogue music is as viable today as most of the nineteenth-century compositions. During his tenure as Music Director of Temple Sinai at Los Angeles, the author has introduced several of Rossi's pieces into the services of this conservative congregation. Rossi's "Bar-chu" has an authentic Jewish flavor and has been sung for many years and is accepted by the worshippers. The 137th Psalm especially is considered by the Los Angeles congregation as a piece of true devotional inspiration (Mus. exs. Nos. 39 and 40). How different they are from such cheap imitation of Italian operatic style as, for instance, the tenor —solo "K'vodo mole 'olam" in DUNAJEWSKI's "Kedusha,"[46] or the soprano solo "Malkut'ha, malkut" in BARUCH SCHORR's "Ein kamoka," which are considered genuinely Jewish. (Many such examples could be quoted.)

The Jewish character of synagogal music, or the lack of it, are more a psychological than an artistic and esthetic phenomenon. The inertia of mind and the inborn opposition by older generations to any change are the main obstacles to the rejuvenation of liturgical music. In addition, another important element must be touched upon, even if briefly, although it is only indirectly related to our subject. This element might well have been the additional reason for the failure of Rossi's reform.

In the last half century of Western musical development the "perception of the ear" (Hörfähigkeit) of large segments of the population increased in an unprecedented degree. Chords and melodies which only fifty years ago were considered unbearably dissonant and awkward are today readily accepted and even enjoyed by wide audiences. This phenomenon is not merely physiological and psychological, but also of an artistic and sociological nature. A deeper delving into this phenomenon would lead us beyond the scope and limitation of the present study.

In our present time the gradual shaping of such "aural" transformation spans approximately half a century; in medieval times the change of the auditive approach to "new" music must have taken longer, possibly centuries. It can be assumed that Rossi's

Mus. ex. No. 39

BENEDICTION A 3 VOIX.

(1) Pour l'intelligence des musiciens Competents j'ai jugé utile de mettre au commencement de chaque morceau
les anciennes clefs telles que le Compositeur les a placées dans l'original. S.N.

Bar'ku, *by Salomone Rossi Ebreo*

281

Mus. ex. No. 40a

על נהרות בבל

Aux bords des fleuves de Babylone
PSAUME 137 À 4 VOIX.

Mus. ex. No. 40b

Mus. ex. No. 40c

(Al Naḥarot Babel (137. Psalm), by Salomone Rossi Ebreo.

audience, in this particular case his congregation, was not yet ready for the new musical language. This inner situation, together with the unpropitious external circumstances, precipitated the unsuccessful outcome of Rossi's reform.

And yet discoveries are sometimes made which tend to show that Rossi's attempt, after all, may not have been entirely without success. A copy of Rossi's synagogal work (or part of it), preserved in the Bodleian Library at Oxford, had a curious fate. It apparently had been used by several northern cantors whose autographs it contains. One of them, Moses ben Abraham of Nikolsburg (Germany), appended a note to it reading: "The Lord favored me so that I studied in this book of music . . . to chant songs and praises in the synagogue and to exalt Him in exultant voice."[48] There are also scraps of musical notation, some written in the tonic sol-fa method, but in Hebrew characters, certainly a bibliographical unicum.[49] This shows that Rossi's music penetrated wider circles than has been generally assumed. Whether it had any influence upon Central European synagogal melody is a matter of conjecture. Comparative studies between his style and that of eighteenth-century synagogal music did not yield any concrete evidence in this respect.

In spite of Rossi's failure, the half century of intensive Jewish music culture in Mantua was the real "golden age" for Jewish music and musicians. It has even eclipsed the successful activity of Jewish musicians in the Iberian peninsula and had its parallel only far back in biblical times in the Levitical music culture. In Mantua, it sprang suddenly by something short of a miracle; it ended just as abruptly by a tragedy.

The Gonzaga dynasty reigned until 1630; in that year the last of the art-loving dukes died. Shortly thereafter Austrian troops invaded Italy and besieged Mantua. At that time the Jews there lived enclosed in a ghetto; but in spite of this discrimination they were summoned with the other citizens to build new walls and to man the fortifications. The Jews fought valiantly side by side with other defenders of the place, but after a seven-months' siege the city succumbed to the overwhelming onslaught of a well-organized army. The ghetto was ravaged and its inhabitants, about 1,800 souls, had to flee. The fugitive Jews sent a delegation to the Emperor FERDINAND II, who received them at Regensburg. Sensing the legitimacy of their claim, he gave orders to the Austrian governor of the conquered city to permit the return of the Jews and to allow them to regain their homes and whatever else remained of their former possessions. Migration and death greatly reduced their number; furthermore, only a few were inclined to return to a devastated city. Thus the permission for the resettlement of the Mantuan Jews was but an empty gesture, almost without practical results. ROSSI was already dead at that time. Of his company of musicians nothing was heard again; maybe they migrated to Venice, where there was intense musical activity in the ghetto. The glorious epoch of Jewish music in Mantua vanished into nothing, just as it had come seemingly from nothing. Not before a century later do we witness a new turn in the history of Jewish music with the advent of *Hasidism* and its novel music culture.

ROSSI's fate was that of many pioneers and innovators. His work was neglected and, following his death, fell into temporary oblivion. Only arduous research in our time has succeeded in assigning him his right place in the development of Jewish and general music history.

Today this place is firmly established; he was a forerunner of great masters, a connecting link in style, technique and spirit between the music of the Renaissance and the early Baroque. In his first "*Sonata a Tre*" ("Triosonata") he initiated the utilization of a popular dance tune for variations, an innovation imitated by many of his followers. Another sonata published in 1613, called by ROSSI himself "*La Moderna*," is the earliest example of a sonata with four movements, which four decades later was called "*Sonata da Chiesa*," (Church Sonata), in contrast to the "*Sonata da Camera* (Chamber Sonata).

Musicology praised ROSSI's role as a pioneer in the field of instrumental music. His songs, however, have only a minor importance in music history and, despite their charm and pleasantness, are classified at best as "utilitarian music" ("*Gebrauchsmusik*") a term which should not be taken in a derogatory sense. All the other merits ROSSI possessed are eclipsed, though, by his achievements in the domain of synagogal music, which assure him lasting glory as the foremost Jewish composer not only of the Renaissance, but throughout the following few centuries as well.

To the musical atmosphere of Mantua belongs R. YEHUDAH MOSCATO, the famous preacher of the community. He published his sermons under the title *"Nefuzoth Yehudah"* (The Dispersions of Judah) in Venice (1588, reprinted many times). The first of these sermons deals with music in a rather peculiar manner. He mingles with it ideas from the Bible, the Talmud, and the Cabala, together with notions of Greek, Latin and Arabic philosophy, and focuses those relationships with the contemporary musical theories of GIOSEFFO ZARLINO (1517-1590), the renowned composer, theorist and *maestro di cappella* of the Cathedral of San Marco in Venice.

YEHUDA MOSCATO's excursion into music was not restricted to this singular endeavor. It seems that in his personal conversations he expressed strong ideas to other musical experts about his approach to music. At any rate, his dabbling into music engendered a curious sequel. One of his friends, Dr. ABRAHAM da PORTA-LEONE, a physician by profession, seems to have been inspired by MOSCATO's ideas, and felt induced to deal copiously with music in an encyclopedic work *Shilṭe ha-Gibborim*, leaving to posterity the very first historical stratification of Jewish music (see below).

Though ROSSI's attempt at a synagogal reform did not achieve the result the composer dreamed of, he had at least the moral satisfaction of finding congenial and understanding friends who were instrumental in helping him in the publication of his liturgical works.

The case of another "innovator" ended less beneficially. Almost a century after ROSSI's reform movement, the *hazzan* at Ferrara, NEHEMIAH ben R. BARUCH ha-COHEN, felt induced to change the melody of the Priestly Benediction in his synagogue, which until then was "traditional," or at least was called so. The effect of this daring step was catastrophic. There arose vehement opposition by the rabbinate, and conceivably by the congregation as well, to such "revolutionary" proceedings. In spite of all protests and the moral coercion which ensued, NEHEMIAH could not be moved to "recant." The fate of this unruly innovator was tragic: he was excommunicated by the rabbinate.

In spite of all protests and ensuing moral coercion, NEHEMIAH tried to defend his action by publishing an apology which contained detailed reasons for his action (published 1715 in Mantua). The title of his pamphlet is *Meziz u-Meliz,* literally translated *Observation and Contemplation;* but a free rendering the title as *Innovation and Interpretation,* comes closer to the meaning of this apology. The pamphlet contains a musical example, the controversial version of the Benediction (Mus. ex. No. 41).[50]

Mus. ex. No. 41

Modern notation of the music (The Priestly Blessing) from Meziz u-Meliz *by Rabbi Nehemiah ben Rabbi Baruch ha-Cohen, of Ferrara, published in Mantua, 1715. (In the Music Library of the Hebrew Union College, Cincinnati).*

It is not known whether it helped to rehabilitate NEHEMIAH and if the ban was lifted. The entire incident is a dismal example of rabbinical intolerance concerning the introduction of new music into the liturgy.

It would be logical to assume that Mantua's fame as a center of musical activity spread to other Italian cities where Jews lived in sizable numbers. However, extant records testify to the musical practices of other Jewish communities prior to the flourishing musical life of Mantua.

ISRAEL ADLER observed that "the scarcity of documents concerning art music in Jewish life during the seventeenth and eighteenth centuries is only apparent. . . . The bulk of such documentation is hidden in "literary" testimonies of this period. Thus, the vast collection of rabbinical responsa, this faithful mirror of Jewish cultural and social life of the period, reveal much precious evidence, particularly apropos of polemics from both supporters and adversaries of music in the synagogue."[51]

We possess records which attest directly or indirectly, to the musical endeavors in smaller communities. Recent discoveries inform us of the intensive musical life in Senigallia, a small city east of Florence on the Adriatic Sea. These documents cover the years 1642-1652, subsequently of the flourishing Mantuan period. Still it is highly improbable that the musical practice of Senigallia, and probably other places such as Padua, Modena, Ferrara, et alia, were stimulated merely by the activities of Mantua, without precursory development. Rather it may be assumed that during the seventeenth and eighteenth centuries, art music (and here we restrict the term to synagogue music) was a normal part of the cultural life of Italian Jewry.

The extant records (except those of Venice) give us information about Padua but for the limited period of a decade, between 1555 and 1565, about Ferrara around 1605, and Senigallia ca. 1642-1652. Yet, like the records of Padua, which refer to a period prior to the Mantuan "golden era" of Jewish musical practice, we have reason to believe that other Jewish communities took advantage of the general musical trend in the cultural life of the Renaissance, and tried to emulate, although on a more modest scale, their Gentile colleagues.

In Venice, for example, we know of the early existence of Jewish music schools, which had to be closed by the Signoria in 1443, because the social intermingling between Jews and Christians seemed too "dangerous" for the authorities. The prohibition was probably not rigorously enforced, because, after only a short interruption, the schools flourished again.

We have testimonies from the second half of the fifteenth and the beginning of the sixteenth centuries from such outstanding Jewish scholars as YOHANAN ben ISAAC ALEMANNO and ABRAHAM FARESOL, concerning their interest in music. ALEMANNO wrote a commentary to "Shir ha-Shirim," in which he describes the delight experienced in listening to a recital of the blind German organist

KONRAD PAUMANN, ca. 1470 in Mantua. FARESOL, *ḥazzan* of the synagogue of Ferrara for nearly fifty years, used to sign his name with three notes *fa-re-sol* (see p. 298, note 59).

Jewish women in Parma taught music and dancing to the ladies of that city, which aroused the ire of the fanatical anti-Jewish monk, FRA BERNARDINO da FELTRE. His Philippica caused the city authorities to expel these Jewish women in 1644, an epoch when the Jewish musicians at Mantua prospered and were highly honored by the princely Court.

Especially revealing are the documents which discuss the musical life of the small Jewish community of Senigallia. This city was ruled until 1631 by the Dukes of Urbino. In that year the city came under the jurisdiction of the Papal State, which resulted in a marked deterioration of the situation of the Jews and enforced their segregation in a ghetto. According to the Italian historian UMBERTO CASSUTO, there were not more than thirty-nine Jewish families in Senigallia. And yet, in this small community, there was an intensive musical life, producing not one, but even two choral societies. How do we know this? From the responsa, which were handed down to the competing associations by the rabbinical authorities. The arbiter in this case was the rabbi of Modena, NETAN'EL ben BENJAMIN ben 'AZRI'EL TRABOTTO (1568/69-1653). His responsum reveals that there existed in Senigallia both an established and a newly formed choral group, the latter under the leadership of MORDEKAY ben MOSES DELLA ROCCA (the name of the leader of the other group is not divulged).

The controversy concerned a liturgical matter: whether the repetition of the Name of God, in choral singing, should be allowed or prohibited? Rabbi SAMUAL ISAAC NORCI (or NORSA), DELLA ROCCA's teacher, defended the practice, while SAMUEL ben ABRAHAM CORCOS, the rabbi of Senigallia, was against it.

Both rabbis gave plausible reasons for their arguments. NORCI pleaded that they sang in this manner in Senigallia for three years since (1642), and that the same practice was established much earlier in Pesaro. CORCOS maintained that the repetition of the most sacred word was already forbidden at the preceding year's Feast of Tabernacles, with the understanding that it would not be rendered again.

Besides TRABOTTO, another rabbi, ABRAHAM ben JOSEPH SOLO-
MON ben MORDEKAY GRAZIANI (d. 1684), disciple of TRABOTTO
and later his successor as rabbi of Modena, took part in the dispute; however, his role was limited to the introduction of TRA-
BOTTO's responsum. Thus, the final decision fell to TRABOTTO.[52]

No other name than that of DELLA ROCCA appears in these
rabbinical responsa; even the number of singers employed in both
choral groups is not revealed. From the extant records it becomes
evident that the established choral society was jealous about the
newly formed group and tried to suppress it by attempting to
unify both. TRABOTTO learned from NORCI that CORCOS first accepted the newer group, but later reprimanded the singers. In
principle, TRABOTTO did not object to music in the synagogue,
but only to the manner in which DELLA ROCCA's group performed
it. Little by little the controversy took on such proportions that
it could provoke the intervention of the non-Jewish, that is, the
ecclesiastical authorities of the Papal State. TRABOTTO tried to
avert such an intervention in every way, even if it meant the
suppression of all choral singing in the synagogue. Luckily, this
was avoided by the arbitration of TRABOTTO, who clearly established the right of the newer group to exist side by side with the
older group. TRABOTTO concluded his appeal with a plea for
peaceful collaboration, and this appears to have tempered the
musical zeal of DELLA ROCCA and his singers, who were content
to continue unhampered by jealousies by the leader of the older
group.

ISRAEL ADLER treats this incident with great detail,[53] which
provides two important factors: first, that a community as small
as Senigallia, maintained an intensive musical culture, and secondly, that neither the Counter-Reformation, nor the enforced
segregation of the Jews could dampen their musical ardor. Furthermore, that Jewish music practice, once established, could not
be extinguished either by outside pressure, nor by internal strifes,
but rather continued, more or less effectively, up to the dawn
of Jewish emancipation.

Another controversy was recorded in the Jewish community of
the Isle of Corfu in the middle of the eighteenth century. In spite

of the fact that this island is of a limited size, more than one thousand Jews lived there. They were descendants of the Jews who were expelled from the Kingdom of Naples (1540-1541). Together with the Spanish refugees, who settled there after the expulsion from Spain, the Jews of Corfu built themselves a synagogue, which is called even in our days the synagogue of Apulia and Spain, to distinguish it from the older synagogues of the Greek Jews. Since that time, the Jews of Corfu were divided into Italian and Greek ethnic groups.

The controversy of Corfu concerned the recitation of the *Shemᶜā*: should it be recited according to the rules of accentuation (*bedikdukeha*), or chanted in the manner of Biblical cantillation (*taᶜame ha-mikraᶜot*). After lengthy disputes and having asked for rabbinical responsa from cities as far as Venice and Jerusalem, it seems that the anti-musical sentiments prevailed, judging from an argument in one of such responsa, which stated that "several voices /i.e. singing simultaneously/ prevent the understanding, which is particularly serious for a holy prayer such as the *Shemᶜā*."[54]

These encounters between the "conservative" and the "liberal" factions concerning relatively minor ritual practices, are even more astonishing when one considers that the community of Corfu was one of the few places where instrumental music in the synagogue has survived despite all Talmudic and rabbinical prohibitions (see p. 346).

Shilṭe ha-Gibborim by ABRAHAM da PORTALEONE

The radiance of the Court of Mantua, together with the toleration shown by the dukes toward Jewish artists and intellectuals, attracted, besides musicians, eminent writers. Among these were dramatist LEONE de' SOMMI PORTALEONE and AZARIAH min ha-ADUMIN or, as he signed himself, BONAIUTO de ROSSI, commonly known as AZARIAH de' ROSSI, author of the "*Meᵓor ᶜEynayim*" (Enlightment of the Eyes), the most famous Jewish literary work of the Renaissance period.[55]

Though these two men accomplished much for Jewish literature, they contributed nothing toward musical science. The man who attempted to further the knowledge in matters musical, and especially in musical archaeology, was not even a literary person by profession, but a layman of incredible versatility and encyclopedic knowledge. He was an excellent physician—in fact, a descendant of the most eminent Jewish medical family of Italy and, in this capacity, served personally the Dukes Guglielmo and Vincenzo I of Mantua. His name in Hebrew was Abraham mi-Sha'ar Aryeh, meaning "from the Lion's Gate," translated into Italian as Abraham da Portaleone (ca. 1540-1612). In his younger years he wrote two medical treatises in Latin, an outline for pious reading and a primer for the education of his children. In his advanced age he became paralyzed on one side of his body, the result of a stroke. This did not keep him from embarking on a work of an enormous scope, which has assured him lasting fame in the history of Jewish literature. In an encyclopedic compendium of almost all the sciences of his days, dabbling in all subjects of learning, such as history, archaeology, philosophy, natural sciences, linguistics, and also music, he proved himself a Jack-of-all-trades. He named his work *Shilṭe ha-Gibborim* (The Shields of the Mighty). It was finished in 1607 and published at his own expense in 1612 at Mantua.

This work reminds one more of an enormous soliloquy than of a scientific contribution, oscillating between erudition and dilletantism, and displaying a verbosity that exceeds all imagination.

Portaleone boasted to have command of ten languages and to have used ninety-eight Hebrew books as his sources, which he enumerates one by one. Furthermore, he used a huge quantity of source material in other languages, ancient and contemporary, from which he quotes freely. In three "Shields" (sections), divided into ninety chapters, he wrote about such unrelated subjects as the ancient land of Palestine, Solomon's Temple, the priests and Levites and their garments, the sacrificial service, prayers, songs, the Biblical accents, the Samaritans, anatomy and zoology, chemistry and pharmacology, tariffs and currencies, political science, wars and weaponry, liquid and dry measures, salt, wood, spices and incense, precious stones—their medical use and their current prices, even about secret writing and how to prepare the ink for scribes for the Torah scrolls. The appendix contains a treatise concerning Greek and Latin letters and language. Each of these subjects furnishes him the occasion to elaborate upon them in an exasperating verbosity, metaphorically called "limitless learned digression."[56]

His opus is certainly an encyclopedic undertaking in which he shows himself a genuine *"polyhistor"* of immense scope. The historical interest of his book in the Jewish literature of European Renaissance is incontestable. Concerning its scholarly value, the opinions are divided. The most famous Jewish historian, HEINRICH GRAETZ (1817-1891), considers him "half-mad," which is evidently a gross injustice; verbosity in the Renaissance epoch was a virtue, and in this respect PORTALEONE was a true child of his time. Modern historiography characterizes his literary output euphemistically as "discursive to the verge of eccentricity,"[57] which is certainly more appropriate and does justice to PORTALEONE's restless mind and superhuman effort.

We are mainly interested in Chapter V of his book, in which he presents a musico-archaeological essay about the music practice of the ancient Hebrews. His approach to music is a curious amalgam of some facts, but mostly according to his fancy and imagination, and treated with consummate amateurism. This must be said at the outset, since in modern times this aspect of his work is considered—rather uncritically—to be a serious musicological treatise.

In his numerous bizarre statements about the music of Biblical times the most glaring mistakes are easily detectable. They are statements which anybody conversant with the Bible and the early rabbinical writings should have avoided easily. His assertions that the Biblical *kinnor* (lyre) had forty-seven strings is one such error. Another one is that he mistakenly equates the *kinnor* with the harp; harplike instruments of Biblical times were called *nebel* (*nabla*, or *nablon*). Furthermore, he did not realize that an instrument with that many strings must have been so voluminous that it could not have been played while marching; yet there are numerous indications in the Bible that the *kinnor* was indeed portable and played in processions and on other occasions where it had to be carried. It is evident therefore that he confused the *kinnor* with the harp of his time, which might have had indeed forty-seven strings.

As for the *nebel*, he first asserts that the *nablon* (the Greek form of the word) is a combination of the harp and the bagpipe, something which must appear incongruous to anybody faintly familiar with the manufacturing of musical instruments. In another interpretation of the *nebel*, he identifies it with the Italian lute of his days. He describes minutely the fingerboard, the sounding box, the arrangements of the strings, and gives in general a portrayal of an instrument that is manifestly the image of the coeval *chitarrone* or *liuto chitarronato*.

Among other misconceptions of PORTALEONE are his statements that the *mahol* is the flute; the *magrephah* are clappers; the *zilzal* (cymbals) is a wind instrument; the *mashrikuta* (sic) a reedpipe; and the *sumponyah* the bagpipe. He explains the *shofar* as "a kind of flute," a queer definition by someone who surely must have heard this instrument in the synagogue services of his day.

For a scholar who was supposed to know his Bible, it is strange to perceive such complete misunderstanding about the role of the *tof* (hand drum) in Jewish usage. PORTALEONE's long description of this Biblical instrument is amazingly inaccurate. Let us examine his statement that "according to the opinion of our rabbis, and also of the sages of other peoples, the *tof* is undoubtedly an instrument of minor value, which is not fit for artistic music." He evidently failed to realize what an important role the hand drum had played in the dances of the Jewish people and that dancing, together with singing and the playing of instruments, was one of the three conspicuous manifestations of musical practice in Ancient Israel.

His most grotesque statements, however, are contained in the description of the musical portion of the New Moon service. They are so unrealistic, even fantastic, that they deserve to be quoted in full:

> Since on the day of the New Moon more trumpets, musicians and singers were employed, I want to submit to you a description of their rightful functions. Eighteen Levites are standing in a straight

line along one of the steps. The first of them sings in *unisono*, the second in *ditono* or *semiditono*, the third sings the part called *diafente perfeto*, the fourth *diapason*, the fifth *doppioditono* or *semiditono*, that is *diapason* together with *ditono* or *semiditono*, the sixth *doppiodiafente*, that is *diapason* combined with *diafente perfeto*. These perform the first part of the singing.

The seventh to twelfth [of the Levites], corresponding to the first and sixth, join in the second part, the thirteenth to eighteenth in the third part.

In front of the singers there are, also in a straight line, eighteen musicians; one of them with a ten-stringed *nablon*, two to five with harps, and the sixth again with a ten-stringed *nablon*. These play during the first part, the seventh to twelfth [musician] and the thirteenth to eighteenth with the same distribution of instruments, during the second and third part, respectively.

The place centrally located in front of the musicians is occupied by the player of castanets [PORTALEONE means the cymbal player]. Right and left of him, in a straight line, there are nine trumpets on each side. You should know, however, that every trumpeter endeavors to play the same tones sung by the singers; thus three trumpets blow *unisono*, three *ditono* or *semiditono*, three *diafente perfeto*, three *diapason*, three *doppioditono* or *semiditono*, and three *doppiodiafente*, in order to achieve harmony and avoid a confused chaos of tones.

Then the castanet player resorts to action, thereby introducing the singing, which begins with six voices, accompanied by two *nablon* and four harps. After they have finished a section, all eighteen trumpets blow together with the sounding of the castanets, which are played three times alone in a simple *diapason*. Thereupon the people prostrate themselves.

Hereafter, the castanet-player again performs alone, in order to carry over the tone of the first six singers to that of the second group of six, likewise accompanied by two *nablon* and four harps.

The same occurs after the next section, whereupon the remaining six singers perform to the accompaniment of the third group of instruments.

When this section approaches the end, all eighteen singers and musicians sing and play together; at the closing, all eighteen trumpets blow, together with the sounding of the castanets, in a simple *diapason* three times—as mentioned before—and the people prostrate themselves."

In this description PORTALEONE indiscriminately mixes fancy with truth, absurdity with reality. The application of his Italian musical terms is just as erroneous as his statement that castanets (i.e., cymbals) had the faculty of "carrying over the tone" to singers from one group to the other. Moreover, his assertion that the trumpets "endeavor to play the same notes as sung by the singers," is a complete misjudgment of the character of the florid Levitical song and a lack of knowledge of the technical range inherent to the trumpets of Biblical times, which only possessed very few tones of the natural harmonic series.

After all these incongruent statements, the assertion of PORTALEONE that the Levites were taught music theoretically and practically from textbooks (Chapter IV) deserves only scant mention.

Through ATHANASIUS KIRCHER's *Musurgia Universalis* (publ. 1650), and the subsequent translation into Latin of the musical portion of PORTALEONE's book in BLASIUS UGOLINO's *Thesaurus antiquitatum sacrarum* (publ. 1744-1767, in its vol. 32), PORTALEONE's treatise received the distinction, although undeserved, of being an authentic "source book" for the music of Ancient Israel.

In view of the eccentricity of his opinions and his many misstatements, it is incomprehensible how PORTALEONE's essay was, in all seriousness, termed as the result of a "fine and comprehensive musical erudition."[58] The voicing of legitimate criticism on musical errors and misconceptions in PORTALEONE's book can in no way minimize its historical value. The book, with all its shortcomings, was the result of a burning energy and an extraordinary industry, and had an immense scope, that was rare even in the achievements of Renaissance Italy.

The luster of the Mantuan court overshadowed other cultural centers in Italy of the Renaissance, where arts, including music, were likewise arduously cultivated, though on a somewhat smaller scale. Evidently not all these places had their ROSSI. The extant records about such activities are few and incomplete. We know, for instance, that in the Duchy of Monferrat Jews were frequently invited to Christian homes "to sing, play music, and dance." An edict from 1577 forbade such social intermingling, however, through special licenses exceptions were made and Christians certainly made ample use of it. A dancing teacher named LEONE EBREO made such an impression upon the female inhabitants of the city of Reggio that, in 1603, they petitioned the duke to allow him and his family to move to that city to enliven the citizenry, and especially the ladies, with his art. In 1621, DAVID FINZI of Modena, "who possesses the virtue of playing instruments," petitioned the duke to leave his service, because he had been "requested by the gentlemen of Carpi" to become their music teacher.

In the Papal States, in the city of Pesaro, there are records, unfortunately very scant ones, about a Jew named SAMUELLE SONATORE ("Samuel the Musician"). In Ferrara we know about a copyist of music, MORDECAI ben ABRAHAM FARESOL, evidently the son, as his name indicates, of the well-known ABRAHAM FARESOL. He signed his name in 1472 as MORDECAI ha-MENAGEN ("Mordecai the Musician"). The family used as a symbol of their surname the musical notes *fa-re-sol*.[59] Another member of this family, ABRAHAM ben ELEAZAR ha-MENAGEN, was in 1545 a citizen of Rome; he was the ancestor of a distinguished family, among them at least one eminent rabbi, who assumed the Italian equivalent of MENAGEN, SONATORE, as his surname.[60]

The prodigious musical activity of the Jews in Venice will be treated in the chapter devoted to ghetto life.

In Florence, also, the musical life of the Jewish community was undoubtedly intensive, judging from the literary output of the rabbi-poet of this town, IMMANUEL FRANCES (born 1618 in Livorno, died after 1710 in the same town).

A number of his poems were set to music, among them

1. An oratorio for the fraternity (or Academy) of the "Applicants" ("*Anelanti*," 1669-70).

2. A cantata in dialogue form for the same fraternity. About this poem FRANCES wrote: "I composed this poem (*shirah*) in Italian, having been asked by the members of the fraternity of the "Anelanti" ... and they performed it with singing and melody, according to the science of song (*'al pi ḥokmat ha-niggun*), in both synagogues."[61]

3. *Zimrat Purim*, a cantata for the Feast of Purim, for the fraternity of the "*ḥadashim li-veḳarim*" ("New Every Morning").

An introductory note enumerates all ten parts of this cantata: (1) Arietta; (2) Recitativo; (3) Arietta; (4) Recitativo; (5) Arietta; (6) Recitativo; (7) Coro; (8) and (9) Arietta; (10) Coro. According to this table of contents, the music of this cantata must have been quite elaborate. The poet indicates that he wrote this cantata for a group of young musicians, singers and instrumentalists (*menagenim, mezammerim u-meshorerim*).[62]

4. A variant of the same cantata, performed on another occasion in 1692.

In addition, we know of several other poems, serving as lyrics for a musical setting. The whereabouts of their music is not known.[63]

Jewish family events, such as weddings, circumcisions and other festive occasions, were always embellished with singing and music. For other joyous gatherings there often were special compositions written by Jewish (and even non-Jewish) authors, or commissions given them for such. Compositions in these categories have lately aroused the attention of numerous scholars. Recently a great number of such compositions for special occasions have been discovered, originating especially from Italian communities.[64]

There is, for instance, a composition for the celebration of the fraternity of *"Shomrim la-Boker"* (The Watchers of the Dawn) in Ancona (end of the seventeenth, beginning of the eighteenth century). In Mantua the same fraternity intoned noctural prayers to celebrate the feast of *Hosh'ana Rabba*, "with the accompaniment of various instruments," and with "a choir of selected musicians."[65] Our records even mention the instruments which were used on this occasion: the *nebel*=viol, and the *minnim*=organ. Both words are medieval metonymies of the analogous Biblical words. *Nebel* in the Scriptures is the term for the harp, and *minnim* stands as a collective designation for all stringed instruments.

About the music practice of Padua prior to the seventeenth century, we have the testimony of BEN ZIYYON ZARFATI (d. 1610), who furnishes us general information about the music performed in the synagogue of this city. It is contained in his approval given to LEONE MODENA about synagogue music in Ferrara (see p. 272). In it, ZARFATI recalls his own experience as a youth when he studied in Padua and sang in the choral group of the synagogue of the illustrious Rabbi MEïR KATZENELLENBOGEN, who was called *"Mahar-ram Padua,"* (an abbreviation for *"Morenu*/our teacher/ *ha-rab Rabbi Meïr,"* 1482-1565).

Furthermore, there are records of a ceremony with music on the occasion of the consecration of the Holy Ark in the Sephardic synagogue in Padua (1728-29). For this festivity, the famous poet and cabalist MOSES ḤAYYIM LUZZATTO wrote several prayers, which were destined to be set to music. The music of another poem by the same author, written for the feast of *Simḥat Torah* in Amsterdam, has been preserved.[66]

Throughout the entire eighteenth century, it was the common practice of Jewish communities to inaugurate a new synagogue with musical performances. Thus, we have records about a new and splendid Sephardic synagogue in Livorno (1742?), at whose consecration music played an important part.

In the township of Siena, in the province of Toscana, Jews lived continuously since 1229. Following the general trend of Jewish discrimination in Italy, the Jews in Siena were segregated in a ghetto in 1571. This, however, did not diminish their commercial activity in the town. They were, subsequently as before, well-to-do artisans and merchants, specializing in the wool and also in the weaving trades.[67] They certainly had their synagogue (or synagogues), although there are no records preserved about the religious practice of the Jews in Siena prior to 1788, when the inauguration of a new and beautiful house of worship took place. Fortunately, the music performed at this occasion was preserved, together with the poems set to music.

The music was written by VOLUNIO (in Hebrew ZEBULON) GALLICHI, singer and composer, who called himself "chief of the singers and musicians" of the congregation. He seems to have been Jewish, although no biographical or other sources about him were discovered. The title page of the score indicates, after his name, "Dilettante," indicating that he was evidently only a gifted amateur. Besides GALLICHI, another musician, FRANCESCO DREI (1737-1801), figures as the composer of some of the pieces, *e.g.,* the Duo, No. 9. Whether he was Jewish, is not known.

On this performance, twenty-five persons collaborated, either as poets, or composers, or singers and musicians, or else had other functions connected with the ceremonial setup for the occasion.[68]

The music for this festivity consisted of fourteen pieces: five arias for solo voices, three duets, one of them superscribed "*Aria concertato de due Soprani*," five pieces for solo and choir, and a "*Recitativo con Violini.*"

ISRAEL ADLER gave a thorough description of the score and analyzed in depth both text and music.[69] Furthermore, he published the entire composition,[70] thus affording an excellent insight into the style of such religious compositions at the outgoing of the Jewish Middle Ages.

The inauguration of the "Italian" synagogue in Florence (1793) took place under quite peculiar circumstances. For this occasion, besides the usual ritual ceremonies, a veritable comic opera was staged. We shall deal with his hybrid opus when we scrutinize the Jewish theatrical comedies (see p. 372).

Although the music to this inaugural comedy has not turned up, we may judge from analogies of similar works by Jewish composers of that time that the style as well as the form of the music of this *pasticcio* may have reflected that of the then current idiom of the comic opera. However, this is a mere surmise, which cannot be verified presently.

Another theatrical representation, coupled with a ball, took place for the festival of *Purim* in Gorizia, in the year 1767. About the music on this occasion nothing is known. The theatrical play might have been similar to *Purim* comedies staged during the seventeenth and eighteenth centuries, though no records concerning their performance were preserved.

Because all these musical manifestations took place at the very threshold of the Emancipation, it would seem to be unwarranted to include them into the musical practice of the Jewish Middle Ages. Nevertheless, they are mentioned, if only for the sake of completeness.

Even closer to the dawn of the Emancipation was the inauguration of a synagogue in Trieste in 1798. The festivities on this occasion were similar to, or identical with, those of the consecration of the synagogue in Siena. The *Seder ḥanukkat ha-bayit* (the Order of the ceremonies set up for both occasions) are identical.

We may assume, therefore, that the music as well may have been alike to that which was employed in Siena.[71]

The facts presented in this section were merely fragments of a huge mosaic which disclosed Jewish musical talent and which earned them rewards in the service of popes, kings and noblemen. In conclusion, it can be said that it was during the Renaissance period that Jews first asserted themselves in the art of music on equal footing with their Gentile colleagues. In Spain and France, Jewish musicians excelled as popular entertainers, but were still considered socially inferior among the established residents of the townships. In Italy, on the other hand, they proved themselves to be masters of their art and were accorded full citizenship by their employers as well as by the populace among whom they co-existed. Thus the real significance of Jewish musical activity, artistically as well as sociologically, could not be better illustrated than that in Italy of the Renaissance.

Jewish Musical Practice in Southern France

The rich musical culture of the Italian Jewish communities in the Renaissance radiated far beyond the boundaries of Italy, especially to regions close to the Appennine Peninsula. Even the French provinces were under the spell of the Jewish achievements in Italy.

A similar situation, although on a smaller scale, existed in other European Jewish centers, particularly in southern France, where Jews lived relatively undisturbed for several centuries and where they could exercise their musical profession on a par with their Gentile competitors.

Besides the Jewish communities of Alsace and Lorraine (especially that of Metz), we witness in the seventeenth and eighteenth centuries such important Jewish centers as Avignon and the Comtat Venaissin, in the South-Western region of France. Included in this Comtat were such towns as Aix-en-Provence, Cavaillon and L'isle-sur-Sorgues. Extant records from these places testify to a wide-spread Jewish musical activity, religious as well as secular. In other towns of the same area, Marseille, Montpellier, Nimes, and others, the Jewish population was rather small in number and their musical practice is of no great significance for the historical development of Jewish musical practice prior to the Emancipation.[72]

The most outstanding musical document of this epoch in southern France is a composition, which was discovered and first described by ISRAEL ADLER.[73] It was written for a circumcision ceremony, probably between 1680 and 1700.

This rather elaborate composition, entitled *"Canticum Hebraicum,"* was destined either for the entertainment of the invited guest at the eve before the circumcision, or for the banquet following the circumcision rite, or both.

The composer, LOUIS SALADIN, was evidently a non-Jew, judging from another of his preserved compositions, a motet entitled *"Concert pour l'Assomption de la Vierge,"* to be performed at this Christian holiday.

The ensemble of the *"Canticum Hebraicum"* required a relatively large number of performers. The instrumentalists were probably Jews living in that area; whereas the singers were undoubtedly Jewish, because the preserved vocal parts were written with Hebrew characters only.

The music of this *"Canticum Hebraicum"* has no "Hebraic" earmarks, and follows the style of the usual vocal works or orchestral suites of that period. It deserves its title merely because some Hebrew *piyyutim* were used as its lyrics. It is rather strange to find in a Hebraic cantata, written for a Jewish religious ceremony, besides arias, duets and orchestral interludes, dance pieces, such as Rigaudon, Gavotte and Bourrée, used generally in instrumental suites of that epoch.

The work was evidently commissioned by a wealthy and influential member of the Jewish community of Avignon. The performance required a large number of musicians and singers, which only rich men could afford for the elaborate circumcision ceremony of their sons. It is an irony of fate, that everything connected with this musical work, the poem, the music, the vocal parts and the name of the composer are preserved, except the identity of the person who sponsored its creation.

About such circumcision ceremonies of the epoch we have the

testimony of an eyewitness, who visited Avignon in 1599. He was
THOMAS PLATTER, a student of Basle, who left detailed reports
about his voyage in Southern France.[74] They contain valuable
information about the musical practice of the Jews in Avignon,
where he stayed two months and was present at the circumcision
of two boys. In these ceremonies he noticed only the musical
rendering of two prayers. But he also attended several synagogue
services and wedding festivities, about which he left more elaborate reports.

He described, for instance, the *Shaharit* service in the synagogue, in which—among many recited prayers—he heard that
"they sing several prayers and [evidently the *hazzan*] often
elaborates the chanting on one single word for half an hour and
even for a whole hour." Even if this assertion is greatly exaggerated, it shows that the *hazzanim* of that epoch abused their
office, often to the detriment of the time allotted to the entire
morning service.

THOMAS PLATTER was invited to a Jewish marriage and described the ceremonies together with the singing and dancing for
this event. He mentions repeatedly that the participants danced
the Bransle, a stately dance common in the sixteenth and seventeenth centuries, which was generally accompanied by singing,
with a *ritornello* after each stanza. As he observed, "the bridegroom took lead of the men, the bride that of the women, and
joining their hands, everyone of the participants indulged in
dancing." Besides the Bransle, which was a dance for everybody,
young men also danced the Gaillarde, which—contrasting to the
ceremonial Bransle—required livelier movements and steps and
was evidently more appropriate for such a joyous occasion.

There are other testimonies about the musical practice of the
Jews in southern France at the beginning of the eighteenth century. Two benedictine monks made extensive travels in this part
of the country and published a report about their journey.[75]
Among others, they mention that they visited the synagogue of
Carpentras in 1710. At that time, there lived about seven hundred
Jews in this city and—according to their observations—all of them
were wealthy. About the music they heard in the synagogue they
say that "in their assemblies they sing psalms in Hebrew, the

melodies of which are charming." This statement is revealing, since by their musical education the Benedictine Fathers were certainly qualified to pass judgment on the singing of the Jews.

We know also of theatrical plays in Carpentras at the end of the seventeenth century, at which Jewish and provençal tunes enlivened the performances.[76]

As we look back on the historical and musical documents shown above, one realization must form, to wit, that whenever Jews lived in an environment unhampered by constant harassment and fear of persecutions, their creative activities manifested themselves spontaneously. Suppressed temporarily, these impulses erupted with increased vigor as soon as the living conditions improved to a degree which allowed them to lead a normal life.

Looking at the exposed facts from a higher vantage point, two more conclusions will emerge.

First, wherever Jews lived in compact groups, be in in fair-sized, or even small communities, their musical urge created the atmosphere which enabled them to pursue their musical activities as before. This, of course, mainly in the religious domain; but they did not neglect the secular field, even though strongly influenced by the music of the peoples with whom they co-existed.

Secondly, during the Italian Renaissance, the favorable living conditions afforded the Jewish musician not only working chances on an equal footing with his Gentile colleagues, but gave him the incentive and opportunity to *compete* with them. This was a healthy competition, in which the Jewish musician asserted his own value and gave him the possibility of proving his creative power, heretofore suppressed. This handicap created the false impression of improductivity of the Jews as creative musicians. The Italian Renaissance destroyed once and for ever this misinterpretation, and this is the real significance of the facts exposed about the activity of the Jewish musician in this fateful period of the history of the Jewish people.

16

Anti-Jewish Musical Plays in the Renaissance

THE ANTI-JEWISH TREND IN MUSICAL PRODUCTION, A SPECIMEN OF which was shown in the "*Kedusha-Motet*" (see p. 166), was not confined to Spain. In Italy of the Renaissance there were other examples of this kind of musical *pasticcios*, while in Germanic countries the persiflage of Jewish manners, especially of dancing, brought forth rude pieces of musical caricature.

The famous Italian composer of the Renaissance, ORAZIO VECCHI (ca. 1550-1605) felt induced to set to music a sort of comic *pasticcio* called "*L'Anfiparnasso*" (presented in 1594 at Mantua, printed in 1597 and 1610 in Venice). In this musical comedy Jewish customs, jargon and business methods were caricaturized and, by implication, the entire Jewish people were pilloried. The text blends perfectly with the surroundings in which SHAKE-SPEARE's *Merchant of Venice*, described the fictitious Jewish practices of Venice. Curiously enough, VECCHI's music has not the slightest parodistic or satiric vein; it is the perfect image of the contemporary madrigal style and, as such, with altered lyrics, could stand as a serious piece in any anthology of Renaissance music.

The title *Amfiparnasso* indicates the lower mountain ridges in approaching the pinnacle, therefore its meaning is close to that of "*Gradus ad Parnassum*." The work was long regarded as an historical precursor of the opera; this may be maintained only in a very limited way. Whereas the first composers of opera (PERI, CACCINI, MONTEVERDI, etc.) had applied the monodic principle to their musical language, VECCHI, in the style of the times, used four- and five-part choruses for the monologues and dialogues. Thus, his opus may be classified as a madrigal comedy, in the proper sense of the word, used for the purpose of entertainment, without the pretense of being on the same artistic level as his numerous collections of madrigals, masses, canzonettas, etc. In his book *Le veigle di Siena ovvero i varii humori della musica moderna* (The Vigils of Siena, or the various moods in modern music), VECCHI gives descriptive characterizations of the human dispositions, such as: *umor grave* (earnest mood); *allegro* (cheerful); *dolente* (complaining); *lusinghiero* (teasing); *affettuoso* (tender), etc. Yet in the Jewish episode of his *Amfiparnasso* not the slightest attempt is made to characterize the Jews in any way.

As was the custom of the time, VECCHI wrote an introduction to his work, in which he said that his *"Commedia harmonica"* was akin to a work of a painter who drew some principal characters in life size, others as portraits, the remainder as figures in the background. Seldom had an author introduced his work with a bigger misrepresentation. All his characters speak the same language (the polyphonic choral setting does not allow a different one), all the situations, lyric, humorous, sentimental, are expressed by the same even flowing and "well-tempered" madrigal style. To be sure, the rhythmic patterns of his vocal settings are rather variegated, but it is hard to believe that his audience, in the year 1600, could have seen individual characterizations in these lackluster musical pieces. Could it be that somehow the public enjoyed the lyrics which may have contained puns that held a meaning only to audiences of those times? Could it be that the mimics, dances and the scenic "embellishments" were the real "humorous" features of the comedy? Possibly this was the case, for such anti-Jewish *pasticcios,* appealing to the low instincts of the masses, must always in the past have been sure hits.

In VECCHI's comedy the actor-singers perform dramatic scenes assigned to human characters, such as master and servant, a man and a woman of ill-repute, a couple of lovers lamenting about their love, and who are plagued by mutual jealousy, etc. Furthermore, there are musical parodies, sung in various dialects, among them the aforementioned scene of the noisy Jews who, during the Sabbath, cannot do business with the clown Francatrippa, anxious to pawn his clothes. All these "funny" events are musically conveyed in a most monotonous fashion, and in a mock-Hebrew which makes no sense, since it is, just as the text of the above mentioned "*Kedusha-Motet*," mostly gibberish.[1]

Here is the original text of the scene:

Tich, tach, toch, O Hebreorum gentibus,
Tich, tach, toch, sù prest' aurì,
Tich, tach, toch, da hom da be, cha tragh zo l'us.
Ahi Barucha, Badanai Merdochai,
Ahi Barnachai, Badanai Merdochai.
An Biluchan ghet milotran, la Baruchaba.[2]
A noi farò vergot maidi negot ch'ì fala Sinagoga,
O che'l Diavol v'affoga.
Tiche, tiche, tach, tiche, tiche, toch.
Ot zorohot as lach muflach,
Jochut zorochot calamala Balachot.
O chi, O messir Aron, bandanai, bandanai.
C'ha pulset' à sto porton? So mi, messir Aron.
Bandanai, bandanai. Che cheusa volit? Che cheusa dicit?
A voraf impegnà sto Brandamant.
O Samuel, O Samuel, venit' à bess.
Adanai, che l'è lo Goi.
Ch'è venut' con le moscogn,
Che vuel lo parachem.
L'è Sabbà, cha non podem.

The last line is repeated over and over again. And particularly here, where the composer would have had the given opportunity for a characteristic tonal picturization of the satirical scenic action, he turned his music into a solemn choral-like setting which, without these mockingly satirical words, could have its place in any sacred composition.

Translation of Scene III of ORAZIO VECCHI's *Amfiparnasso*.[3]

Tich, tach, toch, O Jewish people,
Tich, tach, toch, quickly open up,
Tich, tach, toch, like a good man,
Or I'll knock the door down.

Ahi Barucha, Badanai Merdochai,
Ahi Barnachai, Badanai Merdochai.
An Biluchan ghet milotran, la Baruchaba.
A no farò vergot maidi negot ch'ì fala Sinagoga,
May the devil disown you.
Tiche, tiche, tach, tiche, tiche, toch.
Ot zorohot aslach muflach,
Jochut zorochot calamala Balachot.
Who is it, Mr. Aron, who knocks at this door?
It's me, Mr. Aron, bandanai, bandanai.
What do you want? What are you saying?
I'd like to pawn this coat.
O Samuel, O Samuel, come down.
Adanai, it's a Goi,
Who has come with his coat,
He wants to pawn it.
It is Sabbath, and we cannot.

This anti-Jewish *pasticcio* deserves to be reproduced in its entirety, not because of its musical value, but because it is an example of a tasteless and untheatrical aberration of a famous master of the Renaissance (mus. ex. 42).

VECCHI's *pasticcio* did not remain an isolated case in Renaissance Italy. FILIPPO d'AZAIOLO, in his musical collection *Villotte del Fiore* (1569) published three burlesque pieces,*"Todesca,"* *"Bergamesca,"* and *"Ebraica"* by GHIRARDO da PANICO of Bologna, parodying German, Bergamese and Jewish dialects. We quote a stanza of the last-named poem.

Adonai con voi lieta brigada
De lo valam, de lo valam
Il gran dottore che senza parachin se fat' honore
E noi cantand' per la contrada ai adonai.

(Adonai be with you oh happy group,
De lo valam, de lo valam,
The great doctor who within "parachin" has
    gained honor
And we go singing through the town, ai adonai.)

ADRIANO BANCHIERI, in his musical intermedio *La Barca di Venezia a Padua* (1605) presents two Jewish comic figures, "Betell"[4] and "Samuel" as *Interlocutori di Barca* (The Oarsmen of the Barque). Among his vocal works for three voices there is a *"Mascherata degli Ebrei,"* a comic "Masquerade of the Jews." In his *"Pazzia Senile"* (Aged Folly), considered the first comic opera (1598, republished 1621), there is a song entitled "The Jewish Synagogue," in which the monotonous "tic, tac, tic" (see Vecchi's *pasticcio*) is supposed to reproduce the characteristic buzz of the

Mus. ex. No. 42a

Scena III.
Francatrippa. Hebrei di dentro.

Mus. ex. No. 42b

Mus. ex. No. 42d

Mus. ex. No. 42f

Mus. ex. No. 42g

317

Mus. ex. No. 42i

Scene III from Orazio Vecchi's L'Amfiparnasso *in modern notation.*

Jewish worshippers.[5] All these last-named compositions are anti-Jewish only by implication, insofar as they deal with some peculiarities of the Jewish dialect or other conspicuous Jewish features. In the literature of Renaissance Italy there are additional examples of vocal caricatures of the Jews without musical settings. Basically, all are good-humored and never malicious, so different from the coarse anti-Semitic satires of contemporary Germany.[6]

Thus, as we see, Italy of the Renaissance produced not only great Jewish writers, scholars and musicians but, with all its tolerant and benevolent understanding, had its share in the anti-Jewish manifestations in literature, drama and musical works, muted, however, by the humanistic spirit that permeated the whole epoch.

17

The Ghetto

WHEREVER JEWS LIVED IN THE DIASPORA AS A MINORITY GROUP THEY
clustered together, in order to maintain their ethnic identity, their
religious unity, as well as for the practical needs of everyday
life. In post-Biblical times their existence centered around the
synagogue, where all their activities pivoted. It was their house
of worship and study, the place where all social activities took
place, their court of justice, and meeting hall. It was therefore
natural that they chose their domiciles in the vicinity of the
synagogue. Thus, even before they had to live in an enforced
isolation they chose voluntary segregation for their own protection as well as for social and economic convenience. Jewish
quarters already existed in ancient Alexandria, Antioch and Rome.
Early in medieval times every larger township had its *Judería,*
Juiverie, Giudecca, Judengasse, or *Judenstadt,* where the Jews
carried on their religious and secular life more or less unhampered
by the authorities and the surrounding populace, among whom
they co-existed. In Venice and Salerno there were special Jewish
quarters in the eleventh century, and Prague is said to have had
one as early as the tenth.[1] Occasional hardships and persecutions
did not change this situation, since in good as in bad times the
voluntary cohabitation proved to be a most expedient means for
preserving their religious unity and ethnic togetherness.

The creation of the ghetto, the compulsory residence, did not
bring about discernible changes in the way of life of the Jews—it
simply gave a legal formula to existing conditions. Only when
actual walls had been erected around the Jewish district, only
when the doors of the ghetto had to be closed from dusk to dawn,
only when other harsh measures deprived the inmates of the

ghetto from exercising their civic rights, only then did the ghetto become synonymous with discrimination; it was a kind of enlarged prison, into which human beings were herded against their will, without the slightest consideration of the most elementary moral principles.

Though the institution of the ghetto proper did not start before the sixteenth century, there are numerous records of earlier voluntary concentrations of Jews in secluded quarters, for example, in Spain in the eleventh century, in Germany in the twelfth century, and in Sicily and Aragon in the fourteenth century. Almost all Rhenish cities had their *Judengasse* or their *Judenstadt* early in the Middle Ages. A "Jews' Street" in London is mentioned in 1115. In documents around 1000 c.e. the streets of Venice and Salerno in which Jews lived were called "*Judaca*" or "*Judacaria.*" At Capua there was a place called "San Martino Judaicam," the Latin *Judaicam* being transformed into the Italian *Giudeica;* even today Venice has an island *Giudecca,* named so in the early Middle Ages when Jews established there schools for singing and instrumental music. In Rome, before the official establishment of a ghetto, most Jewish families resided in the *serraglio degli hebrei,* or *septus hebraicus,* as the Jewish district was called in Latin. At the onset of the twelfth century, on the isle of Majorca, to live in the Jewish quarters was considered more a privilege than a restriction. When the *Judería* there was threatened in 1300 to be demolished by the authorities, the Jews stood firm upon their rights to live in that section.[2]

The official creation of the ghetto in Venice took place in the year 1516. The Jewish quarters in Rome were established as late as 1556; they consisted of a few narrow streets, which were annually flooded by the Tiber. Its first name was *Vicus Judaeorum.* Only afterwards was it called ghetto.

Although the enforced residence for Jews was mainly motivated by religious reasons, it was also the purpose of the authorities to reduce, or even eliminate the competition created by Jewish traders and artisans; at times its establishment constituted an act of favor. After having driven out the Moors from Valencia in 1239, King JAMES I of Aragon (1208-76) assigned to the Jews a district of the town as an act of benevolence. It legally became a ghetto in 1390 (although the Cortes vehemently opposed the measure), probably for economic reasons. It seems that if the Jews were allowed to live in freedom, this would mean a better income for the state rather than their being herded together.

The origin of the word ghetto was never established beyond doubt. There are a number of hypotheses, which determined plausible etymologies for the term. Among its various origins one cited the derivation from the Talmudic *get* (bill of divorce), the Syriac *edah* (community), the Greek *geiton* (neighborhood), the Tuscan *guitto* (in Modenese *ghitta,* meaning "sordid"), the Latin *gehectus* (hedged place, taken over by the Germans as *geheckte Orte*), the Italian diminutive *borghetto* (little burgh), as well as a number of still more far-fetched suggestions.[3] The simplest and most obvious explanation is the Venetian origin of the word: in 1516 the Jews in this city were relegated to a district in which, according to old records, dating back to 1306, there existed a cannon foundry, the term for which in Italian was *getto.* The pronunciation of this word is different from the customary "ghetto," however, in all probability either the pronunciation in the spoken language was altered, or the spelling of the word underwent a slight but important modification in early documents.

There can be no doubt about the Venetian origin of the word; that city boasted even two *ghetti,* the *Ghetto Vecchio,* the old ghetto, and the *Ghetto Nouvo,* the new ghetto; the latter was inhabited long before the so-called Old ghetto, an obviously mixed-up nomenclature. From Venice the word spread throughout Italy, then taken up by Central European countries, and ultimately entered into the languages of every civilized nation, as a designation for the enforced residence of Jews.

What formerly was a voluntary congregation, due to the practical necessities of communal organization, henceforth became a constraint. At first this compulsion was not felt too keenly by the Jews, since it was merely the continuation of an existing condition. Later, however, as intolerance and oppressive measures multiplied, the compulsory residence became a scourge, undermining the human dignity of an entire people.

The ghetto was usually situated in an unsanitary section of the city, in narrow quarters, which constituted a fertile field for the

spread of diseases. In some cities, a few privileged Jews were allowed to live outside the ghetto, but these were rare exceptions.
In addition to other restrictions, Jews in Italy were not allowed
to own real estate. They had to pay high rents to the Gentile land-
lords of the hovels where they lived. In Rome, they had to pay
a residence tax and were compelled annually to apply for the
permission to reside there for the coming year.

With their customary resilience and their faculty to adjust
themselves to ever-changing conditions, the Jews learned to
accept every new situation and to make the best of it. Since their
main concern through all these adversities was that their religion
not be menaced, this gave them the courage and determination
to organize their new life to fit the changed circumstances. If at
first the Jews may have found living in scattered and isolated
small groups undesirable, they now began to regard the ghetto
as a blessing in disguise, since it has become their island of refuge.

The ghetto gates, as we know, had to be closed at night. The
secular authorities carried out rigorously this measure to confine
the Jews, thus curtailing their freedom of movement. However,
from the Jewish point of view, this act was considered as the best
protective measure against treacherous attacks. In some localities
Jews were strictly forbidden to leave the ghetto after sunset, and
even on Sundays and especially on Christian holidays. This again
proved to be a protection for the Jews against fanatical mobs,
whose untrammeled hostility against them frequently led to sav-
age excesses and threatened the property and life of the ghetto
dwellers. Thus seclusion from the outside world had not only its
disadvantages, but was, in many respects, beneficial. It developed
an independent civic organization and fostered the religious life
and especially the personal morality. "Constantly within sight of
his neighbor, each person was obliged to keep strict watch of
himself."[4]

For the practice of music, however, the seclusion of the ghetto
was a crucial blow. Cut off from the currents of musical development of the outer world, which were strong especially after the
Renaissance and which determined the future shape of Western
music, the isolated Jews were left pitiably helpless. They had to
rely, in fact, on their own inadequate resources for building a

musical culture of their own. So it happened that for about two centuries there was a hiatus in the history of Jewish music. The creative urge of Jewish musicians, so powerful in Italy of the Renaissance, subsided and almost died out, until the time when the ghetto walls were broken down.

Social life at that particular time developed along the lines peculiar to the ghetto environment. Even under harsh external conditions the yearning of the people for entertainment was kept alive. Singing and instrumental music were only one manifestation of this popular urge. Another, just as powerful, was the fondness for dancing. In fact, dancing was considered the most popular amusement of the Jews in the ghetto. For them this physical expression of merriment released forces for which there was no other outlet in the cramped way of ghetto life. Besides catering to personal satisfaction, it was most opportune for arousing the enthusiasm of the crowd and thereby brightening the drab existence of ghetto Jewry.

We know that the dance played an important role in the musical culture of Biblical times. It may be safely assumed that even in the Diaspora it never lost its enchantment for the Jews. Considered a Jewish social custom, the dance had never assumed such a paramount importance as it did in ghetto life. The pent-up urge for outward expression of their repressed emotions manifested itself in a rather undisciplined manner of dancing, quite unlike the sedate and highly refined way of the dance in Italy of the Renaissance. In the ghetto, dancing was characterized by vehement leaps and bounds, by hopping in a circle and by vigorous movements of the arms. The men danced together, because dancing between two sexes was considered indecent. The women also danced alone, in line or in a circle, without any prescribed steps or choreographically regulated figures. They danced not only for their own pleasure, but possibly more so for that of the onlookers; hence the intensification of the bodily movements might well have resulted in some elements of exhibitionism. It can be stated that the Jewish dance in the ghetto was not so much an artistic performance but rather a mass athletic amusement.

This explains the medieval Christian notion of the *Judentantz*, which has a strong derogatory implication. In the Christian mind the dances of the Jews were a travesty of folk dances, though the popular dances of the German low and middle classes may have been similar, if not worse. A number of *Judentantz* melodies preserved in Christian sources show, in most instances, grotesque rhythms and often are full of cacophonies, thereby proving in what low esteem the Jewish dance was held in the Christian society.

One of such *Judentantz* can be found in HECKEL's *Lautenbuch*, printed in 1562. This is a simple tune over a drone bass, which supposedly indicates the low level of Jewish musicians' skill (Mus. ex. No. 43).

Mus. ex. No. 43

Judentantz, *from Heckel's* Lautenbuch *(1562). (After Paul Nettl*, Alte jüdische Spielleute und Musiker *(Prague, 1923), p. 41.*

Another *Judentantz* may be found in HANS NEWSIDLER's *Ein new künstlich Lautenbuch* (1544), a piece for the lute, consisting almost entirely of intentional cacophonies, which was obviously the composer's conception of Jewish Music (Mus. ex. No. 44).

Mus. ex. No. 44   Der Juden Tantz.

Aus: „Em new künstlich Lautenbuch" (1544).   Hans Newsidler.

Der Juden Tantz, *from Hans Newsidler's* Ein neu künstlich Lautten-
buch *(1544). (After Paul Nettl*, Alte jüdische Spielleute und Musiker,
Prague, 1923), pp. 64–65.

The most joyous events in the medieval ghetto were the *Simhat Torah* (The Rejoicing over the Law), *Purim* (see later) and the wedding festivities. For all these occasions dancing was the most important element for inducing merriment and for enhancing the joy of the participants. Wedding feasts lasted for several days, sometimes for a week, even on the Sabbath; in large communities several weddings might have followed one another, whereby the synagogue was unduly occupied for longer periods than the community leaders thought admissible.

Since dancing, even apart from weddings, had gradually become a general custom, the synagogue turned out to be too small for such events. In time, therefore, the communities began to establish special dance halls for all social gatherings of this type. This institution originated in German ghettos as proven by its name *Tanzhaus*, which for a long time remained its designation in ghetto life. The *Tanzhaus* became a popular establishment throughout Germany and France; in these countries all larger communities had one. Significantly, in Eastern settlements as well as in Spain there were no such places for popular entertainment. In this part of Europe the houses of the Jews were larger, the social gatherings could be held in private homes and the establishment of dance halls seemed to be superfluous.

In Latin documents the dance hall is called *Speilhus* or *Speylhuz*, clearly pointing to instrumental music (*Spiel*) accompanying the dance. A record of 1354 in Speyer mentions the great "Schulhof called *Dantzhus* or *Brutehus* (bride's house)." The *Tanzhaus* in Augsburg dates from 1290, that in Frankfurt, evidently a marriage hall, from 1349, possibly much before. The Ulm *Tanzhaus* dates from the fourteenth century. In Norwich, England, there stands a house named "Musick House," formerly perhaps a Jewish marriage hall, which can be traced to the twelfth, or even to the eleventh century.[5]

The institution of dance halls went hand-in-hand with the relaxation of the rabbinical prohibitions against promiscuous dancing. The rabbis based their opposition upon the misread scriptural text "Though hand join in hand, the wicked shall not go unpunished" (Prov. 11:21); also upon a maxim of the pietists "Men and women shall neither rejoice nor mourn together." But just as the rabbinical prohibitions of singing and playing were unheeded in the Diaspora, so the restrictions against dancing remained ineffective. First it was allowed, officially or unofficially, that a husband might dance with his wife, then a father with his daughter, a mother with her son, even a brother with his sister. Soon the disobedience of the rabbinical rules went further; young men and maidens derived too great a pleasure in dancing to submit to rabbinical intolerance; they not only indulged in dancing together, but did so in the communal dancing hall, even on the Sabbath and festivals.[6]

As time went by the *Tanzhaus* grew into a recreation center where dancing, as a social activity, encouraged and even required dance innovations such as new steps, new figures, new types of dances.

There is no doubt that many interesting and curious dances can be traced back to this center. For instance:

Dance of the May Day, in pairs, like a Polonaise. It was evidently taken over from the Germans who danced around the May pole, a custom which still exists among the Germans, especially in the Rhineland district.

Marching dance, a stately dance similar to court dances.

Springing dance, much like a rugged peasant dance.

Judentanz, a self-persiflage of the dance of the Jews.

Dance of the First Man, the Hebrew term of which is *'Adam ha-Rishon*; probably a pantomime of Biblical content, or a clumsy dance imitating that of primitive tribes.

Doctor Foist (Faust) dance, obviously of German origin.

Fish Dance, the origin and form of which are not known.

Some wedding dance customs during the Middle Ages had a symbolic or mystic meaning. There was, for instance, the custom of the bride stepping into seven circles toward the bridegroom (unmistakably connected with the superstitious belief in the magic power of the number seven), and the bride turning around the bridegroom three times.

A record from the year 1674 shows that at the township of Cleve, Germany, at a Jewish wedding, one person among those present was made to fall to the ground as though dead. Men and women danced around him singing, and prepared him as they would a corpse. At the end of the dance, the "dead" man stood up and joined with the others, evidently a superstitious practice, a revival of the ancient resurrection charm. Other dance customs were intended to insure fertility of the married couple.[7]

Among other dance customs a "Beggars' dance" and a weird "Death Dance" should be mentioned. The *"Danza de la Muerte"* (Death Dance) was a pantomimic dance developed in Spain around the end of the fourteenth and the beginning of the fifteenth centuries. It is said to have been devised by a Jew, R. Santob (Shem Tob) de Carrion (cf. p. 97). Modern scholars assume that only a Jew could have been its author, in view of the many Talmudic implications in its text.

The dance represents members of the various classes of society, the prince, the cardinal, the archbishop, the rabbi, and others, appearing at the moment when each fights with the symbol of death in an attempt to escape its clutches. The Christians performed this dance during processions, the Jews used it at weddings and other family festivals. In German-Jewish annals we find it mentioned in the famous memoirs of Glückel of Hamelin (seventeenth century), where she says that at the wedding of a relative "they concluded their performance with a truly splendid "Dance of the Death."[8]

The dancing hall developed a new figure in Jewish entertainment; the dance-leader (*Tanzführer*), a person capable of taking over the direction of the dancing and introducing new variations and evolutions. The assumption that the dance-leader was the prototype of the later *Marshalik* and *Badhan* is highly improbable, since the dance-leader was not a comic entertainer like these two; furthermore he was not a professional dancing master, but merely a caller of steps and figures such as is customary in folk dancing.

In spite of all the hardships of their existence in the ghetto, a merry spirit prevailed among the Jews, since demonstrations of joy were considered means of achieving piety. This approach reached its glorious heights in Hasidism, particularly in its music and dance. The Jews never allowed their sufferings to mar their unstricken optimism, for the entire history of the Jewish people, especially in the ghetto, reflects this optimistic reliance upon

God's assistance and for a brighter future. The light-heartedness which the Jews manifested in the ghetto made it necessary for the religious leaders to restrain, at certain times, the most joyous outpourings of the people's merriment. But in general, and especially in later centuries, the rabbis did not to any degree curtail the deeply rooted happy conception of life of the Israelites.

The music practice of the Jews in the ghetto took place on three different spheres: in the synagogue, in the home, and in public manifestations.

Synagogue practice was determined by the activity of the *hazzan*, discussed in a preceding chapter.

Music in the home centered almost exclusively in singing the *zemirot*, the origin and development of which was also treated in another part of this study (p. 177).

The music practice in public was closely connected with the activity of the Jews in some cultural centers of medieval life. Here, together with other Jewish intellectuals, Jewish musicians gave eloquent evidence of their creative power and organizational capacities. We shall proceed to demonstrate how music became an important element in ghetto life in such great communities as Venice, Prague and Frankfurt a.M.

The Ghetto of Venice

From the musical point of view the most important of the Jewish ghettos was that of Venice. As far as the music culture of the Jews was concerned, Venice even surpassed Prague, the largest and most famous ghetto in Central Europe.

Venice had a glorious musical history. For centuries the outstanding composers of Italy were the *maestri di cappella* of the San Marco Cathedral, among them GIOVANNI GABRIELI (1557-1612) and his celebrated successor CLAUDIO MONTEVERDI (1567-1643), who held the position from 1613 until his death. It was therefore natural that the lustre of the church music should have also stimulated Jewish musicians living there.

Only scant records testify to the musical activity of the Venetian ghetto at the beginning of the seventeenth century. We know, for instance, of the presentation of a musical comedy in 1607, in which many prominent members of the community took part. Among them was a Jewish singer named RACHEL, endowed with a remarkably beautiful voice, who was a familiar figure in the palaces of the Venetian nobility.[9] A large audience of Jews and Christians attended this performance, which constituted a favorable augury for the musical life in the ghetto, soon to ripen. There are no records, however, attesting that such a dramatic experiment was ever repeated or continued.

Even before RACHEL, the ghetto of Venice prided itself on having a famous Jewish singer. The Italian writer ANDREA CALMO, in his humorous "Lettere Piacevoli" (middle of the sixteenth century), lavishes praise on MADONNA BELLINA HEBREA, whom he calls *"colonna de la musica,"* "a pillar of music." As he states, "she played and composed to admiration, sang like a thousand nightingales, and had no fault other than her religion."[10]

The musical life of the ghetto of Venice did not thrive even on such early stimulating experiences. The situation was changed quite unexpectedly to the better by the siege and capture of Mantua by the Austrian army in 1630, a fact already mentioned. The Jews living there, as we know, helped defend the city, and as it fell to superior forces they were expelled or left the ravaged township by their own volition. It seems that quite a number of them, and especially a large contingent of Jewish musicians, settled in Venice. With the establishment of this settlement we witness a sudden upsurge of the musical activities in the Venetian ghetto. It was sometimes assumed that SALOMONE ROSSI was among those who sought refuge in Venice; this is not very probable, since according to the prevailing records ROSSI died in Mantua in 1628.

We have to revert, however, once more to another man who evidently was instrumental in the unprecedented growth of musical activities in the ghetto of Venice. This man was LEONE MODENA who, as we have already seen, had been rabbi, cantor and choral conductor in Ferrara, and then, in Mantua, had become the most vigorous supporter of SALOMONE ROSSI. LEONE was a typical Renaissance figure, who combined all the virtues and vices of the epoch. He is described as a "Jack of twenty-six trades" (which he enumerates with visible pride), but master of none.

He was cynical enough to write the memorial address to be delivered over his coffin. He attacked his own convictions and precepts. He was a scholar of unusual breadth, as well as a prolific writer and a vociferous preacher, the pride of the Venetian ghetto, despite being at times its shame.[11] This last remark refers to his addiction to gambling, which he condemned repeatedly, vowing never to indulge in it again. Yet he could not resist cards for long, and lost several small fortunes as a result. When the Venetian Jewish community tried to stamp out the vice of gambling, LEONE brilliantly argued that to do so was contrary to Talmudic injunctions.[12] He had an agreeable tenor voice and was chosen ḥazzan of the Italian congregation in Venice, a position which he retained until his death (1648). In addition, the Sephardic (Spanish) synagogue appointed him as its preacher, thus making him the official orator of the Venetian community.[13]

As for his ability as a preacher, his autobiography states that his sermons attracted the most distinguished audiences.[14] Although a model of Jewish enlightenment, he was intensely superstitious, believed in omens, dreams and visions, and was an adherent to the medieval practices of alchemy.[15] His literary interests fluctuated between rendering into Hebrew the first and the 28th canto of ARIOSTO's *Orlando furioso* from the original, and writing dramatic poems, among them a pastoral comedy, *Rachel and Jacob*. The manuscript of the latter work was lost, for on one occasion he was compelled to pawn his only copy to a friend.[16] As an ardent believer in the reform of SALOMONE ROSSI, he supervised and achieved the printing of Rossi's synagogue compositions in Venice in 1622-23, even before LEONE settled in this city.

This is the character, in broad outlines, of the man who was responsible for shaping the musical destiny of the Venetian ghetto. He was the driving force behind the establishment of a musical academy in the ghetto (1629), that may have been modeled upon a similar institution in Mantua. The existence of the latter academy, however, has not been positively documented. The Venetian academy assumed the official name "The Company of the Musicians of the Ghetto of Venice," but in the pseudo-modest fashion of the day it called itself *L'Accademia degli Imperiti*, that is, "The Academy of the Unskilled." It also had a Hebrew name, using a quotation from the 137th Psalm, "*Bezokrenu et Ziyyon*," (When we remembered Zion).

LEONE MODENA became the leader, secretary and *maestro di cappella* of the Academy, which soon exchanged courtesies with other musical organizations outside the ghetto.

A pupil of LEONE's, SAMUEL NAHMIAS di SALONICCO (1612-1680), who in 1649 became converted to Catholicism and changed his name to GIULIO MOROSINI, was a famous preacher in Venice. In one of his literary works, *Via delle Fede* (The Way of the Faith) he mentions that in 1629 an *Academia musicale* was established in the Venetian ghetto which gave concerts twice a week. These concerts must have been of such quality that the fame of the Jewish institution soon spread and attracted visitors from far and wide, Jews and non-Jews alike. In the second part (chapter 46) of the same work, MOROSINI described the Feast of *Simhat Torah* in Venice ca. 1628, of which he remembers the occasion as being particularly brilliant.[17]

Otherwise, the established musical life in the ghetto of Venice was organized along the lines of ancient Biblical practice. As in Ancient Israel, a trumpet was sounded on the Eve of Sabbath in the *Ghetto Nuovo*, an hour before sunset, to signal the cessation of work. A half hour later the signal was repeated, and a short time after this a last warning was given, after which all secular activities had to cease. At the festival of *Simhat Torah* the synagogues, richly decorated, were open all night; girls and young married women wore masks and went from synagogue to synagogue. Gentiles, common folk as well as patricians, visited the ghetto in droves and participated in the scenes of rejoicing. Special hymns were sung, some to Spanish melodies brought by exiles from the Iberian peninsula.[18]

The rich musical life of the ghetto, and especially the activity of the Academy, were greatly endangered by the plague in 1630, which lasted in Venice for sixteen months. The ghetto suffered just as did the rest of the population, and many members of the Academy were among the victims, including some of its leading performers. It appears, however, that the Academy recovered from this calamity, for it is known that it existed for another ten years, although in a greatly reduced fashion. Its concerts became less frequent, their standard was far below the former excellence.

In 1639 a newly organized musical society in the Gentile part of the city suggested an interchange of musical performances such as had taken place in former days. LEONE MODENA, to his utter regret, had declined such a venture, since he did not feel that the previous quality of the performances could be guaranteed. It is most likely that the Academy of the ghetto came to an end shortly thereafter.[19]

One of the most important innovations of the Venetian ghetto was the introduction of an orchestra into the synagogue. We know that even at earlier historical periods and despite strict rabbinical prohibitions instrumental music was sporadically used in the synagogue. Such, for instance, was the case in the twelfth century in Bagdad, as BENJAMIN of TUDELA reports from his travels in the Orient. Nevertheless, a complete orchestra such as was used in the Sephardic synagogue in Venice was a real break-through in the rabbinical conception about instrumental music in the liturgy. One curious fact deserves to be mentioned. In another synagogue of the Venetian ghetto, which undoubtedly could not afford an orchestra, the playing of the musicians was replaced by an "imitation of the gestures" of the performers, a rather naïve but nevertheless significant substitute for live music.

The daring of those responsible for the music in the Venetian ghetto went even further. On the festival of *Simḥat Torah* they introduced an organ into the Sephardic synagogue, in addition to the orchestra. This created such a sensation that Christians and Jews came in multitudes to hear this extraordinary performance. There was such a tumult at the doors that police were called upon to prevent a turmoil. To avoid further disorders, the organ was removed (evidently it was one of those small portable instruments), and the experiment was never again repeated, though the orchestra remained. The music used for this performance (or on a similar occasion) has been preserved and is in the Library of the Hebrew Union College in Cincinnati.

Even before the establishment of the Academy, Jewish musicians were considered to be the best teachers in Venice, and many a patrician family entrusted them with the musical education of their children.

Through their mutual musical exchange the relations between Jews and Christians became so intimate that the Council of the *Pregadi,* afraid of the consequences that might result from such a state of affairs, ordered the Jewish schools closed in 1443. The Jews were forbidden to teach music in Venice under penalty of six months in prison and a fine of 500 talers. These schools were prohibited to Christians, yet were open to Jews, and after a short while the edict was disregarded completely.

In spite of all harassments, the Jews never abandoned their most potent spiritual weapon, the instruction of the new generation, as this was their sole guarantee of religious and ethnic survival. Even in the troubled period of Venice in the second half of the seventeenth century, the Ashkenazic community opened a new school (December 21, 1661). We do not know whether this school was destined for elementary or higher learning; we do know, however, that the festivities of its inauguration took place with rich musical deployment.[20]

In the highly intellectual atmosphere of Venice there lived one of the most outstanding Jewish women of the Renaissance, SARAH COPPIO SULLAM. The SULLAMS belonged to the most cultured families of Italy at that time. MOSES SULLAM was, as mentioned before, an early supporter of SALOMONE ROSSI. It was he who had encouraged ROSSI to publish his synagogue compositions. These works were promptly dedicated to SULLAM. SARAH COPPIO was born in Venice in 1592, and received a humanistic education of the widest range. When she was fifteen years old, she displayed her mastery of Latin, Greek and Spanish, in addition to her native Italian, and Hebrew. She was also gifted in poetry, and although her poems remained unpublished, she enjoyed a high standing in literary circles as the foremost Venetian poet. In 1614 she married JACOB SULLAM, one of the most distinguished members of the Venetian community; from there on her home became the center of the ghetto society and a literary salon frequented by Christians and Jews alike. Famous visitors from other cities, even from Rome and Paris, came to pay her homage. In addition to her literary qualities, she was musically gifted, had a sweet voice and was an ardent lover of music. We can imagine that the frequent excellent concerts in her home were a delight for her guests.

LEONE MODENA honored her by dedicating to her his adaptation of SALOMONE USQUE's Spanish drama *Esther*.[21] Her intellectual qualities and her fame as one of the leading women of the Renaissance made it imperative for her to fight for her religion—all in all a remarkable woman, imbued with all the virtues of the Renaissance spirit. She died in Venice in 1641.

SARAH COPPIO was by no means the only person of talent. In Renaissance Italy there lived a number of other Jewish learned women, among them GRACIA NASI (or MENDES), Señora BENVENIDA ABRABANEL, DEBORAH ASCARELLI, HANNAH RIETI, and others. Some were accomplished writers, helpers in their husbands' literary activity, who copied books for them in their own hand.

A talented German Jewess, GLÜCKEL of HAMELN (1648-1724), whom we mentioned earlier, relates in her memoirs an incident wherein, while playing the clavicembalo (harpsichord), she was able to thwart a blackmail attempt on her father.[22]

The women in Italy of the Renaissance were often accomplished musicians who taught their sisters the hymns to be sung in the synagogue. Of the musical instruments, they preferred the lute and the clavichord,[23] on which they accompanied themselves when singing the verses which their husbands composed.

Apart from engaging music masters to teach their daughters the art of instrumental playing, wealthy Jews would also hire dancing masters for their wives and children. This was a regular practice in every cultured Jewish family.

As can be seen, the ghetto was, in certain respects, far from dull. The intellectual striving of the Jews, and also of the Jewesses, brought sunshine and at times even glamour into an otherwise drab existence.

Benedetto Marcello's "Estro poetico-armonico"

The music culture of the Venetian ghetto brought forth a late and rather unexpected harvest. Almost a century after SALOMONE

Rossi strove for reform in synagogue music, a noted Gentile composer had been attracted to the world of Jewish music. He left
a work for posterity which is of the greatest importance for our
knowledge of traditional synagogue chants. He was BENEDETTO
MARCELLO (1686-1739), a descendant of a patrician family, who
was originally a lawyer and held various offices, political and administrative, and who served fourteen years as a member of the
Venetian "Council of the Forty." In 1730 he was elected Governor of Pola, and in 1738 Treasurer of the city of Brescia which, at
that time, belonged to Venice. He had studied music with the
famous composer FRANCESCO GASPARINI (1668-1727), *maestro di
cappella* at the Lateran who, between the years 1694 and 1724,
wrote no less than sixty-one operas, besides a great number of
oratorios, masses, cantatas, etc. MARCELLO must have had a
thorough musical education, which enabled him to make use of
his astonishing facility of composing large works. We wonder
where he found time and inspiration to write his concertos, sonatas and madrigals, considering his many official functions. His
most famous musical creation was the Italian paraphrase, after
the poems of GIROLAMO ASCANIO GIUSTINIANI, of the first fifty
psalms. He entitled his work *"Estro poetico-armonico"* (Poetic
and Harmonic Inspiration), and added the subtitle *"Parafrasi
sopra li primi 50 Salmi."* It was written for voices in solo and
various combinations, with occasional soli for violin or violoncello and with figured bass, the realization of which was left, as
was usual at those times, to the accompanist. The eight volumes
were published by LOVISO in Venice, 1724-1727.

It was "Inspiration" in the proper sense of the word, an inspiration caused by ancient Hebrew chants, which he may have heard
by attending services in the Venetian synagogues. As a matter
of fact, he had actually notated some of the synagogue melodies
which he found particularly attractive and characteristic. It was
presumed that he had written them down from memory. This,
however, appears rather doubtful in view of the fact that he
indicated with every melody not only the exact title in Hebrew
letters (without vowels), but indicated precisely the ritual in
which these songs were sung. Furthermore, he indicated those
melodies which belonged to the Sephardic and which to the

Ashkenazic tradition. Apparently he received advice in each instance, either from the rabbi or the cantor of the synagogue, or
both. This does not in the least lessen the importance of his work.
On the contrary, it proves that the melodies are authentic, even
though slightly adapted according to the taste of his time, in order
to serve as the *canti firmi* for his elaborate polyphonic designs.

Among the fifty psalm settings, eleven contain a synagogue
song as their Tenor; of these, five belong to the Sephardic and
six to the Ashkenasic rite. He begins each of the eleven compositions with quoting for one voice the traditional melody upon
which it is based. In nine of them he quotes the Hebrew text in
its entirety, and places the Hebrew syllables under each note to
which they belong; in two he indicates only the first Hebrew
phrase. Below can be found the eleven melodies:

Mus. ex. No. 45

The Hebrew Intonations in
Benedetto Marcello's Estro Poetico-Armonico
in modern notation

1. L'David Baruch (Sephardic)

2. B'zet Yisrael (Ashkenazic)

3. Od'ho ki anitani. (Sephardic)

4. Ma'oz Zur (Ashkenazic)

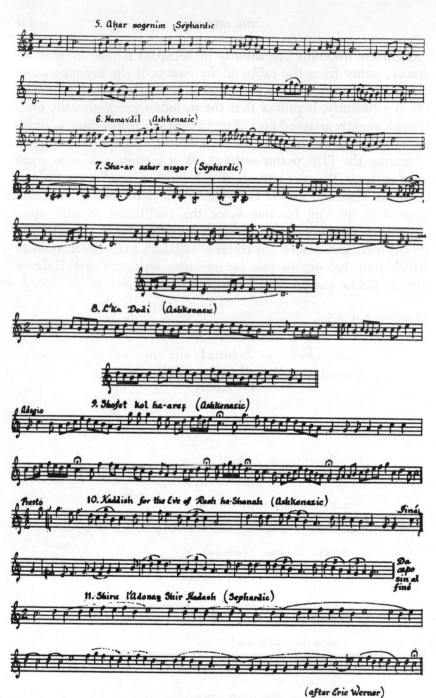

The Hebrew intonations in Benedetto Marcello's Estra poetico-armonico (Venice, 1724–1727). *(After Eric Werner).*

According to the custom of the time MARCELLO wrote a long-winded introduction to the work, wherein he gave an explanation of ancient Greek and Hebrew music, indicating the reasons that induced him to use various Hebrew melodies for his composition. The subsequent volumes of his work are likewise preceded by some introductory remarks.

It is fortunate that most of MARCELLO's Jewish melodies were selected among those sung by the congregations. It might also be that he considered their rhythmic patterns more suitable for contrapuntal treatment. Among them, the Ashkenazic melodies have an unmistakably rhythmic, almost chorale-like quality.[24]

MARCELLO's psalm compositions had a well-earned success. They were frequently performed by famous singers in the Cathedral of San Marco in Venice; the texts were subsequently translated into French and English, and as early as 1728, in Hamburg, they were undoubtedly presented in German. There were several new editions of the work, some as late as the nineteenth century.

During his lifetime, MARCELLO was considered one of the leading composers of the Baroque era; in Rome and Bologna he was called *"Princeps musicae,"* a Prince of Music. Even JOHANN SEBASTIAN BACH was attracted by MARCELLO's music and transcribed his Oboe Concerto for Clavier solo (No. 974 in Schmieder's "Bach-Verzeichnis," Leipzig, 1950).

After the illustrious event of the Mantuan and Venetian era, the musical activity of the Italian Jews declined considerably. The reason was not merely the lack of such outstanding personalities as SALOMONE ROSSI and LEONE MODENA, but was probably the anti-Jewish reaction which set in with the Counter-Reformation. Jewish performers encountered increasing difficulties in the exercise of their profession. Heavy taxes were levied upon them; to these were added all kinds of restrictions pertaining to the number of the participants in each Jewish group of musicians, to the places, days and even hours during which they were permitted to play. Furthermore, owing to the expanding anti-Jewish attitude of certain strata of the population, social contact between Christians and Jews dwindled. When added up, all those circumstances were not of the kind that further the individual's desire to embrace the musical profession. They resulted, in fact, in a situation nearly fatal to Jewish musicians and, in the last analysis, for Jewish music itself.

Eventually only vestiges of the former highly developed musical culture remained and, as a concomitant, the professional ability of Jewish musicians declined. It so happened that in the second half of the seventeenth century a Mantuan religious confraternity, *Shomrim la-Boker* (The Watchers of the Dawn), wished to commission a four-part antiphonal setting for a lively hymn, *")Aḥai ve-Reai* (My brothers and my friends), to be inserted into the feast of *Hoshanna Rabba*. As it turned out, no Jewish composer capable of writing music to the words could be located in the city, so finally a Church musician, CARLO GROSSI of Vicenza, later *maestro di cappella* of Mantua (1687), was entrusted with the composition of the music. The opus, with the Hebrew words transliterated, is included in GROSSI's publication *Il Divertimento de' Grandi . . . Con un dialogo amoroso e uno in idoma Ebraico* (Venice, 1681).

The cantata has eight stanzas, soli and choir alternating. The music, though written with (transliterated) Hebrew words, has nothing Jewish, it follows rather the common idiom of the music of those days.[25]

In spite of the fact that the printed score of GROSSI's cantata indicates expressly that it was published in Venice, printed by GIUSEPPE SALA, ISRAEL ADLER considered the possibility that it was published in Modena, or Verona, since in both places there were fraternities of the same name. However, in view of the fact that the printed score indicates Venice as the place of publication, we must abide by this.

Another writer whose information about the musical life of the Jews would have been of great value, was YEHUDAH ben MOSES SALTARO de FANO (ca. 1550-1627), rabbi of the Sephardic community of Venice. He was one of the authorities who concurred with LEONE MODENA's *Responsum* about choral singing in Ferrara in 1605. In his written opinion about MODENA's *Responsum*, SALTARO mentioned that the fifth chapter of a treatise of his, *Shir Ziyyon* was devoted to the praise of music. His treatise, however, was never published, and it is not even known whether its manuscript still exists.

It is most frustrating that this treatise, which might have given us additional insight into the Jewish life of the Venetian ghetto, is presumably lost.

Still an ancient musical culture, such as that of the Italian Jewry, refused to become extinct in spite of all hardships. Once in a while a spark would glimmer under the ashes. In the eighteenth century several Jewish musicians were known to have lived in Verona. Among them were the famous violoncellist GIACOBBE (JAMES) BASEVI CERVETTO and his son GIACOMO, both of whom settled later in England and were appointed to the English Court.[26] GIACOBBE is said to have introduced the violoncello into England,[27] a rather doubtful statement, since the violoncello, at that time, and even earlier, was a well-known solo instrument all over the civilized world. The master creators of Italian string instruments, AMATI, GASPARO de SALO, MAGGINI and others, are known to have manufactured excellent violoncelli in the sixteenth century, although then the violoncello was still overshadowed by its more popular historical predecessor, the *viola da gamba*. The first cello virtuoso known in music history was PETRONIO FRANCESCHINI of Bologna (seventeenth century); following his leadership, the instrument became solidly entrenched in contemporaneous chamber music. DOMENICO GABRIELI wrote already in 1689 *Ricercari* for violoncello, some even without the accompaniment of the usual *Basso continuo*, thus establishing clearly the reputation of the violoncello as a solo instrument. JOHANN SEBASTIAN BACH's sonatas for solo cello, written in the first half of the eighteenth century, have remained masterpieces of cello literature.

In view of all this historical evidence, it cannot be asserted that CERVETTO may have been the man who introduced the violoncello into England.

A sure sign of Jewish musical activity in the eighteenth century was the translation into Hebrew by a Venetian rabbi, JACOB RAPHAEL SARAVAL, of HANDEL's oratorio *Esther* (composed 1737). The purpose of the translation must certainly have been the performance of the work, possibly in a Jewish musical circle.

Whether the performance actually took place cannot be ascertained. The fact alone that it was planned, would tend to prove that the singers (soloists and choir), as well as the instrumentalists, were available in sufficient numbers and quality for such a project.

As was pointed out earlier, the flourishing Jewish musical activity in Mantua came to an abrupt end after the Austrian army captured the city in 1630. Not for considerable time did Jewish musicians settle there again. A few musicians were granted the privilege in Northern Italy to give instruction in music and the dance, a privilege which the cardinal delegate of Ancona abolished a decade later. Toward the end of the eighteenth century the learned physician BENEDETTO FRIZZI, in enumerating the occupations of the Mantuan Jews, relates that among the general population of about two thousand, there were no less than fifteen professional Jewish musicians.[28] A township of this size might have had only a few Jewish families; therefore, the fifteen musicians counted by FRIZZI must have earned their living by rendering their services mainly to the Gentiles.

Synagogal music, after the ill-fated reform of MODENA, ROSSI, and other pioneers of the sixteenth and seventeenth centuries, reverted to the old routine, borrowing all sorts of melodies right and left and in self-complacency excluded everything that was new or unusual. Records left by MENAḤEM NAVARRA of Verona relate that in the eighteenth century it was customary in this city to sing the *Ḳiddush*, the *Ḳedushah* and the *Tefillah* to the melodies of popular love songs and dance tunes. The religious leaders (particularly the *ḥazzanim*) invoked for this custom the authority of R. YOEL ben SAMUEL SIRKES (1561-1640), the Polish rabbi and great Cabalist. NAVARRA, however, was inclined to side with his countryman SAMUEL ARCHEVOLTI, the rabbi-poet-grammarian (1515-1611), who opposed such practices. Yet his opinions about music were highly unrealistic. In his famous work *'Arugat ha-Bosem* (The Bed of Spices) (Venice, 1602), he maintained that music originated from the celestial spheres. Furthermore, he asserted in all seriousness that, as the Bible "vaguely" suggests, music was given to mankind by Tubal Cain (he evidently confused him with Jubal!), it was lost in consequence of the Flood, was renewed by Pythagoras, and then (!) by King

David.[29] Thus, ARCHEVOLTI might not have been the proper authority to decide about the admissibility of secular tunes in synagogue music.

NAVARRA finally turned to a famous contemporary, R. ḤAI ben AARON RAKAḤ (1690-1768) for an opinion. In a lengthy responsum (publ. 1742), R. ḤAI discussed the whole question and came to the conclusion that the views of R. JOEL SIRKES were misunderstood and that the introduction of foreign tunes in the synagogue should absolutely be forbidden.

All the rabbinical hair-splitting turned out to be futile. In Italy, Germany and France, the ḥazzanim, undisturbed by rabbinic opinions, continued their habit of leaning predominantly on borrowed music in the eighteenth century, as they had been doing in earlier times.

Lorenzo da Ponte

The picture of Italian Jewish music culture would be incomplete without mentioning the man who had earned for himself indelible merits in the general history of music. He is EMMANUELE CONEGLIANO, born in 1740 in Ceneda (province of Venice), but better known under the name of LORENZO da PONTE, a name, which he adopted when he was converted to Catholicism in his fourteenth year, together with his father GEREMIA, and two brothers. He entered a seminary for priesthood and was ordained in 1773. When still a young man he became professor of Italian belles-lettres at Treviso, then in Venice, and wrote poetry and, unfortunately, also a venomous political satire for which he was exiled from Italy.

This exile turned out to be a blessing in disguise, for after an adventurous life he landed in Vienna, where he impressed the Emperor JOSEPH II with his literary qualities. He was employed as a dramatic writer at the Court, a sort of poet laureate, and wrote plays and libretti for opera composers.

By a curious turn of fate, a Jew was instrumental in bringing together DA PONTE and MOZART. Baron RAIMUND von PLANKEN-STERN, a wealthy Jewish banker and patron of art, had been for several years MOZART's landlord in Vienna. MOZART called him his "good and true friend," and he acted as godfather to MOZART's first son who, accordingly, was named RAIMUND LEOPOLD (this second name after MOZART's father).

At a party given by Baron von PLANKENSTERN, MOZART met DA PONTE. The Baron evidently hoped for a fruitful collaboration of the two artists, but MOZART at first assumed a reticent attitude toward DA PONTE. The poet himself was at first also skeptical, since he did not foresee financial advantages in working with MOZART. Again, Baron von PLANKENSTERN proved to be the "guardian angel" of both. He offered to pay DA PONTE a guaranteed sum in case the opera written jointly with MOZART should not be staged in Vienna. Furthermore, he promised that in this case he would see to it that the opera would be performed by another major theater.

The story of the first collaboration of the two artists is well known. MOZART's choice, among other suggestions made by DA PONTE, fell on BEAUMARCHAIS' comedy *The Marriage of Figaro*. This social satire encountered difficulties with the Vienna censorship, and not before some incisive changes have been made in the libretto had the objections been withdrawn. However, the performance was assured only after MOZART played for the Emperor several of the already composed numbers.

After the initial success of the two artists in Vienna and Prague in 1786, their collaboration continued with *Don Giovanni* (1787) and *Così fan tutte* (1790). Through this collaboration DA PONTE's name became immortal in the annals of music history.

As a result of his intrigues, DA PONTE lost the favor of JOSEPH II. He was dismissed and could not regain his employment at the court. The new Emperor LEOPOLD banished him from the country. His further life was equally adventurous. He first went to London, where he became associated with the Italian opera; in that city he was threatened with imprisonment for debts. He left secretly and embarked for the United States.

In New York he occupied the chair of Italian language and literature at Columbia College (1826-1837); he was the first to make Dante known in America. His real vocation, however, was the theater. He tried his luck in 1833 as an impressario for the Italian opera. He brought over an Italian company, in which such great artists sang as GARCIA and the MALIBRAN. In the same year he organized his own company and took over its management. At the age of eighty he composed an opera which was performed by his own company. The music was a weak imitation of the current style of the Italian opera and did not last except for a few performances. He died in New York in 1837.

DA PONTE left to posterity an extensive autobiography entitled *Memorie,* first published in four volumes in New York (1829-1830), reissued many times, and subsequently translated into other European languages. In his memoirs he indiscriminately mixed fact and fancy, magniloquence and self-adulation. The book should be read with reserve and caution.

For us, one facet of his life is significant: his statement that in his youth he was proficient in Hebrew. Who knows how he could have utilized his brilliant literary qualities and his love for music in the service of his people? His talent was lost to Judaism, but on the other hand he inspired MOZART's genius to immortal masterpieces, for which the musical world should be grateful.

In commemoration, Columbia University in New York created, in 1928, a chair in his name for Italian language and literature.

With him, the Italian period of Jewish music history ends, a period that brought to the fore the best qualities of the Jewish genius: the force and perseverance of the Jewish artist, his unbroken will and courage to assert himself under the most adverse conditions. Above all, this period provided ample proof of Jewish musical creativity which was for long denied to the Jewish people and with such ill will.

Klezmorim and Badḥanim

The most numerous and most important practitioners of music in German ghettos were the instrumentalists, called *klezmorim* or *leẓim,* and their counterparts in the field of popular entertainment, the *badḥanim,* jesters, merrymakers. There exist numerous records in official documents and also in contemporary literary works concerning their activity at Jewish and Christian celebrations. Posterity is therefore well informed about their artistry and their social status.

The word *klezmer* (plur. *klezmorim*) is the contraction of the Biblical *kle zemer* (lit. tools for the song; in general, musical instruments) into one word, indicating in Judaeo-German instrumentalists of all categories, without differentiation between them. The word *lezim* is of Talmudic origin. In the rabbinical literature it was a term for the ungodly ones: "Thy children have made me as a harp (*kinnor*), upon which they frivolously play (*lezim menagnim*)."[30] RASHI calls grotesque dancers *lezonim*.[31] In the Middle Ages the term *lezim* meant buffoons and jesters who furnished the merriment at fairs and other popular festivities. In the later centuries these merrymakers were generally called *badhanim*.

It had been said that after the destruction of the Jerusalem Temple by the Romans, Jewish instrumental music had to be abandoned. The strict rabbinical prohibition, however, had one loop-hole: the ban on music making was lifted for weddings, since merriment on this occasion was a Biblical command, and joy without singing and music was unthinkable even for the most zealous rabbis. Therefore, despite all restrictions imposed on instrumental music, a fair-sized number of instrumentalists survived the epoch of national mourning, to be on hand at least for weddings, and probably also for other joyous occasions.

Instrumental music was even kept alive in the synagogue, here and there. It has been mentioned that there was rich musical display at the inauguration ceremonies of the Exilarch in Babylonia, inside and outside the synagogue. A traveler to the Orient in the twelfth century, R. BENJAMIN of TUDELA, reported that, during the intermediary days of *Pesah* and *Sukkot,* he witnessed services with instrumental music in the synagogue of Bagdad. This practice continued sporadically throughout the entire period of the Diaspora. We refer to the examples already mentioned in Ferrara, Mantua, Venice and in Livorno. There also exist records from Germanic countries, attesting to instrumental music in the synagogue. It is reported for instance, that in the township of Nikolsburg there were musical performances in the services with *"sheyne nokhspil welkhes gor oft lang gevert"* ("beautiful postludiums, which often lasted long").[32] Even an isolated place such as the island of Corfu boasted of instrumental music in the synagogue. Thus in a nineteenth-century book, *Noga Ẕedek* (publ. in 1818), reference is made to older historical records stating that as late as the fifteenth century, on this island, the *Shem'ā* was accompanied with music (*b'niggun ha-musiḳa*). What instruments might have been used for the accompaniment is not revealed by this source. Another musical peculiarity on the island of Corfu was the ancient custom of singing certain elegies in the dialect of southern Italy, mixing it with Greek, Hebrew and Venetian words. "In this language they explained also the *Seder* on the Eve of Passover, and they even sang their love songs."[33]

Three eighteenth-century literary works, all written by non-Jews, afford us insight into Jewish customs and furnish numerous observations about ghetto life in general, which might have appeared "strange" to Gentile readers. Considered jointly, the three treatises also contain reflections about Jewish music and musicians, and it would be quite in order to say a few words about them at this juncture.

The author of one is JOHANN JACOB SCHUDT, whose work *Memorabilia judaica; sive Jüdische Merkwürdigkeiten . . .* (Jewish Curiosa), published in four volumes, 1714-17, in Frankfurt a.M., is a veritable compendium of the cultural history of the Jews in the seventeenth century. Its illustrations are especially revealing for the various manifestations of medieval Jewish life. It is worth noting that SCHUDT's opus does not belong to the German anti-Jewish literature common in those centuries. In this respect it differs markedly from the second treatise we are referring to, JOHANN CHRISTOPH WAGENSEIL's *Belehrung der Jüdisch-Teutschen Red- und Schreibart* (Advice about the Judeo-German Manner of Speech and Writing), publ. in Königsberg, 1699. SCHUDT tries to be objective, as much as was possible at that time, adhering to facts. Our knowledge about ghetto life is greatly enhanced by his chronicle.

His characterizations of Jewish musicians are exquisite in their whimsical criticism. Quite revealing, too, are SCHUDT's disclosures about the demands for the services of these musicians, both by Jews and Gentiles. He considers the *leẓim* as common beer-fiddlers in taverns, whose "artistry" was far below that of Christian musicians. Whether this was a fact or the usual bias of Christians against Jewish performers cannot be established conclusively. It may be assumed, however, that the Gentile musicians of the lower categories (playing at Jewish weddings) were not much superior to Jewish *klezmorim.*

The third treatise in question is PAUL CHRISTIAN KIRCHNER's *Jüdisches Ceremoniel* (Jewish Ceremonial), published at Nüremberg in 1726, which contains valuable information about Jewish life. Some of its illustrations enhance our knowledge about Jewish music practice in the ghetto.

The Ghetto of Prague

In Germanic countries the needs of communal organization occasioned at a very early date a voluntary congregation of the Jews in separate districts of the various cities. Even before the establishment of specifically organized ghettos, Jewish quarters were known by the thirteenth century. As we have mentioned earlier, almost all larger German cities had their *Judenstadt* or *Judengasse,* the French their *Juiverie,* the Venetians their *Giudecca.*

The two most important ghettos in Germanic lands, numerically, economically and intellectually speaking, were those of Prague and Frankfurt a.M. As far as the musical culture of the Jews is concerned, Prague definitely deserves the crown.

The ghetto of Prague was a state within the state, and had its own autonomic administration, its town hall, its synagogues, and a musical life which was equal with that of Mantua and Venice.

The first historical records of Jews living in Prague dates back to 906, although at that time there were no ghettos as such. In 1096 the Crusaders inflicted heavy damage upon the Jewish quarters and killed many of its inhabitants. The earliest recorded mention of a synagogue in Prague goes back to the year 1124. The famous *Altneuschul* synagogue was built in the thirteenth century.

The ghetto of Prague must have held so many apparently gainful points in the eyes of the Jews living outside its precincts that in 1437 they decided voluntarily to move into it *en masse.* The *Judenstadt* of Prague not only offered to its inhabitants economic and social advantages, but as time passed living in it became a matter of pride for them. They enjoyed the privilege of their own flag, a right conferred on them in 1357 for patriotic services. The flag is still preserved in the synagogue of Prague. In the sixteenth century the philanthropist MORDECAI MEISEL constructed the famous *Rathhaus* (town hall), an architectural gem. Its tower clock had a dial in Hebrew and Arabic letters, the hands of which moved counterclockwise.

The prosperity of the Jews in the ghetto of Prague, combined with their highly developed intellectual life, resulted in a lofty musical culture. On the tombstones in the old Jewish cemetery of Prague there appear forty-four professions, among them many musicians, whose engraved emblems were a violin or a harp.[34] Some epitaphs indicate the graves of singers.

The intensive practice of music in the ghetto of Prague began to be recorded at an early date. We know, for instance, that at the turn of the fourteenth century it was customary among the Jews to sing certain *Einheitsgesänge* (Songs of Unity); these were hymnlike songs praising the unity of God in the vernacular instead of Hebrew. They were sung in the company of Christians in the streets of Prague, which made a great impression upon the onlookers.[35]

When the ghetto of Prague was burned down in 1689 the ten synagogues were destroyed. One of the oldest, the Pinkas synagogue (built at the end of the thirteenth or beginning of the fourteenth century), had the distinction of being the first to have used a portable organ for its services. The organ was replaced after the conflagration and kept until the middle of the eighteenth century; it was played on festive occasions and carried in processions.

The *Altneuschul* likewise possessed an organ at a very early date. After the fire, a new one was purchased and given to the synagogue by a Jewish donor in 1716.

Still another organ was installed in the Meisel-Synagogue; it was built by R. MAIER MAHLER and, according to contemporary records, "cost more than 400 Gulden." The *Sidur Amsterdam*, printed in 1680 together with the book *Sifte Yeshenim* (The Eyes of the Sleepers) by SHABBETAI BASS, a singer in the synagogue of Prague, mentions instrumental music in synagogue services: "A lovely melody by R. Solomon Singer, which is played in the Meisel Synagogue in Prague with organ (*'ugab*) and string instruments (*nebalim*) before [the singing of] "*Lekah Dodi*" (p. 21b). We know that during the period of the Diaspora certain rabbis, to supplement their livelihood, had to engage in secular professions. Nevertheless, a rabbi like Maier Mahler, who could double as an organ-maker, was not only unique but his case constituted the refutation of the ingrained notion that the organ was a "Christian" instrument. Evidently it was not considered as such during the seventeenth century.

About the aforementioned singer Shabbetai we learn that: "This Isaac is called Bass, because he sings the bass, and sings it well. Therefore his name is R. Sabbatheus, or Bassista Pragensis."[36]

Before, or simultaneously with Prague, instrumental "preludes" to the Friday-night service were also performed in Regensburg, as recorded in 1689.

When Ludwig II, the last Polish king of Bohemia, entered the city of Prague in 1512, the Jews welcomed him with a solemn procession, singing psalms accompanied by musical instruments, while the rabbis carried the Scrolls of the Law. In Schudt's work there are several illustrations showing, among others, a bridal procession and a "Jewish procession in Prague," with musicians, string players, trumpets and drummers (Illustration No. 30).

In honor of the coronation of the Emperor Leopold I of Austria (1658-1705), a solemn procession of the Jews of Prague took place in 1678. On this occasion a number of Jewish musicians and singers participated: a woman playing the cymbals and two fiddlers; a clavicembalo and two fiddlers; three portable organs, one supporting the musicians, the others accompanying three choral groups; three trumpeteers, and three groups consisting of five trumpets each with a set of kettle drums. These latter groups did not take part in the procession, but were distributed along the route of the cortège. The outstanding feature of the procession was the three choral groups of *hazzanim* with their assistant singers (treble and bass voices). The soloist of the whole musical display was the famous Isserl Hazzan.

Still another procession, in 1741, illustrated in Schudt's opus, shows typical figures of the Italian carnival, which was imitated in Prague. The picture shows a harlequin, some jesters, a *badhan*, and other masqueraded comic persons. There are also Jewish musicians in this procession, some of them making noise on large "tin cans." The caption under it explains that an old man in woman's attire played the bassoon; that among the participants there was a *hazzan*, whose singing was accompanied by an organ carried ahead of him.

It is unfortunate that none of this music has survived. The reasons are twofold: first, most of the Jewish musicians of that epoch were probably unable to read or write music (just as was the case with Gypsy musicians in various places only a few decades ago); the other reason might have been the jealously guarded "professional secret" of the *klezmorim*. They were evidently aware of the possibility of "piracy" by non-Jewish musicians. As a precaution, there was no solution except to leave the music unwritten and to transmit it by oral instruction.

There exist records about professional guilds of Jewish musicians having existed in Prague, such as a choral society and also an orchestral society. The latter played in the synagogue before the beginning of the Friday Eve service. A contemporary record reads: "With the help of these instruments they sing not only 'Lekah Dodi,' but after they finish that poem they continue to sing several sweet tunes for about an hour's time," which may have amounted to a veritable sacred concert for the welcoming of the Sabbath Queen.[37]

ABRAHAM LEVY (1705-85) in his *Travels in Israel* mentions that "In Prague there are famous *hazzanim*. Among them I found one who is a great artist and famous throughout Europe. His name is YOKELE HAZZAN. The *hazzanim* employ *meshorerim* (singers) and also flutes and organs and violins and cymbals and various instruments of percussion for every Friday to usher in the Sabbath."[38] Another famous *hazzan* of Prague was LIPPMAN KATZ POPPER, who received a glowing eulogy by R. HIRSCHELE TAUSIG WEINSCHENK (printed in the appendix of J. Chr. WAGENSEIL's *Sota*, Altdorff, 1674, pp. 83-88). In the aforementioned work of WAGENSEIL (p. 347), mention is made of *"Drey Lieder, welche die Juden, sonderlich die Weibsbilder unter denselben, sowol sonsten, als sonderlich an dem Oster-Fest zu singen pflegen"* (Three songs which the Jews, especially the women, use to sing occasionally, but in particular at the Passover festival) (pp. 91-110). Furthermore, WAGENSEIL describes *"Ein schön Lied, hübsch und bescheidlich, für Weiber und Meidlich, zu erkennen Gottes Kraft und Macht"* (A pretty song, comely and modest, for women and maidens. To recognize God's power and might") (pp. 119-145).

These and numerous other contemporaneous descriptions of the life and the musical practice in the ghetto of Prague make it evident that a most intellectual atmosphere existed in this Jewish community. Here thrived such illustrious men as *"Der hohe Rabbi Löw"* (R. YUDAH Löw ben BEZALEEL), who became the center of the legends about the *Golem*,[39] R. YOMTOB LIPPMANN HELLER, the famous author of the *Tosafot Yom-Tob*, the renowned astronomer DAVID GANS, and many others, whose concerted efforts made Prague a spiritual center of the first magnitude for several generations.

The large number of *klezmorim* in Prague in conjunction with their professional skill, resulted in repeated clashes with the civic authorities. Permission to play, and revocation thereof, alternated with maddening regularity. In June, 1641, the Archbishop of Prague confirmed the privilege granted Jewish musicians in 1640 to play at weddings and baptismal rites of Gentiles. This created a great uproar among Christian musicians. Petitions followed petitions, *klezmorim* for, Gentiles against. Eventually the archbishop could no longer hold against the pressure by the Christian music guild and the governor of the city, who took the part of the Gentiles. In 1644 he withdrew the privilege from the Jews; henceforth they were not allowed to play in Christian homes on Sundays and holidays. This prohibition seems not to have lasted long, for in 1648 the Christian musicians petitioned anew against their Jewish competitors. In 1650, and again in 1651, the guild of Christian musicians, this time reinforced by the guild of Church organists, asked for anti-Jewish measures.

The objection of the Christian musicians was motivated by their assertion that *"sie die Music confuse verstupfen, weder Tempo noch Tact führen und der edlen und anmutigen Music mit*

Spott ihre aestimation nehmen" ([the Jewish musicians] corrupt and confuse the music, because they do not follow either tempo or time signature, thus mockingly depriving the noble and charming music of its esteemed quality.)[40]

There are no records as to who sponsored the cause of the Jews, but in October, 1651, the archbishop once again renewed his edict permitting Jewish musicians to play for Christian festivities on Sundays and holidays.[41]

With this edict the "battle of the frogs and mice" was far from settled; the eternal ups and downs continued. Nevertheless, the *klezmorim* appeared to have gained a victory due to their professional efficiency.

It is recorded that for one festive procession the Jewish musicians of Prague furnished nineteen trumpets (probably distributed along the entire cortège route), eight violins, four French horns and four kettle drums, in addition to "other instruments," among them a portable organ. At the same occasion, as SCHUDT reports, a *Teutsch-Lied* (German song) was performed, this being a composition by a Herr ISAAC BASS, who was no one else than the aforementioned synagogue *meshorer*, SHABBETAI BASS.

As early as the fifteenth century contemporary records describe bands of Jewish musicians which boasted women among their members.[42] Such bands traveled in Germanic lands and performed at Christian festivities; frequently they were preferred to Gentile musicians. This, in time, resulted in serious setbacks for the Jews; to handicap them, the authorities imposed heavy taxes upon *klezmorim*. After the sixteenth century a permit to perform music was required for each individual town. This permit was nothing but a means of taxation, and since it was required for almost every city in Germany it can be imagined what hardships the Jewish musicians had to endure.[43] Another restriction was that in some cities, and on certain days, the *klezmorim* were even forbidden to play for Jewish weddings.

At the beginning of the fifteenth century it came about that in one of the small German principalities the wife of the ruling prince died and that a year of mourning was declared. At that time in Eppenstein, a small township in this district, a Jewish wedding was planned but, owing to the mourning period, no music was allowed. Since a wedding celebration was unthinkable without music, the people of the town sent an inquiry on how to proceed to R. JACOB MÖLLN (MAHARIL). He replied that music was absolutely essential for weddings and advised them to celebrate elsewhere. Consequently they transferred the wedding to Mainz, to comply with Jewish practice and the rabbinical decision.[44]

Still another hardship imposed upon Jewish musicians was the compulsory reduction of their number on certain occasions. In Metz, only three musicians were permitted. For weddings an additional man could play, and those who had no permanent residence in the city were allowed only to play alone, even for weddings. In Frankfurt a quartet could be hired, but the music had to stop at midnight. In Fürth and other German cities the limit was three *klezmorim*.[45]

All these restrictions, however annoying they may have been, did not affect to any degree the joy and bliss of the wedding festivities. Since singing and music at weddings were age-old Jewish customs, musicians—Jewish or non-Jewish—were brought in from wherever they could be found. The wedding procession had to be enlivened by music—young people danced around the bridal couple. Musicians and torch-bearers led the procession from the bride's house to the synagogue. As we already know, the burning torches and tapers during daytime were a remnant of old superstitious belief, according to which demons and malevolent spirits who lurked everywhere could be chased by the use of these blazing paraphernalia. The primitive purpose of this custom was, therefore, to protect the bridal couple from the harmful influence of hostile powers.

The wedding rites in the synagogue usually began with the singing of the bridal song *"Mi 'addir"*; during the ceremony the Seven benedictions were chanted, either by the rabbi or the ḥazzan. This ritual was based on the ancient belief already referred to, that the magic number seven would be beneficial to the bridal couple.

In later centuries wedding odes would be recited at marriage ceremonies. These odes were at times rather gaudy and ornate, notwithstanding the intentional puns made about the names of the bridegroom and the bride. Famous writers did not consider it below their dignity to compose such odes, in Hebrew or in the vernacular. MOSES ḤAYYIM LUZZATTO (1707-1747) was well known for his skill in writing metrical Hebrew poetry, an art in which he was inimitable. As a result, the demand for his marriage verses was considerable.[46]

The crowning event at each wedding was the banquet, enlivened by the playing of the klezmorim and the jokes of the merrymakers, the badḥanim. In Bohemia and Poland they were called "Marschalks" or "Marschaliks" (the word is of German origin: Mar-Schalk); they were indispensable at every Jewish wedding. They may be compared to the French jongleurs or the Spanish juglares, with the difference, however, that they were not necessarily instrumentalists at the same time as were their Latin counterparts. Some of them may well have played an instrument, but they mainly represented the buffoons and clowns of later times.

It was natural that during the festivities wedding songs were performed; in some places even dramas were recited during and after the banquet. The wedding ceremonies often lasted a week, and because the klezmorim could not play on the Sabbath, Gentiles were hired instead. The entertainment by the badḥanim, however, went on undisturbed and the slogan remained on the Sabbath: the merrier the better. The grotesque clowning was the domain of a special type of badḥanim, the "Pickelherring," as he was called in Germanic countries. He was, as a rule, dressed in a ridiculous motley garment, his jokes were coarse though not indecent, so as not to offend public morals: he was the embodiment of popular jocularity (Illustration No. 31).

Similarly to female klezmorim there were also female badḥanim,[47] just as in Spain, where the juglares employed juglaresas in their groups.

The number of players customary to make up a group of klezmorim consisted of two violins and a violoncello, to which occasionally a clarinet was added. In KIRCHNER's book an illustration depicting a Jewish wedding shows this number of musicians.[48] A similar illustration of two violins and a violoncello in the bridal cortège is found in an engraving of about 1700, entitled "Exact reproduction of a Jewish wedding" and preserved in the Cabinet of Prints at the Berlin Library. SCHUDT reports that Jewish musicians frequently performed outside the ghetto. It is noteworthy that on such an important event as the visit of the Court of Hessen, Jewish musicians were invited to play the introductions to the singing of a famous *hazzan.*

SCHUDT reports with some indignation that Jewish musicians entertained the customers of certain fashionable resorts. Many people were annoyed by the fact that in the spa of Ems a certain Jew was fond of employing, for his private entertainment, trumpet and horn players. Furthermore, in the resort of Schwalbach four or five Jewish musicians were in the habit of playing near the fountain where the guests consumed the waters; after their concert passed around a plate for donations.[49]

As to their social status, the *klezmorim* and *badhanim* belonged to the lowest class of Jewish society, although they were always in great demand as entertainers. Itinerant musicians and jesters existed at all epochs and in all countries; all of them shared a common fate: since their profession was considered far below the ordinary civic occupations of a sedentary life, which normally constituted the prime source of the livelihood of a settled burgher. The itinerant life, combined with the uncertainty of their existence, stamped the Jewish *klezmorim* and *badhanim* as social pariahs.

What a vast difference when compared to conditions in Biblical times! In the social scheme of Ancient Israel the itinerant musician was held in high esteem; he was a folkbard, the preserver and dispenser of ancient heroic songs and tales, disseminating good and bad tidings, respected and loved by the people, feared by the rulers. The entire population considered it their duty to provide for their minstrels. In the people's consciousness they stood only one rung lower than Israel's prophets, but their authority and political power might have been just as prominent and exalted.

The Ghetto of Frankfurt

Compared with the elaborate musical culture of Prague, the other famous German ghetto in Frankfurt-am-Main is considered of lesser rank. Undoubtedly there were many Jewish musicians in this large community, but their professional skill appears to have been far below that of the Prague instrumentalists. This is pointedly illustrated by a historical fact: in 1716 SCHUDT published a little pamphlet[50] in which he described the solemn processions held at Frankfurt and Prague on the occasion of the birth of the crown prince to the Austrian throne. In both processions Jewish musicians participated, but whereas in Prague the majority of musicians (see p. 353) was provided by local instrumentalists, Frankfurt was compelled to engage Jewish musicians from the neighboring town of Offenbach.

While the records about the activity of Jewish musicians in Prague are abundant, little is known, in comparison, about the musicians in Frankfurt. In this respect it will be revealing to take a look at the hierarchy of the Frankfurt ghetto. In 1694, with 414 Jewish households (probably no more than 2,500 souls), Frankfurt maintained eight rabbis, two slaughterers, five readers (*hazzanim*), one *Schulklopfer* (who summoned the congregants to the services by knocking on their doors), ten teachers, two physicians, one nurse, one notary, two lawyers, two scribes, four watchmen, but only two musicians.[51] At the same time, there were quite a number of *Stadtpfeifer* (Christian town musicians), employed by the city.

If the ghetto of Frankfurt could not keep abreast in musical matters with Prague, it had other artistic accomplishments to its credit. In dramatic art, in theatrical productions, it surpassed not only Prague, but all other ghettos in Germanic lands. This was natural, since Frankfurt had a glorious history in the field of the German theater. It was inevitable that the Jews, in spite of the confining ghetto walls, began to take advantage of this development and emulated the dramatic art of their Gentile neighbors.

About Jewish plays in Frankfurt, as well as in other places, more will be said presently.

Jewish Music and Musicians in Other Ghettos

Like the case of the ghetto of Prague, the life of musicians in other German ghettos was subjected to the same harassment, intolerance, professional jealousy of the Gentile musicians, heavy taxation, plus the other setbacks Jewish performers were forced to endure in order to pursue a profession as free-lance artists.

In spite of all these handicaps, Jewish musicians were active, even if only tolerated, in Eastern Europe, in Cracow (in 1556), in Lublin (1654), Lwow (Lemberg), Rzeszow, Leszbo (Lissa), and Kepno.

In Germany, in the seventeenth and eighteenth centuries, we know of wandering Jewish musicians, through preserved records from Berlin, Halberstadt, Dresden, Frankfurt a.M., Dessau, Breslau, Fürth, and others.

A few of the numerous examples of the vexations Jewish musicians had to live with will throw additional light upon the fate of their brethren inside and outside the ghetto walls.

A police law of Cracow from 1595 decreed that it was forbidden for Jews to go through the streets at night playing instruments.[52] Here "night" evidently meant "after sunset," since it was not probable that Jewish musicians, of all places in an anti-Semitic Polish city, would parade about at night playing music, unless they were accompanying some important Gentile person returning home from a banquet.

A contemporary record dating back to 1742 reveals that the synagogue of Carpentras in France was considered by authorities too ornate and too pompous. Criticism was raised that it was taller than the Cathedral of St. Siffrein. The authorities invoked an ancient ordinance prohibiting the Jews from enlarging or embellishing their synagogues. The excuse was invented that Christianity was offended and humiliated by the ostentatiousness of the synagogue. In addition, it was claimed that the synagogue was too close to the churches of St. John and St. Marie-de-la-Charité, and that the songs of the synagogue worship disturbed the divine service, this being considered an outrage. It seems, however, that this grievance was later abandoned after the Jews promised to reduce the volume of their singing so that it would not intrude upon the Christian services.[53]

Such harassments of the Jews were common in earlier times. Clergy and civic authorities easily found reasons for objecting to the Jews' performing their religious services. Here are a few examples of many:

GREGORY the GREAT (c. 540-604) ordered the removal of a synagogue which was too close to a church, because the loud singing of the Jews interfered with the Christian services. INNO-CENT III prohibited (1100) the "noise" created by the Jews in their services. In 1288 the Jews in Paris were punished for their loud singing. Even in Eastern settlements this Jewish religious practice was sometimes prohibited. The law book of the Shiites of ABBAS II (around 1650) invoked an earlier prohibition against the loud singing of Jewish congregations.[54]

The constitution of the town of Sugenheim (in Franconia), in 1756, stipulated that the only *paid* synagogal official be the cantor who, at the same time, was required to be the spiritual leader, teacher, ritual cattle slaughterer, *Schulklopfer,* hotelkeeper and, of course, the *ḥazzan* of the community.[55] In addition, it was the cantor's duty to call the people to the synagogue regularly, so that no one might have the excuse of ignorance. Should the cantor forget this, he was to be fined ten *kreuzer* for the first time, and if he blundered frequently, fifteen or twenty *kreuzer*, and possibly even be dismissed.[56]

On April 17, 1750, FREDERICK II of Prussia (called "the Great") issued a Charter for the Jews living in his realm. In this Charter he enumerated the "tolerated" officials of the Jewish community in Berlin: (1) One rabbi or vice-rabbi; (2) four assistant judges; and (3) a chief and an assistant cantor with his basses and sopranos, who must not be married.[57]

The charter contains other discriminatory stipulations which prompted MIRABEAU to call it "A law worthy of a cannibal."

In this sea of bias and rancor, a human attitude practiced by tolerant rulers is bound to stand out like an island of bliss. In the Archives of the German town of Aurich there actually exists a veritable letter of safe-conduct for Jewish musicians. In a special edict, Count Edzard II conferred to the Jews Salomon and Lewen (Levi) the right "to make henceforth an honest living in our County Ostfriesland by playing (*spylendo*), and all officials are advised to let them pass and proceed to all places where they are wanted and not hinder them, on pain of heavy punishment and our displeasure."[58]

The beautiful voice of a Jewish girl once captivated princely audiences in Germany. This took place at the end of the seventeenth century. German princes and princesses were thrilled by the superb voice of Brentzen Marcus, the daughter of Isaac Marcus. The Prince of Anhalt heard and admired "her extraordinary voice" and evidently recommended her to the Great Elector (Frederick William of Brandenburg, 1640-1688), who in turn invited her to Berlin. Regarding her visit, the Elector reported to the Prince of Anhalt in July 1680: "she waits upon our beloved spouse with singing and, according to her judgment, she practices and perfects herself in music and learns how to adapt and utilize her rare voice, following the rules of the art and its method."[59]

This is the first mention in the annals that there existed a Court Singer (*Kammersängerin*) belonging to the Jewish faith, for such honorary titles were never before bestowed upon persons of Jewish extraction. This precedent was, however, soon followed by a long list of other Jewish Court Singers, both male and female.

With all the hardships and disgrace which the ghetto brought upon the Jews, one positive aspect of their enforced segregation cannot be overlooked, and this can best be expressed in a negative form: without the ghetto the Jews as an ethnic group would have disappeared long ago, either assimilated or dissolved into their environment, as was the fate of many other minorities.

The ghetto walls forced the isolated Jews to preserve not only their religion, but also their racial identity, their institutions and their culture. Notwithstanding the sufferings the ghetto brought about for them, the Jews should be thankful to providence for having enclosed them into these humiliating boundaries. For the latter have helped them to keep intact the soul of the people and to keep alive the heritage of their fathers, to endow them with spiritual and intellectual powers, to be ready for the hour of liberation.

Looking at it from the higher vantage of general history, one will readily gather the fateful significance of the ghetto for the Jewish people.

In spite of all discriminatory measures, the Jews in the ghetto always tried to be good citizens of the countries in which they lived and never failed to give testimony of their loyalty to the ruling houses. At joyous occasions, such as the birth of an heir to the throne, a wedding in the princely family, a military victory, etc., they always celebrated the event with a "patriotic" poem set to music. The earliest preserved example of such patriotic poetry is the *Zemer über Kaiser Leopold und die Kaiserin mit ihren lieben Prinzen zu Ehren (natal. Joseph I, anno 1676)* (Song honoring Emperor Leopold and the Empress with their dear prince . . .). The poem was composed by ASHER SELIG ben ḤISKIYYA ḤAZZAN, sung to the melody *"Halb schwarz, halb weiss"* (C.B., 3673). Another such joyous occasion was the birth of LEOPOLD, the crown prince of Austria (May 18, 1716). The author of the poem, in which Hebrew and German stanzas alternated, was the same ASHER SELIG of Prague; the melody accompanying the lyrics is unknown.[60]

The victory of FREDERICK II in the Second Silesian war with Austria, which ceded Silesia and the county of Glatz to Prussia, was celebrated on December 18, 1745, in the Berlin Synagogue. The rabbi, DAVID FRENKEL, wrote the poem, which was performed with music. The words were translated into German by AARON ben SOLOMON GUMPERZ, then a student of philosophy and mathematics in Berlin.[61]

The German *"Freuden-Lied"* on the wedding of the Emperor JOSEPH I of Austria, which was indicated to be sung to the air of the *"Baba-Buch,"* belongs to this category (see p. 201). Further examples of patriotic songs are two elegies on the death of King FERDINAND (Prague, 1654), and a song for the coronation of LEOPOLD I (1658); the melody of the latter is said to have been a "Jewish song."[62]

In the Netherlands, MANASSEH ben ISRAEL welcomed Prince

FREDERICK HENRY in Amsterdam (1642) with a Portuguese and Latin address when the Prince visited his synagogue (see p. 380).

In general, the Jews never missed the opportunity to prove their loyalty and show their gratitude to their princely benefactors with poetry and music.

Simḥat Torah and Purim

Apart from wedding festivities, the urge of the Jews for popular rejoicing vented itself on two specific occasions: the festival of *Simḥat Torah* and the semireligious feast of *Purim*.

Simḥat Torah, the "Rejoicing over the Torah" (given on Mount Sinai), was celebrated in all centuries, with singing and dancing and merriment. However, this feast never degenerated into excesses of public frolicking, such as characterized the *Purim* celebrations. *Simḥat Torah* was still a religious feast, and its general tone was kept within the limits of a religious ceremony. This was different at the *Purim* rejoicing, where the rules of the Biblical precepts were more liberal and at times completely abandoned.

The origin of *Purim* can be traced back to the ancient Persian *Farvardīgān* festival, which the Jews adopted in Babylonia. The Hebrew name of the festival is explained by the Akkadian word *purruru*, "to destroy," or by the Babylonian *puru*, "lot," the plural of which is *purim*. The generally accepted explanation for the incorporation of this pagan feast into the calendar of Jewish festivals was the *Purim* tale which, despite its foreign origin and its thoroughly legendary character, had an irresistible fascination for the Jews and has actually assumed the character of a historical narrative in the minds of the people.

The sources of the Esther story may be found in Babylonian mythology, as the names of its principal characters indubitably prove. Mordechai is *Marduk*, Esther is *Ishtar*, both being the names of the supreme god and goddess in the Babyonian pantheon. Haman is identified with *Hamman* (or *Humman*), the supreme god of the Elamites, whose capital city Susa (or Shushan) (today's Shush) is the scene of the Esther story. Even Vashti is supposed to be the name of an Elamite deity, slightly altered in spelling, as *Mashti*.[63]

According to LEWY, MORDECHAI is not even a proper name, but a term denoting worshippers of Marduk, as evidenced by the Greek term in 2 Macc. 15:36: *hē Mardochaikē hēmera*, "the day of the worshippers of Marduk."[64]

The *Purim* festival was probably brought back to the homeland by the repatriates from the Babylonian captivity and continued to be celebrated by the Jews after the return. It never failed to exercise a great attraction upon the mind of a people living under conditions of austerity and in dire need of psychological stimulants such as were able to kindle the imagination and the patriotic sentiments of the nation. The story undoubtedly circulated among the Israelites long before the book was written and, together with the celebration of the feast in Israel, became deeply rooted in the national consciousness of the Jews. The written form probably constituted the final step toward the general acceptance by the Jews of the Esther legend as a historical fact. The story of the canonization of this wholly secular book corroborates our assumption.

The outstanding feature of the *Purim* festival was frolicking, bordering on boisterousness, jokers parading in disguises, human as well as animal, with masquerades, joyous processions and, of course, with a good deal of dancing. On these days everybody danced, rich and poor, men and women, young and old. The casual saying "On *Purim* everything is allowed" became, through the years, a general rule in Jewish customs, even to a point of transgressing the Mosaic laws. Thus, at the popular *Purim* masquerading men would dress up as women and vice versa, a thing strictly forbidden by religious laws.[65]

On *Purim* boys and girls walked from house to house singing comic doggerel and were rewarded with sweets and with cakes that had appropriate names, such as "Haman ears," "*Hamantaschen*," and the like.

The masquerading on *Purim* goes back to the late fifteenth century in Italy, where the Jews, in imitation of the Roman carnival, adopted this custom which eventually spread all over the Jewry of Europe. Thus, in Jewish consciousness, the *Purim* festival became the equivalent for the Christian carnival.

The first mention of it was made by R. YUDAH MINZ (d. 1508 in

Venice). He found an ingenious justification for the masquerading: since its purpose was only merrymaking, it was not considered a transgression of the law.

Purim songs were also introduced into the synagogue. Certain verses from the Scroll of Esther have been sung in chorus on *Purim.*[66]

A pagan practice, the "leap through fire," a thing common to many primitive religions, survived in one of the ceremonies of *Purim.*[67] In Babylonia there existed a custom called in Aramaic *meshavarta depuriya,* the "jumping place of *Purim.*" According to Gaonic explanation, this involved the following procedure: Four or five days before *Purim* young men would make an effigy of Haman and hang it on the roof. On *Purim* itself, they would kindle a bonfire, then cast the effigy into it while standing around, joking and singing. Thereafter, they would jump over the fire through a hoop placed upon the burning stakes.[68] This hoop was called the "place of jumping," *dereh ha-abarah.* The custom itself was a remnant of an ancient fire-dance practiced in many primitive religions. Its magic meaning was the destruction of the demon by fire. The existence of this custom may have been widespread, because in 408 C.E. the Emperor THEODOSIUS II issued a decree forbidding Jews of the Byzantine empire to practice it. In defiance of this prohibition the fire-dance still survived many centuries. It was either so strongly rooted among the superstitious practices of early medieval Jewry that it could not be extirpated, or it simply was so much fun that Jewish youth would not do without it. R. NATHAN ben YEHIEL of Rome mentioned that the custom continued among the Italian Jews in the same manner as among the Byzantine Jews.[69]

A special feature of *Purim* were the theatrical performances which, though contrary to the Mosaic law, originated very early in Jewish history, spread everywhere in the East and the West, and maintained themselves through the entire life of the Diaspora up to our present time.

18

Jewish Plays

THE ORIGIN OF JEWISH PLAYS AS THEATRICAL PERFORMANCES ON a real stage goes back to the Gaonic period and, according to some theories, possibly even to Biblical times. "Drama, of a sort, can be traced to the Bible, for the ancient Hebrews were wont to express their emotion in dialogue and song."[1] This theory, though, cannot be maintained for Biblical Jewry;—their dialogue (antiphonal and responsive singing) and their songs have motivations other than dramatic "performances," which are the essence of plays.

For the existence of early Jewish drama the fact is invoked that the first drama with a scriptural subject was the play *Exodus*, written in Alexandria in Greek by a Jew named EZEKIEL, who lived in the second century B.C.E.[2] Whether it was actually performed is unknown; however, it is wrong to identify this attempt by an undoubtedly Hellenistic Jew with the birth of the "Jewish drama." The Jews in Alexandria at that epoch were in the throes of emancipation and assimilation. This isolated attempt at imitating Greek drama cannot and must not be taken as proof for the creation of Hebrew dramatic productions.[3]

From the very beginning the rabbis were hostile toward the theater and more particularly toward those Jews who performed on a stage. "Making images" was condemned in the Bible (Exod. 20:4, cp. Lev. 26:1), and impersonating or imitating other persons was tantamount to making images. When HEROD built a theater in Jerusalem after Greek models, this "innovation" was met with furious indignation. It is significant that neither JOSEPHUS nor PHILO, the two chroniclers who lived in the last decades of Israel's national existence, make any mention of Jewish theatrical performances, for none appears to have taken place at that period.

The first rabbinical condemnation of the theater was uttered by R. Meïr Baal ha-Nes, *Tanna* of the second century; but the feeling of hostility itself dates back to even earlier times. We read in the Talmud: "Cursed be they who visit the theater and the circus, and despise our laws."[4]

Nevertheless, quite a number of attempts were made during the eighteenth and nineteenth centuries to interpret the Song of Songs as a real Jewish drama which—according to these theories—was staged with persons acting, singing and dancing.

The idea of the dramatic character of the Song of Songs goes back to Origen (c. 185-c. 254 C.E.), whose followers gave this Biblical book an intermediate position between the dramatic and lyric creations. They called it "a nuptial poem composed in dramatic form" and regarded it as "a dramatic epithalamium celebrating Solomon's marriage with Pharaoh's daughter."[5] However, the simplest historical consideration invalidates this assumption. According to modern Biblical exegesis, the time of origin of the *Canticles* is about 250 B.C.E., which in itself disproves Solomon's authorship as well as the use of the poem at Solomon's wedding.

The first attempt in modern times at "dramatization" of the Song of Songs was made by an Englishman, John Bland (d. 1788), who wrote a play about it in seven scenes which was published in 1750. Since then there followed a long series of dramatizations which have continued to the present.

The chief advocates of this theory in the nineteenth century were Heinrich August Ewald and the famous historian Ernest Renan, both of whom published elaborate dramatizations of the *Canticles*.[6]

There exist records of *Purim* buffooneries, reported to have been perpetrated in the East, during the Gaonic age,[7] (ninth to tenth centuries). Conceivably this custom prevailed even in earlier times, owing to the general rejoicing on *Purim*. The narration of the story of Esther assumed semidramatic forms on occasions without, however, being actually a stage play in the true sense of the word.

The existence of the earliest Jewish plays was recorded in the eleventh to twelfth centuries. That they were not plays as yet in the proper sense of the word appears certain. They were more or less dramatic narrations of Biblical subjects, akin to the Mystery and Morality plays of the Christian Church. Such dramatic narrations have cropped up among the Jews in almost every century; influenced by Christian models, they assumed, in an increasing measure, the characteristic features of real plays.

During the fourteenth century the Jews in France and Germany used the Haman plot and the delivery of the Jews as occasions for rejoicing in masquerades. But these improvisations, too, cannot be considered plays, since the dialogue, if any, was extemporized and its fun was enhanced by the participants who dressed up in the attire of the opposite sex and wore all kinds of masks. Rabbinical literature contains indications concerning the masks carried by merrymakers during such popular entertainment. These masks were called 'ankitmin, which was the corrupted Greek term *onos kat'omon*, "donkey on the shoulder," contracted in Aramaic into two words, *onos katmon* and, subsequently, into one: 'ankatmon or 'ankitmin. Its meaning was, according to the Talmud, "ḥamra deyoda" (donkey carried in the hand)[8] or ḥamra dakofa" (donkey on the shoulder).[9]

The earliest information about genuine Hebrew drama belongs to the seventeenth century, about *Purim* plays to the eighteenth century. From earlier times, there are some records of primitive *Purim* plays, performed mostly in the synagogue, with singing, dancing, merrymaking and instrumental music. As pointed out, however, these plays are mostly weak imitations of Christian Morality plays.

The first distinctly Jewish play with a plot was written in Spanish, by a Jew in the sixteenth century, based on the story of Esther. Its author was SOLOMON USQUE (d. after 1567), who called himself SALUSQUE LUSITANO (that is, SALOMON USQUE, the Portuguese), called in Portugal also DUARTE GOMEZ. He wrote the play in collaboration with LAZARO GRAZIANI.[10]

The discussion of Hebrew drama is beyond the scope of our study, since no music has ever been connected with drama in the history of the Jews. Nevertheless, such discussion is rather warranted in a cursory survey of Hebrew drama, for it opens the avenue for the appreciation of the later Judaeo-German plays in which music, song and dance were an essential part of the dramatic action.

The Jargon (Yiddish) play was a product of the ghetto; the plays in Hebrew were mirror images of the dramatic production of the nations among whom the Israelites co-existed. The culture of these nations, even before the crumbling of the ghetto walls, penetrated the ghetto and exerted an irresistible influence upon Jewish playwrights. It inspired them to creations which are more in conformity with the Jewish national spirit than the stereotyped Jargon comedies, the only purpose of which was popular entertainment.

The development of Hebrew drama took different turns outside of the Germanic countries. There were such plays in Italy and in the Netherlands, where MOSES ZACUTO and MOSES ḤAYYIM LUZZATTO, both in their early youth, wrote dramas in Hebrew.

Amsterdam was, at the beginning of the seventeenth century, the center not only of the Dutch national and literary movement, but also the core of Jewish intellectual life, brought along and further fostered by the Spanish and Portuguese refugees (see later).

MOSES ZACUTO (1625-1697) is credited with having written the first drama in Hebrew. Its title was YESSOD 'OLAM (The Eternal Foundation). The play aroused, and still holds, considerable attention as a unique Hebrew literary product.[11]

ZACUTO's pioneering achievement remained without a following for a quarter of a century. The next original Hebrew drama, a Morality play with the title ᾿ASIR TIKVAH (Prisoner of Hope), was written by JOSEPH ben ISAAC PENSO, also known as PENSO de la VEGA, who was born in Spain, the son of a crypto-Jew. He was seventeen years old when he wrote the play, but despite his youth the work shows maturity and real dramatic qualities.

More than half a century elapsed before another Hebrew drama came to the fore. The author of it was the Italian Jew MOSES ḤAYYIM LUZZATTO (1707-1747). When he wrote his first play Samson and Delilah, he was, like PENSO, seventeen years old. There is no record that it was ever performed on the stage, a fate it shared with many other Hebrew dramas. His second work was

The Tower of Strength, followed in 1743 by a Morality play, *Glory to the Righteous,* which was partly based on GUARINI's pastoral comedy *Il Pastor Fido.* Hebrew drama suffered a severe loss by LUZZATTO's untimely death at forty, the victim of the plague.

Up to this point we have followed the development of Hebrew drama, merely to show how Jewish creativity asserted itself in this new medium, even long before the Emancipation liberated the Jewish mind. A further historical survey of Hebrew drama without music cannot be given here; let us rather focus attention on the satirical side of Jewish inspiration, to the *Purim* plays, in which music, in all its manifestations, playing, singing, and dancing, played an important part.

Purim Comedies

At a very early date, the beginning of the fourteenth century, KALONYMOS ben KALONYMOS, who lived in the Provence and Italy, described *Purim* pantomimes, as they were practiced in the Jewish quarters of Italian towns. At those times, pantomimes lacked organized dramatic texture and therefore cannot be considered Purim plays which, in the proper sense of the word, came into being centuries later. They consisted mainly of children's boisterous roamings, adults' marching in the streets with fir branches in their hands, shouting and making all kinds of noises with children's gadgets, and dancing around an effigy of Haman attached to a post which later was burned.

Such pantomimes spread throughout all Jewry and persisted for centuries through their appeal to the primitive instincts of the masses. For the people *Purim* was not merely a day of rejoicing and merrymaking, but a day of historical significance, because it commemorated the liberation from oppression, and stressed the people's longing for freedom and justice.

Later, when *Purimspiele* appeared on the stage, they not only dramatized the Esther story, but developed a specific Jewish trait, satirizing Jewish institutions, both secular and sacred, and caricaturing persons of standing. This was done in a vein of self-mockery and became an outstanding feature for centuries to come, of Jewish, and particularly Yiddish, literature. This may be the origin of the distinct Jewish "humor," so characteristic of the concern of the Jew for himself and the world around him, as well as his view of the frailties and vanities of everyday life.

Jewish comic-parodistic plays were of two types: their subjects were either caricatures of rabbinical arguments, mixed with parodies of the prayers, or else they were simple buffooneries, in which such features were included as, for instance, *Orders of Service for the Night of Drunkenness*, and other parodies.

The long line of such comic plays, of which historical records exist, starts with a satirical poem in Judaeo-German from 1598, called *Spiel von Tab Jäklein mit sein Weib*, which was performed in the small German town of Tannhausen, on the occasion of *Purim* during the sixteenth century. It was not printed, and there is no way to verify whether music was used with it. This can be assumed, however, for a *Purim* play without singing and dancing would not have fulfilled its purpose. The same is true of the very popular *Ahaschwerosch-Spiel*, published anonymously in Frankfurt a.M. (1708, and mentioned by SCHUDT).[12] In order to attract large audiences, it was characterized in the title as *"auf eine neue art gleich einer opera"* (in a new manner like an opera).

Another play, *Mekirat Yosef* (The Sale of Joseph), written by a certain BERMAN in Limburg, was published in Frankfurt a.M. (1711), but publicly performed years before that date. The first performance, of which there is recorded mention, took place in Frankfurt a.M. in 1713 in the house *Zur weissen oder silbernen Kanne*, the landlord of which was R. DAVID ULFF of Mannheim. The actors were Jewish students (*bahurim*) of Prague and Hamburg, a curious fact, since the large community of Frankfurt might have had local students in sufficient number to act in the play. In this comedy, according to reliable witnesses, such scenic effects as "fire, heaven, thunder," together with other theatrical tricks, were employed. The comic-grotesque element in this production was the *Pickelherring*, who introduced many "gags" on topics of local interest.[13] The same comedy was presented at Metz in Lorraine, with most of the actors having participated in it previously at Frankfurt. This gave rise to the fallacy of the existence of Jewish "traveling theatrical companies" at this early date in history. Such a rare repetition of a play in two different localities is no proof for this conjecture. (Jewish traveling companies are the product of the theatrical practice of nineteenth century Eastern Jewry.)

The play *Mekirat Yosef* attracted huge crowds, but when it began to draw large Christian audiences, it was prohibited by the city authorities. In this case, too, we have no positive knowledge whether music was used in the play. The fact, however, that Gentiles *en masse* came to see it may give credence to this assumption.

An anonymous publication appeared in Prague in 1708, with the title *Acta Esther mit Ahaschwerosch*, was another of these *Purim* plays. (It is not identical with the *Ahaschwerosch-Spiel* mentioned above). The original title page of this comedy in Judaeo-German is highly amusing; it is quoted here in English translation:

> A beautiful new *Ahashverush-Spiel*, composed with utmost art, never again will another be made so nicely, with pretty, beautiful lamentations in rhyme. We hope that whoever will buy it will not regret his expenditure; because God has commanded us to be merry on *Purim*, therefore have we made this *Ahashverush*-play nice and beautiful. Therefore, also, you householders and boys, come quickly and buy this play from me; you will not regret the cost. If you read it, you will discover that you have got your money's worth.[14]

The title page has the comment that "it was acted at Prague in a real theatrum, with trumpets and other musical instruments." The significant fact about this production was that the actors were all pupils (*baḥurim*) of the famous R. DAVID OPPENHEIM, which shows that the religious leader of those times had given up their antagonistic attitude toward theatrical presentations. They evidently recognized the great moral value of Jewish plays, especially of those which dealt with the story of Esther, in times of the persecution; such plays were apt to kindle and rekindle the hope of the oppressed people for a miraculous deliverance.[15]

Another play about the Esther story was *Acta Esther*, by an anonymous author, performed in Prague in 1763. The same subject was used for a *Purim* comedy with the title *Aman y Mardochay* (Amsterdam, 1699), the author of which is also unknown.

The narrative of Esther was by no means the only story which served as a subject for *Purim* plays. Another was that of David and Goliath, which enjoyed a popularity equal to the above-mentioned *Ahaschwerosch-Spiel.*

The ghetto entertainment in dramatic form is not only an artistic, but also a social phenomenon, with equal importance for the historian of civilization as for the musical observer. The continuity of Jewish life is marked by the fact that *Purim* plays survived up to modern times. Even today, and in all countries where Jews live in compact groups, they constitute the ineluctable *Purim* entertainment for young and old.

Besides *Purim* plays, in which music played an essential part, there exist a number of small musical comedies from Amsterdam, which were written for celebrations of the numerous fraternities of this town. They are preserved (without the music, of course), in a compilation of poems composed by MOSES ben YEHUDAH PIZA, entitled *Shir 'emunim* (Song of Faithfulness).

There exist records about theatrical performances with music in Pesaro, in the years 1770, 1771, and 1774. Whether these were *Purim* plays or other kinds of dramatic displays, cannot be said with certainty. We can only surmise that with the approaching Enlightenment both types were popular, especially since the attitude of the rabbis toward Jewish theatrical plays became completely relaxed. It is significant that in the year 1793, for the opening ceremonies of a newly built synagogue in Florence, a play was presented at the feast of *Simḥat Miẓvah* (The Joys of the Law). It was written by R. DANIEL TERNI, the music composed by MICHAEL BOLAFFI (1768-1842).

The play's title was *Comedy of Marriage*, a rather curious subject for the inauguration of a synagogue. It seems that it was an adaptation of a sixteenth-century play by LEONE de' SOMMI PORTALEONE, who probably performed it with his troupe of Jewish actors in Mantua. LEONE has been called "the first theatrical impressario of modern times,"[16] which is odd in view of the fact that in his youth he was a pupil of R. DAVID PROVENZAL of Mantua, an orthodox rabbi, who strongly opposed theatrical performances. LEONE de' SOMMI left to posterity a considerable number of literary manuscripts, poetry as well as prose, eleven plays, among them six comedies, three pastoral fables and six intermezzi.[17] It may be assumed that the above-mentioned play was a rewrite of one of these posthumous comedies.

In this new version the burlesque elements prevail; the addition of humorous scenes, of a finale containing a scene of blind man's buff, plus a fighting and singing choir, must have added considerably to its success. In its new adaptation the comedy enjoyed several performances.[18]

Throughout the Middle Ages, and especially in Germanic countries, Jewish actors were more or less second-class citizens, socially a little above the *badhanim,* unless they were talmudic students (*bahurim*), as in a theatrical performance in Frankfurt (see pp. 45, 371). In the 18th century this situation underwent radical changes. The theatrical history of England shows a remarkable elevation of the social status of the Jewish actor. This manifested itself in two ways: first, it opened the doors of the legitimate theatre to the Jewish actors, and secondly, it took into consideration some personal necessities connected with the participation of Jewish actors in theatrical performances. In both cases British theatre furnishes significant examples.

RICHARD BRINSLEY SHERIDAN (1751-1816) engaged two Jews for his plays. The first was ISAAC MENDOZA, in *The Duenna,* the comic opera for which SHERIDAN's father-in-law LINLEY, composed the music. It was produced at Covent Garden on November 21, 1775. The principal singing part of this play was performed by LEONI, the outstanding singer in London in those days. LEONI, whose real name was MEYER LEON, first appeared on the English stage as a boy, playing the role of a sprite in the *Enchanter* on December 13, 1760, at the Drury Lane Theatre. As he grew up, he vacillated between a career of the stage and as a cantor in the synagogue.

In *The Duenna,* he was to impersonate a Jew but, out of consideration for the singer, the character of the part was altered. At that time LEONI was cantor of the Bevis Marks Synagogue. To meet his religious scruples and enable him to officiate on Friday evenings, *The Duenna* was not played that night.[19]

Antonio José da Silva

It is a cruel irony of fate that a famous author, who was born a Jew, baptized by force and, as a Christian, practiced law in his country, should have been accused of "Judaizing" and, on a flimsy testimony, became a victim of the Inquisition.

He did not write *Purim* plays or other Jewish comedies. Nevertheless, it would be a serious omission not to include him among Jewish playwrights, since his plays with music, called "operas," were highly successful.

He was ANTONIO JOSÉ da SILVA, born in Rio de Janeiro, Brazil, in 1705. His father, JOÃO MENDEZ da SILVA, who moved to Portugal, was a well-known lawyer and a renowned poet. His mother, LOURENCA CONTINHO, had been converted by force, but nevertheless raised her three sons secretly in the Jewish faith. In spite of her baptism, she was accused of "Judaizing" and condemned by the Holy Office in Valladolid. After a public *auto-da-fè* she was released, but remained under suspicion and soon was again arrested, this time on the testimony of her own son ANTONIO who, under torture, was forced to testify against his parents. After an *auto-da-fè* in 1726 he regained his liberty, but his mother was kept in prison until 1729. The tortures left ANTONIO so crippled that, for some time, he even was unable to sign his own name. It borders on the miraculous that after all these tribulations ANTONIO succeeded in completing his law studies in 1726 at the University of Coimbra, and was promptly admitted to the bar. Besides practicing as a lawyer, he took an interest in literature and began to write comedies and musical plays, which made his name famous throughout Portugal.

One of the features of his plays was the introduction, or rather re-introduction, of the *modinha*, a song type of Portuguese folk music almost extinct in the mother country, but still surviving in Brazil. During his youth, ANTONIO heard them sung daily,[20] and he was strongly influenced by these Portuguese melodies.

The King of Portugal at that time, Don JOÃO V (1689-1750), was a mixture of benevolence and despotism. He had, however, one thing to his credit: he was a fervent sponsor of the theater. He spent large sums to support an opera company in Lisbon, which employed Italian singers.

The literary repertoire of the Portuguese theater consisted of *autos* (religious plays), *farzas* (comedies), and *intermez* (a medley of whimsicality, facetiousness, even tomfoolery, interspersed with songs and dances.) The most celebrated dramatic author of the times was GIL VICENTE. It was certainly a daring venture to compete with this admired playwright. Yet ANTONIO did compete with him and with marked success.

His first comedies did not immediately divulge his satiric vein in which he was to excel later; they were not even very successful. Then in 1733 his play *The Life of the Grand Quixote de la Mancha and of the coarse Sancho Pansa* created a veritable sensation. In rapid succession he wrote a number of brilliant comedies: *The Life of Aesop* (1734), in which he poured irony and sarcasm upon the class of conceited and arrogant scholars. It was followed by another big success, *The Enchantment of Medea* (1735).

Soon, however, a feeling of hostility arose against him which, curiously, originated among the Italian singers who sang in his plays. Under the pretense that the *modinhas,* which were enlarged to the proportions of real arias, "harmed" their voices, they maintained that this inflicted heavy damage to the performances. A more ridiculous accusation could not have been invented by trained opera singers!

These accusations might have remained inconsequential to his fate, had ANTONIO not committed serious mistakes. He wrote a play, *Jupiter and Alamena* (1736), in which he satirized the King's morals. The King took the criticism with good humor, but ANTONIO alienated the sympathies of the court sycophants. Shortly thereafter ANTONIO dared to hold a mirror to his contemporaries. In his next play, *The Wars of Romarin and Marjolaine,* he castigated with all the satiric force at his disposal the morals of Portuguese society. For the average theatergoers this became his most popular comedy, but it turned the "society" against him.

Since his first release, ANTONIO was permanently under suspicion and it did not take much to denounce him as a Judaizer. In 1737 he was again thrown into the prison of the Inquisition, this time with his young wife, who was pregnant. Neither the intervention of his friends, nor even that of the King, could save him. His wife was freed under the condition of a public *auto-da-fè,* together with ANTONIO's mother, who abjured for a third time. For ANTONIO there could be no clemency; at this stage he had amassed too many enemies who now took their revenge and rejoiced in the downfall of their caustic lampooner.

The principal witness in his trial was a Negro slave girl, who testified that he was in the habit of changing his linen on the Sabbath, and that he even abstained from work on this day. He was under constant surveillance in prison, and his jailers "observed" that he practiced some "unfamiliar" rites. He was again submitted to torture, but this time the expected "confession" did not materialize. Accordingly, he was condemned as a stubborn, convicted, and relapsed Judaizer.[21]

On October 1, 1739, he was released to the "secular arm" (the Church did not "kill"); his mother, his wife and his young child were forced to be present at his execution. Since he was not condemned as a Jew, but only as a Judaizer, he was "favored" with a "mild" execution. The mildness consisted of his being first garroted, then burned at the stake (Oct. 19, 1739). Had he been a *real* Jew, he would have been burned alive.[22]

By a tragic coincidence, on the night of his execution one of his plays was presented in the largest theater of the town. Was it really a coincidence? Some think that it was intentional, which would be quite in line with the great popularity of ANTONIO as a satiric playwright.

In prison he had written his last comedy, *The Downfall of Phaeton*. He did not live to see it produced—it was played shortly after his execution.

After his death the people crowded the theater where the "operas of the Jew" were performed. A further irony of fate was that his plays were published again and again, but always without the name of the author. Nevertheless, the plays of *O Judeu*, "the Jew," lived henceforth on the Portuguese stage and ANTONIO went down in the literary history of his country as "the Portuguese Plautus."

As so often before, the Holy Inquisition snuffed out a great talent whose sole crime might have been his adherence, though in secret, to the faith of his ancestors.

19

Jews in the Netherlands

AFTER THEIR EXPULSION FROM SPAIN AND PORTUGAL, THE JEWS
settled in increasing numbers in the Netherlands, where they
found friendly asylum. Marrano Jews appeared in Amsterdam
shortly after the expulsion, although prior to the end of the seventeenth century there is no actual proof of the exitence of a Jewish
congregation in that city. They brought with them their learning,
their skills, their international enterprises and, most of all, their
unbroken devotion to their Jewish faith despite forced conversions and their long life as crypto-Jews. As they established new
trade centers in Holland there can be no doubt that the decline
of Spanish commerce in the following centuries was due in large
measure to the activities of the refugees in their countries of
asylum, Italy, England, but mainly in Holland. "In this indirect
way the Marranos became a nemesis to the Spanish kingdom.[1]

More direct and especially grievous was the intellectual loss
for Spain. A great number of writers, poets, philosophers of Spanish origin who would have fertilized the native intellectual life,
were lost to Spain. Men like SPINOZA, da SILVA, MANASSEH ben
ISRAEL, the DISRAELIS, the MONTEFIORES, and others, became
bright lights of their newly adopted countries. Especially in the
Netherlands their literary and scholarly activities had contributed
largely to the elevation of such a little country to an intellectual
center of Europe.

"The Dutch Jerusalem," as Amsterdam was called,[2] was indeed
a God-sent refuge for the expelled Iberian Jews. They felt themselves at home in the tolerant atmosphere and soon they prospered
under the protection of benevolent rulers. With the influx of the
Jewish immigration the whole country flourished as never before.

In daily life they spoke Spanish and Portuguese, in worship their language was Hebrew.

However, owing to their "underground" Judaism, the Marranos had been deprived of Jewish education for centuries. When they arrived in the Netherlands, they could not even read Hebrew. In order to be able to follow the Jewish rites, their only solution was to transcribe the Hebrew prayers into Latin characters, at least at the beginning.

In Amsterdam, the Portuguese Jews joined together under the leadership of DON MANUEL del BELMONTO to establish an Academy of Poets which, under the name of "Sitibundos e Floridos" (roughly translated "The Pensive and Ornate") exerted for many years a great influence upon Jewish literature.[3] In this Academy the famous poet ANTONIO (JACOB) CASTILLO read his works to an appreciative audience. Besides being a renowned poet, he was an acknowledged virtuoso on the *vihuela de arco,* the precursor of today's violin. Another expert on this instrument was the poet ISAAC MENDES (mid-seventeenth century).

One of the most illustrious poets of the Sephardic colony was DANIEL LEVI (MIGUEL) de BARRIOS (c. 1625-1701), author of numerous religious plays, or *"mosaic sacred autos"* (auto=act of faith), as he called them. The titles of some are: *Torah ʾOr* (Torah's Light); *ʾAuto Mosayco* (Mosaic Act [of Faith]); *Meirat ʿEnayim* (The Light of the Eyes); *Maskil el Dal* (Wisdom for the Miserable Ones). What makes these religious plays important for us is the fact that they were performed, on religious festivals, with musical accompaniment, evidently with elaborate scenic music.[4]

In his *Coro de las Musas* (publ. Brussels 1672), BARRIOS renders homage to CASTILLO's musical talent in saying: *"Don ANTONIO de CASTILLO perito* [expert] *en las artes liberales y sublima en el toccar la bihuela."*

CASTILLO returns the compliment; in the Prologue to the same play of BARRIOS, CASTILLO inserted a poem (verse 224):

> En la lyra que tocas rare estreno.
> La hazes luzis junto al Ursario Polo.
> Major que la del musica del Hemo.
> Das á las artes en todo solo.

> (Your playing of the lyre is superb
> You make it shine like the Great Bear.
> Even better than the musician of Hemo.
> You add distinction to the arts with
> every piece you play.)[5]

Soon after they settled in Amsterdam (1593), the Marranos built a synagogue, inaugurated on the Day of Atonement, 1608. It was the starting point of a musical culture which eclipsed that of older and more numerous communities in Central Europe in the seventeenth and eighteenth centuries, with the exception of Prague. It may be considered the legitimate succssor to the vibrant musical practice of the ghetto of Venice, without the taint of the restricted ghetto life, since the Jews of Amsterdam were, from the very beginning, free citizens, accepted socially and economically on an equal footing to the rest of the population.

As the community grew, two other synagogues were built. In 1638 the three Sephardic congregations united; in 1671 the Portuguese-Jewish community numbered four thousand families, and to satisfy the religious needs of such a large congregation, a beautiful new synagogue was built in 1675, which still remains one of the worthwhile sights of today's Amsterdam.

In The Hague, the Portuguese Jews, in 1728, built a synagogue which, in the spirit of charity, they named *Honen Dal* (Favoring the Poor). Its inauguration took place, like that of the older Amsterdam synagogue, on the *Sabbat nahamu* (August 9*).[6] For this occasion ABRAHAM CACERES set to music a poem of the *hazzan* DANIEL COHEN RODRIGUEZ, starting with *"Ohillah leka ʾel na heyeh ʿezer"* (I implore you, God, please be of help!).

With the building of synagogues, the education of the young generation went hand in hand. When still a young rabbi in Amsterdam, MANASSEH ben ISRAEL, together with other dedicated members of the community, established a school, in which the children received instruction in Hebrew and in the singing of sacred songs. Soon after its creation, MANASSEH's school counted among its pupils the young BARUCH SPINOZA. Besides this school, AARON ANTUNES in 1718 opened an *esguer* (*hesger* = fraternity) for the study of the Talmud and other rabbinical writings, which

---

* See note on p. 387.

he called *Leḳaḥ tov* ("Good teaching"). ANTUNES was probably identical with the Jewish printer, whose publications contributed to the establishment of Amsterdam as an important center of Jewish learning. Although this fraternity lasted only two years, the anniversaries of its foundation were also later on celebrated with rich musical display. The lyrics of the songs performed on these occasions were by ANTUNES, the music by CACERES. This is the earliest mention of this composer, who played an important role in the music culture of Amsterdam in the first half of the eighteenth century.

Another of the Jewish fraternities dedicated to learning in the Amsterdam community was the *Miḳra Ḳodesh* (Holy Reading), a society created by and for the Portuguese aristocracy. Its members met at the home of JOSEPH SUASSO de LIMA. No direct records have been preserved as to whether music played a part in these conventions. Some poems, however, composed by its members, have direct allusions to music, for instance, the praise of music in one of them, as well as a marginal note referring to the musical rendering in another one. Other poems contain the names of certain tunes to be used for the lyrics, and the introduction of one of the poems gives precise indications for a musical rendering: "ʿArukah be-ḳol zimrah u-neginah" (arranged for voices and instruments).

Just as they cultivated their literary activities, as mentioned above, the Amsterdam Jews cherished their music, sacred as well as secular. When, in August, 1651, the English ambassador to the Netherlands visited MANASSEH, he was welcomed with Hebrew prayers and sacred songs, sung by the pupils of his school.

Around 1665, the false Messiah, SABBATAI ZEVI, was enthusiastically received by the Amsterdam community. The "coming of the Kingdom" was celebrated in the synagogues with music and dancing. In order to expedite the entrance into the Promised Land, special prayerbooks were printed, to teach the adherents of SABBATAI the chants preparatory to the advent of the Messianic Age, which was believed imminent.

Similar mass hysteria occurred in other countries as well. In Hamburg, for instance, worshippers of all ages hopped and jumped in the synagogues and danced with the Torah scrolls in their hands.[7] Even in puritanic England, among the Christian population, the belief of SABBATAI's messianic mission spread rapidly; "many Puritan regiments inscribed their banners with the Lion of Judah."[8]

In their country of origin, the Marranos and the other Spanish and Portuguese refugees enjoyed high social standing. In their new surroundings they kept also their ancient manners and habits and became, so to speak, a Jewish aristocracy, supported not only by their intellectual standard, but also by their soon developing wealth and their ever expanding commercial activity, which soon made their new homeland the foremost commercial power on the continent.

The prosperity of the Sephardic colony soon attracted Ashkenazic Jews from the East European provinces, where they lived under intermittent persecutions. The migration toward the West started gradually around 1638, but gained momentum after the Chmelnicki pogroms (1648). The influx of Eastern Jewry changed the heretofore aristocratic structure of the Jewish community in Amsterdam. The newcomers being of a lower social level, followed humbler occupations and felt themselves in this respect inferior to their Sephardic brethren. On the other hand, they brought with them a thorough knowledge of the Hebrew language and a profound Talmudic scholarship, which the Sephardic community was deprived of. Thus, what the Ashkenazic Jews lacked in social standing, they made up by their other Jewish qualities and learning. They were the first to establish printing shops, by which Amsterdam gained a reputation as a center of extensive Jewish learning.

The Ashkenazim brought with them their own liturgical service, including their own traditional synagogue songs. Thus, socially as well as ritually, the Amsterdam Jewry soon was divided between Sephardic and Ashkenazic ways of living and worship.

The Sephardic community of Amsterdam was not only distinguished by its intellectual life, but it was also notorious for its religious intolerance. Well known are the cases of free thinkers, such as URIEL d'ACOSTA (excommunicated twice, in 1618 and

1640, the second ending with his suicide), and BARUCH SPINOZA
(1656), both dismal examples of parochial prejudice and fanatic
narrow-mindedness.

In this respect, the Ashkenazic community was no better. They
hired a *hazzan* from Lublin, YEHIEL MICHAEL ben NATHAN, who
tried to introduce certain innovations in the ritual music, but was
met with vehement opposition. While nothing is known specifically about these innovations, it has been reported that some
members of the congregation made derisive imitations of the
hazzan's chanting, used derogatory gestures to ridicule him, and
applied disrespectful haste in the congregational responses, using
—within the service—all kinds of acrimonious practices to show
their opposition to his well-meaning changes.[9]

The literary language of the newcomers from the Iberian peninsula remained Spanish and Portuguese. Some poets and drama-
tists, among them MOSES ZACUTO (1625-1967), wrote in Spanish,
while JOSEPH PENSO de la VEGA (ca. 1650-1692) produced literary
works in both languages. Soon, however, the tendency of writing
in Hebrew took precedence among the writers of the Amsterdam
colony. We mentioned earlier (p. 367) that the most important
early religious Hebrew dramas were written in Amsterdam. Why
did their authors refrain from using their native tongue in the
new surrounding? Probably it was their firm belief in the unique
mission of the Jewish people and their desire to cultivate the
ancient Biblical language. Since the majority of the Sephardic
Jews were not familiar with Hebrew, these authors, by their
literary endeavors, initiated an interest in Hebrew and gave proof
that the original language of the Bible was still a living and
flexible idiom.

Among the multitude of writers who produced Hebrew poems
for all occasions, the person of the talented and prolific DAVID
FRANCO MENDES (1713-1792) stands out as a highly qualified
representative of Jewish literary endeavors in the Netherlands of
the eighteenth century.

With the literary activity of the newcomers, their musical activity went hand in hand. In an early established library of the
Amsterdam community, abundant literary sources are preserved,

which shed a light on music in general; furthermore there are, in these archives, manuscripts of musical works, as well as printed compositions. This library, which was given the characteristic name of ʿEẓ Ḥayyim (Tree of Life), is the richest repository of everything concerning music in the seventeenth and eighteenth centuries of the Jews in Amsterdam.

The qualifications of many Jewish persons of social standing included a good musical knowledge and the playing of an instrument. The Sephardic rabbi, hakam ISAAC UZIEL (d. in 1622), was famous not only as a poet, but also well versed in music and an expert harpist. Another renowned rabbi of Amsterdam, ISAAC ABOAB da FONSECA (1605-1693), was also a good harpist. Sometimes scholarship and musicianship went parallel, as in the case of ABRAHAM PEREIRA, who was the head of the Talmudic school Torah ʾOr (Light of the Torah), but also an expert harpist and, owing to his fine voice, a "melodious cantor."[10] MANUEL PIMENTEL excelled as a dancer (and probably also as a dancing master), and was also a famous harpist.

It would seem that the harp was the preferred instrument of the Amsterdam Jews, but we know of outstanding persons who preferred other instruments. We mentioned above (p. 378) two famous poets and dramatic authors, ANTONIO CASTILLO and JUAN MENDES, who were virtuosi on the vihuela de arco. These were some recorded instances of distinguished persons mastering other instruments than the harp. There must have been many more whose names were not transmitted for posterity. Curiously, we have no records from Amsterdam about expert players of a certain instrument, widely used among amateurs as well as professionals, the universal house-instrument of the eighteenth century: the clavicembalo, or harpsichord. There exist only a veiled mention of it in a report about a "spiritual concert," which took place around 1736, and in which the composer CACERES took over the accompaniment, evidently conducting the musicians from the harpsichord, as was customary in those days.

Other records concerning a widespread musical activity refer to the "poet laureate" of the Amsterdam colony, DANIEL LEVI BARRIOS. He lavished praises upon MANUEL (or JACOB) de PINA for his literary gifts as well as for his enchanting singing. BARRIOS also mentions the superb voice of IMMANUEL ABENATAR MELLO, ḥazzan of the Amsterdam synagogue since 1652. We also know of a musician who was master of several instruments, the Portuguese LORENÇO ESCUDERO who, after having settled in Amsterdam, changed his name to ABRAHAM PEREGRINO.

From this list of renowned singers and musicians the name of DAVID de PINNA should not be omitted. He was a famous surgeon of Amsterdam who was asked to furnish the musical notation of the Biblical cantillation (the ta'amim) for JABLONSKI's Biblia Hebraica (published in Berlin in 1699). What coincidence of circumstances brought about the selection of an Amsterdam surgeon to contribute a transcription of the Biblical intonations for a publication of the Bible is not known. The fact remains that through de PINNA's expert notation, the authentic intonations of the Sephardic rite became known outside of the Netherlands and were preserved in an authentic form for posterity (see also p. 213).

As in Italy of the Renaissance, wealthy Sephardim of Amsterdam vied with each other in sponsoring musical arts and artists. The homes of the PEREIRA, CAPADOCE, SUASSO, TEIXEIRA, and others, became centers of musical activity, where regular house concerts took place, affording the artists the opportunity to entertain the Jewish aristocracy and spread musical culture into wider circles. In the country home of the family PEREIRA, the Prince WILLIAM V was honored at a splendid concert, where the famous musicus MAGALLI, an Italian singer very much in vogue at that time, was presented as the main attraction to the aristocratic audience.

A curious fact about the Sephardic colony was that around 1750 the "Portuguese" Jews established a "Spanish" theater, where operas in "French" were also staged. To stress the "aristocratic" side of operatic art of the epoch, the performances of this theater were held in closed sessions, only for invited guests. An ardent addict of the operatic art, FRANCESCO LOPES de LIZ, from 1734 to 1742, in his palatial home in The Hague, gave concerts and opera performances, to which only invited notables had access.

To insure the high musical standard of his concerts, de LIZ

*Facsimile of a page from the Cairuan Codex (ca. 1400). Song of Songs.
In:* Semitic Studies in Memory of Immanuel Löw *(Budapest, 1947),*
p. 131.

לְעָרִים סְבִיבֹתֵיהֶם תִּתְּנוּ לַלְוִיִּם׃ וְהָיוּ הֶעָרִים לָהֶם לָשָׁבֶת
וּמִגְרְשֵׁיהֶם יִהְיוּ לִבְהֶמְתָּם וְלִרְכֻשָׁם וּלְכֹל חַיָּתָם׃ וּמִגְרְשֵׁי
הֶעָרִים אֲשֶׁר תִּתְּנוּ לַלְוִיִּם מִקִּיר הָעִיר וָחוּצָה אֶלֶף אַמָּה סָבִיב׃
וּמַדֹּתֶם מִחוּץ לָעִיר אֶת פְּאַת קֵדְמָה אַלְפַּיִם בָּאַמָּה וְאֶת פְּאַת
נֶגֶב אַלְפַּיִם בָּאַמָּה וְאֶת פְּאַת יָם אַלְפַּיִם בָּאַמָּה וְאֵת פְּאַת צָפוֹן
אַלְפַּיִם בָּאַמָּה וְהָעִיר בַּתָּוֶךְ זֶה יִהְיֶה לָהֶם מִגְרְשֵׁי הֶעָרִים׃
וְאֵת הֶעָרִים אֲשֶׁר תִּתְּנוּ לַלְוִיִּם אֵת שֵׁשׁ עָרֵי הַמִּקְלָט אֲשֶׁר
תִּתְּנוּ לָנֻס שָׁמָּה הָרֹצֵחַ וַעֲלֵיהֶם תִּתְּנוּ אַרְבָּעִים וּשְׁתַּיִם עִיר׃
כָּל הֶעָרִים אֲשֶׁר תִּתְּנוּ לַלְוִיִּם אַרְבָּעִים וּשְׁמֹנֶה עִיר אֶתְהֶן
וְאֶת מִגְרְשֵׁיהֶן וְהֶעָרִים אֲשֶׁר תִּתְּנוּ מֵאֲחֻזַּת בְּנֵי יִשְׂרָאֵל מֵאֵת
הָרַב תַּרְבּוּ וּמֵאֵת הַמְעַט תַּמְעִיטוּ אִישׁ כְּפִי נַחֲלָתוֹ אֲשֶׁר יְ
יִנְחָלוּ יִתֵּן מֵעָרָיו לַלְוִיִּם׃ פ וַיְדַבֵּר יְהוָה
אֶל מֹשֶׁה לֵּאמֹר׃ דַּבֵּר אֶל בְּנֵי יִשְׂרָאֵל וְאָמַרְתָּ אֲלֵהֶם כִּי
אַתֶּם עֹבְרִים אֶת הַיַּרְדֵּן אַרְצָה כְּנָעַן׃ וְהִקְרִיתֶם לָכֶם עָרִים
עָרֵי מִקְלָט תִּהְיֶינָה לָכֶם וְנָס שָׁמָּה רֹצֵחַ מַכֵּה נֶפֶשׁ בִּשְׁגָגָה׃
וְהָיוּ לָכֶם הֶעָרִים לְמִקְלָט מִגֹּאֵל וְלֹא יָמוּת הָרֹצֵחַ עַד עָמְדוֹ
לִפְנֵי הָעֵדָה לַמִּשְׁפָּט׃ וְהֶעָרִים אֲשֶׁר תִּתֵּנוּ שֵׁשׁ עָרֵי מִקְלָט
תִּהְיֶינָה לָכֶם׃ אֵת שְׁלֹשׁ הֶעָרִים תִּתְּנוּ מֵעֵבֶר לַיַּרְדֵּן וְאֵת
שְׁלֹשׁ הֶעָרִים תִּתְּנוּ בְּאֶרֶץ כְּנָעַן עָרֵי מִקְלָט תִּהְיֶינָה׃ לִבְנֵי
יִשְׂרָאֵל וְלַגֵּר וְלַתּוֹשָׁב בְּתוֹכָם תִּהְיֶינָה שֵׁשׁ הֶעָרִים הָאֵלֶּה
לְמִקְלָט לָנוּס שָׁמָּה כָּל מַכֵּה נֶפֶשׁ בִּשְׁגָגָה׃ וְאִם בִּכְלִי בַרְזֶל

Page from the earliest Hebrew book printed with taʿamim: Pentateuch (Bologna, 1482). Original size 7½ x 11 inches. (Courtesy of the Jewish Theological Seminary of America, New York).

INTRODV-
ctio vtiliffima, Hebrai=
ce difcere cupientibus:
cum latiori emenda
tione Iohãnis Bœ
fchenſtain.

Oratio dominica
Angelica falutatio
Salue regina.
Hebraice.

Matthæo Adriano Equi=
te Aurato inter=
prete.

Facsimile of the title page of Böschenstein's Hebrew Grammar. *(Hagenau, 1520).*

Facsimile of the title page of Kirchan's Simḥat ha-Nefesh. *(Fürth, 1727).*

Ḥazzan, *bass and singer in a Jewish service. From a* Maḥsor *(fourteenth century) (Courtesy of the University Library, Leipzig).*

Probably Guglielmo da Pesaro and his pupils. (Bibliothèque Nationale, Paris, Manusc. Fonds Ital., 973).

Facsimile of the tenor part of Allegro Porto's Book of Madrigals. (Courtesy of the University Library, Uppsala).

ALLA
SACRA CESAREA
E REGGIA MAESTA
DI
FERDINANDO II.
IMPERATORE &c.

Questi Madrigali à Cinque Voci
co'l Basso Continuo.

ALLEGRO PORTO HEBREO,

DONA
E
CONSACRA.

TENORE

B

Facsimile of the title page of the tenor part of Allegro Porto's Book of
Madrigals, *dedicated to the Emperor Ferdinand II. (Courtesy of the
University Library, Uppsala).*

Facsimile of the title page of Salomone Rossi's Ha-Shirim Asher
LiShelomoh *(Venice, 1622).*

Marriage Procession. From Kirchner, Jüdisches Ceremoniel. *(Nürem-berg, 1726).*

Musicians in a Purim Procession. (Woodcut, Amsterdam, 1723).

engaged the renowned violonist and composer JEAN MARIE LE-
CLAIR, the elder (1697-1764). In the contract, signed on July 1,
1740, de LIZ stipulated that LECLAIR was obliged "to conduct my
concerts as leader of all the musicians which I have now in my
service, or which I shall have in the future; furthermore, to play
the violin twice a week, namely Thursday and Saturday, or any
other day as suits my pleasure, leaving him complete freedom
to make use of the rest of his time as he choses."[11]

The Sephardim were not the only ones who distinguished themselves as patrons of music. Among the Ashkenazim there were
certainly music-loving circles, although the names of such families
have not been recorded.

Yet the Ashkenazim had other merits to their credit. One of
them, a German Jew, J. H. DESSAUER, in 1784 established a theatrical and musical company, labeled for "Amusement and Culture." It is significant tthat the entire company, which consisted
of actors, singers and twenty-three orchestra members, were all
Jews. This Jewish theater, active until 1838, gave operatic performances of the works of Salieri, Martini, Grétry, Dalayrac,
Nicolo, Méhul, Kreutzer, Süssmayer, "and always, always Mozart."
Beginning with 1795, two weekly performances were given. An-
nouncing a performance of Don Giovanni on Saturday, May,
1796, DESSAUER put an advertisement in the Rotterdam Courant
informing the public that this performance would start at nightfall
when the Sabbath ended. Outside of Amsterdam, the Jewish
troupe gave performances in Utrecht and Rotterdam. DESSAUER
himself was a singer and, furthermore, he created a school to
give dramatic and vocal instruction to young neophytes in the
operatic art.

Just as in the secular field, music in the synagogue enjoyed
an impressive rebirth in the Sephardic as well as in the Ashkenazic
congregations. From the beginning of the seventeenth century on
we have isolated records about the burgeoning musical activity of
the synagogues of Amsterdam. We know, for instance, about a
cantata, Dialogo dos montes, by PAOLO de PINA who, after his
return to Judaism, in 1604, changed his name to ROḤIEL JESSURUN.
The Dialogo was performed on the festival of Shabuot in the

newly built synagogue *Bet Ya'akov* (1624), with musical interludes, sung and played, as a note in the preserved text indicates,
by "*os muzicos.*" Such performances in the synagogues, however,
which too closely resembled secular entertainment, were later
prohibited and relegated to the meeting of fraternities or
academies.

LEOPOLD MOZART, in his records about his voyages in Europe,
mentions that in The Hague (1765) he was lavishly entertained
at the home of the art-loving Jewish brothers ISAAC and ANDRE
PINTO. And while in Amsterdam, in January and February, 1766,
he mentions among his hosts four rich Jewish families (see p.
384), who were ardent music lovers.

In his diary about his stay in London in 1764, we find the
notation: "Juden: Mr. Zuni, Mr. Liebman, Mr. de Simon, Mr.
d'Almaida, Mr. Frenck," with the addresses of most of them, proof
that he was received and entertained in the Jewish circles of
other cities as well.[12]

Well known is the fact that LEOPOLD MOZART, during his sojourn
in London with WOLFGANG and MARIANNE, in 1764, met and be-
friended the violoncellist SIPRUTINI, the son of a Dutch Jew. His
name must have been originally different, and SIPRUTINI was
merely an adopted name, since Italian artists were in vogue in
those days.

The friendship with LEOPOLD MOZART must have had an irresistible fascination upon SIPRUTINI, since MOZART succeeded in
converting him to Catholicism. How MOZART achieved this is not
known. At any rate, it shows the almost mystic allurement which
the name MOZART exerted upon Jews and Gentiles alike at that
time, even before WOLFGANG became the most celebrated composer of the period.

SIPRUTINI evidently was a talented player of his instrument,
since he gave successful concerts in many cities. The news about
his conversion, however, seems not to have been generally known
in the musical world; he gave recitals in The Hague in 1765, and
even in Amsterdam in 1766.[13] It is hardly conceivable that a concert of a converted Dutch Jew could have taken place in Amster-

dam, in view of the notorious religious intolerance of that Jewish community.

The greatest religious, social and musical event in Amsterdam of the seventeenth century was the inauguration of the "Great Synagogue," which took place on August 2, 1675, in the presence of all the notables of the city, with rich choral and orchestral display.

The inauguration started on the even of the *Sabbat nahamu*,* the Sabbath following the Ninth of 'Ab, the date of the destruction by the Romans of the Jerusalem Temple. The poems composed for this occasion by the rabbis ISAAC ABOAB da FONSECA and SOLOMON d'OLIVEYRA contain precise indications concerning their instrumental accompaniment. Another poem written for this event by ISAAC ABOAB, states in a marginal note that "it was sung in the synagogue for four voices."

DAVID FRANCO MENDES, in his introduction to the vocal parts of the inauguration, reports that the choral selections were performed" *(ale higgayon be-kinnor u-be kol kle shir"* (with the sound of the *kinnor* and with instrumental accompaniment).

The special liturgy for this *Sabbat nahamu* is delineated in the *Seder hazzanut*, the manual for the precentor of the Portuguese synagogue, which is preserved in the library *(Ez-Hayyim* of the congregation.

This inauguration was the most outstanding festival event of the Sephardic Jews in Amsterdam, and its anniversary is celebrated even in our own time.

Another religious occasion with rich musical display was the Feast of *Simhat Torah* in 1738. On this festival the Jews celebrate the completion of the yearly cycle of the public reading of the Torah in the synagogue, and the start of a new cycle with the first verse of Genesis. The religious part of the ceremony took place in the sanctuary, after which selected members of the congregation, carrying Torah scrolls, marched in a solemn procession in the streets adjacent to the synagogue.

---

* *Nahamu, nahamu, 'ami,* "Comfort ye, comfort ye, my people." (Isaiah 40:1).

Singing and music were essential parts of this celebration, and with the years, the musical part of the feast assumed such preponderance that it was more a "spiritual concert" than a part of the divine service.

For the inauguration, MOSES ḤAYYIM LUZZATTO, who lived in Amsterdam from 1736 to 1743, wrote the poems and ABRAHAM CACERES the music. The vocal soli were sung by the two famous *ḥazzanim,* SAMUEL RODRIGUES MENDES and AARON ha-COHEN de LARA. The text has five (resp. six) stanzas, the first of which was repeated at the end. Each stanza contains annotations concerning its musical rendering, with precise indications whether it should be sung as a solo, or as a duet for both *ḥazzanim.* This composition was performed repeatedly and was even imitated by other composers in the eighteenth century.

Similar compositions are still preserved in the library of the congregation. The lyrics of one of them is by ABRAHAM ben IMMANUEL da SILVA, who wrote the poem in 1772 for his brother, the famous *ḥazzan* DAVID da SILVA. For this poem there are two different musical versions by the composer M. MANI, who wrote several other synagogue compositions, which are also preserved (*e.g.,* two cantatas and a *Ḳaddish*).

The two regular composers-in-residence of the Amsterdam Sephardim were ABRAHAM CACERES, who was Jewish, and CRISTIANO GIUSEPPE LIDARTI, a Gentile. About CACARES we possess only sketchy knowledge. He seems not to have been a professional musician, but at the best a gifted amateur. Nevertheless, in Amsterdam his music enjoyed great acclaim. In 1726 he wrote the music for the inauguration of the synagogue in The Hague, and from then on, his fame seems to have spread among the Sephardim of the Netherlands.

IMMANUEL ḤAY RICCHI, the noted Italian cabalist (1687-1743), published in Amsterdam (1730-31) a commentary to the *Mishnah,* "*Sefer hon ʾashir*" (The Book about the Wealth of a Rich Man), to which he added some poems in honor of the Sabbath, the circumcision, and the phylacteries. He commissioned CACERES to notate (or compose?) melodies for these poems (Mus. ex. No. 29.) Here is the translation of the Hebrew caption following the music:

To this tune (*niggun*) the author [i.e. Ricchi] composed a poem about Sabbath, Circumcision and Tefillim [Phylacteries]. In order to complete [probably: notate] the tune, he applied to one who is more qualified in this art. This is the honorable person Abraham Caceres, from this town. [He did it] for the pleasure of the patron, Yehuda of Urbino, a lover of this art.

This indication refers to a Maecenas of the town of Urbino, about whom we know only that he sponsored RICCHI's book and that he was a great music lover. This might have been reason enough for RICCHI to add music to a book whose subject was completely nonmusical as well as the pretense of having "composed" the melody himself.

At any rate, the mention of CACERES' collaboration indicates that as early as 1730, he might have been already a well-known composer in the Netherlands. His music for the above-mentioned *Simḥat Torah* celebration was enthusiastically praised by DAVID FRANCO MENDES, whose chronicle, *Memorias do estabelecimento,* the manuscript of which is preserved in the library of the Amsterdam congregation, records faithfully all the important events of the Sephardic community.

About LIDARTI we are better informed. He was born in Vienna in 1730 of Italian parentage; he died presumably after 1793, since his last composition carries this date. After a musical career which took him from Venice, Florence and Pisa to London (1768-1780),[14] he seems to have stayed several years in the Netherlands; but about his sojourn in Amsterdam the sources are rather vague. In this city, he wrote a number of compositions for the synagogue, among them two cantatas, *"Boi-be-shalom"* (Come, bringing Peace), and *"Kol ha-neshamah"* (Every Soul [Ps. 150]), which were for a long time included in the yearly *Simḥat Torah* celebration of the Amsterdam synagogue.

Furthermore, another composer, ABRAHAM RATHOM of London, figures among those who wrote music for the Sephardic congregation of Amsterdam. The only thing we know about him is that he was an amateur musician, probably the son of ISAAC RATHOM, whose name appears in 1712 as the *shamash* (beadle) in the payroll of the Sephardic synagogue of London.

In the repertoire of the above mentioned Portuguese fraternity *Mikra kodesh,* there is a little musical comedy from 1766; the three characters of the cast consist of a poet, a physician, and a pharmacist. They sing ariettas in solo, ending with a vocal trio.[15]

In addition, there are some smaller pieces for the celebration of fraternities for two voices, destined to be performed with accompaniment, always indicating the tune to be used for the lyrics. The author of most of these poems was the above mentioned MOSES ben YEHUDA PIZA (see p. 372).

Furthermore, the same author has to his credit a little musical comedy for four actors, which he wrote for the "*Siyyum*" (Completion) of the society *Limmud ha-talmidim* (Teaching of Students) in 1776. The parts were to be sung using earlier, well-known tunes. For this occasion, however, also some new music was composed; the new tunes were indicated by the note *lahan hadash* (to a new melody).[16]

In the above-mentioned chronicles of DAVID FRANCO MENDES, two important musical events of the Amsterdam congregation are related in colorful details. These refer to the two competitions concerning the cantorial vacancies at the Great Synagogue.

The first of these took place in 1743, upon the death of *hazzan* SAMUEL RODRIGUEZ MENDES (one of the soloists of CACERES' cantata for *Simhat Torah* in 1738). Among the several candidates, DANIEL PIMENTEL sang two selections of CACERES, one from among his earlier compositions, the other written especially for this occasion.

More detailed are MENDES' records about the second competition, that took place in 1776, after the death of the *hazzan* JOSEPH ben ISAAC SARFATIM. At this time, there were no less than seven candidates, whose names, together with the pieces they sang at the competition, are carefully noted by MENDES.

Each of the candidates was introduced to the congregation on consecutive Saturday services, where they sang several selections which included at least one new piece. For these new compositions some of the candidates asked local poets for special poems, for which the candidate furnished the music, either his own, or some borrowed melody, to be adapted to the new lyrics. The third candidate, HAYYIM ben JOSEPH PIZA, sang some new compositions by LIDARTI, and of another composer of the name of CREITZER (or KREUTZER), whose identity cannot be established beyond doubt. The fourth candidate, AARON ben ABRAHAM TOURO, sang a portion of the HALLEL—"*Pithuli sha'are zedek,*" (Open for me the Gates of the Righteous)—composed by LIDARTI, and a new *Kaddish,* composed by M. MANI. The fifth candidate, DAVID ben IMMANUEL da SILVA, must have selected his pieces with particular shrewdness, evidently with a keen eye for their effect upon the congregation, since from the outset he was the favorite and, in the end, the victor.

FRANCO MENDES vividly describes the victory celebration and everything that went before. He stated that the participation of the people at the contests was enormous; not only Sephardim, but also Ashkenazim, and even Gentiles stormed the synagogue, and that six guards had to be employed to control the crowd.

During the weeks preceding the final selection, the community was in perpetual turmoil. The candidates campaigned vigorously by soliciting votes, and members of the congregation took sides for or against the individual competitors. After the proclamation of the election's result, the victor was brought home accompanied by a huge crowd, with lighted torches and blaring trumpets, in a most triumphant manner never seen before. The installation ceremony in the afternoon surpassed even the joy of the morning. The newly elected *hazzan* was led to the synagogue preceded by an instrumental ensemble of two oboes, two Frnche horns and two trumpets, followed by a multitude of celebrants. When the huge doors of the synagogue were opened, the Ashkenazic Jews overthrew the guards and overran the synagogue. They sang their own songs, psalms, and *pizmonim* (liturgical poems), and the ceremony ended in an atmosphere of indescribable merriment.[17]

Similar rejoicings, though on a smaller scale, took place for the numerous fraternities (*hevrot*), philanthropic, religious, or educational, which were just as meaningful for the intellectual life of the Jews in Amsterdam, as they were in Italy during the Renaissance. For these fraternities quite a number of poems were written for all sorts of events, such as anniversaries of their foundation, for initiations and other solemn occasions. Many of them were presented either with music specially composed, or utilizing extant melodies adapted to the new lyrics. A printed collection of the fraternity *Shomrim la-Boker,* entitled *Sefer mishmeret laylah* (Book of the Night-Watchers), published in Amsterdam in 1767-1768, contains a number of poems with indications as to the tune to be used for the melody. Sometimes the same melody was prescribed for different poems, which proves that the poets wrote their lyrics to some well-known tune.

Even more numerous were the musical settings for poems written for family festivities, especially for weddings and circumcisions. For weddings, the use of music (vocal as well as instrumental) was prescribed by a long tradition, going back to Biblical times. The poems composed for such occasions were mostly printed on handbills, some even on silk sheets, which were distributed among the guests. Many of these handbills bear an indication of a musical (vocal) participation requested of those present.

For the wedding ceremonies of the Jewish financial aristocracy such small poems were considered inadequate and replaced by literary products on a scale more in line with the social standing of the sponsor. MOSES ḤAYYIM LUZZATTO, while residing in Amsterdam, composed an elaborate allegorical poem for the wedding of his pupil, the son of his wealthy friend, MOSES de CHAVES. This poem turned out to be a real dramatic production, in which there were seventeen actors, not counting the choir singers (*ḥevrat meshorerim*). In the final apotheosis there appeared some allegorical figures, such as *Yosher* (Justice), *Tehillah* (Praise), *Shekel* (Money, as a metonymy for Prosperity), and also a large choir, which sang as a riturnello the strophe "*kol tofse kinnor 'ugab va-nebel, kumu . . . naggen hetivu*" (everybody who holds a *kinnor,* an *'ugab* and a *nebel,* rise and make good music), indicating a performance with numerous instrumentalists, evidently with a full orchestra.

The wealthy Ashkenazic Jews did not want to be eclipsed in musical showmanship by their Sephardic brothers. They commissioned no less than the famous chronicler of Amsterdam, DAVID FRANCO MENDES, to write a showy musical piece for the wedding of the daughter of BENJAMIN COHEN of Amersfoort, which took place about 1788-89. In order not to be outdone by LUZZATTO, MENDES wrote an allegorical opera in which the characters were Venus (*Nogah*), Apollo (*Yubal*), the Muses (*benot ha-shir*, literally "the daughters of song"), among them Calliope. The second act played at the foot of the Parnasse, thus giving the proper background to the plot.

MENDES titled his play *'Ahavat 'Olam*, the same as the ritual prayer taken from the sacred service, "With everlasting Love." This opera-cantata was staged with a rich musical setting, using soloists, choir singers, instrumentalists, and even dancers. It is not farfetched to assume that the performance was entrusted to DESSAUER's German theatrical group, whose members—as mentioned earlier—were all Jews who evidently encountered no difficulties in singing the Hebrew lyrics of MENDES' piece.

MENDES seems to have been particularly attracted to the dramatic aspect of poetry. He wrote several cantata-like works, which were conceived for the stage, to be performed either in part, or entirely with music. We have knowledge, among others, of a libretto he wrote for a musical work, *Bi'at ha-mashiah* (The Coming of the Messiah), which he considered not as much as an opera than as an oratorio. Further specimens of his dramatic plans are the Biblical subjects *Gemul 'Atalyah* (The Reckoning of Athaliah), based partly on RACINE's *Athalia*, and *Gioas, Re di Giuda* (Joash, King of Judah), modeled after METASTASIO's drama. As was customary in those times, the choral passages of RACINE's tragedy were replaced by MENDES with *canzonette*, a curious procedure in a Biblical oratorio sung in the Hebrew language.

Furthermore, records indicate that MENDES planned to use METASTASIO's *Betulia liberata* as a libretto for an opera or an oratorio. There are also some hints for other musical plans of MENDES which, however, are too vague to be counted among the musical practice of the Amsterdam Jewry.

When we pass in review the outstanding features of the musical life of the Jews of the seventeenth and eighteenth centuries in Italy and France, we come to the conclusion that it was not before the Jewish achievements in the Netherlands, and especially in

Amsterdam, that *art* music gained a permanent foothold in the divine service. Even in the rich musical culture of Mantua and Venice, art music appeared only rarely, on holidays, in the ritual, while the main musical part of the service consisted primarily of chanting and other vocal manifestations of the *ḥazzanim.* "According to the evidence, the Portuguese Jews, these former Marranos, more imbued with the European culture than their Italian brothers, were the first to devote their initial efforts to forge for themselves a rejuvenated Jewish personality."[18]

Beginning with the practice of the Amsterdam Sephardim, and closely followed by that of the Ashkenazim of the same town, art music gained momentum in the synagogue. This achievement, at the close of the Jewish Middle Ages led to a renaissance of great significance, lasting throughout the nineteenth century, continuing with unbroken development until present times.

20

The Jewish Musical Child Prodigy

IT HAS ALWAYS BEEN THE GENERAL BELIEF THAT LIVING CONDITIONS in the ghetto were responsible for suppressing musical activity as well as stifling the personal initiative of Jewish musical artists. We have seen, however, how this assumption was shaken by the rich musical culture created by Jews in such places as Mantua, Venice, and in Prague.

Yet there is an artistic manifestation in the ghetto life which deserves more than a passing consideration. It is the phenomenon which first erupted after the crumbling of the ghetto walls and continued unabatedly throughout the entire nineteenth and twentieth centuries, up to our own days; but its germinal origin may legitimately be traced to the ghetto itself.

We refer to the Jewish musical child prodigy, allegedly the product of modern living and the ever growing influence of Western music upon Jewish musical talent. This is true if we consider only the external circumstances, namely the newly won emancipation of the Jewish musical artist, and his acceptance as full-fledged member of the artistic world. It is well known that literally hundreds of Jewish children with the most extraordinary musical abilities made their appearance in all civilized countries after the Emancipation. It appears as if the pent-up musical energies, repressed for centuries, were to create for themselves a volcanic outburst as soon as the artificial barriers were removed.

Music history, philosophy and sociology consider it as "normal" that the beginning of the artistic phenomenon of the Jewish musical child prodigy coincides with the breaking down of the ghetto walls. As music history teaches, the first exponents of this remarkable occurrence were, in their early childhood, such famous Jewish musicians as GIACOMO MEYERBEER (1791-1864) and FELIX MENDELSSOHN-BARTHODY (1809-1847). But looking closely into Jewish life, we discover that the real beginning of the miracle of Jewish musical child prodigies may be found ultimately far back in the ghetto environment. It is highly significant that the very first of the child prodigies who can legitimately be traced in history was the scion of a famous Jewish family.

LOUIS-CLAUDE D'AQUIN (or DACQUIN) was born in Paris on July 4, 1694, and died there on June 15, 1772. He was the offspring of a Jewish family that emigrated from Italy to Carpentras in southern France. The members of the family, while still residing in Italy, became Christians, and because the conversion took place at Acquino, the newly baptized received the name D'AQUINE (or DACQUIN). A grand-uncle of LOUIS-CLAUDE was Professor of Hebrew at the College de France in Paris. As a Jew, his name was MORDECHAI; under his Jewish name he translated into French YEDADA PENINI's Behinat 'Olam, and published it in Paris in 1629 under the title L'examen du monde. An uncle of LOUIS-CLAUDE was the famous Dr. D'AQUIN, personal physician of King Louis XIV.

LOUIS-CLAUDE began his musical career as a pianist and composer at eight years of age. He was a pupil of the most renowned organist of the time, LOUIS MARCHAND, and became his successor in various positions. At twelve, LOUIS-CLAUDE became organist of the St. Antoine-Cloister at Paris. In 1727 the young artist applied for the position of organist at the Church of St. Paul, and in a musical competition outdid the famous RAMEAU. After having had various other church positions LOUIS-CLAUDE became the organist of France's most famous church, the Cathedral of Notre Dame in Paris.

LOUIS-CLAUDE was the greatest of all Paris organists of the eighteenth century. Huge throngs filled the churches whenever he played, and his superiority dwarfed all other organists of his period, among them COUPERIN. LOUIS-CLAUDE was outstanding not only as a virtuoso, but also as a composer. He wrote a large number of pieces for the clavecin, which to this day are counted among the most famous works of the early French keyboard literature. Among his choral works a cantata, *"La Rose,"* has lasting value.

Now, can we consider LOUIS-CLAUDE a Jewish musician? Just as much, or just as little as SALOMONE ROSSI EBREO, the most famous Jewish composer of the late Renaissance in Italy. The comparison is not quite exact, since ROSSI, among other lasting works, composed psalms for the synagogue liturgy, using for his texts the original Hebrew words; he gave, at least by his synagogue compositions, testimony of his Jewish faith. Nevertheless, as we pointed out earlier, his music is devoid of any Jewish traits; his musical idiom is simply that of the historical Italian period. His psalms sound exactly like Italian madrigals; besides a general religious feeling in them, not a single measure, not even one phrase of his music has a genuine Jewish inflection. The musical tradition of the synagogue, the old Jewish chant (*nussah*) are lacking in Rossi's music. His style has completely integrated into the musical idiom of his time, just as CLAUDE D'AQUIN, too, speaks the fanciful and graceful language of the French Rococo.

Nevertheless, CLAUDE D'AQUIN is of importance to Jewish music history, although he himself was not of Jewish faith. He is the first recorded exponent of the creative power of the Jewish people in the musical field, a power which manifests itself by way of a novel and significant phenomenon: the Jewish musical child prodigy. The fact that he opens the long list of these prodigies assures him a lasting place in the history of Jewish music.

There also lived a female Jewish musical child prodigy prior to the Emancipation. She was MARIA THERESA BLAND, who later became a famous singer in England. She was born in 1769 as the daughter of the Italian Jew ROMANZINI, who settled in London in 1770. In England the vocal talent of the bright girl developed amazingly. After having made a brilliant debut in public at the Royal Circus (a place where singers generally do not make their initial appearance), she was offered the opportunity to appear at a legitimate theater where her voice created a furor. Shortly thereafter, in 1782, at the age of thirteen, she obtained a regular con-

tract for the operatic stage, and a few years later was cast only in
leading roles.

Two of her sons also became famous singers on the English
stage. Although not a unique occurrence, it shows that, even
before the Emancipation, musical talent, instrumental, and sometimes vocal, was hereditary in Jewish families.

21

Ḥasidism and Its Music*

ḤASIDIC MUSIC WAS THE LATEST MANIFESTATION OF JEWISH MUSICAL creativity prior to the period of Emancipation. This music, nurtured in the Eastern European Ḥasidic movement, could not be fully understood without a succinct examination of its roots in the historical, philosophical, and liturgical sense.

Ḥasidism in Poland and the Ukraine was not an entirely new phenomenon of Jewish life. It was the continuation, or, more correctly, the revival of medieval mysticism, which found its adequate expression in the esoteric teachings of the Cabala. In a

* The Jewish people's never-ending love for music would warrant the assumption that even before the burgeoning of Hasidic music, the Polish and Ukrainian Jews might have had, beside their synagogue music, some kind of folk music of their own. Such music would have substantially been borrowed from, or represent an imitation of, the music of the environment, i.e., Russian, Ukrainian, and Cossack folksongs. Since there is, however, no historical documentation to sustain this hypothesis, such theory can only be a surmise.

In a remarkable study, Joseph Yasser furnishes historical, religious and literary proofs for the influence of Jewish music upon the early Russian civilization as far back as the first Grand Dukes of Kiev (eleventh and twelfth centuries). In their courts, minstrels sang "Hebrew verses," "Songs of Jerusalem," and other ballads, the origin of which strongly points, on the one hand, to the Jewish *Hazzanic* tradition and, on the other hand, to Jewish folklore of those times. This folklore may have been cultivated largely in the Khazar state which, as is commonly known, was a religiously Judaic (but ethnically Turkic) commonwealth with its own Jewish culture, especially among the upper classes. As a correlation, it might be assumed that the later developed Russian, and especially Ukrainian, folksong exerted its influence upon the Jewish minority of that region, and thus became a driving force in creating a Jewish folk music, though strongly overshadowed by Slavic musical elements. This might constitute the medieval precursor of the later emerging Hasidic music. (See Joseph Yasser, "References to Hebrew Music in Russian Medieval Ballads," in *Jewish Social Studies*, New York, 1949, vol. XI, No. 1, pp. 21–48.)

survey of the musical culture in the Jewish Diaspora a comprehensive picture of Jewish mysticism would be out of place. Nevertheless, it is necessary to give a brief outline of this phenomenon for an understanding of the Ḥasidic musical manifestations and to assign them their proper place in the history of Jewish music.

The term Ḥasidism comes from the Biblical word *ḥasid,* "pious," "benevolent," which later assumed the additional meaning of "saintly." In the Middle Ages it was applied as the surname of several venerable men; the best-known of them was YEHUDAH he-ḤASID (d. 1217 in Regensburg), author of the famous *Sefer Ḥasidim* (Book of the Pious).

In medieval Germany there was a religious movement as exemplified by the life of certain Jewish groups, whom contemporaries called Ḥasidim. This movement was a decisive event in the religious development of German Jewry. Ḥasidism, in this epoch, was looked upon as the ideally Jewish way of life, even though its principles were never completely followed in everyday life. Yet, it was due to these principles that the German Jews were able to maintain an inner strength and an unbroken resistance during the continuous periods of persecutions.

Medieval Jewish mysticism was based upon the Cabala, a term derived from the Hebrew *ḳabal,* "to receive," in figurative sense "the received or traditional lore." Cabala was also identified with "*ḥokmah nistarah*" (the hidden science, or the hidden wisdom). It was an esoteric doctrine concerning the relation between God and the universe, the knowledge of which was entrusted only to a few chosen individuals.

It is held that Cabala already existed in Biblical times, perhaps not under this name, but encompassing mystical doctrines in general. This is at least how a verse of Ben Sirach has sometimes been interpreted, which warns: "For it is not needful for thee to see with thine eyes the things that are in secret" (Ecclus. 3:22). According to JOSEPHUS, the Essenes possessed mystical writings, which they jealously guarded against disclosure (*Josephus, A History of the Jewish Wars,* 2:8). Gnosticism thrived upon apocalyptic mysticism, which constituted the transition to the "science" of the Cabala.

The chief representatives of this science were the spiritual

leaders of the Jewish communities in the Rhineland, the KALONY-
MOS family, who had come to the Rhine from Italy. The three
men who molded German Ḥasidim all belonged to this family:
SAMUEL he-ḤASID, the son of KALONYMOS of Speyer (mid-twelfth
cent.), his son YEHUDAH he-ḤASID (d. in 1217), and the latter's
disciple ELEAZAR he-ḤASID of Worms (d. between 1223 and
1232). YEHUDAH he-ḤASID in particular was the undisputed religious leader as long as German Ḥasidism remained a living force.

YEHUDAH's book, Sefer Ḥasidim, is not only a remarkable compendium of medieval Ḥasidic thought, but beyond that, one of
the most outstanding products of Jewish medieval literature.

The mystics, both Jewish and non-Jewish, believed in the pre-
existence of the soul and its close relation to God before it enters
the human body. By this, they hoped to establish a bridge between the Creator and mundane life.

In the belief of the mystics the world of the spirit, just as the
external world, had undergone a deep transformation. This necessitated for the basically conservative German Judaism a novel
conception of the Ḥasid, a novel religious ideal, which was considered more desirable than any intellectual achievement. Here
we find the initial germ of the later Polish Ḥasidism and a connecting link between German and Eastern Ḥasidism.

Mystic speculations abound in the Talmud; the Gaonic period
is particularly rich in esoteric mysticism. The famous book of the
mystics, Sefer Yeẓirah (Book of the Creation), written before the
ninth century, was the bridge between the Gaonic mystics and
the Cabala. It is the oldest philosophical work in Hebrew; its main
subject deals with the relationship between God and the Universe.

Medieval German mysticism was nurtured by the esoteric
teachings of the Cabala. The Cabala reached its zenith in the
thirteenth century and created an extensive mystic literature, cli-
maxing in the Sefer ha-Zohar (The Book of Splendor), which
became the authoritative and standard book of the Cabalists.
The Zohar, in the main, was the creation of MOSES ben SHEMTOB
de LEON (1250-1305). One of its most significant tenets, and one
which survived in Ḥasidism, is the doctrine that the pious may
achieve a union between God and himself in this life, if he
knows how to free his soul from the shackles by which it is bound

to his body. Thus, the Cabalists believed that some privileged pious men were able to reveal the mysteries of the world beyond.

The most important doctrine of the Cabala was that of the *Sefirot,* the ten heavenly spheres, which were supposedly replete with creative powers through which the Divine Essence manifested itself in the universe. The interpretation of it created a highly speculative philosophy, presented quite differently in the various cabalistic literary works. Some held that the *Sefirot,* in their totality, were identical with the Divine Being; others looked upon the *Sefirot* merely as tools of the Divine Power.[1]

However, the true movement of Jewish mysticism is considered that which took form in Safed in the Upper Galilee during the period 1570-1630. Here lived and taught many great Cabalists, among them ISAAC LURIA (1533-1572), who is believed to be the creator of the Cabala as a theoretical and practical science. He "heard" the songs of animate as well as of inanimate nature, put his emotions into poems and sang them with tunes, which inspired and elated his followers.

The Cabala, in its ultimate form, appeared simultaneously in two different cultural spheres: Spain, Italy, and the Provence of France, on the one hand, and Germany, on the other. Due to the different political and social conditions of these areas, the doctrines of the two are different in their essence and terminology.

In Germany, the Cabala found its most eloquent spokesman in JOHANNES REUCHLIN (1455-1522), who used it as a potent weapon in the early Reformation. Cabalistic ideas had a strong influence in Germanic countries after large sections of Christians broke with the Church. Many conceptions of the Cabala may be found in Protestantism, as taught by LUTHER, MELANCHTHON, and others.

The Cabala kept mysticism alive in Germany; it is not surprising therefore that it penetrated beyond the eastern borders and established itself firmly in Poland and the Ukraine. Thus, Ḥasidism was the direct continuation, among the Eastern Ashkenazim, of medieval mysticism.

Because of its esoteric nature, the Cabala was full of superstitious beliefs, such as the conception of a heavenly alphabet, the signs of which supposedly constituted the constellations and the stars. It also believed that the Hebrew letters were not merely signs for the formation of words, but implements of divine power, by means of which nature might be subjugated.[2]

In the writings of ELEAZAR of WORMS, the most faithful of YEHUDAH's disciples, mystical doctrines about God and the universe, as well as the effectiveness of God's secret Name, are to be found side by side with speculations on magic and the "hidden science." Most of the superstitions and magical practices of Talmudic and post-Talmudic times were kept alive in the Cabala and were adopted by Hasidism. In fact, there is a close connection between mysticism and magic throughout the entire history of the Hasidic movement.

The basic difference between the German and the Eastern Hasidism may be defined by a simple comparison of the basic approach of both to religion and faith: while the German mystics held that the Hasid must reject and overcome the temptations of ordinary life, the Eastern Hasidim based their conduct of life just upon the opposite principle; their religious devotion demanded the participation, the active co-operation of the body, in addition to the ecstasy of the soul. This boiled down to the simple formula: German Hasidism was a mystic speculation; Eastern Hasidism was an entirely new way of life.

Medieval mysticism was a historical phenomenon, which became powerful only when it developed into a popular "movement." As long as this mysticism remained restricted to its teacher and a relatively small circle of disciples, it had not much effect upon the life of the general Jewish population. Only when its tenets gained a hold on larger masses and wider strata of the people, a profound transformation took place in the faith and in the soul of the people. This, eventually, changed the way of life of many Jewish settlements and of Judaism itself in the Eastern provinces.

East European Hassidism is generally defined as the revolt of "feeling" against religious rationalism, which required the fulfillment of religious commands, such as participating in the services and following to the letter the prescribed laws. Such practices alone were considered by Hasidism as superficial and ineffective.

In Ḥasidism, the doctrine of redemption lived in the heart of the simple man; every Jew, no matter how uneducated, could take an active part in the redemption of the world.

The sixteenth and seventeenth centuries were the hotbeds of the cabalistic movement, spawning all kinds of fanatic dreamers, visionaries and adepts of magic beliefs. It was the "age-old struggle between faith and reason, between emotion and intellect."[3] The mystics at Safed, and later the followers of the Cabala, held that singing was the source of all devotion, that it was the most effective approach to religious inspiration. Thus they made singing a religious duty, a duty only second to prayer.

Long before the birth of European Ḥasidism the Cabalists of Safed used to go out every Friday afternoon in a procession over the hills of Galilee to welcome the "Queen Sabbath" with songs and dances. The Sabbath Eve hymn *"Lekah Dodi"* (Come, my Beloved), composed by SOLOMON ben MOSES ha-LEVI ʾALḲABIẒ (1505-ca. 1580), was the appropriate poetic vehicle for expressing in singing the mystic-devotional expectation for the arrival of the personified Sabbath Queen. It remained up to the present day one of the strongest pillars of every Friday Eve service (see p. 192).

Jewish mysticism of the early Middle Ages passed through several phases of intensity, mitigated by the intellectual awakening of the Renaissance, reinforced by natural catastrophes such as wars, pestilence, persecutions; it went parallel with Christian mysticism; it experienced constant ups and down in the life of medieval peoples, a fluctuation which came to its end at the European Enlightenment.

Ḥasidism was the outgrowth of Jewish mysticism which found a fertile soil in the religious and social conditions of the Eastern Ashkenazim. Among the Eastern Jews, who lived under heavy oppression, Ḥasidic mysticism was not only a state of mind but a way of life. Its aim was to relieve the gloom and hopelessness of the impoverished Polish Jewry, in the midst of which Ḥasidism originated.

Ḥasidism was the answer to the burning desire of the common people for a simple, stimulating and comforting faith. The oppressed masses could not understand the sophisticated rabbinism, the stern and rigid discipline which made life even more difficult. Thus, the soil was prepared for a movement destined to give the people a faith with a source of consolation for their everyday tribulations.

There are striking similarities between early Christianity and Hasidism. In both cases the new religious movement attempted to address itself to the common people, in the Jewish case to the *am ha-)arez*, the uneducated country people. The ignorant masses were treated with contempt by the rabbinical leaders, those rabbis, whose "faith" consisted in learning, and nothing but learning, and who were devoted solely to the knowledge of the Torah and the Talmud, and whose tradition was concentrated in the ritualistic exercise of the divine service. The original impulse of the Hasidic movement arose out of the rebellion of the masses, who were considered by the rabbis as second class Jews because of their lack of learning.

At the beginning, Hasidism was not a sectarian movement and the intention of its founder and adherents was not to abolish age-old customs, but to infuse into them greater warmth and deeper intensity. In its first stage, Hasidism did not discourage learning, but it taught that scholarship alone did not lead to salvation and that the essence of Jewish life was a glowing faith which was the real approach to the Eternal. In the conception of the Hasidim, emotion was placed above reason, and religious exaltation above knowledge, especially rabbinical learning. When later the hasidic movement split into two antagonistic groups, one of them completely rejected the doctrine that rabbinic learning alone led to salvation and retained as basic tenets for Hasidism only the emotional power of music, singing and dancing.

The founder of the movement was ISRAEL BAAL SHEM TOB, "The Master of the Good Name" (1700-1760), abbreviated BESHT (using the initials of his name). He was a son of the people; simple, unpretentious, unselfish and conscious of the spiritual needs of his co-religionists. He began as a practitioner of physical ills; he was a kind of nature healer who by his sound advice and fervent prayer brought relief to thousands. Soon stories about his miraculous cures began to circulate, repeated in the towns and villages, amplified and embellished, until a maze of legends sprang up about him. No wonder that he was ultimately hailed by the masses as a saint, and therein lies the explanation for the unprecedented success of the religious movement he inaugurated.

Here is BESHT's basic credo: not Talmudic scholarship was the criterion of true religion, but rather fervent faith and the belief in the efficacy of prayer. Eventually not only simple people adhered to his teachings, but also a number of rabbis and other learned men who believed in him and lent distinction to his movement. By this, he achieved a complete democratization of Judaism which until then was split into two large segments: the educated and the ignorant.

It was paradoxical that the Ḥasidim, "whose utterances not infrequently throw more light on the nature of the mystical consciousness than anything before them, became the advocates of the simple and untainted belief of the common man, and this simplicity was even glorified by them as the highest religious value."[4]

Ḥasidism was not at odds with the Cabala, as the professional rabbinate were. Ḥasidism continued and attempted to complete the basic tenets of the Cabala by adapting it to the ever changing circumstances of every day life. It took over its ideas and in some cases its methods of teaching, until it achieved a philosophical base which made the principles of medieval mysticism obsolete, and even unpractical. It is true that while some Cabalistic works by Ḥasidic authors did not abandon the tracks of the late Cabala, these are only theoretical writings which do not reflect Ḥasidism as a manifestation of Jewish life. These authors still followed the esoteric doctrine of the Cabala, even when it was supposed to disclose its secrets to the uninitiated. Nonetheless, Ḥasidism was dead set against this principle. Its mysteries and secrets became the common property of all and there was no differentiation between the enlightened and the common man.

With the outgrowth of Ḥasidism the Jews of Poland were immediately attracted to it and soon it spread rapidly to other regions. Within a short time almost half of the world's Jewry were adherents of the new movement.

While the world Jewish community was held together by a common history, common faith, and common ritual, inside of it stood a "chosen community," that of the Ḥasidim. Their leader, their "prophet" (if we may use this term) was the *zaddik*, the *rebbe*, who should not be identified with the *rab* (rav), the rabbi of the congregation, although several *zaddikim* exercised both functions and bore both titles. To distinguish the two, it was the *rab* who was supposed to possess a greater Biblical and Talmudic knowledge, whereas the *rebbe* was basically a simple man of the people, whose only qualification was that he be able "to lead the souls," which by no means excluded that many of the *zaddikim* were also fully conversant with the *Halaka* (the Law) in all its ramifications.

The *zaddik* was not a priest, but a man who dedicated himself to the salvation for all men and all ages. His daily work was the "unification," the *yiḥud*, of God and man.

Nothing was "worldly" to the *zaddik*. Everything could be hallowed, everything, even the most profane actions of everyday life could lead to redemption, to salvation, if they were directed with concentrated immersion of the soul toward one goal: the *yiḥud*, the unity of the creation with the Creator, which was also the aim of the ancient divine teaching of Israel: "Be holy, for I am holy."

Hallowing that which was worldly was the basic motive of the *zaddik*. All his movements and actions had the purport of leading to salvation. It was held that he who performed a *mizvah* (a religious command) with the perfect *kavana* (religious fervor, or intention) directed to God, contributed to the sanctity of the world, and uplifted the divine spark that was inherent in all mundane things.

About Ḥasidism, its inception, expansion, its philosophy and ethics, there exists a wealth of literature. It would exceed the limitations of the present study to go beyond a succinct survey of such a unique phenomenon in Jewish life. For us it is essential to realize that in the eyes of the Ḥasidim worship must be cheerful. Joy was a necessary ingredient for devotional prayer and God must be served with gladness and rapture. The best means toward achieving this was singing and dancing, as written in Psalm 100:2: "Serve the Lord with gladness, come before His presence with singing," and, more emphatically, in Psalm 149:2: "Let the children of Zion be joyful in their King. Let them praise His Name in the dance, let them sing praises unto Him with the timbrel and harp."

Prayer alone was not considered sufficient for Ḥasidim to bring about unity with God, or *Debekut,* as it was called. Physical ecstasy, a rapturous state of mind, was necessary, and the followers of BESHT devised a ritual which included singing and dancing as the means for attaining the desired spiritual exaltation.

Soon specific Ḥasidic songs sprang up, some with lyrics, in which short Biblical phrases, but mostly single words, were repeated over and over again. Some were sung to a rhythmical formula utilizing meaningless words, others were without words, and employed vowels as a "text." This was a late Jewish parallel to the early Christian psalmody of a similar ecstatic nature, in which the consonants of the words were omitted and the worshippers sang only the vowels, for instance AEIUA (for *Alleluyah*), or EUOUAE (for *Seculorum Amen*).

While Ḥasidism added but a few—and mostly rhythmically new—features to Jewish music, it infused an entirely new spirit into the devotional chant and into the folksong as well. In the belief of its adherents, "Song ascends to heaven faster than prayer," because "a divine spark is hidden in each tune." The singers considered themselves "God-intoxicated," and this gave such emotional power to their songs.

BESHT, and after him other Ḥasidic *zaddikim,* or "Righteous Ones," as the Ḥasidim called their leaders, established specific semireligious "courts," in which the followers gathered regularly to have their own services. Unlike the regular synagogue worship, the main feature of these services were not the traditional ritual and prayer, but a new conception of worship based upon joyous, enthusiastic and rapturous experiences which were brought about by singing and dancing. They followed a maxim of the *Tikuni Zohar* (The *Supplement to the Zohar*), which says:

"There are in heaven sacred places, Which open only by song and chant." (p. 45). The authority of the learned rabbis was seriously threatened by the new movement. Its doctrine, that man approached his Creator by exaltation and not by knowledge of the Torah, was apt "to undermine the very foundation of the time-honored hegemony of Jewish learning."[5] It was therefore natural that, as Ḥasidism spread, it should have met with opposition by orthodox rabbinism, for whom the letter of the Law was more important than the religious spirit of the *zaddikim*. The leaders of the opposition called themselves *"Mitnaggedim"* (opponents). They poured on the Ḥasidim their venomous hatred and fought them with all conceivable means such as "accusing them of pantheism, even of paganism, excommunicating them, and burning their books."[6] It accounted to a complete schism of the two groups. The intolerance went so far that orthodox rabbis even informed against one of Besht's successors, the gentle and beloved Ḥasidic teacher Shneor Zalman (1747-1813), who was twice taken in chains to St. Petersburg (in 1798 and 1800) where he was labeled a dangerous "revolutionary," but each time was released as harmless. It was a sad example of Jewish dissension and of the narrow-mindedness of the rabbinical clan that could not understand the high spiritual values inherent in Ḥasidism. Zalman's release was a complete vindication for the Ḥasidic movement, which now spread to even wider regions.

But even among the Ḥasidim themselves there was a cleavage: North against South. In the Ukraine, in such places as Podolia, Volhynia, Galicia, Bukovina and northern Hungary, where the majority of the Jews lived in small villages, entire communities were attracted by Ḥasidism. Everywhere Ḥasidic prayer-houses were erected with services differing from that of rabbinic Judaism. They followed the approach of Besht to faith with its ecstasies, evoked by singing, dancing, bodily movements, even shouting in exaltation. In the north, Lithuania and White Russia, where the bulk of the Jews lived in larger cities, the movement spread only sporadically at the beginning, and its adherents remained for a longer period no more than sectarians. There a system came into being called *Ḥabad Ḥasidism,* a term formed by the first letters of *Ḥokmah,* (wisdom), *Binah,* (understanding), and *De'ah* (knowledge). It was a rational approach to the essence of Ḥasidism, in contrast to the exclusive emotionalism of the followers of BESHT.

The Ḥabad group was often characterized as "mystical intellectualism"; but for both factions singing and dancing as "the ladder to the throne of God," were supreme manifestations of faith. In the religious practice of the Ḥasidim the Biblical term *niggun* acquired a new meaning. In Ḥasidic thinking, the *niggunim* were considered as the purest form of achieving the "Outpouring of the Soul" (*hishtaphut ha-nefesh*), leading the worshippers into the higher spheres which were closer to the Creator.

One of the beliefs of the Ḥasidim was that old songs "from yesterday" lost their effectiveness and new songs should continually be created, because these would rejuvenate the world. There lived in almost every Jewish town, often even in villages, musically gifted amateurs who excelled in the creation of new melodies, especially for the High Holidays, and also for the rabbi's table. Nearly all the courts of the Ḥassidim had their own "court composer," whose *niggunim* and *zemirot* enjoyed wide popularity, particularly if, as in some cases, the *zaddik* himself was the "composer." These songs were picked up by the numerous visitors and brought back to their own communities, thus making them known and famous throughout the land.

Through the methodical work of a number of compilers in the nineteenth century, when the Ḥasidic song was still alive, though in a second generation, a great number of these songs have been preserved in modern notation. IDELSOHN alone published 243 of them in his *Thesaurus,* others, among them GESHURI, collected great many, published in the *Ḥasidic Encyclopedia.*

From this wealth of material, we selected a few songs, which may be considered typical for the mood and spirit of Ḥasidism. It goes without saying that a few examples cannot give the true picture of the scope of ḥasidic music. But they can afford at least an insight into the inspirational power which erupted with elementary force from the depth of the emotional life of Ḥasidism.

The "lyrics" of most of the Ḥasidic melodies are meaningless syllables, such as "doi, doi, doi," "dam, dam, dam," "ba, ba, ba," "oi, oi, oi," and similar patterns, which were easily set to any melodic strain.

Sometimes, such syllables were interrupted by a "real" text, as for instance in the following example, in which the "oi, oi, oi" pattern is interrupted by the words *mazol tov* (good luck).

Mus. ex. No. 46

Ḥasidic song (After Idelsohn, Thesaurus, X, No. 25).

The following example starts with a "text," *Shir hamaalos* (Song of the Degrees), which is but the heading of Psalms 120-134. The composer's addition, *"mit hispalos"* (the Hebrew *hitpalut* in the Polish-Ashkenazic spelling), meaning "with exalta-

Mus. ex. No. 47

Shir hamaalos. Ḥasidic song (After Idelsohn, Thesaurus, X. No. 58).

tion," or "fervor," refers to the "degree" of the emotional uplift manifested while singing the song. The rest of the "text" is filled in with the stereotyped "ai, ai, ai" formula. Furthermore, this example is characteristic for its syncopated rhythm, not uncommon among Ḥasidic songs. The "downbeats" of the melody are mostly rests, which were evidently marked by clapping the hands, indicating that the song may have been danced at the same time.

The following example is characterized by IDELSOHN as one of the "caricatures of a Ḥasidic song." There seems to be no evident reason why IDELSOHN considered this song to be a caricature. It has a regular text, admonishing the participants to *"sha shtil"* (be quiet), because the Rebbe is going to dance, and inviting the onlookers to *"lomir alle plisken mit di hent"* (let us all clap hands).

Mus. ex. No. 48

Sha, shtil

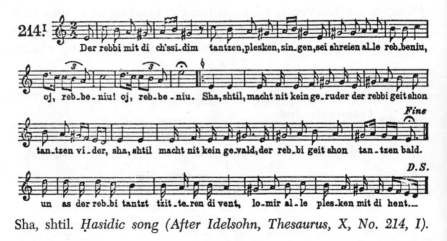

Sha, shtil. *Ḥasidic song (After Idelsohn, Thesaurus, X, No. 214, I).*

Sometimes a *niggun* had a "title," such as in the following example composed by the Rebbe ḤAYYIM of KRASNA, *" ʾAdir hu"* (Mighty Is He). The compiler failed to indicate how the lyrics of the poem were applied to the melody.

Mus. ex. No. 49

ʾAdir Hu ("*Mighty is He*"). *Ḥasidic song by the Rabbi Ḥayyim of Krasna (After Ḥasidic Encyclopedia, (VII, p. 121).*

The following *niggun* was composed by the famous Rebbe SHLOMO of KARLIN. The "text" was probably the stereotyped formula "oi, oi, oi."

Mus. ex. No. 50

Niggun *by the Rabbi Shlomoh of Karlin (After Ḥasidic Encyclopedia, VII, p. 161).*

In some cases, *niggunim* used words of Hebrew hymns, such as in the following example, whose lyrics are taken from the famous medieval *piyyut*, *"Yah Ribbon 'Olam"* (God of the Universe).

Mus. ex. No. 51

Yah Ribbon 'Olam *("God of the Universe")*, Niggun Mizrahi *(After Ḥasidic Encyclopedia, VII, p. 45).*

The following *niggun* from the Ukraine also used words from a *piyyut*, composed in the seventh century by the Hebrew poet

"V-'kol ma'aminim" ("And all believe. . .")

Mus. ex. No. 52

V'kol ma'aminim ("And all believe . . ."), Niggun from the Ukraine
(After Ḥasidic Encyclopedia, VII. p. 447).

YANAI. The poem (with other musical settings, of course) is part
of today's New Year's Additional (Musaf) service.

The following melody of the Ḥabad-Ḥasidim, called "Dem
Rebben's Niggun" (The Rebbe's Tune), is ascribed to SHNEOR
ZALMAN of LADI.

Mus. ex. No. 53

Ḥasidic song of the Ḥabad-Hasidim, called Dem Rebben's Niggun
("The Rebbe's Tune"), ascribed to Shneor Zalman of Ladi (After Idelsohn, p. 422).

IDELSOHN gives an "analysis" of this *niggun,* applying all the artifices of hermeneutics for his purpose. At the beginning of the melody he discovers "the outpouring of the soul"; beginning with the fifth bar, he sees the "spiritual awakening"; the third part, beginning with the ninth bar, "reaches the stage of ecstasy"; while the fourth part, from the thirteenth bar on, presents the stage of the "disembodied soul."[7] With all interest that Ḥasidic *niggunim* represents for the musical observer, and even taking into account IDELSOHN's understandable enthusiasm for Ḥasidic music, such dissecting of a simple folk melody is like overshooting a near target with a big gun.

It is significant that the Ḥasidic *niggunim* were sung exclusively by men. This rule, however, did not apply to *zemirot,* for whose performance—in the intimacy of the family circle—women, and even children participated.[8]

The Ḥasidic song strongly influenced the *ḥazzanut* of the Eastern Ashkenazim. The *ḥazzanim* of Poland, Lithuania and other districts where Ḥasidic singing was practiced, were under the spell of the *niggunim,* which they heard daily about them. The *ḥazzanic* manner of singing, and even more so, the melodies which they were able to write down, were imbued with the spirit of the Ḥasidic song far into the nineteenth century. In the published compositions of such nineteenth-century *ḥazzanim* as NISSI BELZER (NISSON SPIVAK), ZEIDEL ROVNER (JACOB SAMUEL MARGOWSKY), and others, it is easy to discover the same mood that permeated the Ḥasidic song. In their own creations, the nineteenth-century *ḥazzanim* could not help but infuse the peculiar style of the Ḥasidic *niggunim.*

A special place among the achievements of Ḥasidic art must be assigned to the dance. The Ḥasidic dance is unlike any other Jewish dance manifestations. It has a strong rhythmical impact and, because it was accompanied mostly by appropriate melodies, a special type of *niggunim* developed, which came to be known as the Ḥasidic dance-song. The dances combined spontaneity with profound inner exaltation and were mainly improvised by the dancers, who represented their individual ecstatic experiences, either alone or in groups, without any intention to show off or to entertain before spectators.

Ḥasidic dances began slowly, and gradually became faster until they climaxed in a state of ecstasy, where a flowing together of all senses and faculties was attained.[9]

The following *niggun,* with its lively rhythmical pattern, may be classified as a typical dance song. It was composed by the Rebbe Mordechai of Korshow (or Koristishow), surnamed "the Righteous." It was probably accompanied by clapping the hands.

Mus. ex. No. 54

Ḥasidic dance song, by Rebbe Mordechai of Korshow (or Koristishow), surnamed "The Righteous." (After Ḥasidic Encyclopedia, VII, p. 362).

The great-grandson of Besht, R. Naḥman of Bratzlav (1771-1811), taught his followers that every part of the body had a rhythm of its own: "as the melody brings out the beauty in poetry, the dance brings it to a climax."[10]

There were special dances for the Sabbath. Among the BESHT Hasidim it was usual that on Friday afternoon the entire village would go out, singing and dancing, to welcome the Queen Sabbath (see also p. 404).

During the ceremonial procession of the feast of *Simhat Torah*, the rebbe used to dance with the Torah scroll. Wrapped in his *tallit* (prayer shawl), carrying the Torah "close to his heart," the rebbe poured out his ecstatic feelings in a rapturous dance, while his followers formed a circle around him, singing appropriate dance songs and clapping their hands rhythmically. A typical *Simhat Torah Niggun* follows.

Mus. ex. No. 55

Simchas toroh niggun

Simḥat Torah Niggun *(After Idelsohn,* Thesaurus, X, *No. 199).*

Just as their division into two heterogeneous groups amounting to the difference between the Northern and Southern Hasidim, so also the style of their dancing showed marked dissimilarities. The "rationalists" in the North performed their dances in a rather stately, more refined mood, while the dances in the South had greater vigor, abandon, and frequent pantomimic features.

In some instances the Hasidic dancers indulged in a rather curious custom. The followers of the famous ẓaddik, R. AARON KARLINER (d. 1792), used to roll on the ground in dance rhythm each morning before the *Shaharit* service. They were called *"Kullyikes"* (Rollers) and were highly praised by the congregation for their devoted and saintly practice. At first Ḥasidic dances were performed only in the prayer-houses; but later such dances took place outside the synagogues for varied occasions, such as weddings, circumcisions, or even in commerorating the anniversary of a beloved *zaddik*. Ḥasidim who emigrated to Palestine danced annually at the grave of R. SIMEON ben YOHAI, supposedly the author of the "*Sefer ha-Zohar*," and, thereby, the first "prophet" of the Cabala.

As long as the struggle between rabbinism and Ḥasidism continued, both factions differed in their approach to religion. The former gave prime importance to dogma and ritual, and the latter to sentiment and emotion. Little by little reason prevailed on both sides and the established enmities were mitigated, especially when Ḥasidim and Mitnaggedim began to intermarry. But it was not until the middle of the nineteenth century when the intrinsic value of Ḥasidism was recognized, and unfortunately this came at a time when the movement was already on the decline. Only then were the poetic and artistic potentialities of Ḥasidism appreciated, and from then on a great number of writers, religious and secular, attempted to interpret the momentous spiritual revolution that had exerted such a powerful influence upon the religious and social life of the Eastern Ashkenazim.

The most profound and most thorough-going evaluation of the tenets and ethics on Ḥasidism may be found in our century in the writings of MARTIN BUBER who, better than anybody else, has delved into the very depths of Ḥasidism and whose lucid penetration of this unique phenomenon paved the way for the recognition of this type of Jewish revelation.[11]

BUBER sets forth cogently the driving forces which led to the emergence of Ḥasidism: "In an otherwise not very productive century . . . the Polish and Ukrainian Jews brought forth the greatest phenomenon in the history of the spirit, greater than any individual genius in art and in thought: a society that lived by its faith."[12]

Ḥasidism was the last original creation of the Jewish people in general and of their musical genius in particular. As long as it lasted, Ḥasidism was a victorious and overwhelming experience in Jewish life. Its beliefs and rituals, its saints and their courts with their followers, its mystic grandeur and rapturous enchantment belong to a world that passed into oblivion. Two World Wars wiped out the last vestiges that might have survived the decline of the once flourishing movement. There might to this day exist some adepts of Ḥasidism, if only in the modernized form, in the United States and in Israel. The movement as such, however, is extinct, and what has remained is nothing more than the incentive for creative artisic expression in poetry, literature, drama, beaux-arts, and mainly in music and dance.

In all these fields, Jewish philosophy and thought, Jewish ethics, and not the least, Jewish religious practice, will be fertilized for a long time to come by the unique, cheerful and fervent conception, as Ḥasidism envisaged the relationship between God and man.

Thus comes to a close the highly eventful epoch of Jewish music history in the Middle Ages which, despite its reaching chronologically the revolutionary period of the eighteenth-century "Enlightenment," retained to the end many of the most distinctive marks of medievalism. Looked upon as a whole, it was an epoch which encompassed more than seventeen centuries of severe handicaps, terrible frustrations, alternate bloom and decay. And yet, it preserved the intrinsic force leading to final recovery. During this period, Jewish music was frequently on the brink of complete extinction. Nothing proves more conclusively the innate musical genius of this people who, despite this prolonged era of tribulations, clung tenaciously to "their" music, often for years on end, utilizing elements appropriated or adapted from the outside world, but imbuing them with a unique character of their own.

But just as most of the religious and secular institutions of the Hebrews were of foreign origin, adjusted to suit their own national needs, so their music, though greatly influenced by that of the environment, preserved obvious Jewish traits. And, just as the ghetto walls had prevented the ethnic and religious assimilation of the Jews within their host nations, so was their music surrounded by imaginary walls, which disappeared together with their enforced isolation.

It was no mean triumph for a minority to have kept alive the driving forces of musical creativity, which was exposed most of the time to every adversity. Not until they were able to come into their own again, did Jewish music revive, especially in Israel in the present century.

Notes

Introduction

1. Spengler, Oswald, *The Decline of the West*. Engl. transl. in one vol. (New York, 1939), p. 16.
2. How arbitrary this rigid time table "Antiquity, Middle Ages, Modern Times" is, becomes evident if we realize that by it the past is divided into three completely unlike sections as to their duration: the first covering hundred thousands of years, the second about a millennium, and the third about five centuries. (*Ibid.*, p. 16.)
3. *Ibid.*, p. 12.
4. Toynbee, Arnold, *Civilization on Trial* (New York, 1948), p. v.
5. *Ibid.*, *A Study of History*. Abridged Version (New York, 1957). 2 vols. II, pp. 171–72.
6. *Ibid.*, *Civilization on Trial*, p. 14.
7. *Ibid.*, p. 235.
8. *Ibid.*, p. 238.

Chapter 1

Eastern Settlements

1. *J.E.* I, 146.
2. T.B., *Shabbat* 20b.
3. T.B., *Shabbat* 58a.
4. T.B., *'Aboda Zarah* 38b; *Gittin* 67b.
5. T.Y., *Megillah* 74b.
6. *J.E.*, V, 292.
7. T.B., *Megillah* 32a; cp. T.B., *Shabbat* 106b; cp. Rash's commentary to the passage.
8. T.B., *'Arakin* 11b.
9. T.B., *Sanhedrin* 14a.
10. *Ibid.*
11. M., *Sukkah* V:4; M., *Middot* II:5; T.B., *Sukkah* 51a, b.
12. T.B., *Berakot* 30b, 31a.
13. *Ibid.*
14. T.B., *Ketubot* 16b; *Sanhedrin* 14a.
15. T.B., *Ketubot* 17a.

16. T.B., *Ḥagigah* 14b.
17. T.B., *Shabuʿot* 15b.
18. T.B., *Berakot* 14a.
19. T.B., *Soṭah* 48a.
20. T.B., *Sanhedrin* 101a.
21. T.Y., *Soṭah* IX:12 (15b).
22. T.B., *Soṭah* 48a.
23. T.B., *Giṭṭin* 7a.
24. T.B., *Pesaḥim* 85b; T.Y., *Pesaḥim* VII:11 (35b).
25. T.B., *Ḥullin* 91b.
26. *Ibid.*
27. *Ibid.*
28. Midrash, *Lamentations* III:23.
29. Midrash, *Song of Songs* VIII:13.
30. *Ibid.*, VIII:14, par. 1.
31. Midrash, *Lamentations (The Proems of the Sages)* XIV.
32. T.Y., *Soṭah* VII:2 (21c).

Western Settlements

1. DurantFaith, p. 365.
2. *Ibid.*, p. 364.
3. *Ibid.*, p. 356.
4. *Ibid.*, p. 359.
5. T.Y., *Ḥagigah* 76c; *Pesikta* (ed. Buber), f. 120b.
6. DurantFaith, p. 349.
7. *Ibid.*, p. 350.
8. *J.E.*, IV, 194.
9. Abrahams, p. 276.
10. DurantFaith, p. 374.
11. *Ibid.*, p. 382.
12. Moore, G. F., *Judaism in the First Centuries of the Christian Era* (Cambridge, Mass., 1927), I, 318.
13. T.B., *Megillah* 32b.
14. T.B., *Sanhedrin* 99b.
15. T.B., *Nedarim* 37a.
16. T.Y., *Shekalim* V:2 (48d).
17. *J.E.*, III, 537.
18. *Ibid.*, III, 538.
19. Comparative tables for Jewish accent-motives are to be found in *J.E.*, III, 540–46, and *Idelsohn*, pp. 44–46.
20. *J.E.*, III, 638.
21. T.B., *Berakot* 62a.
22. *Ibid.*
23. Komroff, Manuel, *The Contemporaries of Marco Polo* (New York, 1928), pp. 253–322.
24. Zunz, Leopold, *Die Ritus des synagogalen Gottesdienstes* (Berlin, 1859), p. 57.
25. Grünhut, Lazar, *Die Rundreise des R. Petachjah aus Regensburg* (Frankfurt a.M., 1904), sect. 18.

26. *SteinLiter,* (1905) p. 82.
27. Cf. Maimonides' Responsum on Music, *infra.*
28. Baron, Salo W., *A Social and Religious History of the Jews* (New York, 1937), 3 vols. I, p. 353.

Chapter 2

1. Sachs, Curt, *Geist und Werden der Musikinstrumente* (Berlin, 1929), Foreword.
2. T.B., *Soṭah* 48a.
3. T.B., *Pesaḥim* 111b.
4. Jastrow, Marcus, *A Dictionary of the Targumim, the Talmud Babli and the Midrashic Literature* (New York, 1943), I, p. 458.
5. M., *Kelim* XV: 6.
6. SachsHist, pp. 117–18.
7. Gur, Jehuda, *Hebrew Lexikon* (Tel Aviv, 1947), p. 66.
8. Midrash, Genesis XXIII:3.
9. T.B., *'Arakin* 10b.
10. *Ibid.*
11. M., *'Arakin* II:3.
12. T.Y., *Sukkah* V:6 (55c, d).
13. T.B., *'Arakin* 10b, 11a.
14. *Ibid.*
15. *Ibid.*
16. T.Y., *Sukkah* V:6 (55c, d).
17. M., *Tamid* V:6.
18. *Ibid.*
19. Yasser, Joseph, *The Magrephah of the Herodian Temple,* in *Journal of the American Musicological Society,* vol. XIII, (1960), Nos. 1–3, pp. 24–42.
20. Midrash, Genesis L:9.
21. SachsHist, p. 109.
22. Tosefta, *Shabbat* XIII.
23. To M., *Kelim* XV:6.
24. M., *Soṭah* IX:4; *Kelim* XV:6.
25. SachsHist., p. 289.
26. The Dura-Europos Synagogue, built around 245 c.e., discovered in Syria in November 1932, contains on its Westwall a fresco depicting "The Ark versus Paganism." This painting shows a destroyed pagan temple; strewn on the floor are some heathen ritualistic objects. Two of them evidently are musical instruments. One is easily recognizable as a long-necked lute, the only could be a sistrum or some shaking or rattling instrument. (Illustration in Erwin Goodenough, *Jewish Symbols in the Graeco-Roman Period,* New York 1964, vol. II, plate XII). Since all these objects were meant to be used in a heathen cult, the inclusion of these instruments into Hebrew musical relics is not warranted. The same is true for a mosaic found in the Monastery of the Lady Mary in Beth-Shean, showing a man playing the pipe to his dog. This mosaic originates about 567 c.e., and cannot likewise be considered a material relic of Hebrew music.

Chapter 3

1. *J.E.*, XI, 484.
2. *Ibid.*
3. *Ibid.*
4. *Ibid.*
5. *Ibid.*
6. DurantFaith, p. 371.
7. *Ibid.*
8. *Ibid.*
9. *J.E.*, XI, 489.
10. Baer, Yizḥak, *The History of the Jews in Christian Spain* (Philadelphia, 1961), I, p. 257.
11. Idelsohn, p. 112.
12. *J.E.*, IX, 121.
13. Cohen, Boaz, *The Responsum of Maimonides concerning music* in *Law and Tradition in Judaism* (New York, 1959), pp. 167–77.
14. Cohen, *op. cit.*, p. 168.
15. T.B., *Sanhedrin* 37a.
16. Cohen, *op. cit.*, p. 173.
17. *Loc. cit.*
18. Idelsohn, p. 126.
19. Cohen, *loc. cit.*
20. Baer, *op. cit.*, p. 65.
21. *Ibid.*, p. 64.
22. *Ibid.*, p. 65. Although it is not a part of Jewish history in Spain, the fate of R. MEIR of ROTHENBURG (1215–1293) is an illustration how the royal houses considered their Jews as valuable property. Under the pressure of persecutions in Germanic lands, R. MEIR escaped clandestinely in 1285, to go to Palestine. In the Lombardy he was recognized by a Jewish convert, who denounced him to the ecclesiastical authorities. He was apprehended and extradited to the Emperor RUDOLF of HABSBURG, who jailed him in the citadel of Ensisheim and asked a huge ransom for him. The Jews offered 20,000 marks, a considerable sum by monetary standards of those days, but this was not enough for such an illustrious prisoner. The small community probably could not raise more, and so R. MEIR languished seven years in prison until his death (1293). Even his body was still an object of value to the Emperor; fourteen years after his death the Emperor, who went down in history as "chevaleresque, wise, and pious," sold the body to the Jew SÜSSKIND of WIMPFFEN. According to a later source (Solomon Luria), R. MEIR forbade his community to pay any ransom for his release in order not to create a precedent that would lead to the imprisonment of other Jewish notables for purpose of extortion. This report does not conform to the fact that in the beginning R. MEIR was consoled by the hope of speedy release; later on he resigned to the thought that it was the will of God, whose ways were always just. Furthermore, it is unlikely that his community would not have tried the utmost to liberate this beloved rabbi, whose scholarship and authority were such that he was called the "Light of the Exile," *Me-ʾOr ha-Galut*, a distinction he shared only with Rashi and Rabbenu Gershom of Mayence (960–1040).

23. *J.E.*, XI, 495.
24. British Museum, Manuscript Or. 2227.
25. Abrahams, p. 179.
26. Millgram, Abraham E., *An Anthology of Medieval Literature* (New York, 1961), p. 54.
27. *Ibid.*, p. 67.
28. Menéndez Pidal, Ramón, *La epopeya Castellana a través da la literatura Española* (Buenos Aires, 1945), p. 166.
29. Avenary, Hanoch, *Études sur le Cancionero Judéo-Espagnol (XVIe et XVII siècles),* in *Sefarad,* (1960), vol. XX, pp. 377–394.
30. Danon, Abraham, *Recueil de romances Judéo-Espagnoles chantés en Turquie, avec traduction française et notes,* in *Revue des Études Juives* (1896), vol. XXXII, pp. 102–123, 263–275, vol. XXXIII (1986)m/, pp. 122–139, 255–268.
31. Katz, Israel J., *Toward a Musical Study of the Judeo-Spanish Romancero,* in *Western Folklore,* vol. XXI (Apr. 1962), pp. 83–91. See also Katz, Israel J., *Judeo-Spanish Traditional Ballads Collected in Jerusalem. An Ethnomusicological Study* (Los Angeles, University of California, 1967).

Chapters 4 and 5

1. Faral, Edmond, *Les jongleurs en France au Moyen Age* (Paris, 1910).
2. We possess historical records about such "puys" held in the Auvergne, in Picardie, in Artois, in the Champagne and in Normandie. One such "puys" is vividly described by Faral, *op. cit.,* p. 140 ff.
3. Faral, p. 307.
4. *Ibid.*, II, p. 23.
5. Chabaneau, Camille, *Les biographies des Troubadours en Langue Provençale* ... (Toulouse, 1885), p. 360.
6. Baron Salo Wittmayer, *A Social and Religious History of the Jews.* Second, enlarged edition (Philadelphia, 1958), 8 vols. VII, p. 204.
7. Schirman, Hayyim, *Yizhak Gorni, Meshorer Ibri mi-Provence* [A Hebrew Singer from the Provence], in *Orlogin,* III, pp. 91 ff. French translation in *Lettres Romanes,* III, pp. 180, 184.
8. Faral, pp. 160 ff.
9. *Ibid.*, p. 123.
10. Published in the Edition Kessner (11, verses 61–66), and in a more recent edition of Rutebeuf's works by Edmond Faral and Julia Bastin (Paris, Picard, 1960), II, p. 258.
11. The author is indebted for the translation by Prof. Stephen G. Nichols, University of California at Los Angeles.
12. Chabaneau, *op. cit.,* p. 193.
13. Ticknor, George, *History of the Spanish Literature* (Boston and New York, 1871), 3 vols. I, pp. 93 ff.
14. Abrahams, p. 396.
15. Menéndez Pidal, *op. cit.,* p. 98.
16. *Ibid.*, p. 62.
17. *Ibid.*, p. 64.
18. Baer, Fritz, *Die Juden im christlichen Spanien* (Berlin, 1936), 2 vols. I, p. 968.

19. Neumann, Abraham A., *The Jews in Spain. Their Social, Political, and Cultural Life during the Middle Ages* (Philadelphia, 1942), 2 vols. II, p. 224.
20. Jacobs, Joseph, *An Inquiry into the Sources of the History of the Jews in Spain* (London, 1894), p. 101.
21. Baer, I, p. 975.
22. *Ibid.*, I, p. 413.
23. *SteinLiter*, p. 104.
24. Gross, *Gallia Judaica*, p. 467.
25. Baer, *passim*.
26. Abrahams, p. 175.
27. Baer, I, p. 150.
28. Abrahams, p. 275.
29. Baer, p. 414.
30. *Ibid.*
31. *Ibid.*
32. Anglés, Higini, *Cantors und Ministers in den Diensten der Könige von Katalonien-Aragonien im 14. Jahrh.* In *Bericht über den musikwissenschaftlichen Kongress in Basel* (Leipzig, 1925), pp. 55–66.
33. Baer, I, p. 262.
34. Cf. Ibn Said, Manuscript 80, folios 25–26.
35. Al-Makkari, transl. by Gayangos, II. p. 117.
36. *U.J.E.*, III, 461.
37. Anglés, Higini, *Hispanic Musical Culture*, in *MQ* (Oct. 1940), vol. 26, No. 4, pp. 523–24.
38. Baer, I, p. 414.
39. *MenéndezPoesía*, p. 96.
40. *U.J.E.*, III, 462.
41. Jer. 9:16, 17, 19; Am. 5:16; M., *Mo'ed Katan* III:9; T.B., *Mo'ed Katan* 8a, 28b; *Nedarim* 66b.
42. Ribera, *La Música de las Cantigas* (1929), p. 144.
43. Baer, II, p. 160.
44. *Ibid.*
45. Ward, Mary, *A Medieval Spanish Writer*, in *Fortnightly Review*, vol. XX, new series (July-Dec. 1876), p. 809.
46. Menéndez, p. 326.
47. Quoted from JUAN RUIZ' works, ed. Ducamin, p. 281.
48. Farmer, p. 187.

Chapter 6

1. T.B., *Ketubot* 105a; T.Y., *Megillah* III:1 (73d).
2. M., *Tamid* V:1.
3. T.B., *Sukkah* 53a.
4. Baron, Salo W., *A Social and Religious History of the Jews* (1937), I, p. 290.
5. St. Augustine, *Sermo 374, 2*, in *PL*, XXXIX, 1667.
6. We follow here the outlines of H. G. Farmer's *History of the Arabian Music* (1929), pp. 10 ff.
7. See the author's *Music in Ancient Israel*, "The Nature of Oriental Song."
8. Farmer, p. 17.

9. Baer, Yiẓḥak, *op. cit.*, I, pp. 198, 202, 205.
10. 'Al-Mas'udi, *op. cit.*, vol. VIII, p. 90.
11. Farmer, p. 221.
12. We follow here, in its bare outlines, Werner and Sonne's investigations of medieval Jewish music theory, in *HUCA* (1941–1942).
13. T.B., *Shabbat* 31b.
14. Steinschenider, Moritz, *Hebräische Bibliographie*, VIII, p. 70, XIX, pp. 40 ff.
15. Sholem, Gershom G., *Major Trends in Jewish Mysticism* (New York, 1941), p. 134.
16. *Ibid.*

Chapters 7, 8, and 9

1. Zinberg, Israel, *History of Jewish Literature* (Vilna, 1929–37). II.
2. Graetz, Heinrich Hirsch, *History of the Jews* (Philadelphia, 1898). V, p. 195.
3. Zunz, Leopold, *Die Ritus des synagogalen Gottesdienstes geschichtlich entwickelt* (Berlin, 1859), p. 66; J.E., II, 191–93.
4. Rabinovitch, Israel, *Of Jewish Music*. Translated from the Yiddish by A. M. Klein (Montreal, 1952), p. 44.
5. Bäumker, Wilhelm, *Das katholisch-deutsche Kirchenlied* (Freiburg, 1883–1911), 4 vols. I, p. 6.
6. Chrysander, Friedrich, *Nachwort zu F.W. Arnold's "Lochamer Liederbuch,* in *Jahrbücher für musikalische Wissenschaft* (Leipzig, 1867), II, p. 231.
7. Epstein, A., *Die Wormser Minhagbücher* (Breslau, 1900), XIII.
8. *Sefer Ḥasidim*, ed. Freimann (Frankfurt a.M., 1924), p. 332.
9. *Ibid.*
10. *Ibid.*, p. 106.
11. Idelsohn, p. 133.
12. Avenary, Hanoch, *The Musical Vocabulary of Ashkenazic Ḥazzanim*, in *Studies in Biblical and Jewish Folklore* (Bloomington, Ind., 1960), pp. 194–95.
13. Strauss, Raphael, *Was Süsskint von Trimberg a Jew? An Inquiry into 13th Century Cultural History*, in *Jewish Social Studies* (Jan. 1948), No. 1, pp. 19–30.
14. ". . . *magister Burchardus hospitalis Sancti Egidii et Sancti Theoderici procurator, judaeo Suzkint nomine vendit particulam areae infine hujus hospitalis prope locum . . .*"
15. Von der Hagen, Friedrich, *Minnesinger* (Leipzig, 1938) IV, p. 537.
16. Among others: Israel Abrahams, *Jewish Life in the Middle Ages*, even *The Jewish Encyclopedia*.
17. Reprinted from Gustav Karpeles, *Jewish Literature and other Essays,"* Philadelphia, 1895). This is a very free adaptation of Süsskind's poem. For the sake of comparison, we quote here Kastein's translation from the Middle-High-German to today's language:

> *Da bin ich eines Toren Fahrt*
> *mit meiner Kunst gefahren!*
> *Die Herren geben mir nichts mehr—*
> *Die Höfe will ich fliehen.*
> *Ich will mir einen langen Bart*
> *lahn wachsen grieser Haare.*

Nach alter Juden Lebensart
will ich jetzt weiter ziehen.
Mein Mantel, der soll wesen lang,
tief unter einem Hute.
Demütiglich soll sein mein Gang,
und nie mehr sing ich höfischen Gesang
seit mich die Herren schieden von dem Gute.
(Josef Kastein, *Süsskind von Trimberg*, 1934, pp. 157–58).

18. His findings are published in the *"Jahrbücher für musikalische Wissenschaft"* (Leipzig, 1867), II. pp. 1–234.

19. Arnold could not reply to Chrysander's allegations, because he died three years earlier.

Chapter 10

1. The manuscript is in the Library of the Jewish Theological Seminary of America at New York. The reproduction and description of it can be found in the *"Catalogue of Hebrew Manuscripts in the Collection of Elkan Nathan Adler,"* No. 4096 (Cambridge, England, The University Press, 1921).

2. Werner, Eric, "The Oldest Sources of Synagogal Chant," in *Proceedings of the American Academy for Jewish Research* (New York, 1947), XVI, p. 227.

3. Friedlander, Arthur M., *Facts and Theories Relating to Hebrew Music* (London, 1924).

4. Werner, *op. cit., ibid.*

5. *Ibid.* Recorded in the collection *Israel Sings*, issued by the Hebrew Union College, Cincinnati, before 1947 (n.d.).

6. Werner, *op. cit., ibid.*

7. Published in *Anthology of Music. Hebrew Music* (Arno Volk Verlag, Köln, 1961, p. 9).

8. Golb, Norman, "Obadiah the Proselyte: Scribe of a Unique Twelfth-Century Hebrew Manuscript Containing Lombardic Neumes," in *The Journal of Religion*, XLV, No. 2 (April 1965). p. 153.

9. *"Who stood on Mount Horeb . . ."* The earliest notation of a *piyyut* melody. 12th century. In Hebrew, with a brief English abstract. In *Tatzlil* (1964, No. 4), pp. 5–9.

10. Recently, Avenary's assumption has been confirmed by Norman Golb. "Manuscript E. N. Adler 4096 *b* is written in an Eastern handwriting and on Egyptian paper and is, at the same time, provided with Lombardic neumes because it was written by 'Obadiah, the Norman proselyte, who was born and raised as a Christian in Italy, who learned how to write Hebrew in Bagdad and who finally settled in the land of the Nile, probably in its chief city of Fustāt-Misr, toward the middle of the 12th century." (See Norman Golb, *op. cit.*, ["'Obadiah the Proselyte: Scribe of a Unique Twelfth-century Hebrew Manuscript Containing Lombardic Neumes," in *Journal of Religion*, XLV (April, 1965), No. 2, pp. 153–156.] Another music page by the same 'Obadiah has been discovered by N. Allony in Genizah fragments.

11. The information about 'Obadiah's conversion is contained in the fragment of a prayerbook written by 'Obadiah himself, which is in the Genizah Collec-

tion of the Hebrew Union College at Cincinnati. The phenomenon of proselytism took place frequently throughout the eleventh and into the twelfth centuries (see Norman Golb, "A Study of a Proselyte to Judaism Who Fled to Egypt at the Beginning of the Eleventh Century" (in Hebrew), in *I. Ben-Zwi Memorial Volume* (Jerusalem, 1961), pp. 87–104.

12. Goitein, S. D., "Obadiah, a Norman Proselyte," in *The Journal of Jewish Studies*, IV (1953), pp. 74–84.

13. *Ibid.*

14. The popes themselves looked with equanimity upon the killing of thousands of Jews during the Crusades, without lifting a finger to check such savagery.

15. Scheiber, Alexander, "The Origins of (Obadiah, the Norman Proselyte" in *The Journal of Jewish Studies*, V, (1954) No. 1, p. 33.

16. Goitein, *op. cit.*, p. 82.

17. Adler, Israel, *Les chants synagogaux notés au 12me siècle (ca. 1103–1150) par Abdias, le Prosélyte Normand*, in *Revue de Musicologie* (Paris, 1965), vol. 51, No. 1, pp. 19–51; Adler, Israel, "Synagogue chants of the Twelfth Century. The Music Notations of (Obadiah the Proselyte, in *Ariel* (Jerusalem, 1966), No. 15, p. 27–41.

18. The "recto" and "verso" can easily be identified by the custos, a sign which anticipates the first note of the following line.

19. Avenary, Hanoch, "Genizah Fragments of Hebrew Hymns and Prayers set to Music (Early 12th century), in *The Journal of Jewish Studies*, vol. XIV, Nos. 3–4 (1966), pp. 80–104.

20. *Op. cit*, p. 91.

21. *Op. cit.*, p. 100.

22. *Op. cit.*, p. 102.

23. *Ibid.*

24. *Op. cit.*, p. 104.

25. Among others: "Hispanic Musical Culture from the 8th to the 14th centuries, in *MQ*, XXVI (Oct. 1940), pp. 494–528.

26. Werner, *op. cit.*, pp. 228 ff.

27. *Ibid.*, p. 230.

28. *Ibid.*, p. 231.

29. Monsignor Higinio Anglés, in a letter to the author, ventures the hypothesis that this motet might have been part of a dramatic production, an assumption which is very probable. In Italy of the Renaissance we know of similar anti-Jewish outbursts which were incorporated into dramatic plays (see below). Whether part of a play or not, however, the *"Kedushah-Motet"* does not thereby alter its manifestly anti-Jewish character.

30. One is the Hebrew manuscript from the thirteenth century, the *Codex Adler* (see Note 1 of this chapter), the other is contained in a fourteenth-century manuscript, the *Codex Shem* in the Parma Library (No. 74), also in Juan da Gara's *Mahzor Vitry* (publ. in Venice, 1587), p. 190. The Parma notation is reproduced in Solomon Sulzer's *Shir Zion* (Vienna, 1838, 1865), II, p. 257.

31. See pp. 306 ff.

32. In *MGWJ* (1937), No. 2, pp. 192–209.

33. Szabolcsi, Bence, "A Jewish Musical Document of the Middle Ages: the most Ancient Noted Biblical Melody," in *Semitic Studies in Memory of Immanuel Löw*. Ed. by Alexander Scheiber (Budapest, 1947), pp. 131–133.

34. Vol. I, mus. ex. 74, p. 70.
35. Fuks, Leib, *The Oldest Known Literary Document in Yiddish Literature (ca. 1382)*, (Leiden, 1957).
36. *Op. cit.*, p. XXVI.
37. *Op. cit.*, p. XXV.

Chapter 11

1. Idelsohn, p. 39.
2. *Ibid.*, p. 34.
3. *Ibid.*, p. 400.
4. Marcus, Jacob R., *The Jew in the Medieval World. A Source Book. 315–1791.* (Cincinnati, 1938), p. 242.
5. M., *Soṭah* IX:11.
6. T. B., *Soṭah* 48a.
7. J. E., XII, 656.
8. Idelsohn, p. 112.
9. Saminsky, Lazare, *Music of the Ghetto and the Bible* (New York, 1934), p. 39.
10. *Abrahams*, p. 148.
11. *Ibid.*
12. Loewe, Herbert, *Mediaeval Hebrew Minstrelsy. Songs for the Bride Queen's Feast.* Sixteen Zemiroth arranged according to the Traditional Harmonies by Rose L. Henriques (London, 1926), p. 125.
13. *Ibid.*, p. 1.

Chapter 12

1. *MGG*, pp. 235–36.
2. Marcus, Jacob R., *op. cit.*, p. 123.
3. Idelsohn, p. 171, 173. See also W. Tappert, *"Wandernde Melodien;* Berlin, 1890).
4. Emil Breslaur discovered a "strong" likeness between the opening strain of the *Kol Nidre* melody and the first five bars of Beethoven's string quartet in C sharp minor, Op. 131, in its sixth movement, "Adagio quasi un poco andante."
    It is unimaginable that Beethoven might have "heard" the *Kol Nidre* theme in a synagogue or elsewhere, since at the time of the creation of this quartet, in the last years of his life, he was completely deaf. It is quite obvious that a similarity, if there is one, which is very questionable, is nothing more than a coincidence.
5. Idelsohn, p. 116.
6. J. E., VII, 675.
7. Cp. Eric Werner's transcription of Benedetto Marcello's *Lekah Dodi* on p. 338.
8. The manuscripts of all these songs are preserved in the Library of the Jewish Institute of Religion in New York.
9. Incidentally, Johann Sebastian Bach used Luther's melody for one of his chorales.
10. Kaufmann, David, *R. Baruch, called Benedict, Arvil and his poem*, in *Ha-asif* (Warsaw, 1885), vol. II, p. 298.

11. Bachrach, Ya'ir Hayyim, *"Havat Ya'ir"* (Frankfurt a.M., 1699), p. 167b.
12. Zlichubar, Judah Leib, *"Shirei Yehudah"* (Amsterdam 5497 /1696/), p. 9a.
13. Avenary, Hanoch, *Neimah Maos-Zur ("The Melody of Maos-Zur")*, in *Tatzlil* (Haifa, 1967), pp. 125–128.
14. Fuks, Leib, *The Oldest Known Literary Documents of Yiddish Literature* (Leiden, 1957), p. XXV.
15. ———, *op. cit.*, p. XXVI.
16. ———, *Das Schemuel-Buch des Mosche Esrim Wearba* (Assen, 1961).
17. ———, *op. cit.*, p. 6.
18. *Ibid.*, p. 11.
19. Steinschneider assumed that the name of the town was rather Ancona than Antona (*Stein C. B.*, p. 935).
20. *Stein C. B.*, No. 3634.
21. ———, p. 921.
22. ———, Nos. 3639, 3040, 3686.

Chapter 13

1. See Friedrich Chrysander, "Postscript to F. W. Arnold's Locheimer Lieder-buch," in *Jahrbücher für musikalische Wissenschaft* (Leipzig, 1867), II, p. 231.
2. It has been speculated that Böschenstein was of Jewish descent (See Lazare Saminsky, *Music of the Ghetto and the Bible*, New York, 1934, p. 196). This fact, however, cannot be established beyond doubt.
3. In Johannes Reuchlin's *Hebrew Grammar* (Hagenau, 1518).
4. In Abraham ben Meír Balmes' Grammar *Mikne Abram,* (publ. in Venice, 1523).
5. In his *Sefer Magen 'Abot* (publ. in Livorno, 1785).
6. In his *Shilte ha-Gibborim* (publ. Mantua, 1612).
7. See the facsimile of Böschenstein's Buch. Also of the tenor part and its transcription in modern notation.
8. *MGG*, p. 247.
9. *Ibid.*
10. The story how this important literary product came into being is told in this author's *Bibliography of Jewish Music*, pp. XXXI-XXXII.
11. *SteinLiter*, (1965), p. 208.
12. See Note 10.
13. There are four pages of musical examples, which are partially transcribed in modern notation in Idelsohn, *Thesaurus*, vol. V. item 302.
14. For a modern transcription see Idelsohn, *Thesaurus*, vol. VII, p. 106.
15. Partially transcribed in Idelsohn, *Thesaurus*, vol. VII, p. 107.
16. *Idelsohn*, p. 380.
17. In *Musica Hebraica* (Jerusalem, 1938), pp. 28–31.
18. It is reproduced in Idelsohn, *Thesaurus*, vol. VI, p. 234.
19. See Eric Werner, "The Eduard Birnbaum Collection of Jewish Music," in *HUCA* (1943–44), XVIII, pp. 397–428.
20. *Idelsohn*, p. 218.
21. *Ibid.*, p. 219.
22. *Ibid.*, p. 220 ff.

Chapter 14

1. Winkler and Zimmern, *Die Keilinschriften und das Alte Testament* Berlin, 1903, pp. 194, 196, 198.
2. T. B., *Baba Meẓiah*, 93b; *Ketubot* 8b; *'Arakin* 6b.
3. T. Y., *Berakot* IV (7d).
4. *Maccabees* III:12; cp. T. Y., *Sanhedrin* V (23a).
5. M., *Tamid* V:3; *Yoma* VII:1.
6. M., *Soṭah* VII:7–8; T. Y., *Soṭah* VII (21d); T. Y., *Megillah* IV, 15b (75b).
7. T. Y., *Ma'aser Sheni* (56a).
8. Tosefta, *Bikkurim* II:101.
9. M., *Shabbat* I:3; see Maimonides' commentary.
10. G. B. de Rossi, *Roma sotterranea* (Rome, 1877), III, p. 159.
11. Mgr. P. Batiffol, *History of the Roman Breviary* (London-New York, 1912), p. 34 ff.
12. T. Y., *Yebamot* (13a).
13. Baron, Com (1942), II, p. 140. For further relevant facts about the ḥazzan's situation in the Middle Ages see Baron, Com (1942), II, p. 100–105.
14. Grad, p. 103.
15. Abrahams, p. 107.
16. *J. E.*, VI, 287.
17. *Tachkemoni-Maḳams* (ed. A. Leminka, Warsaw, 1899), XXIV, p. 220–227.
18. *Roth*, p. 282.
19. VII, p. 676.
20. *J. E.*, IX, 130.
20a. Idelsohn, p. 309.
21. *J. E.*, IV, 41.
22. Responsum No. 81.
23. Neumann, II, p. 160.
24. T. B., *'Arakin* 13b; *Yoma* 38a.
25. They were appropriately termed as "Flötsinger," "Saitbass," "Fagottbass," etc.
26. Idelsohn Thes, I, p. 16.

Chapter 15

1. Roth, pp. 274–75.
2. Ibid., p. 275.
3. Publ. before 1463.
4. Roth, pp. 176–77.
5. *Ibid.*
6. For a detailed description of this *divertimento* see Roth, pp. 277–78.
7. Roth, p. 278.
8. Ibid.
9. Roth, p. 279. A detailed description of Guglielmo's *"Trattato"* is given by Roth, pp. 279–80.
10. See the author's *"Music in Ancient Israel"*, Sect. VIII.
11. Otto Kinkeldey, "A Jewish Dancing Master of the Renaissance," in *Studies in Jewish Bibliography. In Memory of Abraham Solomon Freidus* (New York, 1929), pp. 344 ff.

12. *Op. cit.*, p. 349.
13. *Ibid.*
14. *Op. cit.*, p. 360.
15. Roth, p. 281.
16. *Ibid.*
17. *Roth*, p. 282.
18. "*Cornetto*," in the parlance of those times was the collective term for all the wind-instruments, just as today's jazz-musicians call their wind instruments "horns," whether they are trumpets, trombones, clarinets, saxophones, etc.
19. Roth, p. 213 note.
20. *Ibid.*, p. 284.
21. *Ibid.*
22. *Ibid.*, p. 285.
23. *Ibid.*
24. *Ibid.*, p. 286.
25. *Ibid.*, p. 287.
26. *SteinLiter*, (1905), p. 112.
27. G. O. Pitoni, *Notizia de' contrapuntisti e Compositori di musica* (Bibl. Vatic., Capp. Giul. I, No. 1 & 2).
28. Israel Adler, *The Rise of Art Music in the Italian Ghetto* (Brandeis University, 1964), p. 331.
29. *Roth*, p. 288.
30. *Ibid.*, p. 318 ff.
31. *Ibid.*, p. 289.
32. Alfred Einstein, *Salomone Rossi as Composer of Madrigals*, in *HUCA*, XXII, part 2 (1950–51), p. 388.
33. *Ibid.*, p. 389.
34. *Roth*, p. 289.
35. *Ibid.*
36. Einstein, *op. cit.*
37. Einstein, *op. cit.*, p. 383.
38. *Ibid.*
39. *Ibid.*, p. 390 ff.
40. *Ibid.*, p. 383.
41. *Roth*, p. 149.
42. *Ibid.*, pp. 42–43.
43. These rabbinical authorities were Ben Ziyyon Zarfati, [Judah] Leb Saraval, Baruch ben Samuel, Ezra da Fano, and Judah ben Moses [Saltaro] da Fano. Modena addressed his responsum to the last-named rabbi. For a complete English translation of Modena's responsum see *Grad*, pp. 146 ff.
44. Lazare Saminsky, *The Music of the Ghetto and the Bible* (New York, 1934), pp. 170–71. At least, Sulzer named the composer, Franz Volkert who, at that time, was conductor of the Leopoldstädter Theater in Vienna and had written the music to some 150 popular plays, all enjoying great acclaim at the Austrian metropolis.
45. *IdelJewMus*, p. 239.
46. See Gershon Ephros, "*Anthology*," vol. III, pp. 288–89.
47. See "*Neginot Schorr*," p. 85.
48. *Roth*, p. 299.

49. *Ibid.*
50. In the Library of the Hebrew Union College in Cincinnati.
51. *AdlerRise*, p. 326. One of the choral pieces is preserved; it was published in 1893 by Eduard Birnbaum.
52. ———, p. 352.
53. ———, pp. 349–360.
54. *Adler*, pp. 118, 120.
55. *Roth*, p. 318.
56. *Ibid.*, p. 316.
57. *Ibid.*, p. 318.
58. Eric Werner, *The Oldest Sources of Synagogal Chant*, p. 228.
59. *Roth*, p. 300. In a short article, published in MGWJ (1936, vol. 8, pp. 489–90), entitled *"Faresol nicht Peritsol,"* M. Gaster informs us that he saw this manuscript in the Library of Turin, but he did not cite the exact reference. The author, desirous to reproduce this siglum as a facsimile in the present study, wrote to the National and University Library of Turin for a photocopy. The director of the Library, Prof. Stelio Bassi, replied that there is not, nor ever was in the Library, a manuscript or a printed book by Peritsol (or Faresol), not even before the fire in the Library of 1904.
60. *Adler*, p. 48.
61. *Ibid.* p. 85.
62. *Ibid.* p. 86.
63. *Ibid.*, p. 111.
64. *Ibid.*, p. 111.
65. Ibid., p. 112.
66. *Ibid.*, p. 113.
67. *Ibid.*, pp. 132–133.
68. *Ibid.*, pp. 136–137.
69. *Ibid.*, pp. 138 ff.
70. *Adler*, II, pp. 77–172.
71. ———, pp. 130–131.
72. A collection of Hebraic songs of the Provence under the title *"Zemirot Yisrael"* was published by Jules Salomon and Mardochée Crémieux ca. 1887 in Marseille.
73. See the thorough description in *Adler* (pp. 166–188), as well as the musical analysis of the work (pp. 290 ff).
74. S. Kahn, *Thomas Platter et les Juifs d' Avignon*, in *REJ*, (Paris, 1892), pp. 81-96.
75. Martène et Durand, *Voyage littéraire de religieux Bénédictins de la Congrégation de Saint Maur* (Paris. 1717).
76. *Adler*, p. 162.

Chapter 16

1. This scene might perhaps be considered as the prototype of the Jews quarreling about religion in Richard Strauss' *Salome*, although Strauss himself may have not been aware of it.
2. The Jewish traditional salutation *Baruch ha-ba* (Blessed be he who comes).

This gave the title to a famous anti-Jewish Italian comedy of the eighteenth Century (Roth, p. 295).

3. The text is written in the Venetian dialect, intermingled with corrupted Hebrew words. The author is indebted to Prof. Carlo L. Golino of the University of California for the translation.

4. Betell is the corruption of the Hebrew *Beth-El*, "the House of God"!

5. Roth, p. 295.

6. *Ibid.*

Chapter 17

1. *J. E.*, V, 652.
2. Abrahams, p. 81.
3. RothVen, p. 53.
4. *J. E.*, V, 652.
5. Abrahams, p. 90.
6. *Ibid.*, p. 405.
7. *U. J. E.*, III, 458.
8. *Ibid.*, III, 461.
9. RothVen, p. 200.
10. Roth, p. 300.
11. *Ibid.*, p. 13.
12. *Ibid.*, p. 27.
13. RothVenice, p. 217.
14. Roth, p. 36.
15. *Ibid.*, p. 60.
16. *Ibid.*, p. 269.
17. AdlerRise, p. 345.
18. RothVenice, p. 150.
19. Roth, p. 303. About the Academy see also Cecil Roth, *L'Accademia musicale nel Ghetto Veneziano*, in *Rassegna mensile*, III, No. 4, pp. 152–162.
20. Adler, p. 82.
21. RothVenice, p. 237.
22. *Die Memoiren der Glückel von Hameln*, ed. by D. Kaufmann, (Frankfurt a.M., 1896).
23. David Kaufmann, *A Contribution to the History of the Venetian Jews*, in JQR, II (1890), p. 198.
24. Eric Werner, *"Die hebräischen Intonationen in B. Marcellos Estro poetico-armonico,"* in *MGWJ*, LXXXVI (Nov.-Dec., 1937), pp. 393–416.
25. A thorough musical analysis of this composition has been made by Israel Adler, *La pratique musicale* . . . pp. 89–109.
26. RothVenice, p. 200.
27. Roth, p. 304.
28. *Ibid.*
29. *Ibid.*, p. 274.
30. Tal. Bab., *Sanhedrin* 101 a.
31. To Tal. Bab., *Baba Kamma* 86 a.
32. J. Zinberg, *The History of Jewish Literature* (Vilna, 1929–1937), vol. VI, pp. 270–271.

33. RothVenice, p. 317. As a contrast to this liberal attitude, it should be mentioned that one of the remaining enclaves of isolated Jewish groups, on the Island of Djerba in the Mediterranean, music is altogether banned in the services. At Hara Saghira, a sacred place of pilgrimage, even the mere presence of a musical instrument is not tolerated. Robert Lachmann reports the amusing story that the old-fashioned Edison phonograph used by him for recording was mistaken by the inhabitants for an instrument on account of its horn. The synagogue authorities had to be consulted; their verdict was that on payment of a fee for expiatory prayers, the machine may be used (R. Lachmann, *Jewish Cantillation and Song in the Isle of Djerba*. (Jerusalem, 1940).

34. Abrahams, p. 96.

35. A. Berliner, *Aus dem Leben der deutschen Juden im Mittelalter* (Berlin, 1900), p. 54.

36. Schudt, *op. cit.*, p. 71.

37. Anton Margarite's report in *Mitteilungen zur jüdischen Volkskunde*, 1900, p. 60.

38. Idelsohn, p. 509.

39. A mysterious audience with the Emperor Rudolph II in the Hradshin gave rise to the rumor that Rabbi Löw performed miracles before the Emperor.

40. Paul Nettl, *Alte jüdische Spielleute und Musiker* (Prague, 1923), p. 38.

41. *Ibid.*

42. Cp. the analogy in Spain, where the *juglares* employed woman singers and dancers.

43. Albert Wolf, *Fahrende Leute bei den Juden* (Leipzig, 1909), p. 53 ff.

44. Boaz Cohen, *Law and Tradition in Judaism* (New York, 1959), p. 177.

45. Idelsohn, p. 457.

46. Abrahams, p. 106.

47. Abraham Berliner, *op. cit.*, p. 62.

48. P. Chr. Kirchner, *op. cit.* (see Illustr. No. 41).

49. Schudt, *op. cit.*, vol. IV, chap. 2, p. 159.

50. "*Jüdisches Frankfurter und Prager Freundenfest*" (Frankfurt a.M., 1716).

51. BaronCom, (1942), II, p. 119.

52. Marcus, p. 195.

53. Isidore Loeb, *Les Juifs de Carpentras*, in *REJ*, vol. XII, p. 230.

54. *MGG*, p. 245.

55. Marcus, p. 212.

56. *Ibid.*, p. 213.

57. *Ibid.*, p. 86.

58. K. Anklam, *Die Judengemeinde in Aurich* (Frankfurt a.M.,n.d.).

59. Meyer Kayserling, *Die jüdischen Frauen in der Geschichte, Literatur und Kunst* (Leipzig, 1879), p. 319.

60. SteinCB, 3673.

61. SteinLiter (1965), p. 247.

62. *Ibid.*

63. Julius Lewy, "*The Feast of the 14th Day of Adar*," in *HUCA*, XIV, (1939), p. 146.

64. *Ibid.*, p. 131.

65. "The woman shall not wear that which pertaineth unto a man, neither shall man put on a woman's garment" (Deuter. 22:5).

66. Abrahams, p. 33.
67. T. B., *Sanhedrin* 64 b.
68. Louis Ginzberg, "Genizah-Studies," in *JQR*, XVI, (1903–1904), p. 650.
69. *U.J.E.*, III, pp. 458.

Chapter 18

7. M. J. Landa, *The Jews in Drama* (London, 1926), p. 23.
2. N. Bentwich, *Hellenism* (Philadelphia, 1918), p. 137.
3. Clement of Alexandria and Eusebius of Caesarea have preserved numerous fragments of this work. These fragments are included in a collection of ancient manuscripts entitled *Poetae Christiani Graeci*. A Latin translation exists in the Bibliothèque Nationale, Paris.
4. T. B., *'Abodah Zarah* 18b.
5. Robert H. Pfeiffer, *Introduction into the Old Testament* (New York, 1941), p. 715.
6. This theory was refuted in this author's *"Music in Ancient Israel"*, sect. VIII.
7. Moritz Steinschneider, *Purim und Paradie* (Frankfurt a.M., 1903).
8. T. Y., *Shabbat* VI:8 (Vilna ed. p. 76).
9. T. B., *Shabbat* 66b.
10. It was mentioned above (p. 335) that Leone Modena dedicated his Italian adaptation of the play to Sara Coppio Sullam.
11. According to modern research, the author of *Yessod 'Olam* was not Moses Zacuto, but presumably Leone de' Sommi (See J. Schirmann, *Eine hebräisch-italienische Komödie des XVI. Jahrhunderts*, in *MGWJ* (1931), vol. 75 (n. s. vol. 39), p. 109.) This assumption is corroborated by the fact that de' Somi wrote a number of theatrical plays in Italian and had his own Jewish theatrical company in Mantua (*Roth*, p. 255 ff). For an analysis of *Yessod 'Olam see Abrahams*, p. 190 ff.
12. Abrahams, p. 286.
13. *Ibid.*
14. Abrahams, p. 286 ff.
15. A great number of other *Purim* plays, comedies and dramas in Judaeo-German, Hebrew and Arabic are listed in Moritz Steinschneider's *"Purim und Parodie"* (Frankfurt a.M., 1903).
16. Roth, p. 254.
17. Roth, p. 261.
18. J. Schirmann, *op. cit.*, p. 116.
19. S. A. Hirsch, *Book of Essays* (London, 1905), p. 272.
20. Ernest David, *Les opéras du Juif Antonio José da Silva*, in *Archives Israélites* (Paris, June 1876), p. 440.
21. Cecil Roth, *A History of the Marranos* (Philadelphia, 1947), pp. 165–67.
22. Webster's *Biographical Dictionary* (Springfield, Mass., 1966, p. 1364), asserts that Antonio's mother and wife were burned together with him at the stake. This statement is manifestly based upon a mistranslated passage of a German article by Dr. M. Grünwald in *MGWJ* (1880, vol. XXIX, pp. 241–257). It was taken over uncritically by the *Encyclopedia Americana*. The *Jewish Encyclopedia* (XI, 324–43) states that, according to some authorities, Antonio's wife survived her husband by several months. Besides, there is a bizarre (and spurious) statement in the *Universal Jewish Encyclopedia* (IX,

536): "For the purpose of dissipating the rumors that he still adhered to Judaism, Antonio joined the Franciscan Order." Such a step, if carried out, would have automatically thwarted Antonio's execution.

Chapter 19

1. DurantLouis, p. 501.
2. *Ibid.*, p. 457.
3. Meyer Kayserling, *Die Geschichte der Juden in Portugal* (Leipzig, 1867), p. 320.
4. Meyer Kayserling, *Sephardim* (Leipzig, 1859), p. 285.
5. *Ibid.*, p. 253.
6. Adler, p. 197.
7. DurantLouis, p. 472.
8. *Ibid.*, p. 461.
9. Salo W. Baron, *The Jewish Community* (Philadelphia, 1942), vol. III, p. 150.
10. Adler, p. 193.
11. *Ibid.*, p. 196.
12. Arthur Schurig, *Leopold Mozart. Reiseaufzeichnungen 1763–1771* (Dresden, 1920), p. 30.
13. Adler, p. 195.
14. His autobiography, however, does not mention any sojourn in London.
15. Adler, p. 208.
16. *Ibid.*, p. 209.
17. *Ibid,* p. 205.
18. *Ibid.*, p. 238.

Chapter 21

1. *U. J. E.*, III, 471.
2. Cp. the legend of the Golem, a human figure of clay, which came to life when a piece of parchment with the letters of the Ineffable Name was put into its mouth.
3. *U. J. E.*, V, 237.
4. Gershom G. Scholem, *Major Trends in Jewish Mysticism* (New York, 1941), p. 346.
5. *U. J. E.*, III, 462.
6. Idelsohn, p. 413.
7. *Ibid,* p. 419.
8. A veritable treasure of Ḥasidic songs is to be found in Idelsohn's *Thesaurus,* vol. X. It contains no less than 243 Ḥasidic tunes (plus seven melodies from old manuscripts).
9. *J. E.*, III, 458.
10. *Ibid.*
11. Especially in his *Tales of Rabbi Nachman,* transl. from the German by Maurice Friedman (New York, 1956), and *The Origin and Meaning of Ḥasidism,* edited and translated by Maurice Friedman (New York, 1960).
12. Martin Buber, *"The Origin and Meaning of Ḥasidism"* (New York, 1960), p. 27.

Bibliography

Aaron ben Mosheh ben Asher, *Dikduke ha-ta'amim* (c. 900) (1st ed. *Grammatica Hebraea de accentibus,* Venice, 1515).

Abraham ben Meïr Balmes, *Mikne Abram* (Venice, 1523).

Abrahams, Israel. *Jewish Life in the Middle Ages.* New edition enlarged and revised on the basis of the author's material by Cecil Roth (London, Edward Goldston, 1932), XXII, 478, illustr.

Ackermann, Aron. *Der synagogale Gesang in seiner historischen Entwicklung.* In: Winter und Wünsche, *Die jüdische Literatur seit Abschluss des Kanons* (Berlin, M. Poppelauer, 1897). 3 vols. III, pp. 477–529.

Adler, Elkan Nathan. *Catalogue of Hebrew Manuscripts in the collection of Elkan Nathan Adler* (Cambridge, The University Press, 1921). XII, 228. Frontispiece, 25 tables.

Adler, Israel. *La pratique musicale savante dans quelques communautés juives en Europe aux XVIIe et XVIIIe siècles* (Paris, La Haye, Mouton & Co., 1966). 2 vols. 1. Text. 2. Music.

———. *Les chants synagogaux notés au 12me siècle* (ca. 1103–1150) par Abdias, le Prosélyte Normand. In: *Revue de Musicologie* (Paris, 1965), vol. 51, No. 1, pp. 19–51.

———. *The Rise of Art Music in the Italian Ghetto.* In: *Jewish Medieval and Renaissance Studies,* ed. by Alexander Altmann, pp. 321–364. (Harvard University Press, Cambridge, Mass., 1967).

———. *Synagogue Chants of the Twelfth Century. The Music Notations of 'Obadiah the Proselyte.* In: *Ariel* (Jerusalem, 1966), No. 15., pp. 27–41. Illustr., mus. ex.

Allony, Nehemyah. *Ha-Mahzor le-'Obadiah ha-Ger mi-Normandia.* In: *Sinai* (Jerusalem, 1965), No. 57, pp. 43–55.

———. *'Ovadiah ha-Ger mi-Normandia umahzoro.* In: *Ha-arez* (Tel-Aviv, 1965), No. 13, p. 947.

ʾAl-Masʿudi. *Livre des Prairies d'Or et des Mines de Pierres Précieuses*. Texte et traduction par C. Barbier de Meynard (Paris, L'Imprimerie Nationale, 1874), vol. VIII.

Ameisenowa, Zofja. *Eine spanisch-jüdische Bilderbibel um 1400*. In: *MGWJ* (Breslau, 1937). vol. 81, N.S. vol. 45, pp. 193–209, illustr.

Anglés, Higinio. *Cantors und Ministers (minstrels) in den Diensten der Könige von Katalonien-Aragonien im 14. Jahrh*. In: *Bericht über den musikwissenschaftlichen Kongress in Basel* (Leipzig, 1925), pp. 55–66.

———. *Hispanic Musical Culture from the 8th to the 14th centuries*. In: *MQ* (Oct. 1940), vol. 26, pp. 494–528.

Anklam, K. *Die Judengemeinde in Aurich* (Frankfurt a.M., M. J. Kauffmann, n.d.), 15 pp.

Apel, Willi, see Davison, Archibald T. and Apel Willi.

Arnold, Friedrich Wilhelm. *Das Lochamer Liederbuch*. In: *Chrysanders Jahrbücher für musikalische Wissenschaft* (1867), vol. II, pp. 1–234.

Aronstein, R.F. *Süsskind of Trimberg* [in Hebrew], in ZION (Jerusalem, 1943), April, No. 3., pp. 135–155.

Augustine, St. *Sermo 374, 2*, in *Patrologia Latina*, XXXIX, 1667.

Avenary, Hanoch. *Études sur le Cancionero judéo-espagnol (XVIe et XVIIe siècles*. In: *Sepharad* (1960), vol. XX, pp. 377–394.

———. *Genizah Fragments of Hebrew Hymns and Prayers set to Music*. In: *The Journal of Jewish Studies* (London, 1966), vol. XIV, Nos. 3–4, pp. 87–104, facsim., mus. ex.

———. *Geschichte der jüdischen Musik*. In: *MGG*, vol. VII, pp. 225–261.

———. *The Musical Vocabulary of Ashkenasic Ḥazzanim*. In: *Studies in Biblical and Jewish Folklore* (Bloomington, Ind., 1960), pp. 194–95.

———. *Neimah Maos-Ẓur (The Melody of Maos-Ẓur)* [In Hebrew]. In: *Tatzlil* (Haifa, 1967), pp. 125–28.

———. *"Who stood on Mount Horeb"* . . . *The earliest notation of a piyyut melody. 12th century*. [In Hebrew]. In: *Tatzlil* (Haifa, 1964), No. 4. pp. 5–9. Engl. abstract, p. 65. Illustr., mus. ex.

Bachrach, Yaʿir Ḥayyim. *Havat Yaʿir* (Frankfurt a.M. 1699). p. 167 b.

Baer, Fritz. *Die Juden im christlichen Spanien* (Berlin, Akademie Verlag 1936). 2 vols. I. Aragon und Navarra. II. Castile. Records of the Inquisition.

Baer, Yizhak. *The History of the Jews in Christian Spain*. (Philadelphia, 1961).

Baron, Salo Wittmayer. *The Jewish Community, its History and Structure to the American Revolution* (Philadelphia, The Jewish Publication Society of America, 1942), 3 vols.

———. *A Social and Religious History of the Jews* (New York, Columbia University Press, 1937), 3 vols.

———. *A Social and Religious History of the Jews*. Second edition, Revised and Enlarged. (Philadelphia, The Jewish Publication Society of America, 1958), 8 vols.

Bartolocci, Giulio de Celleno. *Bibliotheca magna rabbinica* (Rome, Typographia Sacrae Congregationis de Propaganda Fide, 1675–1693), 4 vols.

Batiffol, R. *History of the Roman Breviary* (London, New York, 1912).

Bäumker, Wilhelm. *Das katholisch-deutsche Kirchenlied*. (Freiburg i. B., 1883–1911), 4 vols. Appendices 1913.

Bellermann, J. Joachim, see Arnold, Friedrich Wilhelm, *Das Lochamer Liederbuch.*

Bentwitch, Norman de Mattos. *Hellenism*. (Philadelphia, The Jewish Publication Society of America, 1920). 386 pp.

Berliner, Abraham. *Das älteste bekannte dramatische Gedicht in hebräischer Sprache von Mose Sacut (1576–1642)* ... (Berlin, 1874).

———. *Aus dem Leben der Juden Deutschlands im Mittelalter* (New ed. Berlin, 1927). 104 pp.

———. *Beiträge zur hebräischen Grammatik im Talmud und Midrasch* (Berlin, 1879). 59 pp.

Binder, Abraham Wolf. *Jewish Music*. In: *The Jewish People, Past and Present*. (New York, Jewish Encyclopedia Handbooks, 1952), vol. 3, pp. 324–376.

Blume, Friedrich, ed. *Die Musik in Geschichte und Gegenwart* (Kassel, Bärenreiter Verlag, 1949), 13 vols.

Buber, Martin. *The Origin and Meaning of Ḥasidism* (New York, Horizon Press, 1960).

———. *The Tales of Rabbi Nachman*. Transl. from the German by Maurice Friedman (New York, Horizon Press, 1956).

Chabaneau, Camille. *Les Biographies des Troubadours en Langue Provençale* ... (Toulouse, 1885), 204 pp.

Chrysander, Friedrich. *Nachwort zu F.W. Arnolds "Lochamer Liederbuch."* In: *Jahrbücher für musikalische Wissenschaft* (Leipzig, 1867). vol. II, pp. 231 ff.

Cohen, Boaz. *The Responsum of Maimonides concerning Music*. In: *Law and Tradition in Judaism* (New York, The Jewish Theological Seminary of America, 1959), XII, 243 p.

Danon, Abraham. *Recueil de romances judéo-espagnoles chantées en Turquie, avec traduction française, introduction et notes.* In: *REJ,* vol. XXXII (1896), pp. 102–123, 268–275, vol. XXXIII (1896), pp. 122–139, 255–268.

David, Ernest. *Les opéras du Juif Antonio José da Silva.* In: *Archives Israélites* (Paris, June, 1876).

———. *Sara Coppia Sullam.* In: *Archives Israélites* (Paris, June 1876), p. 440.

Davison, Archibald T., and Apel Willi. *Historical Anthology of Music* (Cambridge, Mass., Harvard University Press, 1946), 2 vols.

Dom. Devie, Claude and Dom. Vaisette, Jean Joseph. *Histoire générale de Languedoc* (Toulouse, 1885). Vol. X. *Biographies des Troubadours,* pp. 209–323.

Durant, Will. *The Age of Faith. A History of Medieval Civilization, Christian, Islamic, and Judaic—from Constantine to Dante.* (New York, Simon & Schuster, 1950). XVII, 1196 pp., illustr.

———. *The Age of Louis XIV* (New York, Simon & Schuster, 1963). XVIII, 802 pp., illustr.

Einstein, Alfred. *Salomone Rossi as Composer of Madrigals.* In: *HUCA* (1950–51), vol. XXIII, part 2, pp. 383–396, with mus. ex. of one of Rossi's madrigals.

Ephros, Gershon. *Cantorial Anthology of Traditional and Modern Synagogue Music* . . . (New York, Bloch Publ. Co., 1940–1952), 5 vols.

Epstein, Abraham. *Die Wormser Minhagbücher* (Breslau, S. Schottlaender, 1900), 30 pp.

Faral, Edmond. *Les jongleurs en France au Moyen Age* (Paris, Honoré Champion, 1910), X, 339 pp.

Faral, Edmond et Julia Bastin. *Les Oeuvres de Rutebeuf* (Paris, 1960).

Farmer, Henry George. *Historical Facts for the Arabian Musical Influence* (London, William Reeves, n.d.), XII, 376 pp.

———. *A History of Arabian Music to the XIIIth Century* (London, Luzac & Co., 1929), XV, 264 pp.

———. *Maimonides on Listening to Music.* From the *Responsa* of Moses ben Maimon (d. 1204) (Hartford, Conn., 1941).

Friedlander, Arthur M. *Facts and Theories Relating to Hebrew Music* (London, 1924), 16 pp., illustr., mus. ex.

Friedman, Lee M. *The first Printed Picture of a Jew.* In: *HUCA* (1950–51), vol. XXIII, part 2, pp. 433–448, illustr., bibliography.

Fuks, Leib. *Das altjiddische Epos Meloķim-Buķ* (Assen, Van Gorkum, 1965, 2 vols.

———. *The Oldest Known Literary Documents of Yiddish Literature* (ca. 1382). (Leiden, E.J. Brill, 1957), 2 vols.

———. *Das Schemuelbuch des Mosche Esrim Wearba* (Assen, Van Gorkum, 1961). (*Editio princeps*, Augsburg, 1544).

Fürst, Julius. *Bibliotheca judaica. Handbuch der gesamten jüdischen Literatur* (Leipzig, Wilhelm Engelmann, 1849–1863), 3 vols.

Geshuri, Meir Shimeon, ed. *Enzyķlopedia shel ha-ḥasidut* (Tel-Aviv, 7th vol., 1957). *Haniggun v'hariķud be-ḥasidut* (Music and dance in Ḥasidism), vols. 1–3.

Ginzberg, Louis. *Genizah-Studies.* In: JQR (1903–1904), XVI.

Goitein, S. D. *ʿObadiah, a Norman Proselyte.* In: *The Journal of Jewish Studies* (1953), vol. 4, pp. 74–84.

Golb, Naḥum. *Binyian ʿObadiah ha-Ger v'avodato hamusikologith.* In: *Tarbiz* (Jerusalem, 1965), vol. 35, pp. 81–83.

Golb, Norman. *ʿObadiah the Proselyte: Scribe of a Unique Twelfth-Century Manuscript Containing Neumes.* In: *The Journal of Religion* (Chicago, April 1965), vol. 45, No. 2, p. 153.

———. *A Study of a Proselyte to Judaism Who Fled to Egypt at the Beginning of the Eleventh Century.* In Hebrew. In: *I. Ben-Zwi Memorial Volume* (Jerusalem, 1961), pp. 87–104.

Gradenwitz, Peter. *The Music of Israel, Its Rise and Growth.* (New York, Norton 1949), 334 pp., illustr., mus. exs.

Graetz, Heinrich Hirsch. *History of the Jews* (Engl. ed.). (Philadelphia, The Jewish Publication Society of America, 1891–1896), 6 vols.

Gross, Heinrich. *Gallia Judaica* (Paris, 1897).

Grünhut, Lazar. *Die Rundreise des R. Petachjah aus Regensburg* (Frankfurt a.M., J. Kaufmann, 1904).

Güdemann, Moritz. *Das Jüdische Unterrichtswesen während der spanisch-arabischen Periode* (Wien, Carl Gerold's Sohn, 1873). vol. II, German part, 198 pp., Hebrew part, 62 pp.

Gur (Grasowski), Jehudah. *Milon ʾIbri* (Hebrew Lexicon). 2nd ed. (Tel-Aviv, 1947).

Hagen, Friedrich Heinrich, von der. *Minnesinger* (Leipzig, Joh. Ambros. Barth, 1838), 5 vols., facs., mus. exs.

Hanoch ben Abraham ben Yeḥiel. *Reshit Bikkurim* (written about 1650, printed 1708).

Hickmann, Hans. *Musicologie Pharaonique.* Études sur l'évolution de l'art musical dans l'Égypte ancienne (Librairie Heitz, Kehl am Rhein, 1956), 165 pp., illustr.

———. *Musikgeschichte in Bildern. Band II. Musik des Altertums. Ägypten.* (Leipzig, VEB Deutscher Verlag für Musik, 1961). 187 pp., 121 illustr., mus. ex.

Hirsch, S. A. *Book of Essays* (London, 1905).

Idelsohn, Abraham Zevi. *Collections of and Literature on Synagogue Song.* In: *Studies in Jewish Bibliography . . . In Memory of Abraham Solomon Freidus* (New York, The Alexander Kohut Memorial Foundation, 1929), pp. 388–403.

———. *Jewish Liturgy and its Development* (New York, Sacred Music Press, 1932), XIX, 404 pp.

———. *Jewish Music in its Historical Development* (New York, Henry Holt & Co., 1929), XIII, 535 pp., facs., mus. ex.

———. *Thesaurus of Oriental Hebrew Melodies* (Leipzig, Berlin, Vienna, Jerusalem, 1914–1932). 10 vols. Also in a German and Hebrew edition.

Jacobs, Joseph. *An Inquiry into the Sources of the History of the Jews in Spain.* (London, David Nutt, 1894), XLVII, 263 pp., illustr.

Jastrow, Marcus. *A Dictionary of the Targumim, the Talmud Babli, and the Midrashic Literature.* (New York, 1943).

(The) Jewish Encyclopedia, ed. Isidore Singer (New York and London, 1901–1906), 12 vols.

Joseph ben Judah ibn ʾAknin. *Tabb-al-nufus* (Recreation of the Soul), Chap. 27.

Kahn, S. *Thomas Platter et les Juifs d'Avignon.* In: *REJ* (Paris, 1892), pp. 81–96.

Karpeles, Gustav. *Jewish Literature and other Essays* (Philadelphia, The Jewish Publication Society of America, 1895).

Kastein, Josef. *Süsskind von Trimberg, oder Die Tragödie der Heimatlosigkeit* (Jerusalem, The Palestine Publishing Co., 1934), 185 pp.

Katz, Israel J. *Judaeo-Spanish Traditional Ballads Collected in Jerusalem. An Ethnomusicological Study.* (Los Angeles, University of California Press, 1967). 2 vols. Vol. I text, vol. II mus. exs.

———. *Toward a Musical Study of the Judaeo-Spanish Romancero.* In: *Western Folklore* (Berkeley and Los Angeles, April 1962), vol. XXI, No. 2, pp. 83–91, mus. ex.

Kaufmann, D[avid]. *R. Baruch, called Benedict, Arvil and his Poem.* In: *Ha-Asif* (Warsaw, 1885), vol. II, p. 298.

Kaufmann, David. *A Contribution to the History of the Venetian Jews.* In: *JQR* (1890), II, pp. 297–302.

—— ed. *Die Memoiren der Glückel von Hameln.* (Frankfurt a.M., J. Kaufmann, 1896).

Kayserling, Meyer. *Die Geschichte der Juden in Portugal.* (Leipzig, O. Leiner, 1867), XI, 367 pp.

——. *Die jüdischen Frauen in der Geschichte, Literatur und Kunst* (Leipzig, Brockhaus, 1879), VIII, 375 pp.

——. *Sephardim . . .* (Leipzig, H. Mendelssohn, 1859), XII, 370 pp.

Kinkeldey, Otto. *A Jewish Dancing Master of the Renaissance (Guglielmo Ebreo).* In: *Studies in Jewish Bibliography . . . In Memory of Abraham Solomon Freidus* (New York, The Alexander Kohut Memorial Foundation, 1929). CXXX, 518 pp.

Kirchner, Paul Christian. *Jüdisches Ceremoniell.* (Nürnberg, Peter Conrad Monath, 1726), 226 pp.

Komroff, Manuel. *The Contemporaries of Marco Polo . . .* (New York, Boni & Liveright, 1928), pp. 253–322: The Oriental Travels of R. Benjamin of Tudela.

Lachmann, Robert. *Jewish Cantillation and Song in the Isle of Djerba.* (Jerusalem, Archives of Oriental Music, 1940), 115 pp., mus. ex.

Landa, M. J. *The Jewish Drama.* (London, P. S. King & Son, 1926), 340 pp.

Leminka, A. ed. *Tachkemoni-Makams.* (Warsaw, 1899).

Levi ben Gerschom (Leo Hebraeus). *De numeris Harmonicis* (1343).

Levita, Elias, transl. *Baba-Buch* (1507).

——. *Sefer Masoret ha-Masoret* (The Tradition of the Tradition).

Lewy, Julius. *The Feast of the 14th Day of Adar.* In: *HUCA* (1939), vol. XIV.

Lipschütz, Shlomo. *Sefer Teʿudat Shelomoh.* (Offenbach, Seligman Reiss, 1718), 46 fol.

Loeb, Isidore. *Les Juifs de Carpentras sous le gouvernement pontifical.* In: *REJ* (1886), vol. XII, p. 230.

Loewe, Herbert. *Mediaeval Hebrew Minstrelsy. Songs for the Bride Queen's Feast.* Sixteen Zemiroth arranged according to the Traditional Harmonies by Rose L. Henriques. (London, James Clark & Co., 1926). 134 pp., mus. ex.

Loewenthal, Marvin. *A World Passed By. Scenes and Memories of Jewish Civilization in Europe and North Africa.* (New York, Harper Bros., 1933), XXXV, 500 pp., illustr.

Maimonides. *Responsum on Music,* see Cohen, Boaz.

ʾAl-Makkari, Ahmed ibn Mohammed. *The History of the Moham-medan Dynasties in Spain*. Transl. by Paṣcal de Gayangos. (London, 1840–1843), 2 vols.

Marcus, Jacob R. *The Jew in the Medieval World. A Source Book. 315–1791*. (Cincinnati, The Sinai Press, 1938), XXIV, 504 pp.

Martène and Durand. *Voyage littéraire de deux religieux bénédictins de la Congrégation de Saint Maur* (Paris, 1717).

Masʿudi (see ʾAl-Masʿudi).

Mendel, Arthur. *Spengler's Quarrel with the Methods of Music History*. In: *MQ* (April 1934), vol. 20, No. 2, pp. 131–171, mus. ex., portrait.

Menéndez Pidal, Ramón. *L'épopée castillane*. (Buenos Aires, 1945).

———. *La epopeya castellana a través de la literatura Española*. (Buenos Aires, Espasa-Calpe, 1945), 245 pp.

———*Poesía juglaresca y origenes de las literaturas romanicas*. (Madrid, Instituto de Estudios Politicos, 1957), VIII, 413 pp., illustr.

Millgram, Abraham E., ed. *An Anthology of Medieval Hebrew Literature*. (Philadelphia, The Associated Talmud Torahs, 1961), XIX, 469 pp.

Monatsschrift für Geschichte und Wissenschaft des Judentums (Krotoschin).

Moore, George Foot. *Judaism in the First Centuries of the Christian Era*. (Cambridge, Mass., Harvard University Press, 1927), 2 vols.

Musical Quarterly.

Nadel, Arno. *The Hannoverian Compendium*. (The Oldest Collection of Hebrew Music). In: *Musica Hebraica* (Jerusalem, 1938), I–II.

Nettl, Paul. *Alte jüdische Spielleute und Musiker*. (Prague, Josef Flesch, 1923), 65 pp., mus. ex.

Neuman, A. Abraham. *The Jews in Spain. Their Social, Political, and Cultural Life during the Middle Ages*. (Philadelphia, The Jewish Publication Society of America, 1942), 2 vols., illustr., maps.

Nostradamus (Notredame), Jean de. *Les vies des plus célèbres et anciens poètes provençaux*. Nouvelle édition préparée par Camille Chabaneau. (Paris, H. Champion, 1913). 176 and 407 pp.

Orel, Dobreslav. *Kanzional Franushov*. (Prague, 1922), p. 43.

Paralikova, Verdeil R. *La musique Byzantine chez les Bulgares et les Russes*. In: *Monumenta Musicae Byzantinae Subsidia*. (Copenhagen and Boston, 1953), vol. 3.

Pedrell, Felipe. *Canconiero musical popular español* (Boileau, Casa editorial de música, n.d.), 2nd ed., 4 vols.

Pfeiffer, Robert Henry. *Introduction to the Old Testament.* (New York, Harper & Brothers, 1941), XIII, 917 pp.

Pitoni, G. O. *Notizia de' Contrapuntisti, e Compositori di Musica.* (Bibl. Vatic., Capp. Giul. I), 1 and 2.

Portaleone, Abraham da. *Shilṭe Ha-Gibborim.* (Mantual, 1612).

Rabinovitch, Israel. *Of Jewish Music.* Translated from the Yiddish by A. M. Klein. (Montreal, The Book Center, 1952), 321 pp., mus. ex.

Reuchlin, Johannes. *De accentibus et orthographia linguae Hebraicae . . . libri tres . . .* (Hagenau, Thomas Anshelm, 1518), 83 f, 9 pp., mus. ex.

Ribera y Tarragó, Julian. *La Música de las Cantigas* (Music in Ancient Arabia and Spain). Transl. by Eleanor Hague and Marion Leffingwell. (Stanford University Press, California, 1929), XVI, 183 pp., illustr., mus. ex.

Ricchi, Immanuel Ḥay. *Sefer hon ᵓashir* (Commentary to the Mishnah). (Amsterdam, 1730–31), mus. ex.

Rossi, G. B. de. *Roma sotteranea.* (Rome, 1877), 3 vols.

Roth, Cecil. *L'accademia musicale nel Ghetto Veneziano.* In: *La Rassegna mensile,* III, No. 4.

——. *The History of the Jews in Italy.* (Philadelphia, The Jewish Publication Society of America, 1946), XIV, 575 pp., illustr.

——. *A History of the Jews in Venice.* (Philadelphia, The Jewish Publication Society of America, 1930), 380 pp.

——. *A History of the Marranos.* (Philadelphia, The Jewish Publication Society of America, 1947).

——. *The Jewish Contribution to Civilization.* (London, Macmillan & Co., 1938), XIII, 357 pp., illustr.

——. *The Jews in the Renaissance.* (Philadelphia, The Jewish Publication Society of America, 1959), XIII, 380 pp., illustr., mus. ex.

——. *The Spanish Inquisition* (New York, Norton, 1964).

Rothmüller, Aron Marko. *Die Musik der Juden. Versuch einer geschichtlichen Darstellung ihrer Entwicklung und ihres Wesens.* (Zürich, Pan-Verlag, 1951). XII, 193 pp., illustr., mus. exs.

Ruiz, Juan (Archipreste de Hita). *El Libro de buen amor* (1389).

Rutebeuf. *Oeuvres complètes.* Recuellies . . . par Achille Jubinal (Paris, 1839), 2 vols. German edition by Adolf Kressner (Wolfenbüttel, 1885).

Sachs, Curt. *Geist und Werden der Musikinstrumente.* (Berlin, D. Reimer, 1929), XI, 282 pp. 48 tables, bibliography.

——. *The History of Musical Instruments.* New York, (Norton, 1940). 505 pp., illustr.

————. *World History of Dance.* Transl. by Bessie Schönberg. (New York, Seven Arts, 1937). XII, 469 pp., illustr.

Saminsky, Lazare. *Music of the Ghetto and the Bible.* (New York, Bloch Publ. Co., 1934), VIII, 261 pp., mus. ex.

Scheiber, Alexander. *The Origins of 'Obadiah, the Norman Proselyte.* In: *The Journal of Jewish Studies* (1954), vol. V., No. 1, p. 33.

————. *'Obadyah ha-Ger ha-Normani, ha-roshem ha-rishon shel manginah yehudith.* [In Hebrew]. In: *Tarbiz* (Jerusalem, 1965), pp. 366–371.

Schirman, Ḥayyim. *Yizhak Gorni, Meshorer 'Ibri mi-Provence* [A Hebrew Singer from the Provence]. In: *Orlogin,* III, pp. 91 ff. French translation in *Lettres Romanes,* III, pp. 180, 184.

Schirmann, J. *Eine hebräisch-italienische Komödie des XVI. Jahrhunderts.* In: *MGWJ* (1931), vol. 75, N.S. vol. 39, pp. 97–118.

Schmieder's. *Bach Verzeichnis* (Leipzig, Breitkopf & Härtel, 1950).

Scholem, Gershom G. *Major Trends in Jewish Mysticism.* (New York, Schocken Books, 1941).

Schorr, Baruch. *Neginot Baruch Schorr.* Synagogen-Gesänge für die hohen Feiertage . . . Hrsg. von seinem Sohn Israel Schorr. (New York, Bloch Publ. Co., 1906). 2nd ed. 1928.

Schudt, Johann Jacob. *Jüdische Merkwürdigkeiten* . . . (Frankfurt a.M. und Leipzig, Samuel Tobias Hocker, 1714), 4 vols. New ed. Berlin, 1922.

————. *Jüdisches Frankfurter und Prager Freuden-Fest* . . . (Frankfurt a.M., Matthias Andreä, 1716), 84 pp., ill.

Schurig, Arthur. *Leopold Mozart. Reiseaufzeichnungen* 1763–1771. (Dresden, Laube 1920).

Sefer Ḥasidim. ed. by Aron Freimann (Frankfurt a.M., F. Kaufmann, 1924).

Sendrey, Alfred. *Bibliography of Jewish Music.* (New York, Columbia University Press, 1951), XLI, 404 pp.

————. *Music in Ancient Israel.* (Philosophical Library, New York, 1969). 674 pp., illustr., mus. exs., bibliography.

Spengler, Oswald. *The Decline of the West.* Transl. by Charles Francis Atkinson. (New York, Alfred A. Knopf. 1939), 2 vols. Vol. I, XV, 428. Vol. II, XXXII, 507.

Steinschneider, Moritz. *Allgemeine Einleitung in die jüdische Literatur. Vorlesungen.* 3d. ed. (Jerusalem, Wahrmann Books, 1964). 148 pp.

————. *Catalogus librorum Hebraeorum in Bibliotheca Bodleiana* (Berlin, Ad. Friedlaender, 1852–1860), 3 vols.

——. *Die Geschichtsliteratur der Juden in Druckwerken und Handschriften.* (Frankfurt a.M., 1905).

——. *Hebräische Bibliographie* (Berlin, 1858–1882), 21 vols. Vols. VIII, XIX.

——. *Jewish Literature from the Eighth to the Eighteenth Century.* (New York, Hermon Press, 1965).

——. *Purim und Parodie.* (Frankfurt a.M. 1903).

Strauss, Raphael. *Was Süsskint von Trimberg a Jew?* An Inquiry into 13th Century Cultural History. In: *Jewish Social Studies* (January 1948), vol. X, No. 1, pp. 19–30.

Szabolcsi, Bence. *A Jewish Musical Document of the Middle Ages: the Most Ancient Noted Biblical Melody.* In: *Semitic Studies in Memory of Immanuel Löw.* Ed. by Alexander Scheiber. (Budapest, 1947), pp. 131–133, illustr., mus. ex.

Ticknor, George. *History of the Spanish Literature.* (Boston and New York, Houghton Mifflin Co., 1871), 3 vols.

Toynbee, Arnold J. *Civilization on Trial.* (New York, Oxford University Press, 1948), VII, 263 pp.

——. *A Study of History.* Abridged version. (New York, Oxford University Press, 1957), 2 vols.

Ugolino, Biagio (Blasius). *Thesaurus antiquitatum sacrarum . . .* (Venice, Joh. Gabriel Hertz and Seb. Coletti, 1744–1767), 24 vols.

(The) Universal Jewish Encyclopedia, ed. by Isaac Landmann. (New York, 1939–1942), 10 vols.

Ursprung, Otto. *Vier Studien zur Geschichte des deutschen Liedes.* In: *Archiv für Musikwissenschaft* (1922), vol. IV, pp. 413–419.

Vallensis (Valentius), Johannes Hieronymus. *Sefer Tob Taʿam. Opus de prosodia Hebraeorum in quatuor libros diuisum . . .* (Paris, J. Bogardus, 1545), 61 f., mus. ex.

Ward, Mary A. *A Medieval Spanish Writer.* In: *Forthnightly Review,* vol. XX, New Series (July-Dec. 1876), pp. 809–832.

Werner, Eric. *Anthology of Music. Hebrew Music.* (Köln, Arno Volk Verlag), 1961).

——. *The Conflict between Hellenism and Judaism in the Music of the Early Christian Church.* In: *HUCA* (1947), XX.

——. *The Doxology in Synagogue and Church.* In: *HUCA* (1945–46), XIX.

——. *Die hebräischen Intonationen in B. Marcellos Estro poeticoarmonico.* In: *MGWJ* (Breslau, 1937), vol. 81, N.S. vol. 45, pp. 393–416, mus. ex.

——. *The Jewish Contribution to Music.* In: *The Jews, Their His-*

tory, Culture, and Religion. (Philadelphia, The Jewish Publication Society of America, 1949), 4 vols. III, p. 950 ff., mus. ex.

——. *Leading Motifs in Synagogue and Plain Song.* In: *Papers of the American Musicological Society,* Detroit Congress (1946).

——. *The Music of Post-Biblical Judaism.* In: *New Oxford History of Music,* vol. I, pp. 313-335.

——. *Musical Aspects of the Dead Sea Scrolls.* In: *MQ,* vol. XLIII, January 1957, No. 1), pp. 21-37.

——. *Two Obscure Sources of Reuchlin's "De accentibus linguae hebraicae."* In: *Historia Judaica* (April, 1954), vol. XVI, pp. 39-54.

——. *The Oldest Sources of Synagogal Chant.* In: *Proceedings of the American Academy for Jewish Research* (New York, 1947), vol. XVI, pp. 228 ff.

——. *The Sacred Bridge.* (London, Dennis Dobson & New York, Columbia University Press, 1959). XX, 618 pp., mus. exs.

Winter, Jakob, und August Wünsche. *Die jüdische Literatur seit Abschluss des Kanons.* (Berlin, M. Poppelauer, 1897), 3 vols.

Wolf, Albert. *Fahrende Leute bei den Juden.* (Leipzig, M. W. Kaufmann, 1909), 68 pp.

Yaakob Halevi Molin (Mölln). (Maharil), *Sefer Maharil* (1556).

Yasser, Joseph. *The Magrephah of the Herodian Temple.* In: *Journal of the American Musicological Society* (1960), vol. XIII, Nos. 1-3, pp. 24-42, illustr.

——. *References to Hebrew Music in Russian Medieval Ballads.* In: *Jewish Social Studies* (1949), vol. XI, No. 1, pp. 21-48.

Zinberg, Israel. *The History of Jewish Literature.* [In Yiddish]. (Vilna, "Tomor" Farlag, 1929-1937), 8 vols.

Zlichubar, Judah Leib. *Shirei Yehudah.* (Amsterdam, 5497 [1696]).

Zunz, Leopold. *Die Ritus des synagogalen Gottesdienstes geschichtlich entwickelt.* (Berlin, Julius Springer, 1859), 249 pp.

Index